Ancient Marbles to American Shores

Ancient Marbles to American Shores

Classical Archaeology in the United States

Stephen L. Dyson

PENN

University of Pennsylvania Press

Philadelphia

DE
60
.D97
1998

Published by
University of Pennsylvania Press
Philadelphia, Pennsylvania 19104–4011

Library of Congress Cataloging-in-Publication Data
Dyson, Stephen L.
   Ancient marbles to American shores : classical archaeology in the
United States / Stephen L. Dyson.
      p.   cm.
   Includes bibliographical references and index.
   ISBN 0-8122-3446-4 (cloth : alk. paper)
   1. Classical antiquities.   2. Archaeology — United States —
History — 20th century.   3. Archaeological museums and collections —
United States — Influence.   I. Title.
DE60.D97   1998
938 — dc21   98-21208
                                                       CIP

39007147

For Jacob and Simona

Contents

Preface

The aim of this book is to explore the emergence and growth of an academic discipline within a changing American culture and society. Classical archaeology of all of the subfields of archaeology in the United States has the longest history. Through much of the nineteenth and early twentieth centuries it played a major shaping role within the discipline of archaeology, creating research models and setting research agendas. Since classical art was central to the aesthetic values of the American cultural elite during much of this period, classical archaeology had a wider influence than many other humanistic disciplines. However, no comprehensive history of North American classical archaeology exists. This situation contrasts with that of American archaeology,[1] European prehistory,[2] American Egyptology,[3] Mesopotamian archaeology,[4] Christian archaeology,[5] and African archaeology.[6] Scholars and amateurs interested in the history of American classical archaeology have had to be content with limited discussions in more general histories of archaeology, studies of special themes like the discovery of Greece,[7] and histories of such institutions as the American School of Classical Studies in Athens[8] and the American Academy in Rome.[9] Biographies and autobiographies have been rare and limited in scope.[10] So have the few histories of major

1. Willey and Sabloff 1980; Meltzer, Fowler, and Sabloff 1986.
2. Daniel 1962, 1976; Grayson 1983; Graslund 1987.
3. Wilson 1964.
4. Lloyd 1980; Kuklick 1996.
5. Frend 1996.
6. Robertshaw 1980.
7. Stoneman 1987.
8. Lord 1947; Meritt 1984.
9. Valentine and Valentine 1973.
10. Dyson 1994. Only Richard Seager (Becker and Betancourt 1997) and Harriet Boyd Hawes have received full biographies and that for Hawes was written by a family member-

excavations that have appeared.[11] Important anniversaries like the centenaries of the Archaeological Institute of America and the *American Journal of Archaeology* produced very limited published commemorations, which contrasted sadly with the scholarly celebrations for similar anniversaries at the Society for American Archaeology.[12] Much of the limited history that has been written is a rather odd blend of hagiography and antiquarianism.[13]

This book attempts to fill part of this void, not only for classical archaeology but also for the history of archaeology and the history of American scholarship. Its aim is not to chronicle famous discoveries in the manner of many popular histories of archaeology. In fact, relatively little is said here about what was found at a particular site or during a particular project. Rather my goal is to narrate the framework for a history of American classical archaeology, highlighting those individuals, actions, and institutions I see as key to the development of the field. I am concerned with pioneers like Charles Eliot Norton and Joseph Thacher Clarke and with consolidators like Howard Crosby Butler. I consider the formation and early development of academic departments, museums and foreign schools that supported and advanced classical archaeology in America.

At the same time, I attempt to place the developments in classical archaeology within the context of educational reform, institutional formation and changing cultural values and ideologies in the United States of the late nineteenth and twentieth centuries. My approach reflects the influence of such scholars as the American historian Peter Novick[14] and the anthropological archaeologist Thomas Patterson.[15] In many respects American classical archaeology provides an ideal subject for this type of study. It is one of the oldest American academic disciplines and one of the most important within the humanities. Today as in the past it serves as a link between art history and classics in the humanities, history and anthropology in the social sciences, and diverse disciplines in the natural sciences. American classical archaeologists from the largest national group within their profession. Classical archaeology has a place at all levels of American academic culture from the introductory college survey to the research institute.

American classical archaeology is not just an academic enterprise. Be-

(Allesbrook 1992). The recent publication of *An Encyclopedia of the History of Classical Archaeology* (1996; henceforth designated *EHCA*) has provided an important new reference tool.

11. Camp 1986; Hopkins 1979.

12. Sheftel 1979; Thompson 1980; Donahue 1985; Dow 1985. For the history of the Society for American Archaeology, see Meltzer, Fowler, and Sabloff 1986.

13. Dyson 1989.

14. Novick 1988.

15. Patterson 1986, 1995.

cause of its association with the mysterious and exotic, and because its research produces objects that are often things of beauty and have a tangible association with an otherwise dead past, archaeology has always held a special fascination for the nonacademic as well as the academic public. This is fitting and necessary, since archaeology is an expensive enterprise that requires extensive, nonprofessional patronage from either the government or society's economic elite. The elite private connections have been especially important for American classical archaeology, because until relatively recently the United States did not have a tradition of government support for Old World archaeology.

But the role of classical archaeology within U.S. society has been more complex and important than that of an eccentric scholarly activity that could have become just the plaything of the rich. Unlike many other branches of archaeology, classical archaeology, because of its role in explicating ancient Greece and Rome, has long enjoyed a close association with core American cultural and ideological values. The Founding Fathers and the leaders of the early Republic identified closely with ancient Greece and Rome.[16] The study of Classics was placed at the center of both secondary and higher education during the eighteenth and early nineteenth centuries. Greek and Roman artistic imagery shaped the public and private architectural and sculptural taste of the new Republic.[17] Jefferson's Rotunda at the University of Virginia and Hiram Powers's "Greek Slave" represented different aspects of the identification with antiquity.

The ideological association of classical art and elite American values has proved extremely fluid and flexible even in our Republic's short history. Charles Eliot Norton, the major founding figure in American classical archaeology, was a Helleno-Romantic seeking to escape from the grim realities of the post-Civil War industrial age into Ruskinian evocations of the beauties of a past epoch.[18] Yet the same era in which Norton lived and preached his aesthetic saw the proud advocates of triumphant capitalism take over the imagery of Roman imperial architecture that survived in the Baths of Caracalla for new railroad terminals like Pennsylvania Station in New York. In the period between the world wars classical archaeology derived strength from conservatives who saw it as a bulwark in the struggle against cultural modernism. After World War II, the America that had saved democracy from the Nazis and Fascists poured millions of dollars into the excavation of the perceived birthplace of democracy, the Athenian Agora.

16. Gummere 1963; Reinhold 1984; K. Lehmann 1985.
17. Wills 1984; Cooper 1993.
18. Vanderbilt 1959; Duffy 1996.

As noted above, classical archaeology in the United States by its very nature must have a close economic association with the ruling economic elite. It is a very expensive enterprise for an essentially nonscientific discipline. From Richard Norton organizing his 1914 Cyrene expedition from the yacht of the Chicago millionaire Allison Armour anchored off Libya's shore to Agora archaeologists obtaining large grants from major private foundations, classical field archaeologists have always cultivated sources of great wealth in the American elite. The same has been true of the major art and archaeology museums, which had to build their classical collections at a time when opportunities for cheap looting in Greece and Italy and the acquiring of bargains in Greek and Roman art were few and far between.

For these reasons the study of the development of classical archaeology has to be both a history of research, of the scholars who did that research, of the museums and universities that fostered the discipline, and of the nonacademic individuals and groups who shaped those cultural institutions. It also has to consider wider trends in American history, society, and ideology. The fact that the two most dynamic periods in American classical archaeology were those immediately following the Civil War and World War II relates closely to the intellectual, cultural, and political concerns of those eras.

This study is organized in six chapters. In the first, I discuss the ways the exploration and exploitation of the classics and ancient art and culture in America before the Civil War laid the foundations in education, public interest, and ideological identification on which the discipline of classical archaeology was built. Much of this ground has been covered by other scholars, but the general review is necessary to understand how the field emerged after the Civil War. The second and third chapters are concerned with the founding of the discipline in the post-Civil War period, its incorporation into the academic world, the first programs of research, and the creation of the institutions needed to sustain that discipline. In the fourth chapter, I explore the creation and development of classical collections within the American art museum as a separate, rather special institution within classical archaeology. Since I argue that American museum archaeology's attitudes and approaches began to change significantly only during the 1970s, this chapter has the greatest chronological range, moving from the years immediately after the Civil War to those following World War II. In the fifth chapter, I deal with the period between the world wars and look at ways in which classical archaeologists and their supporters adjusted to a rapidly changing social, ideological, and institutional world. The final chapter takes the story into the post–World War II period and what was in many ways another golden age of American classical archaeology. This chapter ends with important changes in the world of classical archaeology ranging from shifts in the funding base to growing concerns about the antiquities trade that began to be manifest in the 1970s and early 1980s. More recent events are too close to allow a clear historical perspective. However, I have provided an Afterword in which I set out some of my own personal views on the current state and the future prospects of the discipline.

Since this is the first history of American classical archaeology, it has to be very much a prolegomenon. As I have observed, very little fundamental groundbreaking research on individuals and institutions has been done. I have undertaken some of that myself, using important archives such as those of the Archaeological Institute of America in Boston. However, rather than spending the decades necessary to track down and explore the many potential archives and oral historical sources, delaying the appearance of a much needed historical overview, I have decided to produce a historical synthesis based largely on printed sources. These are rich and diverse, allowing me to provide a framework for more detailed investigations. I foresee and hope that this study will stimulate the specialized research that will fill lacunae and question many of its conclusions.

This history is also in many respects a personal evaluation of what has been important in the past and is important in the present of the discipline. In this age of academic postmodernism, a claim of total scientific detachment on the part of the historian is almost impossible to substantiate and of uncertain value. Ironically, the motto for writing history of the *sine ira et studio* type came from Tacitus, one of the most engaged Roman historians. I have attempted to marshal my evidence as fully and accurately as possible. I have also tried throughout to understand and interpret individual actions of individuals in their times rather than judging them ex post facto. I have attempted to articulate my own points of view in a clear and evident manner.

A number of people and institutions have made this work possible. The start for research on this project was made possible by a fellowship from the American Council of Learned Societies. My project also benefited from research support from Wesleyan University and the State University of New York at Buffalo. Mark Meister, executive director of the Archaeological Institute of America, was very helpful in accessing the AIA archives. Dr. Susan Hueck Allen provided me with important material related to Joseph Thacher Clarke and Francis Bacon. For archival and library help I am deeply indebted to library staff at the American Academy in Rome, the Stone Science Library of Boston University, Lockwood Library of the University at Buffalo, and Olin Library of Wesleyan University. My wife Pauline read, edited, and critiqued the manuscript with great care. I owe a great deal to the many observations and corrections of the anonymous readers of the University of Pennsylvania Press. They saved me from a large number of errors and embarrassment. I also must give thanks to the staff of the University of Pennsylvania Press, especially Eric Halpern and Alison Anderson. It is fitting that a book concerned with the past should also look to the future. Therefore I dedicate this book to my two young grandchildren.

1. Prehistory

Classical archaeology gradually emerged as a formal discipline in the United States during the 1870s and the 1880s with the appointment of Charles Eliot Norton to teach the history of art at Harvard, the organization of the Archaeological Institute of America (AIA) in Boston, and the foundation of the American School of Classical Studies (ASCA) in Athens. However, these developments would not have been possible if Americans had not already considered classical art and architecture as central to their visual and cultural experience. The founding figures of American classical archaeology were raised and educated in pre-Civil War America and expressed many of its values. Theirs was a world of Greek and Latin in the schools, neoclassical churches and courthouses, and the new middle-class Grand Tour. They looked back to the controlled classicism of the revolutionary generation, absorbed the lessons of Romanticism, read Ruskin, and reflected on the impact of the Industrial Revolution. A brief consideration of the roots of the appreciation of Greek and Roman visual culture is necessary to understand what Norton, W. J. Stillman, and others did in the decades after the Civil War.

Americans came relatively late to the material world of Greek and Roman antiquity. During the Renaissance, when Europeans were discovering the physical remains of ancient Rome and privileging classical values in architecture, sculpture, and painting, the later territory of the United States was largely the preserve of the native Americans.[1] Certain settlers of Jamestown, including Captain John Smith, possessed some classical learning, but education in general was not high a high priority among the early Virginians.[2] The Pilgrims of Plymouth were not deeply concerned with high culture and advanced education either. In contrast, the Puritans of Massachusetts Bay were greatly concerned with education, and that meant in part classical learning.[3] Boston Latin School, founded in 1635, was the first educational institution established in what

1. Haskell and Penny 1981; Reinhold 1984.
2. Gummere 1963: 20–36; Mumford Jones 1964: 238–39.
3. Gummere 1963: 37–75.

is now the United States, and classical authors were central to the early curriculum of Harvard College.[4] However, the Puritans' religious beliefs demanded a worldview of stark simplicity, in which the allure of the visual and the ornate was largely rejected.

This attitude toward material possessions changed markedly with the emergence of a mercantile and agricultural elite along the east coast during the mid-eighteenth century.[5] Many of the restraints of Puritan religious culture had broken down, and merchants and plantation owners in the North and the South had increasing sums of money to spend on public architecture and on private housing and furnishings. This new elite naturally looked to Europe, and especially to England, for their ideas of artistic refinement and status goods. There they encountered an aesthetic that reflected the classical order both in the microworld of furniture and in the universe of public and private architecture.[6] It was the world of Lord Burlington and Robert Adam.[7]

For Americans of the seventeenth and eighteenth centuries, direct exposure to the classical remains of Italy, let alone Greece or the eastern Mediterranean, was clearly very limited. By the eighteenth century, the traditions of the Continental Grand Tour were well established, especially in Britain.[8] Generations of young English noblemen had gone off with their tutors to explore the countries of the Continent with a special concentration on Italy. They generally returned with some culture, improved social graces, and often a collection of antiquities that graced their town or country houses.[9]

A number of Americans did go to England and even to France before the Revolution. In some cases they saw the pieces of classical art that were becoming increasingly abundant in private collections, and the public and private neoclassical structures that were coming to dominate the English architectural landscape in both the city and country. However, before the American Revolution, very few colonials went to Italy, and almost none went to Greece.[10] America did not have England's idle, young nobility. Its elite inhabitants went to England and Europe older and with a purpose. Significantly the first American to leave an account of his travels in Italy, Dr. John Morgan of Philadelphia (1735–1815), went there to study medicine.[11] When in Rome, he was guided around the

4. Mumford Jones 1964: 240–41.
5. Mumford Jones 1964: 243–44; Montgomery and Kane 1976.
6. Arnold 1994.
7. Lees-Milne 1947; Kennedy 1990: 431.
8. Hibbert 1987.
9. Haskell and Penny 1981: 84–88; B. Cook 1985; Ford 1985.
10. Prezzolini 1933: 21–49; Baker 1964: 13–19.
11. Prezzolini 1933: 24–28; Monga 1987: 1–5, 188.

museums and monuments by the famous British cicerone James Byres, had his portrait painted by Angelica Kauffmann, and was presented to the pope.[12] He also became a friend of the young Thomas Jefferson.[13] Most Americans, however, did not have the leisure or economic resources for long periods of cultural wandering.

The rarity of an American presence in Italy is illustrated by the reception accorded to the ambitious and talented young American painter Benjamin West (1738–1820). West learned the fundamentals of painting in his native Pennsylvania.[14] He had been taught, in the words of one West scholar, "to blend Christian morality with classical imagery, to insert political issues into theatrical setting and to merge European style with American concerns."[15] He also had strong ambitions that first took him to Philadelphia, where he cultivated patrons and raised the resources and connections that would allow him to travel to Rome. When West arrived in Rome from Pennsylvania on 10 July 1760, he was treated as a cross between a celebrity and a natural curiosity. He was immediately taken into the circle of antiquarians that surrounded the cultured Cardinal Alessandro Albani.[16] The cardinal had created one of the most important classical collections in Rome and patronized that pioneer of classical archaeology, Johann Joachim Winckelmann.[17] West not only visited the expected sites, museums, and collections, but also set out to make himself into a distinguished artist in the neoclassical style. He apprenticed himself to the German painter Anton Raphael Mengs, and befriended the English artist and antiquities dealer Gavin Hamilton and the Swiss painter Angelica Kauffmann. He achieved sufficient artistic distinction in Italy to be elected to academies in Bologna and Florence.[18] His later paintings on subjects like *Agrippina Landing at Brundisium with the Ashes of Germanicus* and *The Departure of Regulus from Rome,* with their classical themes, the architectural accuracy of their backgrounds, and the echoes of sculptural works in the figures (the Agrippina group recalls a section of the Ara Pacis frieze), played a significant role in introducing the Winckelmann-Mengs classical artistic values into the Anglo-American world.[19] However, West spent most of his later adult life in England and thus had a more limited influence in shaping the American classical consciousness than one might otherwise have expected.

12. Brooks 1958: 5 n. 1; Baker 1964: 17; Manners and Williamson 1976: 219.
13. W. H. Adams 1976: 81, 96–97.
14. Abrams 1985: 45–71.
15. Abrams 1985: 71.
16. Brooks 1958: 1–5; J. T. Flexner 1969: 6–11; Abrams 1985: 73–88.
17. Potts 1994: 189–216.
18. Dinsmoor 1943: 73–74.
19. J. T. Flexner 1969: 10–18; Craven 1979: 7–9; Abrams 1985: 21–43.

At West's urging, the even more talented Boston portrait painter John Singleton Copley (1738–1815) visited Italy in 1774–75.[20] He traveled with Mr. and Mrs. Ralph Izard, a wealthy, cultured couple from Charleston, South Carolina. Not only did the American group explore Rome, but they went as far south as Pompeii and Paestum.[21] Paestum, which had been brought to European consciousness only some twenty years before, was their only major point of contact with classical Greek architecture.[22] For Copley, the site was "older than Rome . . . with its singular style of architecture" and represented "the first dawning of that science among the Greeks.[23] One result of this tour was Copley's portrait of the Izards, the first pair of American classical art collectors (Figure 1).[24] The painting, now in the Boston Museum of Fine Arts, portrays the prosperous Charleston couple in a Roman setting. They are seated at a table. Through a break in the curtains in the background one can see the Colosseum, the first appearance of that monument in American painting. On the table is a miniature copy of the Hellenistic statue group of Electra and Orestes and a Greek red-figured vase. Copley depicted the illustrations on the vase with sufficient precision that it can be identified as a now lost work of the artist that John Beazley designated the Niobid Painter.[25]

The outbreak of the Revolution cut off most Americans from Europe and undermined the mercantile and agricultural prosperity this early classical revival was based. But the events leading up to the Revolution and the establishment of a secure national government produced a strengthened interest in the classics, as philosophers, orators, and politicians sought exempla and justifications for the actions in the Greek and Roman past. Virtually every aspect of the movement, from the ideas that justified rebellion and shaped the government that replaced the British Crown to the historically shaped identities of the leaders, derived from classical antiquity, especially from republican Rome.[26]

The Revolution also brought the most famous American classical archaeological tourist, Thomas Jefferson, to Europe in 1784. Jefferson arrived in France with a good classical education, proficiency in architectural design, and a lifelong enthusiasm for Greece and Rome.[27] His direct exposure to classical architecture was limited to a visit to the Roman

20. Brooks 1958: 6–8; Monga 1987: 188–89.
21. Dinsmoor 1943: 75–76; Reinhold 1984: 266–67.
22. Serra 1986.
23. Brooks 1958: 8.
24. Vance 1989: 55–57.
25. Dinsmoor 1943: 75–76; Vance 1989: 55–57.
26. Gummere 1963: 97–119, 161–90; Mumford Jones 1964: 251–65; Richard 1994.
27. Gummere 1963: 191–97; W. H. Adams 1976: 13, 24; K. Lehmann 1985; Kennedy 1990: 431–56.

Figure 1. *Mr. and Mrs. Ralph Izard (Alice Delancey)*. The Izards of Charleston, South Carolina during their Grand Tour visit to Rome in 1775. Oil painting by John Singleton Copley. Courtesy of the Edward Ingersoll Brown Fund, Boston Museum of Fine Arts.

temple known as the Maison Carrée in Nîmes in southern France.[28] He approached this cultural pilgrimage with almost religious devotion. Jefferson described the 1787 visit in a letter to Mme de Tesse: "Here I am, Madam, gazing whole hours at the Maisson Quarrée like a lover at his mistress. The stocking weavers and silk spinners around consider me as a hypochondriac Englishman about to write with a pistol the last chapter of his history."[29]

Jefferson had, however, carefully studied the Roman and Renaissance authors who had written on architecture and the neoclassical architecture of eighteenth-century France. He began acquiring the most impor-

28. W. H. Adams 1976: 95, fig. 150; Kennedy 1990: 433–34.
29. W. H. Adams 1976: 95.

tant architectural publications produced during that period.[30] He also
had his young friend William Short visit and send back descriptions of
Roman monuments in Italy.[31]

Since the opportunity for Americans to experience the Greek and
Roman monuments of Italy and Greece personally was still limited, a
cultivated amateur like Jefferson had to learn about the fine points of
classical architecture largely through illustrated books. Many of those
expounded abstract classical principles based on the traditions of Vitruvius and Palladio.[32] A new type of work based on direct observation and
illustration of classical structures was also beginning to appear on the
market, however. By the 1760s prints of Roman monuments by Piranesi
had made their way to colonial Virginia and the *Pennsylvania Gazette* advertised complete sets of "Roman antiquities."[33] Jefferson himself owned
a copy of the *Antichita di Ercolano.*[34]

Book prints also provided a fuller visual image of antiquity including
renderings of famous scenes. Such a book illustration from an ancient
history text appears to have inspired the earliest classical painting done in
what was soon to become the United States, Benjamin West's *Death of Socrates* painted in 1756.[35] The first casts of ancient statues were also beginning to trickle into American cities. The English painter John Smibert arrived in Boston in 1729 with reproductions of a bust of Homer, the Venus
di Medici, and the Laocoön. This paltry selection of casts could again be
supplemented by book illustrations. Among the books in Thomas Jefferson's library was François Perrier's *Signa et Statua Antiqua.*[36] This certainly
inspired the list of classical sculptures Jefferson drew up in 1771 for his
projected art gallery at Monticello, a scheme that was never realized.[37]

For the promotion of the true Hellenic style (as opposed to Palladian
neo-Roman classicism) in the Anglo-American world of the later eighteenth century, no work was more important than James Stuart and Nicholas Revett's *The Antiquities of Athens*, the first volume of which was published in 1762 and the third in 1799.[38] The London-based Society of
Dilettanti, a group of upper-class British antiquarians, had dispatched the
two young draftsmen to Greece, where they studied and sketched a range
of Greek architectural monuments, providing accurate visual informa-

30. W. H. Adams 1976: 98–99, 125–35, 167–89.
31. Brooks 1958: 10 n. 4; K. Lehmann 1985: 30.
32. W. H. Adams 1976: 25.
33. Dolmetsch 1970: 55, and Fig. 3.
34. Winkes 1993.
35. J. T. Flexner 1952.
36. W. H. Adams 1976: xxxv; Haskell and Penny 1981: 90.
37. W. H. Adams 1976: 81–82; K. Lehmann 1985: 25–27.
38. Wiebenson 1969; Watkins 1982; Jenkyns 1991: 49–51.

tion on Hellenic originals that was not previously available in the Anglo-American world. They produced their beautifully illustrated volumes in a format that combined the abstract architectural renderings derived from the Renaissance tradition with contemporary sketches of the monuments as they existed, renditions that blended architecture and local color in the proto-Romantic manner normally associated with Piranesi's Roman prints.[39]

Stuart and Revett's collection had a profound impact not only in England but also in America. By 1767, the first volume had been deposited in the Library Company of Philadelphia, a collection that included Thomas Major's *Ruins of Paestum*.[40] Thomas Jefferson purchased Stuart and Revett's first volume for his library, and the work strongly influenced his promulgation of the classical architectural style in the United States.

Jefferson's interest in the aesthetics of classical architecture was part of a belief shared by many of the Founding Fathers that antiquity, especially Roman antiquity, had special relevance for the new Republic. Most of the leading figures of the period knew their ancient languages and were highly knowledgeable about Greek and Roman antiquity.[41] Citations from classical authors abound in documents like the Federalist Papers, and continued in eulogies given after the deaths of Washington, Jefferson and Adams.[42] Jefferson therefore found a generally sympathetic audience for his efforts to have classical models shape the architecture of the new Republic. He himself brought the Maison Carrée to America in the form of the new capital building he designed for the state of Virginia at Richmond,[43] and the Pantheon to his own University of Virginia with the Rotunda that he placed at one end of the campus.[44]

Thomas Jefferson also served as patron for other American artists working in the classical style. The most important was Benjamin Latrobe (1764–1820), an Englishman who arrived in Virginia in 1796.[45] His 1799 Bank of Pennsylvania building was the first Greek revival structure in America.[46] After the British burned Washington in 1814, Latrobe was put in charge of rebuilding the capital. Another classicizing architect of the early Republic was Charles Bulfinch of Boston (1763–1844). Bulfinch studied at Harvard, whose library already housed such works as Stuart and Revett, Robert Wood's *Ruins of Palmyra* and Robert Adam's *Ruins of*

---

39. Wiebenson 1969: 1–18, 25–35.
40. Dinsmoor 1943: 71.
41. Wills 1984; Richard 1994.
42. Mumford Jones 1964: 263–68.
43. W. H. Adams 1976: 225–29, 393–99.
44. W. H. Adams 1976: 294–97.
45. Hamlin 1955; Andrews 1964: 75–81.
46. Hamlin 1955: 152–57; Kennedy 1990: 437–378.

the Palace of the Emperor Diocletian at Spalato in Dalmatia.[47] He took his own architectural grand tour in 1785–87, during which he visited the Maison Carrée and then went on to Florence and Rome.[48] He returned to the United States to promote the classical revival through his buildings in Boston and Hartford and eventually Latrobe as architect of the capital.[49]

Greek and Roman portraiture also strongly influenced the sculptural iconography of the early Republic. Public sculpture does not enjoy a good reputation today. Many examples of the early post-independence period have been destroyed or relegated to museum storerooms. This allows us to forget the great role that such works played in the civic life of eighteenth- and nineteenth-century America, when other types of public icons and visual images were more limited in availability. The connection between political ideology and official images can be seen in the vehemence with which an equestrian statue of George III was attacked by a New York mob at the outbreak of the Revolution.[50]

The government of the new Republic had to create new official icons to replace those of the discredited British monarchy. Much of this early image formation focused on George Washington, the father of his country and a statesman who rose above the rapidly emerging party politics of the period. Gary Wills, in his book *Cincinnatus*, has explored the way this new public iconography of Washington was created and how the sculptural traditions of Greece and Rome were pressed into service to give Washington greater heroic historical associations.[51] This process culminated in 1841, when the neoclassical American sculptor Horatio Greenough unveiled his highly controversial statue of Washington rendered seminude in the manner of the seated Olympian Zeus of the fifth-century B.C. sculptor Phidias.[52] The statue demonstrated Greenough's considerable knowledge of ancient sculpture and his sympathy for the increasingly popular classical Greek art style.[53] However, public indignation at the undress of the *pater patriae* and the close association of the image of the first president with pagan divinity and autocracy rapidly rose. This view was summarized by the diarist Philip Hone of New York:

It looks like a great Herculean warrior-like Venus of the bath, a grand Martial Magog-undraped, with a huge napkin lying on his lap and covering his lower extremities and he is preparing to perform his ablutions in the act of consigning his sword to the care of the attendant. Washington was too prudent and careful of

47. Kirker 1969: 4–5.
48. Andrews 1964: 96–99; Place 1968; Kirker 1969: 6–13.
49. Dinsmoor 1943: 73; Kirker and Kirker 1964: 29–52.
50. Marks 1981; Dimmick 1991: 5.
51. Wills 1984: 55–84. See also P. Anderson 1980.
52. Brooks 1958: 43–46; L. B. Miller 1966: 61–65.
53. Crane 1972: 69–85.

his health to expose himself thus in a climate so uncertain as ours, to say nothing of the indecency of such an exposure on which he was known to be exceedingly fastidious. (quoted in Crane 1972: 83)

Nathaniel Hawthorne, writing in 1858, reflected a similar sentiment:

Did anybody ever see Washington nude? It is inconceivable. He had no nakedness, but I imagine he was born with his clothes on and made a stately bow on his first appearance in the world. (quoted in P. Anderson 1980: 17)

In spite of certain semifiascoes of the Greenough type, classical iconography and classical prototypes continued to influence public sculpture during much of the nineteenth century. Images of American orators reflected Greek representations of Demosthenes and other great Athenian speakers. The New Englander Daniel Webster kept reproductions of Demosthenes and Aeschines in his house, and everyone quoted classical orators. In one of the standard rhetorical handbooks of the period, *Living Orators of America* (1849), the author, E. L. Magoon, employed images of classical statues to describe the style of famous American orators.[54]
Even more pervasive was classicism in architecture. By the middle years of the nineteenth century the classical revival style had spread throughout the Northeast, South, and Middle West and was employed both in public buildings like courthouses and churches and in opulent and not so opulent private dwellings of the cultivated and the culturally pretentious.[55] Even cemetery art reflected the change as urns and other classical notifs replaced the skulls and winged spirits of traditional tomb decoration.[56] Initially the neo-classical architecture showed more of an association with the artistic and historical experience of Rome, but during the first half of the nineteenth century its iconography and associations increasingly reflected a growing knowledge of and appreciation for Greece. The so-called Greek revival architecture which arrived with Latrobe was usually a hybrid style blending both Greek and Roman elements, but the popular label reflects the reality that America was gradually coming to identify more with Greece and what was seen as its purer political, intellectual, and artistic values.[57]
This diffusion of Greek revival architecture throughout the pre-Civil War United States was associated with a slow but steady increase in Americans' direct acquaintance with Greece itself.[58] In 1806 the young Nich-

54. J. S. Crawford 1974. See Mumford Jones 1964: 268–69 for the classical quality of Webster's oratory.
55. Hamlin 1944: 159–314; Nye 1960: 268–73; Pierson 1970: 395–460; Kennedy 1990.
56. Deetz 1977: 68–72; Bushman 1993: 21.
57. Hamlin 1944; Nye 1960: 272–74.
58. Larrabee 1957: 3–26.

olas Biddle of Philadelphia (1786–1844) took advantage of his status as a low-level American diplomat to travel widely not only in Napoleonic-dominated Europe but also to Greece itself. He was virtually the first American to make such a trip. His letters, unpublished until quite recently, provide the first extensive reaction of an educated, cultivated American to the Greek experience.[59]

Although Biddle published little on his Greek trip during his lifetime, he was able to use his immediate experience with classical art and architecture in other ways. While in Paris he secured Napoleon's cooperation in acquiring and shipping a large collection of classical casts and copies to the United States.[60] He then returned to a highly successful career in banking and finance, which culminated in his controversial presidency at the Bank of the United States during Andrew Jackson's administration.[61] Biddle was able to use his public position and private wealth to promote the Hellenic style in architecture. The Bank of the United States building he commissioned for Philadelphia was modeled on the Parthenon, and he strongly influenced the neoclassical design of the the Girard College buildings. Biddle's mansion on his Andalusia estate near Philadelphia also incorporated many classical elements.[62]

The neoclassical architectural style was complemented and to a certain degree challenged in the later decades before the Civil War by buildings, especially residences, built in the Italianate and neo-Gothic manner.[63] Still, American public architecture, not only in big cities but also in the small towns of areas as separate as Maine, Ohio, and Georgia was predominantly classical. Cultivated Americans felt that true architectural beauty was classical and especially Greek beauty. It is not surprising that the first generation of archaeologists that emerged after the Civil War had strong architectural backgrounds and went seeking the roots of classical beauty in the public monuments of ancient Greece.

This same admiration for Greek art extended to sculpture, although the carved marbles produced by artists of the same nineteenth-century classical revival aroused controversy. Horatio Greenough's Washington depicted in the guise of Olympian Zeus was seen as ridiculous and Hiram Powers's Greek Slave as scandalous. Nonetheless, the public demand for classical images kept many American sculptors well employed. As taste changed from classical to modern the works of these artists became objects of ridicule and were generally relegated to museum storerooms.

59. Larrabee 1957: 11–18; Biddle 1993.
60. Crane 1972: 11.
61. Govan 1959.
62. Dinsmoor 1943: 81–82; Andrews 1964: 140–42; Pierson 1970: 437–38; Biddle 1993: 11–12.
63. Nye 1960: 273–74: Andrews 1964: 103–37.

Recently there has been a revived interest in nineteenth-century sculptures, especially nude females, but such research is usually focused on efforts to deconstruct them as expressions of ambivalent Victorian sexual attitudes. Bound, nude females depicted as Turkish slaves and Indian captives are seen as playing to a whole range of male fantasies in a somewhat repressed and hypocritical era.[64]

The work of painters and sculptors was of considerable importance in promulgating the classical style in the visual arts when there were few other means available to shape public taste. The leaders were a group of American expatriate artists residing in Florence and Rome. First came the painters, led by John Vanderlyn (1775–1852) and Washington Allston (1779–1843). Vanderlyn first studied in Paris, where he learned to draw from classical casts. In 1803 he was back in Paris, buying casts for the American Academy of Fine Arts. By 1805 he was in Rome, where he painted his *Marius amid the Ruins of Carthage* with its background pastiche of the Parthenon and the aqueduct ruins of the Roman Campagna.[65]

Washington Allston became interested in the fine arts at Harvard when he read Joshua Reynolds's *Discourses Delivered to the Students of the Royal Academy*. He traveled to Europe, where he not only drew from the antique but also fell under the influence of the grand masters.[66] He worked in Rome from 1804 to 1808 and was strongly influenced by the neoclassicism of the Europeans Flaxman, Canova, and Thorvaldsen. In Allston's Italian landscape paintings one sees the restored architecture of antiquity, not the brooding ruins of a Piranesi that painters like Thomas Cole soon made popular in the United States. There is a certain irony that these American painting pioneers, much praised and lionized during their stays in Europe, had what they felt was a disappointing impact when they returned to the United States.[67] Still, they were part of the larger movement that impressed the visual vocabulary of antiquity deeper onto the American consciousness.

Slightly later American sculptors came to Italy. Horatio Greenough (1805–1852) arrived in Rome in 1825.[68] Born in Boston, he studied the casts at the Boston Athenaeum and learned the rudiments of sculptural technique from artisans in that city. He pursued classics at Harvard, and absorbed the ideology of neoclassicism from Washington Allston. After an initial trip to Europe, Greenough returned to the United States, but in

64. L. B. Miller 1966: 222–24; Hyman 1976; Vance 1989 1: 232–237; Jenkyns 1991: 26–27.

65. Brooks 1958: 17–8; J. T. Flexner 1969: 143–47: Craven 1979: 10–20; Cooper 1993: 87–89.

66. Brooks 1958: 18–25; J. T. Flexner 1969: 124–42; Craven 1979: 20–34; Vance 1989 1: 105–13.

67. Craven: 1979: 42–43.

68. Crane 1972: 21–28.

1828 set out for Florence, which was to be his long-term home and work-place.[69] In Florence his artistic production focused on busts of contemporaries and the occasional close imitation of classical works. His nudes such as his *Venus Victrix* reflect a complex combination of classical humanism and German idealism, blending Winckelmann with New England transcendentalism. Interestingly enough, Greenough was critical of much superficial, flexible neoclassicism in the United States, where Greek temple forms were turned into banks. He sought to apply the principles, not the elements, of Greek art in America. His complex dialogue between past and present in some ways anticipated the aesthetic program of Charles Eliot Norton, the founder of American classical archaeology.[70]

Hiram Powers (1805–1873) is best known to American art historians today as the creator of the Greek Slave, a nude bound female that derived its form from the classical Aphrodite of Praxiteles and sought to capture the suffering of the Greek people under Turkish oppression. Powers himself was born in rural Vermont, from which his family moved to Cincinnati, a center of some culture on the frontier.[71] There Powers learned the sculptor's craft and received his first exposure to classical art through casts. After stays in Washington and Boston, he moved to Florence in 1837.[72] Although his reputation had been based on his marble busts of famous contemporaries, he sought to expand his range of subjects and became especially attracted to the female nude. This was the city of the Venus di Medici, a statue that fascinated Powers. He described her qualities thus: "It is my opinion that no entirely original statue of a female can ever equal the Venus di Medici. No other attitude embodies so much grace. There is not an angle in it. From head to foot, all the movements are curves and in strict accordance with Hogarth's line of grace" (quoted in Crane 1972: 195).

In 1839–42 Powers produced a nude, classical Eve and in 1843 the famous Greek Slave. The form is that of the classical Venus, but the chains and the cross on the garment thrown off at her side make her into a figure of contemporary Greek innocence soon to be violated by the Turks. As William Vance has pointed out, the addition of chains and cross create an implied narrative and "the narratives that justify . . . nudity invariably focus the mind on sexuality more than an autonomous Venus so identified would."[73] Evoking a range of emotions, from kinky sexuality to sympathy for the cause of Greek independence, the *Greek Slave* proved enormously popular. Its tour of the United States in 1847–49 yielded some

69. Crane 1972: 35–67, 87–123.
70. Crane 1972: 148–66.
71. Brooks 1958: 47–50; Crane 1972: 175–79.
72. Crane 1972: 180–90.
73. Vance 1989, 1: 235.

$22,000. The statue was exhibited within a curtained booth at London's Crystal Palace exhibition of 1851. Eventually eight copies were made.[74] The Greek Slave launched a small industry in Eves, female captives, and even a nude rendition of California, which made the Venus type and the ideals of the classical nude very familiar on the American scene.[75]

Thomas Crawford (1814–1857), the third of the major American neoclassical sculptors, made his career in Rome, not Florence. Arriving there in 1835, he quickly moved into the orbit of the Danish neoclassical sculptor Bertel Thorvaldsen.[76] Crawford had learned the sculptor's craft in New York, where he could also study casts of classical and neoclassical sculpture at the National Academy of the Arts of Design. In Rome he produced a long series of busts, sentimental child images, and statues based on classical themes, including the Orpheus and Cerberus of 1838–43 and the Anacreon of 1842.[77] In his later career Crawford was also a very successful producer of public art for such cities as Washington and Richmond.[78]

All these sculptors were drawn to Italy by its artistic treasures, appreciation for artistic life, inexpensive materials, cheap lifestyle, and a tradition of sculptural production and copying that allowed them to produce their creations rapidly and inexpensively. The sculptors came to know well the collections of classical sculpture in Italy, and these provided models for their own creations, which often closely reworked Greek and Roman themes.

A fourth figure who deserves mention in this context is William Wetmore Story (1819–1895), because he represented the link between the sculptor's world and the expanding world of the cultivated American tourist.[79] His memoir, *Roba di Roma*, first published in 1862, captured the era in Rome as seen through the eyes of a cultivated American. Story settled in Rome, occupying an apartment in the Palazzo Barberini. This apartment became a pilgrimage place for most cultured Americans who came to Rome. They also visited his studio in great numbers.[80] Such visits to artists' studios became a part of these tourists' repertoire and often resulted in the resident artists' neoclassical works being purchased and shipped back to the United States. Story as a sculptor focused on producing classical draped female figures, representing such historical personages as Cleo-

74. Larrabee 1957: 250–51; Crane 1972: 203–22; Vance 1989, 1: 233–43.
75. Crane 1972: 223–38; Hyman 1976.
76. Crane 1972: 273–88.
77. Crane 1972: 289–333; Vance 1989, 1: 344–52.
78. Crane 1972: 335–408.
79. Brooks 1958: 100–107; the significance of Story for the Roman community of that era is best captured in the memorial volume compiled by Henry James (James 1903).
80. Dinsmoor 1943: 81; Vance 1989, 2: 145–52, 187–93.

patra and Agrippina. He also composed verse letters and dramatic mono-
logues based on such ancient figures as Phidias and Praxiteles.[81]

Important too in the creation of public views of antiquity was a slightly
later group of painters, who also traveled to Italy and brought back Romantic landscape scenes often focused on Roman ruins. Central to this
group was Thomas Cole (1801–1848). Cole was English in origins but
made his artistic career in the United States. Cole was deeply influenced
by his time in Italy. Two of his most striking Italian landscapes with ancient remains were his *Ruins of Aqueducts in the Campagna di Roma* and *Mt.
Aetna from Taormina*, both done in 1843.[82]

By 1836 Cole had completed a cycle of grandiose paintings titled *The
Course of Empire*. His patron for this project was the pioneer New York
collector Lumond Reed.[83] The series depicted Cole's vision of the rise
and fall of an ancient empire (a thinly disguised ancient Rome), which
he used to comment on contemporary American politics and society.[84]
The central painting portrays the historical culmination of this fictional
empire. The focus is an opulent triumph set against a fantasy background, which is a complex blend of Greek and Roman architecture. The
cycle continues with the fiery destruction of the imperial city and con-
cludes with *The Course of Empire: Desolation*, a depiction of ruins in a
pastoral setting that took the viewers back to the landscape traditions of
Poussin and Lorrain. Many who saw the cycle, which received an enthusiastic reception, interpreted it as Cole's hostile commentary on the hubris
of Jacksonian America, which he saw heading to the same fate as ancient
Rome. The themes and imagery of *The Course of Empire* certainly demonstrated the ongoing centrality of classical reference in American intellectual and cultural life.

Americans and the New Grand Tour

The increased interest in neoclassical architecture, painting, and sculpture in the United States was stimulated by the expansion of tourism in
the first half of the nineteenth century. It has already been noted that in
the period before the Revolution relatively few North Americans had
undertaken the Grand Tour of Italy. America lacked the aristocratic leisure class central to the development of the Grand Tour mentality in
England. American youths may have received the foundations of a classical education in secondary school and college, but they generally went
on to study law or serve an apprenticeship in a mercantile house.

81. Vance 1989, 1: 247–55.
82. Cooper 1993: 91–92; Truettner and Wallach 1994: figs. 70–71.
83. L. B. Miller 1966: 151–55; Bender 1987: 123; Cooper 1993: 99.
84. Wallach 1994: 85–98, figs. 103–7.

International tensions also discouraged American tourism in Europe. Between the outbreak of the Revolution and the defeat of Napoleon and the end of the War of 1812, there were few periods when both the seas and the continent were safe for any but the most intrepid Americans. It is significant that two of the major explorers of Europe's classical heritage were Nicholas Biddle and Thomas Jefferson, men whose military and diplomatic activities took them to the Continent, and whose official status gave them a certain degree of protection.

Waterloo and the collapse of Napoleon's empire, America's peace treaty with Britain, and the reduction of the Barbary pirate menace, owing in part to a vigorous American military effort, opened up Europe and the Mediterranean to American visitors. The introduction of regular packet boats and then steamships made the Atlantic passage quicker, safer, and more comfortable. By the middle of the century, the expanded railroads provided a better means of land transportation within Europe itself.[85]

American society was also changing. During this period, there developed a growing middle class, which was increasingly well educated and felt the need for exposure to European culture that would come only with European travel. Interest in the historical sites of the Mediterranean was stimulated by an education that was still classically based, but also by an increasingly sophisticated travel literature, by the classical and Italian painting and sculpture to be seen in copies and occasionally even in originals in cultivated households, and by such visual showpieces as the painted dioramas of Athens and Rome that went on display in a number of American cities during this era.[86]

During the mid-nineteenth century, new middle-class tourists from both England and America displaced the Grand Tour English gentlemen as the dominant foreign travelers in Italy. Indicative of the importance Mediterranean travel held for educated Americans was the fact that almost all the Boston-Cambridge-Concord literary figures of the American Renaissance visited Italy. This formative New England experience of Italy was immortalized in Nathaniel Hawthorne's *Marble Faun*, published in 1860.[87] Significant also was the fact that these new tour groups included women as well as men; for in America, by the mid-nineteenth century, women played an increasingly important role in cultural patronage.[88]

Tour structures and the reactions to the monuments and art works of all but the most sophisticated and independent American tourists were

85. Baker 1964: 20–45.
86. Dinsmoor 1943: 79; Baker 1964: 20–45; McNeal 1995.
87. Brooks 1958: 135–44; Vance 1989, 1: 113–25.
88. Vance 1989, 2: 41–42, 116–17, 218–20, 276–83. Prezzolini 1933: 245–300 lists a dozen women who published accounts of their travels in Italy during this era.

orchestrated by guides and guidebooks and were generally rather stereo-typed. Rome and Florence were the principal cities visited. The Rome tourists saw was the pleasant, sleepy, papal Rome soon to be transformed by the unification of Italy and Rome's designation as the national capital. In this era before systematic excavation, much fewer classical monuments in sites like the forum and Palatine could be seen; and more could be left to the imagination.[89]

Also extremely important were visits to the museums and private collections of antiquities in Rome.[90] The number and duration of these visits depended on a tourist's gender, connections, and interests. Women generally outlasted men in the cold, stone corridors of the Roman galleries. But the Capitoline and Vatican sculpture galleries were required stops, and certain pieces like the Apollo Belvedere and the Laocoön had to be especially admired.

For the more scholarly tourist, there were new discoveries to be investigated and scholarly contacts to be made. A considerable amount of excavation was taking place in Rome during this period. The years of Napoleonic occupation had seen extensive archaeological work in areas like the Forum of Trajan.[91] The papal government was also developing its own archaeological agenda, trying to use excavations and museum modernization to advance its own special identity with the classical past.[92] The impact of new German classical and archaeological scholarship also began to make itself felt. In 1829 the German Eduard Gerhard had founded his Istituto di Corrispondenza Archeologica at the Capitoline. Gerhard's intent was to bring to the Istituto an international community of scholars, who would exchange ideas and publish the results of their research in his new archaeological journal.[93] Although the antiquarian tradition of classical archaeology, which had flourished in the eighteenth century, was declining in many Italian centers, local figures like Bartolomeo Borghesi of San Marino (1781–1860) still produced scholarship that impressed rising academic stars like the young German Theodor Mommsen.[94]

The remains of ancient Rome were intertwined with medieval, Renaissance, Baroque, and modern structures. This did not allow quick and easy comprehension of Rome as an ancient Roman center. If Americans wanted to see better preserved and more comprehensible archaeological sites, they had to go south to the Bay of Naples and visit Pompeii and

89. Vance 1989, 1: 3–42; James 1995: 122–92.
90. Vance 1989, 1: 182–257.
91. Ridley 1992.
92. Springer 1987: 21–114.
93. *EHCA* s.v. Gerhard, Friedrich Wilhelm Eduard (1795–1867); Rieche 1979: 1–54; Schnapp 1982: 767–71; Marchand 1996: 53–62.
94. Fraschetti 1982.

Herculaneum.[95] In the Campanian ruins the nineteenth-century tourist experienced not the slowly decaying remains of the ancient capital, but a Roman town stopped dead at a single tragic moment. As far back as the era of Copley and the Izards, Americans had visited Pompeii. This tourist flow increased, and the influences of those visits made their way back to America. By the early nineteenth century, motifs from Pompeian paintings had been incorporated into a variety of American decorative arts. Bulwer-Lytton's *The Last Days of Pompeii* published in 1834 was widely read in the United States, and Americans of the period began to produce their own small body of Pompeii literature.[96] Statues of Nydia, the blind flower girl of Edward Bulwer-Lytton's novel, became very popular in the United States.[97]

Not far south of Pompeii were the ruins of Paestum, among the most important examples of Greek architecture to be found anywhere in the Mediterranean. The landscape was desolate and malarial, and few of these early nineteenth-century travelers to Pompeii and Herculaneum followed Copley and the Izards south to see these authentic Greek remains. The trio of New Englanders who were the first to study at Göttingen University in Germany—Edward Everett, Joseph Green Cogswell, and George Ticknor—did seek out the Greek temples in 1817–18. Cogswell praised the collection of temples there as "the sublimest monument anywhere to be found of the destruction of time."[98] In 1832 Thomas Cole visited and painted the ruins. Eighteen years later, in his funeral eulogy for Cole, the American poet and journalist William Cullen Bryant described the temples of Paestum as "the grandest and most perfect remains of the architecture of Greece."[99]

Even more impressive Greek remains were to be seen in Sicily, but that island remained almost as inaccessible to Americans as Greece. However, in 1802 a young Charlestonian, Joel Roberts Poinsett, traveled there and was very impressed by the classical remains at places like Agrigento. In the theater at Taormina he recalled Euripides and Sophocles, and on Etna he evoked the spirit of the philosopher Empedocles.[100]

95. Baker 1964: 70–74; Reinhold 1984: 265–79.

96. Reinhold 1984: 271–76.

97. Rogers 1974; Winkes 1993: 129.

98. Baker 1964: 73. In the discovery of Paestum, Goethe led the way. He visited the site on his way to Sicily in 1787 and found the ruins "offensive and even terrifying." By the time he returned, his views on the architecture of the temples had become much more positive and heralded a new era in the appreciation of Greek architecture (Jenkyns 1991: 51–52).

99. Reinhold 1984: 268–70.

100. Rippy 1935: 11–14; Larrabee 1957: 9–10. Poinsett had hoped to visit Greece, but war between Russia and Turkey prevented it. While sympathetic to the cause of Greek independence, he evoked the principles of the Monroe Doctrine to limit American involvement (Rippy 1935: 80–82). Poinsett later in life wrote on Etruscan remains (Rippy 1935: 198).

One American intellectual in this pre-Civil War epoch moved beyond archaeological tourism to more serious scholarly investigations: John Izard Middleton of South Carolina (1785–1849).[101] Educated at Cambridge, he spent much of his life on the continent as a man of leisure. While in Italy he became fascinated with the remains of the so-called cyclopean walls to be found in several towns of Latium. These constructions of large, irregular stone blocks, now dated to the middle of the first millennium B.C., were then attributed to the obscure early Italic race of the Pelasgians. Middleton went to towns like Segni and studied those wall structures carefully. In 1812 he published *Grecian Remains in Italy, a Description of Cyclopian Walls and of Roman Antiquities. With topographical and picturesque Views of Ancient Latium.* This volume, with its vivid, detailed descriptions and color plates of the remains, was the first real American published work in classical archaeology.[102]

Between 1815 and 1861, many educated Americans came to know the classical remains of Italy well. The Forum, the Colosseum, the famous Greek and Roman statues in the various museums, and the houses of Pompeii became familiar landmarks for virtually every cultured American. Yet the nature of their reaction to the classical heritage was changing during those decades. Americans no longer identified with the heroes of Roman history to the degree that they had in the 1780s. They discovered that contemporary Italy, whatever its charms, bore little resemblance to ancient Rome.[103] The new generation that reached maturity in the years after the War of 1812 looked for a classical inspiration different from that of the Founding Fathers.[104] Helleno-Romanticism came to dominate in England and Germany, the two European cultures that most shaped American thinking in the early nineteenth century.[105] Despite Garibaldi's appeal and the journalistic efforts of Americans like Margaret Fuller, the mid-nineteenth-century Italians' struggle to attain independence and national unity did not provide the same degree of romantic identification for classically oriented Americans as the often barbarous Greek wars of independence.[106]

American sculptors and architects increasingly turned toward a Greece that was idealized but still little known, and away from the evocative but somber brick and cement ruins of Rome and the charming but often

101. Brooks 1958: 16–17.
102. Norton 1885. Appropriately enough, this article on Middleton as the first American classical archaeologist appeared in the first issue of the *American Journal of Archaeology*.
103. Baker 1964: 46–101.
104. Larrabee 1957: 24–25; Biddle 1993: 12 n. 12.
105. Jenkyns 1991. On Germany, cf. E.M. Butler 1958; Marchand 1996: 4–35.
106. Cooper 1993: 36–37.

decadent world of contemporary Italy with its poverty and papist supersti-tions.[107] The reasons were both aesthetic and ideological. Americans who studied in Germany became increasingly familiar with Winckelmann's viewpoint that one had to seek the purer world of Greek art beyond the Roman remains. Moreover, ancient Greece had democratic associations that not even republican, let alone imperial Rome could claim. As Benjamin Latrobe stated in 1811, "the history of Grecian art refutes the vulgar opinion that the arts are incompatible with liberty."[108] Greece slowly displaced Italy as the focus of American classical identity, and when American classical archaeology was created it was on a Hellenic base.

More politically conscious Greeks had identified with the goals of the American Revolution, and Demetrios Ypsilantis sailed from Greece to fight for the American cause.[109] Yet very few Americans went to Greece before or immediately after that country gained its independence from the Ottoman Turks in the wars of 1821–33. Even the boldest of the young were daunted by the threats of war, banditry, and disease. The father of the pioneering American philologist George Ticknor, who was one of the party that had visited Paestum, prohibited his son from going to Greece, saying "To see Athens, my son, is not worth exposing your life, nor the time nor the money you must spend to see it."[110] Still some Americans did make the trip. In 1800 the first American naval vessel appeared in Aegean waters, starting a continuing, if little investigated, contact between American naval personnel and the classical Mediterranean.[111] Joseph Allen Smith, a relative of the South Carolina Izard family, seems to have been the first citizen to have visited Greece. Smith was an enthusiastic classicist who had earlier collected casts of ancient statues to be sent to Philadelphia. His trip took place around 1804. The date remains uncertain, for Smith never published an account of his travels.[112]

In 1806 the young Philadelphian Nicholas Biddle undertook an extensive journey to Greece.[113] At the opening of his first Greek journal he described the motives that inspired this ardous and even undertaking:

I had long felt an ardent desire to visit Greece. The fate of a nation whose history was the first brilliant object that my infancy and the first foundations of my early studies was so interesting that I had resolved to avail myself of any opportunity of witnessing it. The soil of Greece is sacred to Genius & to letters. The race of beings

107. Prezzolini 1933: 50–78; Reinhold 1984: 214–20; Cooper 1993: 15–19.
108. Quoted in Cooper 1993: 76.
109. Pappas 1985: 27.
110. Dinsmoor 1943: 82.
111. Larrabee 1957: 7–9; Pappas 1985: 29.
112. Larrabee 1957: 10–11; Biddle 1993: 99 n. 141; Cooper 1993: 81.
113. Biddle 1993.

whose achievements warm our youthful fancy has long disappeared. But the sod under which they repose, the air which listened to their poetry & their eloquence, the hills which saw their valour are still the same. (1993: 49)

Biddle's tour of Greece was impressive, given the wretched communications of the era. He even reached such remote sites as Bassae in the Peloponnesus. His comments on what he saw revealed a perceptive, well-educated mind reflecting on new experiences. Although Biddle engaged in occasional effusions of Helleno-Romanticism, his opinion of contemporary Greece and the Greeks on the whole was rather low. "Are these men, the wretches little superior to the beasts whom they drive heedless over the ruins, are these men *Athenians.*"[114] Yet when the Greek War of Independence broke out, Biddle became a supporter of the Hellenic cause.[115]

In 1818 Edward Everett (1794–1865), who had studied classical archaeology in Germany and became the first professor of classics in the United States, traveled to Greece with an American friend, Theodore Lyman.[116] The direct experiences of the monuments acquired in Greece and the academic knowledge of the emerging discipline of classical archaeology gained at Göttingen were incorporated into the lectures on Greek antiquities that Everett presented in Boston on his return. They earned the approval of no less an emerging intellectual luminary than the young Ralph Waldo Emerson.[117]

Everett's love of Greek art and culture persisted even during a later career that was focused mainly on politics and diplomacy. He also became a strong advocate for the cause of Greek independence.[118] It was Everett along with another Bostonian, Charles Sumner, who urged Horatio Greenough to complete his infamous statue of George Washington rendered as Phidian Zeus. The accomplishments as well as the failures of the ancient Greek and Romans remained a mirror for Everett's activities in American politics.[119] Fittingly he incorporated a small frieze of ancient marble from some classical monument, no doubt a souvenir of his travels in Greece many years before into his tomb monument in Boston's Mt. Auburn Cemetery.

American interest in Greece increased with the start of the Greek War of Independence.[120] Americans had read Shelley, Keats, and Byron and

---

114. Biddle 1993: 112.
115. Pappas 1985: 34–35.
116. Larrabee 1957: 34–40; Pappas 1985: 29–30; Bartlett 1996.
117. Dinsmoor 1943: 82; Reinhold 1984: 205–6; Bartlett 1996: 432–33.
118. Larrabee 1957: 69–73; Pappas 1985: 29–30, 34, 55, 62–66.
119. Bartlett 1996: 434–35.
120. Larrabee 1957: 93–175; Pappas 1985.

were as Helleno-Romantic as the British. Educated opinion was strongly sympathetic to the Hellenic struggle. Highly biased accounts of the Greek rebellion and Turkish repression and evocative works of art like Powers's Greek Slave rallied Americans to the Greek cause. Groups in cities like Boston provided financial aid to the Greeks.[121] Some Americans, like Dr. Samuel Gridley Howe, went off to fight for the cause of Greek independence.[122]

After the end of the war of Greek independence and especially in the 1840s and 1850s, the number of American visitors to Greece increased. The way was led in 1848 by James Masson Hoppin, later to be professor of art history at Yale and author of *Greek Art on Greek Soil* (1897).[123] In 1851–52 Henry Baird became the first American scholar to study in Greece. In 1856 Baird published *Modern Greece*, an account of his impressions of the country.[124] He was followed by a growing group of American academic Hellenists such as Cornelius Felton (1807–1862), future Harvard professor and president.[125] Several of these pioneering Hellenic explorers played a key role in the professionalization of American classics after the Civil War.

The Promotion of Art and Taste in the United States Before the Civil War

The expanding exploration of the wellsprings of Greek and Roman civilization was part of America's expanding cultural horizons. The period between the War of 1812 and the Civil War saw many active, if often futile, efforts to elevate public artistic taste in the United States. Cultural leaders felt that the new democracy, if it was to succeed, needed to have an educated, culturally elevated electorate. To achieve this goal, advocates of the social role of taste sought to promote public art institutions, which would not only provide art instruction but also offer the public both permanent collections and temporary exhibitions of works of art. These institutions would serve to educate the general public and provide appropriate examples of taste for the emerging artist and artisan community. They became especially important as America expanded westward, away from the Atlantic seaboard and into regions where the artistically and culturally ambitious did not have easy access to England and the Continent.

America did not have the traditions of private collecting found in Europe since the Renaissance. Large concentrations of wealth were rare,

121. Pappas 1985: 32–43; St. Clair 1972: 337–47.
122. Schwartz 1956: 7–38; St. Clair 1972; Pappas 1985: 118–20.
123. Larrabee 1957: 255.
124. Seymour 1902: 9; Larrabee 1957: 256–57.
125. Larrabee 1957: 258–59; Wiesen 1981–82.

and the new Republic's laws of partible inheritance discouraged the intergenerational perpetuation of great fortunes and the continuation of great art collections.[126] Cultural entrepreneurs like Charles Willson Peale did develop private museums, but these tended to focus more on natural history and ethnography.[127] The first public art museum in the United States, the Wadsworth Athenaeum of Hartford, opened in 1844, but it focused mainly on painting.[128] In 1855 the young artist W. J. Stillman started the *Crayon*, the first art journal published in America. In spite of the financial and journalistic support of many Northeast cultural luminaries, the journal lasted only a few years, but during that period it played a major role shaping the arts in America.[129] Stillman's interest in art and archaeology continued, and he became an important figure in the emergence of American classical archaeology after the Civil War.

Central to the advancement of aesthetic taste were the artistic academies that began to be founded in American cities. Their aim was to promote quality artistic production in the United States. This was to be achieved in part by supplying aspiring young artists with worthy examples of art from the past. The American Academy of Fine Arts was founded in New York in 1802. In 1826 the National Academy of Design was established.[130] Many citizens of the new Republic got their first, if rather indirect, contact with classical art through art academies.

Original works of Greek and Roman art were rare indeed in America before the Civil War. A few fragments of sculpture and examples of Greek vases were brought back by the crews of American warships, and Lucien Napoleon sent a gift from his excavations at Vulci.[131] One of the more unusual ancient imports was a Roman sarcophagus that Jesse Elliott, captain of the U.S.S. *Constitution*, acquired in Beirut in 1839, and presented to the U.S. government to serve as the future burial place of Andrew Jackson. The associations were judged too imperial for that most democratic of presidents, and the sarcophagus ended up in the newly established Smithsonian.[132] Most of these antiquities were curiosities rather than objects of great beauty, and they were scattered in a great various small public and private collections.

More important for promoting interest in the art of Greece and Rome were casts of famous Greco-Roman originals. Europeans had begun col-

126. L. B. Miller 1966: 141.
127. L. B. Miller 1966: 103–5; Cooper 1993: 79.
128. Silk 1982: 1–14.
129. Stillman 1901: 223–31; Stein 1967: 101–23.
130. L. B. Miller 1966: 90–102; Stein 1967: 2; Bender 1987: 62.
131. Dinsmoor 1943: 87–92; Cooper 1993: 98–99.
132. Ward Perkins 1958.

lecting casts of famous works like the Laocoön as far back as the late seventeenth century.[133] The painter John Smibert of Boston appears to have brought the first classical casts to America. In 1784 a cast of the Venus di Medici arrived in the United States.[134] In 1802 Robert and Edward Livingstone contracted to have plaster casts made of such famous sculptural pieces as the Laocoön, the Apollo Belvedere, and the Venus di Medici for the proposed Society of the Fine Arts in New York.[135]

Artistic and cultural academies took the lead in creating usable cast collections available to both aspiring artists and the general public. In 1805 Nicholas Biddle was commissioned to purchase a suitable cast collection for Philadelphia.[136] By 1822 the Boston Athenaeum had a small collection of "ancient statues" and casts; by 1825 it was the best cast collection in America.[137] By the 1850s, the southwestern Ohio city of Cincinnati, which saw itself as the Athens of the frontier, was able to muster a room of nude statues complete with fig leaves and to provide a collection of casts for its School of Design for Women.[138]

The display of casts, especially nudes, often stirred a lively debate among genteel patrons. Some of the elite public responded with expected prudishness; even artists reacted with a certain ambivalence to the growth of the cast galleries, but their reasons were more practical. The presence of the cast collections did allow them to study and copy masterpieces from Greek and Roman antiquity without extensive and expensive periods of study in Europe. At the same time, artists feared that the presence of casts of famous Greek and Roman sculptures would reduce the demand for original works of art and thus affect their livelihood.[139]

Other instruments for cultivating refined popular taste, such as the historical novel, supported the spread of classical values. As has already been noted, *The Last Days of Pompeii* (1834) by the Englishman Edward Bulwer-Lytton became immensely popular in America, since more and more tourists were visiting the ruins of Pompeii and Herculaneum.[140] Expressive of the enthusiasm for the novel was the fact that the first public statue set up in the Mississippi valley was the 1839 rendition of the Bulwer-Lytton character, *Nydia, the Blind Girl of Pompeii*, by the Cincinnati

133. Connor 1989: 192–93, 200–206.
134. Dinsmoor 1943: 72; Cooper 1993: 77.
135. Dinsmoor 1943: 84–85; L. B. Miller 1966: 91–92.
136. Dinsmoor 1943: 85; L. B. Miller 1966: 106.
137. L. B. Miller 1966: 115–20; Cooper 1993: 83.
138. L. B. Miller 1966: 192–200.
139. L. B. Miller 1966: 107, 194–200.
140. *EHCA* s.v. Bulwer-Lytton, Edward George Earle, First Baron Lytton (1803–73); *Pompeii as Source and Inspiration* 1977.

sculptor Edward Brackett (1818–1908).[141] The image became immensely popular and more than fifty copies were made. Even more popular was the Nydia of Randolph Rogers (1825–1892), of which some one hundred copies were sold. A visitor to Rogers's studio in Rome saw seven of these Nydias "all in a row, all listening, all groping, and seven marble-cutters at work, cutting them out."[142]

The dominance of classical values in the arts, literature, and education by no means went unchallenged. In the post-revolutionary years, certain prominent figures like the Pennsylvanian physician Benjamin Rush expressed concern about the centrality of classics in the new Republic.[143] Arguments of practicality, used against the classics in education ever since, were raised. Many held that the young Republic needed real farmers with scientific knowledge, not those whose understanding of the land was the result of reading of Vergil's *Eclogues*. Such a cultured figure and phil-Hellene as Albert Gallatin of New York questioned the centrality of the classics in the modern college and university.[144]

The defenders of classics countered with their own arguments. In 1828 the professors of Yale University produced a detailed defense of the classical curriculum.[145] Yet the disagreements continued. Indicative of this ongoing controversy about the worth of a classical education in America was a debate held in 1834–45 at the Cincinnati College of Teachers. It pitted one educator, Alexander Kinmont, who argued that the classics were the "pillar and foundation of solid learning," against another, Thomas Smith Grimke, who favored an "American education in opposition to the recognized and almost universal basis of instruction — mathematics and classics."[146]

In spite of a widespread, pragmatic opposition to classics, Greek and Latin remained central to the secondary and college curricula of much of the United States. However, even the advocates of the classical curriculum felt that instruction based on rote mastery of Greek and Latin fell short of the ideals inherent in a classical education. In the early nineteenth century, American colleges and universities were primitive, backwater educational institutions with archaic curricula, poorly prepared teachers, and few library or museum resources.[147]

But the winds of change were blowing. Americans were becoming

141. L. B. Miller 1966: 189, 194; Craven 1968: 187–89.
142. Quoted in Craven 1968: 313–14.
143. Reinhold 1984: 59–108; Richard 1994: 196–202.
144. Larrabee 1957: 189–90; Bender 1987: 100–104.
145. Bender 1987: 97–98.
146. Quoted in L. B. Miller 1966: 208.
147. McCaughey 1974: 246–263; Bartlett 1996: 433.

aware of the revolution in education and scholarship taking place at German universities like Göttingen. Professors there promoted rigorous textual analysis in the new type of classes known as seminars. Supported by large libraries and often by research fellowships, these academics also produced a new kind of high-quality scholarship. Scholars at German universities laid the foundations for modern classical scholarship in philology, but there was also an interest in ancient history, archaeology, and antiquities. *Altertumswissenschaft* represented an all-encompassing approach to classical scholarship that included material culture. For the spiritual heirs of Herder, Winckelmann, and Lessing, Greece as a temple of beauty played a major role in shaping both German classical archaeology and classical philology.[148]

One of America's first German-educated classical scholars was Edward Everett.[149] A brilliant undergraduate, he was appointed professor of Greek at Harvard in 1815 but almost immediately was granted leave to study in Germany and travel in Europe. Although much of his work at Göttingen focused on philology he had an archaeology course five times a week with Friedrich Gottlieb Welcker (1784–1868), one of the most distinguished early German classical archaeologists.[150] Welcker was at Göttingen for a brief period between appointments at Giessen and Bonn. At the latter university, he was entrusted with developing the library and the Kunstmuseum. In Welcker, Everett would have observed an energetic scholar who embraced both philology and archaeology, what the Germans described as the *Totalitätideal*.

Welcker was also a strong eighteenth-century idealist in his approach to Greek art. It was in this milieu that Everett became acquainted with the writings of the founder of classical archaeology, J. J. Winckelmann. In Italy Everett came to know distinguished German intellectuals and classical scholars like Karl Josias von Bunsen, B. G. Niebuhr, and William Gell.[151] Everett returned to Harvard in 1819. There he tried to introduce German scholarship and German teaching methods such as the lecture course to Harvard undergraduates. He also sought to promote Hellenism through his popular audience oriented publications and lectures. None of these efforts was notably successful, and Everett soon turned to a career in politics, university administration, and diplomacy. He is remembered in American popular history mainly as the man who gave the other Gettysburg address.

148. E. M. Butler 1958; Diehl 1978: 13–25; Connor 1989: 202–8; Marchand 1996: 3–24.
149. Reinhold 1984: 204–13.
150. *EHCA* s.v. Welcker, Friedrich Gottlieb (1784–1868); Lullies and Schiering 1988: 18–19; Bartlett 1996: 432–33; Marchand 1996: 41–42.
151. Dinsmoor 1943: 80.

By the time of the Civil War a number of American classicists had studied in Germany including Basil Gildersleeve, the founder of American classical philology, who received his doctorate from Göttingen in 1853.[152] This trend accelerated after the Civil War. By the end of the century an estimated 10,000 Americans had studied in Germany including many of the leading figures in classics.[153] The focus of American student interest shifted from the old German university centers like Göttingen to powerful newer institutions like the university at Berlin. Programs of study became more formalized, and in 1850–1870, an increased number of students took the German Ph.D.[154] This group brought German scholarly values and the German system of graduate seminars and degrees to the United States and gave them institutional life with the formation of Johns Hopkins University.

The foundations for the appreciation of classical art and for the informal study of classical archaeology had been laid in America by the time the Civil War broke out. America's cities, towns, and villages were graced with thousands of structures both public and private reflecting the influence of Greek and Roman architectural styles. Although original works of Greek and Roman art were still rare, cast collections were to be found in most major cities, and the prevailing sculptural style was blatantly classical. American tourism in Italy flourished, and the travel literature on that country was enormous. By the 1850s authoritative books on Greece based on the personal experiences of budding American classicists, such as Felton's *Diary in Greek and Turkish Waters* (1855), were beginning to be published.

Prospects and Problems in the Decades Just Before the Civil War

The foundations of classical professionalism were also being laid. New types of scholarly societies, more rigorous and specialized than the older philosophical and artistic associations, were being established. Here the Americans were following in the footsteps of England and the Continent.[155] In 1843 the American Oriental Society was founded, and in 1848 a classical archaeology section was added to it.[156] By 1858 the developing American interest in coin collecting led to the formation of the American Numismatic and Archaeology Society.[157] From the beginning, the society had a department of archaeology as well as numismatics, but the

152. Briggs 1987: 4–6.
153. Diehl 1978: 1; Jarausch 1995.
154. McCaughey 1974: 264–65; Diehl 1978: 68.
155. P. Levine 1986.
156. Kuklick 1996: 21.
157. *EHCA* s.v. "American Numismatic Society"; Adelson 1958: 11–32.

former section never flourished. The archaeology department was abol-
ished in 1894.[158]

Despite the efforts of pioneers and the significant progress made in
promoting the serious study of Greece and Rome, America was still sadly
underdeveloped in many areas of classical scholarship, especially in art
history and archaeology. In the words of Charles Eliot Norton, who was
educated at Harvard just before the Civil War:

> Our libraries were insufficiently stocked with the older books essential for thor-
> ough investigations in any department of learning, and not one of them possessed
> the means of securing a regular provision of those new books which might enable
> the student at home to keep up with the progress of learning from year to year in
> other lands. There was not a single museum containing a collection of casts from
> which even an imperfect knowledge of the historic development of ancient art, or
> the character even of its chief works could be acquired (1909–10: 252)

In some categories, such as the presence of casts in American collections,
Norton was exaggerating the deficiencies of the American scene. Still,
the United States had nothing like the British Museum or the great
universities, libraries, and museums of Germany. Even if American educational institutions had scholars trained in the new German methods,
they did not have the support structure for their research. Most frustrat-
ing of all, young returning scholars found the colleges and universities ill
prepared to accept the European innovations they sought to import.

158. Adelson 1958: 108–9.

2. The Creation of Classical Archaeology in America

In April 1865, the bloodiest and most tragic war in American history came to an end. Casualties on both sides had been especially heavy among the classically educated elites. Young men used examples from Greek and Roman history to give some sense and meaning to the battlefield experience and its aftermath. For Basil Gildersleeve, Pindar and the Persian wars and his own service as a Confederate officer in the Civil War were interconnected.[1] Even the prairie lawyer from Illinois become president evoked Greece in the most famous military funerary speech since Thucydides.[2]

The Civil War changed much on the American scene. The most immediate and visible outcome of the four-year struggle was economic development. Despite its vast human toll, the war had greatly stimulated the economy of the North and accelerated the processes of industrialization. Even with periodic recessions and depressions, the Northern economy continued to expand rapidly in the postwar decades, creating enormous wealth, much of it concentrated in the hands of relatively few men and women. Boston had a only handful of millionaires in the 1840s. By 1890 there were 400.[3] This new wealth led to greatly increased conspicuous consumption and the excesses of what came to be known as the Gilded Age.

The postwar years also increased class divisions and the gap between rich and poor in American society. The most vivid expressions of poverty were the expanding slum areas that became a part of every major city. These slums contrasted with the often ostentatious displays of the new rich, represented by the mansions being built on Fifth Avenue in New York and the seashore "cottages" of fashionable watering holes like Newport, Rhode Island.[4] Class divisions in cities like Boston and New York

---

1. Kopff 1986.
2. Wills 1992.
3. Dimaggio 1982a: 39.
4. Andrews 1964: 152–204.

were compounded by increasing numbers of uneducated immigrants, mainly from non-Anglo-Saxon countries. Upper-class society, which believed strongly in racial theories of the time with their concepts of naturally superior and inferior ethnic groups, felt threatened socially, economically, and even biologically.

These years also saw developing a heightened sense of ennui among America's cultured elite. Many people felt that the ideals for which so many of the best educated in both the North and South had fought and died had been betrayed. Ugliness, philistinism, and a loss of community seemed to dominate the American scene. All that was cultured and beautiful in American life was being lost to a new materialism. A considerable number of citizens fled into self-imposed exile in Europe.[5]

The artistic and cultural legacy of Greece and Rome was once again called into service by very different constituencies in this changing society. The newly wealthy employed architecturally eclectic styles for their New York town houses and Newport cottages. But the captains of industry, seeking appropriate architectural expression for the emerging American imperial age as well and creating large new public spaces such as railroad stations, turned to the Roman architectural tradition. To Daniel Burnham, the architect of Washington's Union Station among other structures,

the pomp and power and bigness of Rome appealed. The main entrance to his Washington station he made of three arches, the opening of each being higher than that in the arch of Titus. (Moore 1929: 275)

Charles McKim of the historically oriented architectural firm of McKim, Mead, and White drew his inspiration for New York's Pennsylvania Station from afternoons spent admiring the ruins of the Baths of Caracalla in Rome.[6]

Some of the individuals who rejected the values of this vulgar if muscular age turned to nostalgia and aestheticism, seeking in an idealized past what had been lost in the present. Very influential for this group were the writings of the English cultural reformers John Ruskin (1819–1900) and William Morris (1834–1896). Both men emphasized a past beauty that grew out of an art based on community. Ruskin, a tense, complex figure who during his later years passed increasingly into madness, believed strongly in the redeeming power of art, in both creation and contemplation, for personal and social ills.[7] He wrote powerfully and evocatively about both contemporary art and the medieval cities of Italy, especially

5. Cashman 1984: 1–41.
6. Moore 1929: 273–77; Roth 1983: 317–24.
7. J. Evans 1954, Abse 1981.

his beloved Venice, and emphasized the interconnection of experiencing art and making art. Ruskin was also active in workers' education.[8] Although he generally did not like Americans, he could relate to older Boston intellectuals and to sympathetic young artists like W. J. Stillman. Stillman retained an affectionate if critical appreciation for Ruskin and his ideas, even after their friendship formally ended.[9] Ruskin found an especially kindred soul in Charles Eliot Norton.[10] Charles Waldstein, one of the most important and successful of the first generation of American classical archaeologists after the Civil War, also wrote appreciatively on Ruskin and his aesthetic ideals.[11]

For William Morris, the salvation from industrial blight came through the revival of craft traditions and the underlying values that supported them.[12] Morris is remembered today mainly for the innovative yet traditional design patterns he and his artisans created that have since been reproduced in a variety of media. More important for Morris himself was restoring the craft community that had once created those designs. His well-articulated concerns for the health of the craft tradition in England reflected and stimulated wide-ranging debates about the quality of British industrial design. This contributed to the creation of such institutions as the South Kensington (later Victoria and Albert) Museum in London.[13]

The complex social, economic, and cultural changes of the times were bound to impact American higher education. This was a period of major college and university change and expansion within the United States. The Morrill Act of 1862, with its provision for land-grant institutions, reinforced public university education in America's heartland. In spite of their agricultural and technical origins, many of these new institutions emphasized the basic classical education in their curricula. They added to the number of colleges and universities with classical programs already flourishing in the South, Midwest, South, and Far West, and further enhanced the study and appreciation of Greek and Roman culture in those parts of America.[14]

Major curricular reforms began to be undertaken in even the most traditional of eastern educational institutions. In 1869 Charles Eliot (1834–1926) was made president of Harvard, a position he held until 1909. As one contemporary put it, Eliot flipped over Harvard over like a "flap-

8. C. E. Norton 1904: 40–42.
9. Stillman 1897: 92–127; 1901: 116, 128–30, 308–20.
10. C. E. Norton 1904; Abse 1981: 146–47, 218–22, 314–15.
11. Waldstein 1893.
12. Pevesner 1975: 24–30; Bradley 1978.
13. Goodwin 1990.
14. Solberg 1968: 53–58.

jack."[15] A narrow, rigid mode of teaching based on rote recitation was replaced by the elective system, which offered a range of academic subjects. Students no longer had to follow a narrow, set curriculum, but could pursue diverse intellectual interests during their college years. This innovation led to the introduction of new academic subjects like art history, and ultimately made possible the development of classical archaeology as a discipline within the college and university curriculum.

The era also saw the development of higher levels of professionalism and institutionalization in many sectors of American society. Training for many professions like law and medicine had remained more medieval than modern for much of the nineteenth century. Now medical education was reformed, and lawyers could no longer simply clerk in offices to earn their professional credentials. Informal associations were replaced by professional organizations, which set and promoted standards and had less time and space for amateurs.[16]

A small but influential group of intellectuals interested in classical art and archaeology had long been aware of the disciplines' deficient academic professionalism. They had seen another academic world in the German universities, which many American classicists continued to attend for advanced education. Germany had advanced university programs in classical archaeology as well as libraries with holdings many times those of even Harvard and Yale. Its museums displayed large, comprehensive collections of study casts, which allowed an in-depth appreciation of the development of Greek and Roman art. The casts were increasingly complemented by original ancient art objects brought from different parts of the Mediterranean. This German enthusiasm for collecting had received a major stimulus when original Greek sculptures from the temple of Aphaia at Aegina arrived at the Glyptothek of Munich in 1828.[17]

The Germans also developed scientific excavation as a technique for advancing of knowledge rather than for acquiring art objects. Their excavations at the great Hellenic shrine of Olympia, which started in 1875, did not produce material for German museums the impressive art found there remained in Greece, but they trained a new breed of field technicians.[18] Excavations at Pergamon in Turkey, which began in 1878, did both. The famous sculptures from the Great Altar made their way to Berlin and ultimately were housed in their their own museum.[19] The

15. Oliver Wendell Holmes Jr., cited in Brooks 1940: 102.
16. Wiebe 1967: 113–17.
17. *EHCA* s.v. "Aigina (Aegina)"; "Glyptothek, Munich"; Stoneman 1987: 182–99.
18. *EHCA* s.v. "Olympia, Greece"; Marchand 1996: 77–91.
19. *EHCA* s.v. "Pergamon (Pergamum)"; Marchand 1996: 92–103, 288–94.

cosmopolitan group of Bostonians who were to found institutions like the Archaeological Institute of America and the Boston Museum of Fine Arts followed closely the development of German museums and excavations. They appreciated German contributions to scientific scholarship and envied the financial and diplomatic support Germans received from their government.[20]

A key group of American cultural leaders increasingly felt the need not only to develop a discipline of classical archaeology in America to do it in the new professional German manner. This position was described in retrospect in an essay titled "Recent Progress in Classical Archaeology" published by Alfred Emerson in the 1889 annual report of the Archaeological Institute of America.[21] Emerson (1859–1943) was one of the first professional classical archaeologists in the United States,[22] educated at Princeton and in Germany, where he studied with Heinrich Brunn, perhaps the foremost German archaeologist of that era.[23] Emerson became fellow and instructor of archaeology at the new graduate-oriented Johns Hopkins University, where he soon impressed the philologist Basil Gildersleeve. In a letter of recommendation Gildersleeve summarized what he thought were Emerson's strengths and those of a classical archaeologist of his generation in general:

> He has had . . . unusual advantages, long residence abroad, a good training in the school of Heinrich Brunn, familiarity with Greece and other classic lands, experience in archaeological work. He has, it is true, more artistic and literary sensitiveness than power of literary and artistic expression. . . . he has a good knowledge of Greek, a knowledge, that is, in my judgement, equal to any range of archaeological research, though he would not claim to be an accomplished epigraphist. His strength lies rather in the archaeology of art. (Briggs 1987: 179–80)

Emerson became involved in some of the first American excavations in the Mediterranean. He spent his academic life in a various universities and at the Art Institute of Chicago, although his career in the end showed more promise than accomplishment. The 1889 paper in which Emerson set out to assess the accomplishments of the first generation of classical archaeologists in the United States opened with a ringing affirmation of the new professional, scientific direction of classical archaeology that was emerging in both Europe and the United States, one that would take scientific archaeology well beyond the world of Lord Elgin.[24] Thirteen years later Professor Thomas Day Seymour of Yale (1848–1907), in an

20. A. Emerson 1889: 49–55.
21. A. Emerson 1889.
22. Fowler 1944.
23. *EHCA* s.v. "Brunn, Heinrich Von (1822–94)."
24. A. Emerson 1889: 47.

account of the foundation and early years of the American School of Classical Studies at Athens, advanced similar, science-based arguments for the future of American classical archaeology and its need for overseas study and research programs:

We need the use of laboratory methods, and are reminded of the three stages of instruction in chemistry and physics. At first the student read of experiments, and recited the account to his instructor. Later, early in the nineteenth century, the student saw his instructor perform experiments to illustrate the law of gravity or the tendency of oxygen to unite with various other elements. Considerably later, toward the close of the nineteenth century, the student was set to work to perform experiments and discover principles for himself. (1902: 19)

Direct experience with Greece and its archaeological monuments was thus to become the laboratory of budding classical archaeologists. This position suited the spirit of the age, in which science was challenging humanities for intellectual hegemony, and funding for research projects and institutional support had to be obtained from men of money who appreciated the post-Darwinian mindset.

Seymour also recalled the institutional problems and limitations faced by students of classical archaeology in the United States even in 1881, the year when the American School at Athens was founded:

Twenty years ago the opportunities for the study of classical archaeology in our country were very limited. The Museum of Fine Arts in Boston was only four years old as an institution; the Metropolitan Museum of New York was still in narrow temporary quarters on Fourteenth Street. No university in the country offered courses of instruction in archaeology. (1902: 24)

The individual who did most to correct these intellectual, academic, and institutional deficiencies within American classical archaeology was Charles Eliot Norton (1827–1908)[25] (Figure 2). Norton was a vintage Bostonian of the era designated by Van Wyck Brooks as the "New England Indian Summer."[26] His family was deeply rooted in New England, and his education was that of a Boston Brahmin, culminating in a B.A. from Harvard College. He was a wide-ranging litterateur, whose passion for Dante was as great as his enthusiasm for Greek archaeology. The Harvard philosopher George Santayana described Norton in this manner:

Norton, with ten generations of local magnates behind him, had his inspiration and sympathy far away. He worshipped Greek art, he worshipped Christian art, he loved refined English life. He spoke rarified English. He loved Turner and Ruskin. His personal friends were Burne-Jones, Carlyle and Matthew Arnold. (1945: 163)

25. Vanderbilt 1959; Stein 1967: 240–54.
26. Brooks 1940: 24–28, 250–55.

Figure 2. Charles Eliot Norton, teacher of the fine arts at Harvard University. Courtesy of the Harvard University Archives.

Although Norton had spent long periods of time in Europe, he did not have a formal graduate education of the German type and was in many ways ambivalent about its impact on scholarship and the life of the mind. Norton was a transitional figure between the amateur scholars of the age of Ralph Waldo Emerson and Francis Parkman and the new academic professionalism that developed toward the end of the century.[27]

After a brief spell in a Boston merchant house following his graduation from Harvard and an extended period of world traveling, Norton turned

27. Duffy 1996.

to editing and social reform. One of his special interests was providing better housing and schooling for Boston's increasing population of immigrant poor.[28] Having some independent means, he also traveled widely in Europe and even considered joining the band of American expatriates who found life in the Old World much more congenial than that in the still young and raw Republic. When not abroad, Norton lived mostly in Cambridge and was well known in Harvard's inner circles. He seemed destined for a genteel and somewhat isolated life as the last of the Cambridge sages.

Charles Eliot's installation as president of Harvard changed Norton's fate. As part of his wide-ranging reforms of Harvard's curriculum, Eliot sought to introduce the German humanistic vision of education advocated by continental figures like Alexander von Humboldt into American higher education.[29] This identification with the ideals of the German university made sense for him and his institution, since nine of his twenty-three Harvard professors had studied in Germany.[30]

Nonetheless Eliot did not have enough academics with a German-style professional education to teach all the new subjects he was introducing. To fill the void, Boston intellectuals of general culture but with little formal advanced education in specific fields were recruited into the classroom. Henry Adams describes his own hiring by Eliot to teach medieval history in his *Autobiography*. Adams protested that he did not have the qualifications for the appointment:

"But Mr. President," urged Adams, "I know nothing about Medieval History." With the courteous manner and bland smile so familiar for the next generation of America, Mr. Eliot mildly but firmly replied, "If you will point out to me any one who knows more, Mr. Adams, I will appoint him." (1961: 293)

President Eliot similarly persuaded Norton to start teaching art history to Harvard undergraduates. The subject had no real academic standing in the United States and nothing equivalent to what the discipline was developing in Germany. Sporadic efforts had been made to introduce archaeology and art history into the colleges and universities: Princeton as early as 1831 offered the opportunity to study Roman antiquities, and various courses in fine arts were offered at a few institutions in the pre-Civil War period.[31]

Certain Americans were beginning to do art historical scholarship. James Jackson Jarves not only collected Italian primitives but also wrote

28. E. W. Emerson 1912: 9; Vanderbilt 1959: 37–49, 67–102.
29. Morison 1930: xxxix–xlvii; McCaughey 1974: 275–324; Diehl 1978: 105.
30. Diehl 1978: 116.
31. Hiss and Fansler 1934: 6–10.

on Italian art, dedicating his major study to Norton.[32] Even more distinguished was the Bostonian Charles Perkins, who had already established an international reputation for himself in the field of Italian Renaissance sculpture.[33] But it was Norton who stimulated the growth of the field in American higher education through his teaching. He was well read and deeply cultured, and had refined taste. He had traveled extensively in Europe and published a volume of his impressions.[34] This intense first-hand contact with paintings and monuments was essential for a teacher in an era before slides and photographically illustrated art books. As a friend and admirer of John Ruskin, Norton shared Ruskin's vision of art as a potential redeeming force in contemporary life.[35] Teaching Harvard's undergraduate elite could become an important mission in combating philistine trends in late nineteenth-century America.

Norton's general cultured, humanistic background was enough for Eliot to appoint him professor of fine arts. Eliot's judgment proved correct. Norton's courses in art history became enormously successful and attracted large numbers of students. His learned, gentle personality went over very well in the classroom. He introduced several generations of Harvardians to the joys of art appreciation. These included intellectual and scholarly figures, like the art historian Bernard Berenson, the novelist Henry James, the philosopher George Santayana, and the art agent E. P. Warren, as well as graduates who pursued business and professional careers but who also went into amateur collecting and the development of cultural institutions at a time when museums and private collections were being founded at a pace unparalleled in the history of the Republic.[36]

The courses Norton taught at Harvard were a complex blend of humanistic art historical scholarship, connoisseurship, and personal ruminations on the nature of beauty and the sad state of the world. The historian of New England culture Van Wyck Brooks summarized the Norton style thus:

His aesthetic feeling was weak and derivative, but his scholarly feeling was strong, while his ethical feeling dominated all others; and Ruskin had taught him that art had an ethical basis. To preach art as ethics was thus the soul of Norton's mission and to preach the scholarly virtues as the soul of art. If the modern world was also ugly, the modern world was also base: its baseness and its ugliness went together. Taste alone could redeem it and taste was therefore Norton's gospel. He preached it as his forebears preached salvation. (1940: 251)

32. Hiss and Fansler 1934: 10–13; Stein 1967: 76–77, 124–46.
33. C. Perkins 1864; Brooks 1958: 108–9.
34. C. E. Norton 1859.
35. C. E. Norton 1904; Vanderbilt 1959: 53–64, 170–72.
36. James 1904: 422; Santayana 1945: 163; Samuels 1979: 32–36; Shand-Tucci 1995: 22–24, 231.

The curricular emphases of Norton's courses were an expression of his taste and values and did not always follow accepted judgments.[37] Reflective of his Pre-Raphaelite sympathies and enthusiasm for Dante was the fact that he favored later Italian medieval art over that of the Renaissance. Also striking were his claims for the superiority of Greek art, especially that of fifth-century Athens, over that of Rome. Norton had grown up in pre-Civil War New England with its strong Helleno-Romanticism and a built environment dominated by neo-classical structures. He used the classroom to evoke the spirit of Hellas to oppose the vulgar new capitalists with their neo-Renaissance mansions and neo-Roman railroad stations.[38]

Before turning to Norton's organizational accomplishments, one should recall that he was not alone in his attitudes toward art and society. Closest in many ways was James Hoppin of Yale.[39] Hoppin had started out as a theologian and throughout his life his strong religious convictions shaped his attitudes toward art. He has already been mentioned as an early, intrepid traveler to Greece. Yet his interest in art grew progressively stronger and in 1879, five years after Norton starting lecturing on the art history at Harvard, Hoppin resigned his chair at Yale Divinity School and became professor of the history of art at the Yale School of Fine Arts.[40] Like Norton, he was strongly influenced by Ruskin and wanted to use art to fight industrial vulgarity. He also placed Greek art at the center of his art historical considerations. Unlike Norton, Hoppin had been to Greece several times and had written a sensitive if dated book on its land, people, and culture.[41] But Hoppin did not have the same organizational impulse and in the end played only a marginal role in the development of classical art and archaeology studies in the United States.

The Foundation of the Archaeological Institute of America

Norton's educational ambitions extended beyond the amusement and enlightenment of Harvard undergraduates. He was, after all, a great friend and admirer of John Ruskin and shared Ruskin's concern about the deterioration of artistic taste in Europe and America. Norton was dismayed by the growing crass materialism and expanding ugliness of the increasingly industrialized world of Gilded Age America. Not incapable of self-parody, he opened one lecture by proposing "this afternoon to

37. Hiss and Fansler 1934: 179–81 provides samples of Norton's final examinations.
38. Vanderbilt 1959: 72–73, 132–39; Damrosch 1995; Duffy 1996: 106–7.
39. Stein 1967: 234–39.
40. Stein 1967: 236.
41. Hoppin 1897; Stein 1967: 234–39, 242.

make a few remarks on the horrible vulgarity of everything."[42] He shared
with Ruskin and the Pre-Raphaelites a belief in the redeeming qualities of
beauty and humanistic studies as an antidote to the corruption he saw
around him. He expressed these beliefs held for a lifetime in his last
major address to the Archaeological Institute of America (AIA) in 1902:

> At such a period as this, the need is great that those who prize the humanities as
> the strongest forces in the never-ending contest against the degrading influences
> of the spirit of materialism, as the best means of development and discipline of
> the intelligence, as the source of knowledge most useful for the invigoration and
> elevation of character, and most abundant in nutriment for the noblest intellec-
> tual qualities, the need is great, I say, for those who hold the humanities in this
> esteem, and above all for those who recognize in classical studies, largely inter-
> preted and rightly understood, the quintessence of the supremacy of these stud-
> ies among the general elements of the higher education. (1909–10: 258)

Norton was an intellectual with a scientific scholarly, as well as a humanistic vision. He had the genuine if slightly chauvinistic desire to make
the United States an equal partner in the emerging international world
of classical archaeology and art history. He felt that America owed an
enormous scholarly debt to Europe and that it must be ready to repay
that intellectual debt with its own high-quality scholarly contributions.
For archaeology, this required trained scholars, research and professional institutions, and excavations. Norton early on used the German
field research at Olympia as the archaeological model that the Americans should try to emulate in establishing their own excavations. A good
nineteenth-century Bostonian activist, he set out to make his vision a
reality.

Norton's career as a teacher of art history at Harvard would assure him
an honored place in the history of art and archaeology in the United
States. However, he played an even more important role as an archaeological institutional builder. In the 1870s and 1880s he was a prime
mover in the formation of the Archaeological Institute of America and
the American School of Classical Studies in Athens. He also participated
actively in the development of the Boston Museum of Fine Arts and the
American School of Classical Studies in Rome, which was the ancestor of
the American Academy in Rome. Not only did Norton help found those
institutions, but he also continued to serve them throughout his long and
extremely active life.

The first and in many ways most important of Norton's creations was
the AIA. He described his thoughts and motives for taking that initiative
in a letter of 20 May 1879 to John Ruskin:

42. Stein 1967: 247–48; Shand-Tucci 1995: 23.

I have been occupied of late in getting up an archaeological Society in the hope of encouraging classical studies, Greek studies I mean; and of training some of our College-bred boys to take part in investigations in Greek regions, & regions farther east. (Bradley and Ousby 1987: 429)

Other friends were also subjected to Norton's enthusiasm about the new archaeological venture. Oliver Wendell Holmes wrote to James Russell Lowell in May 1879:

I had some talk (at the Saturday Club) last time with Charles Norton, who is greatly interested in an archaeological association of which he is the moving spirit. It is going to dig up some gods in Greece — if he can get money enough. (Harris 1908: 50)

The Archaeological Institute of America got its start on 10 May 1879, when a group of Bostonians gathered at 50 State Street to discuss the formation of an archaeological society. Martin Brimmer chaired. The meeting had been announced in a flyer issued in April, which had laid out the need for, and possible future agenda of, such a society. The society's creation was justified in the following terms:

The increasing interest in archaeology . . . the importance of the historic and artistic results of properly conducted exploration and the immense extent of the field of work embracing the sites of ancient civilization in the New World as well as the Old make it plain that such a society is needed in order to encourage and aid the efforts of individual explorers and to send out special expeditions such as no individual could easily undertake. (AIA Archives Box 1)

Those who attended the meeting represented the elite of Boston and Cambridge intellectual society, figures like the historian Francis Parkman, the art historian Charles Perkins, and the curator Frederic Ward Putnam of Harvard's Peabody Museum.

The Bostonians who met on that spring day in 1879 to discuss the foundation of this new archaeological society certainly had some European precedents in mind. Antiquarian societies had long existed in England, France, Germany, Italy, and other European countries. Most of them had a local base and were concerned with the study of local antiquities.[43] More national in its mission was the French archaeological society founded as the Société Française pour la Conservation et la Description des Monuments Historiques in 1834. Its annual congress, the thirty-sixth of which was held in 1879, aimed to move French archaeologists beyond

43. P. Levine 1986. For the role of such local societies in Germany, cf. Marchand 1996: 162–80.

the parochial world of the local archaeological society and to induce them to pool information on a national level.[44]

More classical and cosmopolitan in organization was London's Society of Dilettanti of London founded in 1733 by a group of young Tory aristocrats, which Norton cited as an important model for the future Archaeological Institute of America. The Society of Dilettanti had sponsored the research and publication of Stuart and Revett's Grecian architectural designs and drawings, which had played a major role in inspiring the classical revival in the United States.[45]

America was not without its own learned societies interested in archaeological research, although much of their activity had been focused on remains found in North America. The American Philosophical Society dated back to the days of Benjamin Franklin and had regularly published papers on archaeological topics.[46] The American Oriental Society, founded in 1842, had a section on archaeology, as did the American Numismatic Society, established in 1858.[47] Other local archaeological groups met regularly and had their own publications. None of these organizations were in a position to shape a national agenda for developing the discipline of American archaeology, however, especially in areas outside the United States.

The discussions at the May meeting in Boston rapidly revealed among the participants deep philosophical and ideological differences about the aims of American archaeological research and the archaeological organization they hoped to create. These disputes challenged the diplomatic skills of even the suave Norton. Some participants, like Francis E. Parker, argued that a society that hoped to promote cultural improvement could ignore the archaeology of savages in the United States.[48] Parker asserted that

if knowledge was the true aim of the society, then the knowledge should be useful and not simply curious. That knowledge which was useful to us was not that of barbarians, but that of cultivated races which had preceded us. The Indians were low on the scale of civilization. (AIA Archives Box 1)

Parker advanced two positions widely shared by the American elite. The first was that research could promote useful knowledge, in this case "useful" in Ruskin's sense of the word. The second was that America's

44. Summaries of these conferences, held in different cities of France were published in *Bulletin monumental* starting in 1834 and then in separate proceedings.

45. *EHCA* s.v. "Society of Dilettanti."

46. Bell 1967.

47. On the American Oriental Society, cf. Kuklick 1996: 21. For the American Numismatic Society, cf. Adelson 1958.

48. Hinsley 1985.

natives, whose past had limited interest for Americans who hoped to compete on the European scene, were racially inferior. For Parker, the new organization was to be a learned society that would focus on the archaeology of the superior cultures of Greece, Rome, and the Near East. He was not alone in this view.

Others present, such as the distinguished American frontier historian Francis Parkman and the Harvard archaeologist Frederic Ward Putnam, argued that the archaeology of the native Americans in the United States offered a wonderful laboratory for studying social and cultural evolution at a time when Darwinian approaches to the historical reconstruction of human society were becoming very fashionable.[49] They argued strongly that the rapid development of many parts of the western United States made such archaeological undertakings both opportune and urgent. It was becoming easier to explore those regions, but with the arrival of white settlers important information on society's early history would soon be lost.

The implication that North America's natives represented an opportunity to study the earlier stages of human social evolution was no more flattering to America's indigenous peoples than Parker's views, but it at least offered the new archaeological society the potential of wider horizons. The Parkman/Putnam view prevailed for the moment, and the newly founded institute adopted a more geographically open archaeological agenda. Support for Adolph Bandelier's research in Mexico was especially important. Indeed, in the decades prior to World War I, the AIA supported as much New World as Old World archaeological research, and, it can be argued that the New World research conducted was of greater long-term significance than that undertaken in the Mediterranean.[50]

Arguments also erupted about the relative importance of basic research, as opposed to the collecting of antiquities. Many of the AIA's founders were also helping launch the fledgling Boston Museum of Fine Arts, and they were concerned about building those collections at a time when access to classical antiquities was becoming more limited. The art historian Charles Perkins stated that, since

we read every day of foreign governments taking out and carrying off works of art, he would suggest that as soon as possible we open a credit with some person upon the other side to act as agent for the Institute in looking about to see what can be had in order that we may lay our hands upon something to be placed in our museums. (AIA Archives Box 1)

49. For Putnam, cf. *Dictionary of American Biography* s.v. "Putnam, George Palmer" (hereafter cited as *DAB*) viii.276–78; Hinsley 1985.

50. *Annual Report AIA* 1882: 19; 1885: 309; Hinsley 1986; Lange and Riley 1996: 29–40, 55–56.

Francis Parkman responded that "the object of the Society as he understood was the acquisition of knowledge and not the acquisition of objects
or works of art." Such dual concerns emerged again when the AIA began
to undertake field research. These tensions between collector and field
researcher have remained part of American classical archaeology up to
the present day; the role they played in dividing the AIA from significant
segments of the collecting and museum communities is discussed more
fully in later chapters.

In the end the mandates given the new institute were very general. The
regulations stated that

It was founded for the purpose of promoting and directing archaeological investigation and research, by sending out expeditions for special investigation, by
aiding the efforts of independent explorers, by publication of reports of the
results of the expeditions which the Institute may undertake or promote, and by
any other means which may from time to time appear desireable. (AIA Archives
Box 1)

The emphasis on explorers and expeditions reflects the gun-and-camera
approach of the late nineteenth century. However, the general research
mandate provided the basis for further institution-building Norton and
his colleagues were to undertake in the next decade.

The original AIA was a Boston-based organization, even though its
founders were clearly thinking in broader terms. It soon became obvious
that here, as in so many other areas of educational and intellectual endeavor, Boston could not hope to continue to dominate the cultural
scene. After all, it was the New England Indian Summer. At one of the
Institute's first meetings, William Everett proposed establishing local
chapters outside Boston. This would make the AIA an innovative federal
organization combining the central purpose of a national society with
the flexibility and sense of local initiative and identity that comes with
individual chapters in different regions of the country. The AIA soon
adopted this model. It remains one of the organization's great strengths
to the present day.

Boston became the first official chapter, but it was soon followed by
New York (1884), Baltimore (1884), Philadelphia (1888), and others on
the east coast. This evolution into a more complex organization led to the
first meeting of a council formed of representatives of the Boston, New
York, and Baltimore chapters held on 20 November 1884 in New York. A
truly national organization was established as a result of that meeting.
Appropriately, Charles Eliot Norton was chosen as its first president.[51]

The Institute's continued geographical expansion mirrored important

51. AIA Archives, Box 1.

demographic changes in American society. The movement toward creating new local chapters followed the movement of American financial power and cultural development westward. Naturally Chicago became the first bridgehead for this westward expansion. On 4 November 1889 a group of prominent Chicagoans assembled to hear William Lawton, secretary of the institute, talk about the possibility of American excavations at ancient Delphi in Greece and urge the formation of an AIA chapter that would assist in the financial support of those excavations.[52] By 1890 midwestern chapters had been established in Detroit and Wisconsin. In 1891 and 1892 Pittsburgh and Cincinnati chapters were founded. Some of these became the largest and most vigorous groups within the AIA.

These developing archaeological power centers in the Midwest were viewed with great ambivalence by the eastern elite, and especially by New Englanders. Some regarded the new rich of places like Chicago as a rather vulgar, yet necessary addition to the organization, new rich whose money was needed if the institute was going to expand its research activities but whose cultural credentials were suspect. Polite acknowledgment of this economic power shift appeared in the AIA's eleventh annual report in connection with a fund-raising appeal for the proposed American excavations at Delphi:

It is not to be admitted that our West, full of energy and intelligence and wealth, will fail to do her part. If she will but add as much as has been now subscribed in the East, the completion of the sum is certain. (*Annual Report AIA* 11)

Charles Eliot Norton was sometimes less tactful in his private correspondence, referring to the "great calamity" and "grave danger" that could come to the institute from domination by midwesterners.[53] Norton, of course, knew little of that part of the country, and when in old age he traveled west to the Chicago Exposition of 1893 he was very impressed with what he saw.[54]

No person embodied the importance the Westerners' rise in the world of classical scholarship better than Francis Kelsey (1858–1927). Born in upstate New York, Kelsey had studied at the University of Rochester and then in Europe. He taught first at Lake Forest College in Illinois but then moved on to the University of Michigan, where he spent the rest of his career. The archaeological museum in Ann Arbor bears his name. Kelsey enjoyed considerable independent means and admired the dynamic business ethos so widespread in the Midwest. Photographs of him with his strong features and close-cropped hair suggest a man who could just as

52. Guralnick 1990: 1–2.
53. Hinsley 1986: 222.
54. Vanderbilt 1959: 199–204.

easily have become a tycoon as a classicist. He had a strong sense of adventure, as was demonstrated by his extensive travels in the Near East in the aftermath of World War I.[55]

Kelsey played a very important role in the development of the early twentieth-century AIA. He became corresponding secretary in 1906 and from 1907 to 1912 served as president. He clearly was one of the most dynamic presidents in the organization's history. Members of the eastern establishment were suspicious of his scholarly values, but had to admit his energy and popular appeal. In a 1906 letter, Thomas Day Seymour of Yale stated his opinion that Kelsey "does not value a high standard of work for the Institute so much as he does 'influence' with the masses (but) no man from the faculties of Harvard, Yale or Columbia could draw such an audience as he in Kansas, Missouri, or Utah."[56]

Kelsey pushed for the development of a national identity for the AIA and a wider vision of American archaeology in its activities. This was articulated in an unpublished lecture preserved in the Kelsey Museum archives at the University of Michigan:

We must beware and not limit the field of archaeology too much; the arrow-head found around Ann Arbor, the wall in Central America—almost as much of a puzzle today as a hundred years ago—the relics of the Mound Builders, all these fall in the range of archaeology just as much as Greek and Roman relics. There is no object that bears the imprint of human mind, that shows purposeful expenditure of human energy in past ages, that does not come under this science. This opens an immense field, a bewildering one; it may seem strange to compare the statues of Phidias with an arrow-head, yet each shows the purpose of the maker; the same set of muscles made the two objects; they have something in common. Such is the breadth of the subject, that while the limits are fairly clear, it is hard to fix them. . . . Again, where does the ancient stop and the modern begin? This is equally hard to answer; in general, men will extend it to the close of the classical period. But too we have the Christian archaeology later; this has a wide range running into the middle ages and even into modern times. (Thomas 1990: 10)

Although his scholarship focused on the classical world, Kelsey advocated broader research interests for the AIA as a means of expanding its popular base in the Midwest and Far West. As he put it in a 1906 letter to Thomas Day Seymour,

In Colorado, Utah, New Mexico and other states of the West, there is a large body of college men from the East who cherish the classical traditions. Naturally enough the first impulse of the people in this region is along the lines of immediate interest; but I am convinced that the interest in American Archaeology, which is a field almost barren of the ideal, will lead to the development of an interest

---

55. *EHCA* s.v. "Kelsey, Francis Willey (1858–1927)"; Thomas 1990.
56. Hinsley 1986: 222.

along the lines of the Institute's present work in classical and Oriental lands. (Hinsley 1986: 223)

This process of local-chapter formation continued westward to California, where the Southwest Society was established in Los Angeles in 1903.[57] By 1912 it had 414 members as opposed to New York city's 160. The society's officers noted with pride that the 1909–10 Norton lecturer, the British archaeologist David Hogarth, described the Southwest Society as "the most live and best organized thing that I found in the United States."[58] Its president, Charles Lummis (1859–1928), was an even more outspoken frontier populist than Kelsey. Although a graduate of Harvard, he identified with the West and with the problems and concerns of its Native American populations.[59] In the midst of one of his policy disputes with the AIA's central organization, he attacked his eastern opponents in vivid language: "I have no doubt that most of your inadequate Greek and Latin professors who are the secretaries that mismanage the dormant and moribund societies would go with the Institute" (AIA Archives Box 19: Lummis to Carroll 31 Jan. 1912). He had equally sharp things to say about the AIA's goals:

You folks back east had grandfathers. We hadn't. We have to build our own towns, sewers, car lines, libraries, museums, jails, schools. You could probably dig up fifty people who could pay ten dollars a year each to help your classical studies in Greece and Rome, but I am too busy. You have been going twenty-four years and have a dozen societies. You haven't a museum or even a museum case. You have "added to knowledge" — but nobody knows it. (Fiske and Lummis 1975: 122)

Lummis was not unexpectedly a supporter of more local research and expressed his views in very pungent terms. He asked:

whether its [the AIA's] only worthy activity is to excavate objects never exhibited in America and never seen by one American in a million and exploited only by publications that not one American in ten million ever reads. (AIA Archives Box 19: Lummis to Carroll 31 Jan. 1912)

By the outbreak of World War I, there were forty-eight local AIA societies of the AIA with a membership of nearly three thousand. They spanned the entire nation. In spite of the tensions and problems that had arisen during the previous forty years over the Institute's purpose and direction, the founders' vision of a national society had been realized.

During this period some of the local societies, especially on the East Coast, became such powerhouses in their own right that they threatened

57. Fiske and Lummis 1975: 122–23.
58. AIA Archives Box 19: Lummis to Carroll 31 Jan, 1912.
59. *NCAB* 42: 578–79; Fiske and Lummis 1975.

the hegemony of the national organization. One such society was that of Washington, D.C., founded in 1895. It listed foreign ambassadors and high cabinet officials among its members and held meetings on a member's yacht sailing up the Potomac. Among its accomplishments were the establishment of the first American popular archaeology journal *Art and Archaeology* in 1905, and the sponsorship of archaeological activities in Europe and the Mediterranean.[60] The chapter used its influence with Congress to give the AIA a national legal identity. In 1906 the AIA was chartered by Congress as a Washington-based organization, and by World War I its general headquarters were located in the Octagon building there.

The Creation of the *American Journal of Archaeology*

The AIA's executive committee minutes for 18 October 1884 noted that a Mr. Frothingham of Baltimore had suggested publishing an archaeological journal.[61] The first major publication venture undertaken by the new institute was launching the *American Journal of Archaeology* (*AJA*) in 1885.[62] Here again the Americans were inspired by the developing world of scholarly publication in Europe. An important aspect of the growing professionalism of the second half of the nineteenth century was the creation of specialized scholarly journals. These soon began to compete for educated readership with the more general cultural-political magazines like the *Athenaeum* in England and the more narrow and amateurish local and regional antiquarian journals. The French *Revue Archéologique* started in 1844 and the German *Historische Zeitschrift* in 1859.[63] These journals promoted an increasingly high level of scholarly professionalism. They provided serious research articles, reviews, and reports on the latest research, keeping academics abreast of the latest developments in their fields.

It is not surprising that an organization like the AIA, which was founded to promote quality scholarship in the European mode, would see the need for its own scholarly periodical. Arthur L. Frothingham Jr. (1859–1923), a young instructor at Johns Hopkins, proposed the creation of such a journal in 1884. Frothingham was one of the first American Ph.D. students in classical archaeology, and he went on to teach the first graduate courses in classical archaeology at Princeton. An American scholarly journal in archaeology suited his sense of emerging professionalism.

60. Kelsey 1926c: 106–10.
61. AIA Archives Box 1.
62. Donahue 1985; Kleiner 1996.
63. P. Levine 1986.

Frothingham became the driving force behind the establishment of the journal, and initially he and his friend and colleague Allan Marquand were the actual owners. The venture's early success owed much to the energy of the younger Frothingham, who not only edited the journal but wrote a great number of the articles, reviews, and newsletters.

The first issue of the *American Journal of Archaeology* appeared on 1 February 1885. The full title was *The American Journal of Archaeology for the Study of Monuments of Antiquity and the Middle Ages*. Norton was listed as advisory editor and Frothingham as managing editor. One of its declared aims was "to afford to American Schools the means of taking active part in the progress of archaeological sciences by the publication of papers embodying the results of original research." The first issue contained articles on classical topics, but also an article titled "The Revival of Sculpture in Europe in the Thirteenth Century" and scholarly notes on the art of Arnolfo di Lapo, Jacopo Torriti, and Antonio da San Gallo, as well as book reviews, summaries of periodicals, and news of the most recent archaeological discoveries. The second issue ranged even more widely, with articles on New World archaeology, the mosaics of Ravenna, and the medieval abbey at Jumieges in France. It reflected the eclectic art and archaeological interests of the new Archaeological Institute of America.

AJA claimed to have advancing the AIA's mission of sponsoring research in all parts of the world as a principal aim, but it was clear from the beginning that the editors' hearts were in the Old World. This soon became painfully clear to one reader (the editors would not reveal his identity), who on 13 July 1888 wrote the editors a strongly worded letter. He opened his letter by stating that

As a subscriber to *The American Journal of Archaeology* I feel it my duty to write you the sense of disappointment which every number produces. Its name appears to me strikingly inappropriate, and it would be better to drop the superfluous "American" and call it the "Journal of Old World Archaeology." (*AJA* 1888: 259)

He went on to accuse the journal of a "lack of real earnestness and to be pervaded by dilettantism." The most recent issues according to the enraged correspondent, had shown a "contempt for the great field offered by its own continent."

The editors (presumably Frothingham and Norton) were clearly stung by the charges of dilettantism and responded by noting the number of distinguished European and American scholars who had contributed to the new periodical. They continued with their own toughly worded ideological statement on the innate superiority of Old World archaeology. The rebuttal started with a statement of the journal's scientific scholarly goals:

One of the main objects in the establishment of our journal was that it might afford to the genuine students of archaeology in America such acquaintance with the progress of science elsewhere as should supply them with the means for comparison of their own work with that done by others, and enable them to draw just conclusions in regard to the true value and significance of the object of their special study. (*AJA* 1888: 260)

They then went on to attack the premises that might support a real archaeology in North America:

. . . there is a common popular delusion which had its source partly in ignorance, partly in a foolish misdirection of national conceit. The archaeology of America, even when it has to do with the remains of the former life of still existing native tribes, is essentially prehistoric archaeology, that is, it is busied with the life and work of a race or races of men in an inchoate, rudimentary, and unformed condition, who never raised themselves, even at their highest point, as in Mexico and Peru, above a low stage of civilization, and never showed the capacity of steadily progressive development. Within the limited of the United States, the native races attained to no high faculty of performance or expression on any field. They had no intellectual life. (260–61)

The final rebuff thrown at the correspondent focused on the quality of archaeological research in North America. The editors denied that they had a "contempt for the great field offered by our own continent" but asserted that "much of the archaeological work done in this country has been and still is unscientific in method, mistaken in aim, and extravagant in its pretensions." The views expressed by Francis E. Parker at the AIA's founding meeting had won in the end, at least in the pages of the *AJA*.

Between 1885 and 1896, the *American Journal of Archaeology*, although sponsored by the AIA, was owned and edited by Frothingham and Marquand. In 1897 the second series started, now formally under the aegis of the AIA. The editor was John Henry Wright of Harvard (1852–1908), who continued to guide the journal until 1906. Wright was trained more in philology than in archaeology, but that seemed to have mattered less in the early days of the discipline when many of the most prominent philologists had received a solid grounding in Greek archaeology at the American School.[64] The start of the new series provided the occasion for the editor to define his editorial policy more clearly. The focus was to be on papers, proceedings, reports, and bulletins of the institute. Interestingly enough, the commitment to publication in New World archaeology was affirmed.[65]

From 1907 to 1916, the editor was Harold Fowler of Western Reserve

64. H. N. Fowler 1909.
65. Kleiner 1996: 3.

College in Cleveland, Ohio.[66] One of his early tasks was to record the death and note the accomplishments of his Harvard mentor and AIA founder Charles Eliot Norton.[67] During Fowler's editorship the *AJA* moved decisively toward becoming a classical and Mediterranean archaeology journal. The first volume he edited in 1907 contained contributions on American and Renaissance material, as well as many classical articles, and the editorial board included representatives in the fields of medieval, Renaissance and American archaeology. His final volume in 1916, although still retaining the special editors, had only articles outside the classical field. In 1917 the editorship passed to James Morton Paton who, carried it through the difficult period of World War I. Paton (1863–1944) had a Harvard and German education and had studied at the American School in Athens. He was a veteran of one of the early American archaeological research projects centered on the Erechtheum and did extensive investigations on early travelers to Greece.[68] The journal's fate in the complex interwar period is considered in a later chapter.

The AIA Lecture Program

Public lectures by renowned religious, cultural, and scholarly figures were an important part of American cultural life throughout much of the nineteenth century. The rituals surrounding these public lectures acquired many of the qualities of a secular sermon. The early nineteenth-century American lyceum movement did much to promote the public lecture in the young Republic.[69] New Englanders were familiar with such prestigious lecture series as those of the Lowell Institute in Boston, which was founded in 1836.[70] The Chautauqua Institute of western New York sent intellectually edifying speakers on tour throughout the east and the midwest.[71]

The archaeological lecture's popularity in America became manifest during the years that followed the founding of the AIA. In 1880 John Holmes of Boston expressed his enthusiasm for a lecture on Ancient Rome complete "with plenty of stereopticon."[72] In 1886–87 the distinguished Italian archaeologist Rodolfo Lanciani came to the United States to give a series of twelve presentations on archaeology in contemporary Rome for the Lowell Institute. Lanciani was a charming, urbane scholar,

66. Donahue 1985: 13–15.
67. H. N. Fowler 1908a.
68. Lord 1947: 47, 78, 124–25, 164, 266; Donahue 1985: 15.
69. Hiss and Fansler 1934: 6.
70. Weeks 1966.
71. Hurlbut 1921; Morrison 1974.
72. Hiss & Fansler 1934: 6.

deeply involved with the latest archaeological discoveries in rapidly developing postunification Rome. Demands for repeat performances of his lectures came from many quarters.[73] The progress of Lanciani's circuit provides a good geographical picture of the emerging classical archaeology scene in the United States. In addition to the Lowell lectures, he presented the same series at Harvard and before an overflow crowd in Baltimore. He gave additional lectures at the University of Pennsylvania, Wellesley, Princeton, Bryn Mawr, and Columbia. Also very successful during this same period were the archaeology lectures presented by Charles Waldstein, the pioneering Anglo-American classical archaeologist from Cambridge, whose impact on American classical archaeology is considered below. The *AJA* editor commented on the speakers' success with enthusiasm, stating that "the rapidity of the growth of archaeology in this country cannot be better proved than by the great interest taken in two courses of lectures which are being delivered during the season throughout the United States."[74]

During the 1890s, the AIA set out to create its own lecture program, one that would combine elements of the local antiquarian presentations familiar to European audiences and of the Chautauqua speaking circuits. By 1896 a program of AIA traveling lectures had been established, which linked the national organization and the local societies. The nascent lecture program provided local societies not only with information on the latest archaeological discoveries but also with direct contact with the leading personalities in the emerging field of classical archaeology. It was a bold venture in an America that had only recently been united by the railways, and often left speakers exhausted. Laments in the AIA archives about missed connections, hurried visits, and general fatigue still ring true with a jet-age lecturer of a century later.

The lecture program was given a more secure financial base and greater prestige in 1909, when James Loeb, a wealthy, cultured Harvard alumnus who lived in Germany, made a donation of $20,000 to establish a lecture series in honor of the recently deceased Charles Eliot Norton.[75] The endowment was a fitting appreciation for Norton's long history of service to the AIA and American archaeology. As Loeb himself expressed it in a letter to the institute:

Two generations of Harvard students were privileged to hear from Professor Norton's inspiring lips what "man's sacrifice to beauty," as Mr. Henry James has well called man's artistic effort, has done for the uplifting of the race. To them the

73. Lanciani 1889, 1988; *EHCA* s.v. "Lanciani, Rodolfo (1847–1929)."
74. *AJA* (1886) 2: 54.
75. For Loeb, cf. *ECHA* s.v. "Loeb, James (1867–1933)."

establishment of the Charles Eliot Norton Memorial Lecture Fund will, I hope, be a welcome event. To that larger circle who knew and valued Mr. Norton for his fearless devotion to his country, for the delightful essays and scholarly public addresses which marked the stages of a long and singularly distinguished life given to the pursuit of *res humaniores*, it may serve as a token of the devotion and admiration of one of his pupils. (*Annual Report AIA* 1909: 128)

Loeb intended that the Norton lectureship would be offered mainly to foreign scholars and hence increase the international visibility of the institute and the growing American archaeological community. His wish was largely fulfilled. The list of pre-World War I Norton lecturers included such distinguished European scholars as J. L. Myers, Christian Hülsen, David Hogarth, Franz Cumont, and Eugenie Sellers Strong.

The lecture program was also used to improve the financial base of archaeological research in the United States. The lecturers were supposed to inspire interested amateurs and thus urge them to contribute to ongoing projects. The 1930–31 annual report on the lecture program summarized this aim:

Our lecturers carry, in the liveliest and most entertaining fashion, the archaeological story to the many laymen and others who compose our societies, and through the splendid work which they are doing they are constantly arousing and quickening interest all over the land. This interest shows itself in substantial ways by the willingness of laymen of means to contribute to the support of the Institute. (*Annual Report AIA* 1930–31: 27)

The lecture program is now one hundred years old and continues to fulfill the diverse and important mission laid out by the founders.

The Annual Meeting

The last of the internal institutions established by the Archaeological Institute of America was the annual meeting of members. In developing such annual meetings the AIA was again following the example of other professional societies in Europe and America in developing such annual meetings. European precedents dated back to the first assembly of the Congrès Archéologique in 1834. The AIA's first annual meeting was held in New Haven, Connecticut in late December 1899. The program consisted of six sessions during which forty-three papers were read. Most of the presentations focused on Greek archaeology, but there was a solid session on New World archaeology and a smattering of papers on Roman and medieval topics. Many of the key figures in late nineteenth- and early twentieth-century classical archaeology, such as Francis Kelsey, T. W.

Heermance, Edward Robinson, F. B. Tarbell, George Chase, Joseph Hoppin, Allan Marquand, J. R. S. Sterrett, A. L. Frothingham, and J. R. Wheeler were on the program. Five of the presenters were women.[76] Charles Eliot Norton was selected to give the keynote address on the evening of the first day. He chose the Institute's progress during the twenty years since its foundation.

The meeting passed two resolutions related to archaeology. One urged the federal government "to care for the preservation of monuments of the earlier inhabitants of this country" and marked the AIA's early involvement in the fledgling archaeological preservation movement in the United States. The second resolution called on the government "to modify the existing regulations affecting the importation of objects of archaeological interest." This grew out of changes in the U.S. tariff rules that now exempted objects destined for a specific museum. Sara Yorke Stevenson, an important, early patron of archaeology in the United States, had argued in a paper presented earlier that such a customs rule would hamper individuals' and groups' ability to import antiquities, and place the United States at a further disadvantage in relation to the Europeans.[77]

Such annual gatherings have become such a routine part of academic life that we tend to forget the important role they have played in promoting academic interchange in a large and diverse country. These meetings were especially key in the late nineteenth-century United States, where there were no large, geographically concentrated collections of classicists as at Oxford or Cambridge. American classical archaeologists were often separated by great distances and for most of the year had to depend on postal correspondence for the exchange of ideas. Now for a few days after Christmas they could gather in some comfortable academic setting, hear presentations on the latest discoveries, and bond with other academics who shared their interests.

The establishment of the annual meeting in 1899 concluded two highly creative decades in the history of the Archaeological Institute of America. A strong, flexible organization had spread across the country. Speakers brought news of the latest archaeological finds to interested audiences throughout the academic year. The *American Journal of Archaeology* had established an international reputation as a serious scholarly journal. The annual meeting provided a forum for professional business and scholarly presentation, and for more informal social and intellectual interaction. The combination of scholarly enterprises under the AIA's auspices exceeded anything that existed in Europe. Yet these were not

76. The full program was printed in *AJA* NS 4 (1900): 149–82.
77. *AJA* NS 4 (1900): 149, 153–55.

the only accomplishments of the founding generation of American classical archaeologists.

The Foundation and Early Development of the American School in Athens

In 1882 the American School of Classical Studies in Athens opened its doors to a small group of students. This was the first American venture into the world of foreign study and research centers, which are such an important part of our higher educational landscape today. The history of such institutions can be traced back to the 1666 foundation by Louis XIV and his minister, Colbert, of the French Academy in Rome as a subsidized center for aspiring painters, sculptors, musicians, and architects.[78] Such noted artists as David and Ingres worked there. The center was designed to promote artistic creativity, not scholarship, but given the strong classical orientation of the French art world, the resident artists were much involved with problems of Roman art and archaeology. Detailed reconstructions of Roman monuments, which were part of the training programs of aspiring French architects, contributed much to a general understanding of the appearance of ancient Rome.[79]

By the mid-nineteenth century such fine arts centers had been complemented by archaeological research institutes in both Athens and Rome. Here Germany and France led the way. In 1829 the Istituto di Corrispondenza Archeologica had been established on the Campidoglio in Rome by German scholars. It enjoyed the support of the Prussian government and was patronized by such political-cultural figures as Baron Bunsen.[80] International in its initial outlook, the Istituto became an important gathering place for archaeological savants working in Rome, while its *Bollettino*, which provided monthly reports of archaeological discovery in Rome and Italy, was the first scientific archaeological periodical.[81]

Greek national independence and the growth of interest in ancient Hellenic culture during the nineteenth century led to the establishment of similar institutions in Athens. In 1846 the Ecole Française d'Athènes, an institution specifically devoted to the study of Greek art and archaeology, was founded in the small, bleak, provincial Greek capital that was mid-nineteenth-century Athens.[82] It provided the model and stimulus for

78. *EHCA* s.v. "French Academy in Rome (Académie de France à Rome)."
79. Egbert 1980; *Roma Antiqua* 1992.
80. Rieche 1979: 11–81; Marchand 1996: 53–62.
81. *EHCA* s.v. "Instituto di Corrispondenza Archeologica"; Emerson 1889: 56–57.
82. *EHCA* s.v. "French School at Athens (Ecole Française d'Athènes); Stoneman 1987: 251–54.

the establishment of other foreign schools in Athens. By 1874 the Athenian branch of the German Archaeological Institute was in operation.[83]

As has already been observed, the number of American scholars visiting Greece increased markedly in the years immediately before the Civil War. This flow continued to expand after the war, even though such travel was not without its discomforts, dangers, and adventures. When the young American classicists Thomas Day Seymour and Martin D'Ooge went to Greece in 1872, they found the Greek authorities very nervous about rural security, for an English party had recently been attacked by bandits near Marathon and a British nobleman killed.[84] The American journalist and amateur archaeologist W. J. Stillman published an amusing account of his own trip to Marathon under army escort.[85] Banditry and unrest continued to be problems in rural Greece into the 1920s. In 1925 John W. Logan, a fellow at the American School, was mortally wounded in an ambush near Arta in Epirus.[86]

Such sporadic lawlessness was considered to be part of the Greek adventure, and added to the spirit of those who worked in Hellas. The important thing for the aspiring classicist was to go and appreciate the beauties and sense of place first-hand. In 1885 the young Alfred Emerson noted that:

The classical archaeologist who has not trodden Greek soil is becoming a curiosity and the little capital of the kingdom of Hellas is one of the principal centers of archaeological investigation. (*AJA* 1885: 2)

In this atmosphere it is not surprising that pressure to establish an American school in Athens developed soon after the foundation of the Archaeological Institute of America.

The initiative for the creation of an American school in Athens came out of the same group that had founded the AIA; Charles Eliot Norton was again one of the prime moving forces. Professor John W. White (1848–1917) of the Harvard classics department also played a major role. White was a philologist, but he had been educated in the German *Wissenschaft* tradition in classics for which the study of monuments and material culture played an important role in reconstructing antiquity. He not only pushed hard for the establishment of the school but also served as the first chair of the managing committee from 1881–87.[87] In his obituary

83. *EHCA* s.v. "German Archaeological Institute" (Deutsches Archaeologisches Institut) Athens); Stoneman 1987: 262.
84. White 1908.
85. Stillman 1897.
86. Lord 1947: 179–80.
87. *DAB* X. s.v. "White, John Williams"; Lord 1947: 1–47.

notice of White in the 1916–17 report of the American School James R. Wheeler observed that

It is not too much to say that he and Professor Charles Eliot Norton were really the founders of the School, for though the idea of starting such an enterprise originated chiefly with the latter, it was Professor White's enthusiasm and driving power which made the realization of the idea possible, and he it was who organized the School and established the methods which still prevail in its management and support. (*Annual Report ASCS* 1916–17: 26)

The choice of Athens over Rome as the site of the first American overseas school came naturally to this post-Civil War Hellenophilic circle of academics and educated amateurs. Greek values in art, literature, and general culture were now considered superior to those of Rome. The goals and achievements of the American School founders were summarized in an 1890 speech given before the AIA's Wisconsin chapter by Professor Charles Edwin Bennett of the University of Wisconsin to celebrate the school's first decade:

Most of them (former students of the school) now hold positions as instructors in the leading colleges and schools of the country, where they are making themselves felt as the vehicles of a higher and better culture. They are making their students feel as they have been made to feel themselves, that a classical education does not end with the grammatical interpretation of a prescribed round of Greek and Roman authors, but that its province is broader, including the whole domain of Hellenic and Roman civilization. It was to secure such results as that that it was founded; to subserve the practical end of a higher education of our people rather than to enable individuals to win distinguished reputation by purely scientific work. (1890: 22)

From the beginning money was a problem for the new enterprise. The other foreign schools in Athens enjoyed direct governmental subsidies. That was not to be the American system. The American School in Athens had to learn to combine direct college and university support with private philanthropy, if it was going to survive and prosper. The School's initial operational organization was based on a consortium of colleges and universities that supplied the funds, students, and faculty. The early program of study was informal with the handful of students housed in temporary quarters and left largely to their own explorational devices.

During the first years, the combination of no fixed abode, the lack of a clearly defined program, and a constantly changing faculty contributed to a sense of instability at the American School. However, a greater sense of order began to emerge in 1888, when the first new American School building opened on a plot of land near Mt. Lykabettos. Although the expanding city of Athens today has enveloped its grounds, the School was then located well away from the small urban core. Trustees had some reservations about the new facility's distance from the major classical monuments, such as the Acropolis, that were to be the prime object of the students' studies; however, the school's elevated location offered a healthier environment and fewer distractions to the fledgling academics. Moreover, Athens at that time offered few attractions besides archaeological monuments. As is clear from photographs taken during that era, it was a small place, whose poverty and lack of class only the most ardent Hellenophiles could ignore.[88]

In its first years, the school employed a cadre of rotating directors and faculty members loaned by member institutions. Although this policy helped reduce costs, it did not provide the best environment for developing long-term programs, especially archaeological field research. The school clearly needed a permanent director in the same way it needed a permanent building. In 1888 Charles Waldstein (1856–1927) was appointed director, although the limited funding made available by the school allowed him to occupy the position for only a few months a year.

Waldstein had the cosmopolitan educational and professional background to lead the new American overseas enterprise.[89] Of German Jewish origins, he had received his early university education in the United States. However, he had left Columbia University after his junior year, and like many of his contemporaries had gone to Germany for his advanced education. He earned a Ph.D. at Heidelberg, where he studied international law and philosophy as well as classical archaeology. A former student of his at Cambridge described him as "a man of broadly cosmopolitan views with a special bent for philosophy. It was, in fact, as an ethical teacher that he first came here at the invitation of Henry Sidgwick" (A. B. Cook 1931: 50). In that era, it was most unusual for an American of Germanic-Jewish background to be appointed at an English university. But Waldstein's academic career flourished at Cambridge. He was appointed fellow of prestigious Trinity College. In 1880 he was made lecturer in classical archaeology, in 1882 reader, and in 1883 director of the Fitzwilliam Museum. In 1895 he became Slade Professor of Fine Arts at Cambridge. Waldstein's success was in part the result of his strong effort to assimilate to English culture. During World War I he changed his name from Waldstein to Walton to reinforce that identity. His rise was also a reflection of the fact that England had even fewer scholars with graduate training in the new German discipline of classical archaeology than America.

As an archaeologist Waldstein focused on Greek art, with a special

88. Lord 1947: 26–30. For photos of Athens, cf. Tomlinson 1991.
89. *EHCA* s.v. "Waldstein (changed to Walston in 1918), Sir Charles (1856–1927)"; A. B. Cook 1931: 49–52.

interest in Greek sculpture.[90] Like Norton, he was strongly influenced by the teachings of John Ruskin, even going so far as to write a small book on his English mentor.[91] Waldstein stressed the centrality of the "beauty-side of life" for the understanding of Greek art.[92] The Cambridge classicist A. B. Cook summarized Waldstein's outlook by noting that "he had the seeing eye. Rhythm and symmetry and everything that spelt or even misspelt Hellenic perfection he loved."[93]

Waldstein also felt strongly that the study of Greek art should be solidly based on the careful study and analysis of the monuments themselves. He did not sympathize with those who tried to write histories of Greek art by using mainly the ancient literary texts. He was suspicious of philologists and feared that they would try to reduce classical archaeology to a subordinate status in relation to philology.[94] Waldstein considered archaeology equal to philology and ancient history in studying the "Science of Antiquity."[95]

Like many of the figures in the first generation of American classical archaeology, Waldstein was a man of broad general culture, anxious to relate the discoveries of archaeology to larger issues and ideas current in Anglo-American intellectual circles. He was an open-minded traditionalist who could praise Rodin while still stressing the centrality of the Greek sculptural experience to contemporary art students.[96] In a review of Waldstein's 1885 book *Essays on the Art of Pheidias* A. R. Marsh observed:

In the history of any science, nothing is rarer than the appearance among its professors of a man with the impulse to connect it with knowledge as a whole. It is therefore always noteworthy when a book appears the author of which shows appreciation of the fact that his subject stands in close relation with all knowledge. Briefly the author of such a book is a moral teacher, as well as an advancer of learning. (1886: 182–87)

Marsh compared Waldstein's breadth of vision to that of the German Karl Otfried Müller (1797–1840), who in his *Archäologie der Kunst* had demonstrated himself to be a scholar for whom "classical archaeology and the history of classical literature were . . . parts of the knowledge of ancient moral life and this of moral life as a whole interpreted by science."[97] Marsh argued that since Müller's era archaeology had tended to become a scholarly world apart, and that archaeologists were "apt to regard as

90. Waldstein 1885, 1914.
91. Waldstein 1893.
92. Waldstein 1914: viii–ix.
93. A.B. Cook 1931: 51.
94. Marsh 1886: 182–87.
95. Waldstein 1885: 27.
96. Waldstein 1914.
97. For Müller cf. *EHCA* s.v. "Müller, Karl Otfried (1797–1840)."

empty enthusiasm anything meant to show the general uses and bearing of the facts to their sciences."[98] These words could have been spoken by Charles Eliot Norton himself and reflected the vision of a humanistic classical archaeology that was soon to be buried in the flood tide of empirical research.

Waldstein appears to have had mixed success as director of the American School. He had been away from America too long and understood Europe better than his rapidly changing native land. He was also a person of restless, not always clearly directed energy. One observer noted that "He is a man of such impetuous mind, that he needs a long time to get settled in any new business. He is never quiet long enough to be of real solid substantial help to the students of the School."[99] The German archaeologist Georg Karo dismissed his scholarly significance by asserting that "As an archaeologist, Waldstein never achieved distinction, though he undoubtedly was well grounded and possessed artistic taste. He had the misfortune of not recognizing the epochal changes brought about in our field both around 1880 and during the closing years of the century."[100] These judgments on Waldstein's archaeological expertise were not totally fair. The French certainly harbored lingering resentment against Waldstein because of the Franco-American struggle over the Delphi archaeological concession. Georg Karo had learned his field archaeology from Wilhelm Dorpfeld and would have had little sympathy for the old Ruskinian Waldstein. Karo, who strongly opposed blaming Germany for World War I also likely had little personal sympathy for someone who changed his name from Waldstein to Walton to appear less German.[101] Waldstein did undertake a number of important archaeological projects for the fledgling school and tried for more.

With a permanent facility and a permanent director, the school's founders could take great satisfaction in their first decade's work. An advertising circular, published in *The Nation* of 12 September 1889, proudly described the school as "provided with a fine edifice, a permanent director of European reputation as an archaeologist, Dr. Waldstein, and an endowment fund of over fifty thousand dollars." These successes had been achieved "through the efforts and sacrifices of a few liberal-minded people, chiefly in Boston and New York." The school's cultural mission was succinctly described in its twelfth annual report: "There can

98. Marsh 1886.

99. Amandry 1992: 105.

100. Quoted in Lord 1947: 88. Karo was a distinguished classical archaeologist. Although of Jewish descent, he was a strong conservative nationalist, who initially favored the Nazi rise to power, even though in the end he was forced to flee to the United States. *EHCA* s.v. "Karo, Georg(e) (1872–1963)"; Marchand 1996: 247–48, 261, 273, 344–45.

101. Marchand 1996: 247–8, 261, 344–5.

be no better influences brought to bear upon our own artists and architects than a close acquaintance with and study of the still unrivalled
productions of Greek masters."

The early generation of students at the school combined serious scholarship with a macho phil-Hellenism. This spirit of the pioneers was
evoked in an obituary notice about Walter Miller (1864–1949), longtime
professor at the University of Missouri and one of the American School's
first student:

Miller was passionately devoted to Hellas. He was an outdoor man and he had
wandered, mostly on foot, over most of Greece. He had climbed Mt. Parnassus
and Mt. Olympus. He had swum the Hellespont. He had been waylaid by Alba-
nian bandits and, commissioned a captain in the Greek army, had hunted them
down and captured them. But he was especially proud of his modern Greek,
which he spoke with his lips and both hands so well that he was frequently mistaken for a Greek. (Lord 1949–50: 19)

The school's first students undertook a variety of topographical, epigraphical, and architectural projects. The serious study of ancient Greek
topography was soon made a central part of the school curriculum, and
extended field trips throughout Greece became a standard feature of the
academic year. The founders felt that a direct, detailed knowledge of the
countryside was essential to a student of Greek history, especially in an
era before extensive photography and high-quality mapping.[102] As Louis
Lord observed in his history of the school's early years. "For the next half-
century the staff of the School would give to the students courses of
instruction on Greek authors whose work dealt with the land of Greece
rather than Greek ideals."[103]

The circular on the school published in the *The Nation* in 1889 stressed
that of the thirty pupils enrolled there so far four had been women. The
first of these was Annie Peck (1850–1935), who arrived in Athens in 1885
with a B.A. and M.A. from Michigan. She later taught briefly at Purdue
University and Smith College and went onto a career of giving "parlor lectures on Greek and Roman archaeology" and "climbing mountains."[104]
In 1886 Wellesley College became the first women's college to join the
ranks of American School cooperating institutions.[105] By 1899–1900,
eight of the school's fifteen students at the School were women. In the
period up to the outbreak of World War I, nine women held fellowships at
the school. Six of these were recipients of the Agnes Hoppin memorial
fellowship, offered from 1898 to 1904. This fellowship for women had

102. Seymour 1902: 16–19.
103. Lord 1947: 47.
104. *Who Was Who in America* (herafter *WWW America*) 1951 s.v. Peck, Annie Smith.
105. Lord 1947:14–15.

been set up by Professor Joseph Hoppin and his wife, because they felt that "the activity of the School for women students was limited to a certain degree."[106] Ironically, the fellowship was withdrawn after a few years, because the founders believed that the obstacles to women's participation had to a great degree been removed.[107] Although this evaluation of women's the progress in classical archaeology may have been optimistic, the high percentage of women at the school was a tribute to the vigor of classical studies at the women's colleges and coeducational institutions.

With the establishment of the institute, *American Journal of Archaeology*, and the American School of Classical Studies at Athens, Americans had laid three very important foundation stones of the profession. Organizationally they had placed themselves on the same level as colleagues in France and Germany and ahead of scholars in England. The institutions were small and fragile, but they became important instruments for creating a new generation of professional archaeologists and the cornerstones of one of the most impressive classical archaeological establishments in the world. However, creating that new discipline and profession required other teaching and research institutions and opportunities for excavation. Here too the generations between the Civil War and World War I proved to be extremely dynamic and creative. That is the story of the next chapter.

106. Sherman 1981: 35; cf. Lord 1947: 82.
107. Sherman 1981: 35. The holders of the Hoppin fellowship were May Louise Nichols (1898–99); Harriet Boyd (later Harriet Boyd Hawes) (1900–1901); Lida Shaw King (1901–2); Agnes Baldwin (Brett) (1902–3); Leila Clement Spaulding (Kent) (1902–3), and Edith Hall (Dohan) (1903–4).

3. From Amateur to Professional

By the 1880s the professionalization of academic institutions at the service of American classical archaeology had in many respects advanced beyond the professionalization of individual academics. The mid-nineteenth-century Americans first involved in classical archaeology in the Mediterranean were very much amateurs. They were drawn to the area for health reasons, journalism, minor diplomatic assignments, or just the opportunities that independent means provided to indulge interests and eccentricities. Even as formal education and professional training increased, many important figures blended what we would today call elements of amateurism and professionalism. These individuals were significant, both for their own accomplishments and for the fact that they helped pave the way for more scholarly American involvement. They also demonstrated that there was an ongoing role in classical archaeological research for serious amateurs that continues today.

Important in this group of archaeological pioneers was W. J. Stillman (1828–1901).[1] Born in Schenectady, New York and graduated from Union College, Stillman took to painting under the aegis of the Hudson River school painter Frederick Church.[2] He went to Europe in 1849 and fell under the influences of the English Pre-Raphaelites and Ruskin. He owed much to Ruskin, although he was realistic about the English critic's intellectual weaknesses.[3] During the 1850s Stillman made an effort to improve the American art and culture scene by founding and editing the *Crayon*, America's first serious art journal. Major cultural figures like the poet James Russell Lowell gave the endeavor strong support, but it lasted only three years.[4] Stillman received early support from Charles Eliot Norton, and Stillman in turn shared the Norton's humanistic vision of Norton. He dedicated one of his books, *The Old Rome and the New* (1897), to

---

1. The most important source for Stillman's life is his autobiography (1901); cf. also *DAB.* ix.29–302.

2. Stillman 1901: 110–15.

3. Stillman 1897: 92–127; Stillman 1901: 116–41, 309–20; Lindquist-Cook 1979.

4. Szegedy-Maszak 1987: 133.

Norton as the "sole survivor of that luminous circle in which once shown Lowell, Longfellow, Emerson, Holmes, Agassiz."

Like many nineteenth-century American cultural figures, Stillman entered the consular service, which provided both income and the opportunity to live overseas. Stillman served as American consul in Rome during the Civil War, and from 1865 to 1869 as American consul in Crete, where he was an avid supporter of the struggle for Cretan independence from the Turks.[5] He also was a *Times* correspondent in the Balkans and in Rome.

Stillman was one of several consuls important in developing American archaeological interests in the Mediterranean during the nineteenth century. Their responsibilities were not arduous and provided plenty of leisure time for such activities as archaeology, as well as good local contacts and a degree of diplomatic protection. The most famous of these archaeological consuls was Baron Cesnola of Cyprus, whose career is discussed in the next chapter. The Englishman Frank Calvert represented American interests from 1874 in Turkey and was also involved in early archaeological research in the Troad.[6] The American consul in Malta John Worthington was visible as a contributor to the early issues of the *American Journal of Archaeology*, reporting regularly on new archaeological discoveries on that island. In 1912 another American consul on Malta, James O. Laing, published a short account of the excavation of a Roman villa on the island in the AIA bulletin.[7]

Stillman's interests extended well beyond those of the casual reporter of new finds. He published semischolarly and popular works on Greek sculpture, archaeology, and topography.[8] However, in the early history of American classical archaeology he is best remembered as the man who almost got the archaeological concession for the Americans at Knossos and as the first serious American archaeological photographer in the Mediterranean.[9] Charles Eliot Norton helped support Stillman in part because of the latter's growing interest in the emerging medium of photography. In 1869, after the termination of his consulship in Crete, Stillman moved to Athens. There he found a photographic community already established. The first archaeological photographer had opened shop in Athens in 1858.[10] Stillman systematically photographed the major ancient monuments of Athens, as well as the evolving urban landscape of the developing city. His photographs, which sold well, depicted the

5. Stillman 1901: 375–450; 1976.
6. S. H. Allen 1995.
7. Laing 1912.
8. Stillman 1888, 1897, 1901.
9. Tomlinson 1991: 31.
10. Feyler 1987.

classical ruins set against a changing Athens with its blend of disappearing Turkish past and emerging neoclassical present.[11] This was the Athens the first American School students saw when they arrived in 1882.

Stillman entered the world of archaeological photography at a key
moment in the development of this new touristic and scholarly medium.
Photographers had been active at archaeological sites from the 1840s,
working with archaeological missions and as independent recorders.[12]
Increasingly, tourists became accustomed to bringing back from their
travels photographic images of places and monuments they had visited.
In Italy, these often high-quality photographs were supplied to them in
growing numbers by photographers like Giorgio Sommer, the brothers
Alinari, John Henry Parker, and Anderson.[13] An 1871 edition of *The
Roman Times: An English and American Journal* advertised "American Photographs of Roman Monuments, Statues of the Galleries and Views of the
Environment." By 1873 a visitor to Pompeii could purchase a special
souvenir album of photos of that site.[14] The sheer number and diversity
of these photographic images became overwhelming: Parker's final catalogue listed three thousand photos.[15]

Photographs provided a wealth of detail unlike the old souvenir
sketches that had been pre-Civil War tourist fare. Memory and recollec-
tion of sites visited became very different with precise images before
one's eyes. Not only were photographs means of memory recall for the
tourist, but they also became central teaching tools for the emerging
archaeology and art history programs in American colleges and universities. Large photo archives were created, such as that developed at the
University of Michigan between 1891 and 1903 by William Kelsey and
Thomas Spencer Jerome.[16] Along with plaster casts of classical sculpture
and architecture, the archaeological photographs made it possible for
students to obtain a much more accurate and detailed view of ancient
sites and monuments than had ever been possible before. Moreover,
photographs could be collected in much greater numbers than casts and
could be used with greater depth and flexibility for comparative studies.
Not surprisingly the great German expert on the identification and classification of Greek sculpture Adolf Furtwängler was in the forefront of
creating scholarly photographic archives.[17] They did not create the space
problems of large cast collections, and even individuals and institutions

11. Stillman 1901: 454–5; Szegedy-Maszak 1987: 133–38; Tomlinson 1991.
12. Feyler 1987.
13. Einaudi 1979: 9–12; Watson 1980; Saibanti 1991: 35–37.
14. Saibanti 1990.
15. Einaudi 1979: 9–12.
16. Gazda 1983: 9.
17. Furtwängler 1990: 85; Marchand 1996: 106–7.

of relatively modest means could acquire decent working collections. The photographic archives in American classics, archaeology, and art history departments helped lay the foundation of a German-inspired positivistic archaeological scholarship that has played a central role in the discipline ever since the last quarter of the nineteenth century.

Stillman's interest in the progress of American classical archaeology remained strong throughout his life. When the future of the Assos expedition was threatened in 1881, he wrote to the *New York Post* expressing his consternation. He noted sadly that "In any other civilized country, the government would have come to the aid at once." He described the site as more important than Hissarlik or Mycenae, and although claiming to be a poor man, he sent a donation of $25. He was one of the last of the major transitional figures who bridged the old world of the educated amateur and the new world of the trained professional.

The 1880s saw the emergence of a new generation of more professionally educated young American archaeologists. They took advantage of study opportunities provided in the graduate programs of the German universities, at the American School in Athens, and on the new archaeological field projects being organized by American institutions. Some became teachers in classics and art history departments, but others found their career options very limited. Some had the independent means to spend their lives as independent scholars, often in Europe. Others, with a certain bitterness returned to family businesses.

Representative of this often troubled transitional generation were the two directors of the Assos excavations, Joseph Thacher Clarke (1856–1921) and Francis Bacon (1856–1940). Clarke emerged as a young archaeological star in the 1880s. Born in Boston, educated as an architect in Germany, he attracted Charles Eliot Norton's with his early research on the lighting of the Greek temple in an essay that impressed Norton sufficiently for him to send a copy to John Ruskin.[18] The AIA establishment thought well enough of Clarke to make him while still a very young man, director of the first major American excavation in the Mediterranean. Yet after the directorship at Assos and the aborted attempt to find another excavation project in Italy, Clarke never again held a regular academic post. He lived in Europe for years, working for George Eastman and Eastman Kodak.[19] He failed after long delays to meet his Assos publication obligations, and by the turn of the century he had disappeared from the American archaeological landscape.

Francis Bacon came to archaeology through the architecture profes-

18. Bradley and Ousby 1987: 428.

19. I owe much of this information to a 22 March 1996 letter from Helen Bacon Landry to Dr. Susan Hueck Allen, a copy of which Dr. Allen kindly supplied me.

sion, a combination of interests and talents with a long and honorable tradition in American classical archaeology. He graduated from the Massachusetts Institute of Technology and practiced architecture for a few years before going to Assos. He appears to have avoided or been unable to find regular academic employment. Bacon worked for many years in the family furniture business while slowly but successfully moving forward the Assos publications. However, in later life he returned to Turkey and his love of archaeology. Bacon died at his house in the town of Chanak Kale overlooking the Dardanelles.[20] His obituary summed up the contributions of this last surviving archaeological pioneer of the Assos era:

In fact, it may be truthfully said that, had it not been for Bacon's enterprise and perseverance, the Archaeological Institute of America would not have been able to undertake, just at the beginning of its career, such an important work as the investigations and excavations at Assos in the Troad, which Bacon visited at the very moment when Charles Eliot Norton and his associates were founding the Archaeological Institute of America in 1879. (*Annual Bulletin AIA* 1940: 41–42)

The obituary goes on to describe Bacon's contribution to the development of an archaeological drafting tradition in the United States and his mentoring role as "Uncle Bacon" for younger generations of archaeologists.

More representative of the slowly emerging academic community of professionally educated classical archaeologists were Alfred Emerson (1859–1943), John R. Sterrett (1851–1914), and Augustus C. Merriam (1843–1895). Emerson received all his early education in Germany, earning a Ph.D. from Munich at the early age of twenty-one. He held fellowships at both Princeton and Johns Hopkins and taught for relatively brief periods at Miami University in Ohio, Lake Forest College, and Cornell. For many years he was curator of antiquities and assistant to the director at the Art Institute of Chicago.[21] H. N. Fowler, whose exceptionally long life gave him the dubious honor of writing the obituaries for most of his contemporaries, summarized Emerson thus:

Emerson was one of the vanguard of classical archaeologists in the U.S. and one of the ablest, but his published work, after his dissertation *De Hercule Homeris*, consisted only of relatively few competent articles in professional periodicals. He was a remarkable linguist, speaking seven languages fluently, and his knowledge of the monuments of antiquity and the facts of history was exceptional. He was a gentle, absent-minded scholar without too much common sense. He possessed a

20. Again I owe much of this information to Dr. Susan Hueck Allen, who is currently editing for publication Bacon's diaries.
21. Fowler 1944; Lord 1947: 92–93.

good sense of humor and enjoyed telling of his unacademic exploits in Munich. (1944: 77)

Sterrett started his classical studies with Basil Gildersleeve at the University of Viriginia and then went on to advanced work in Germany. Like many other bright young men of his generation, he attracted the attention and support of Charles Eliot Norton, to whom Sterrett sent a copy of his University of Texas inaugural lecture. When Sterrett went to the American School in 1882–83, he was, with his Ph.D from Munich, the only student with formal academic training in archaeology.[22] His skills as an archaeological topographical surveyor and epigrapher were sufficiently well developed that he won the confidence of William Ramsay, the famed British investigator of classical and postclassical Anatolia.[23] Ramsay asked Sterrett to join him in his pioneering explorations of Asia Minor. Sterrett continued this research on his own and can be regarded as the father of both American classical epigraphical studies and American survey archaeology.[24]

Unlike many of his academic contemporaries, Sterrett was not a man of independent means, and small sums had to be found constantly to support his work.[25] After his youthful epigraphical research in Asia Minor, he went on to a long and distinguished teaching career at Miami University of Ohio, the University of Texas at Austin, Amherst College, and Cornell University, and played an extremely important role in the introduction of classical archaeology into the American college curriculum.

Sterrett also retained his interest in field research, although he was hamstrung by his lack of a personal fortune or access to a major patron. In 1911, toward the end of his life, he decided to resolve his financial problems by launching a general appeal for funds to support an ambitious topographical research project in Asia Minor. To begin this campaign he published a book entitled *A Plea for Research in Asia Minor and Syria. Authorized by Men Whose High Achievements and Representative Character Make the Project a Call for Humanity at Large for Light in Regard to the Life of Man in the Cradle of Western Civilization.* It is a fascinating work that says much about the potential and limitations of American classical archaeology on the eve of World War I. The first part is a detailed description of Sterrett's proposed long-term research design. Much of it has a very modern sound. The initial emphasis of the project was going to be on the location, identification, and mapping of archaeological sites in the tradi-

---

22. *WWW America* 1897–1942: 1179 s.v. "Sterrett, John Robert Sitlington"; Lord 1947: 38; Briggs 1987: 163–64 n. 3.

23. Frend 1996: 91–107.

24. Sterrett 1888a, b.

25. *Annual Report ASCS* 1884–85.

tion of William Ramsay. An area of Asia Minor was going to be selected, and all the sites and inscriptions were to be mapped and recorded. Unlike many contemporary classical archaeologists who had little interest in material beyond the Roman or even the Hellenistic period, Sterrett wanted to study remains down to the Seljuk and Crusader periods. He noted that the project had a certain urgency, since the area experienced a continuing destruction of monuments.[26] That section closed with a plea for financial support for what would be a twenty-year project and a somewhat depressed statement of the financial limitations hindering American archaeology at that time:

The work done hitherto by America in archaeological research has always been unsatisfactory, has always been incomplete, and with few exceptions it will have to be done over again by more scientific, more systematic expeditions working with larger resources; for the research done by America has always been crippled by slender and inadequate means. It is time to do really scientific, systematic, exhaustive work pursued to a final work that may safely be compared by that done by France, Germany, and Austria, whose governments, understanding the value and importance of real idealism in molding national character supply the scholars with ample means wherewith to carry on research. (1911: 12)

The bulk of the book consisted of written endorsements that had been solicited from the international archaeological community. Advocates ranged from archaeologists like the German Wilhelm Dörpfeld and the British Flinders Petrie to the future American president Woodrow Wilson. In spite of this well-organized appeal, the project never reached realization and Sterrett died a few years later.

Augustus Merriam was described at the time of his death as "the first scholar in the country to devote himself mainly to classical archaeology."[27] He graduated from Columbia University, where he was taught Latin and Greek, until his appointment in 1890 as professor of archaeology and epigraphy. His main research interest was epigraphy. A colleague observed that he "belonged to an almost ideal type, combining as he did the receptivity and progressiveness of the American with the conservatism of the English. In his love of accuracy and in the patience necessary to its attainment he resembled a German.[28] Merriam was appointed director of the American School for 1887–88. He was also its first designated professor of archaeology. In Athens he developed a systematic course of instruction for the fellows and conducted excavations at Sicyon and an Attic site called Dionyso, identified as the location of the ancient deme of Icaria. He returned to Athens in 1895 with the plan to dig at

26. Sterrett 1911: 3–11.
27. *Annual Report ASCS* 1895: 16.
28. C. H. Young 1895: 229.

Koukounari near Icaria, but died suddenly, cutting short a very promising career.[29]

The Assos Excavations

This first group of young American archaeologists faced the challenge of creating a field tradition. Even as the planning for the AIA and the American School in Athens were moving ahead, serious thought was being given to the possibility of a major American excavation in the Greek Mediterranean. Almost from its foundation the organizers of the AIA wanted the institute to engage in active field work. Charles Eliot Norton believed passionately that Americans should not just be the passive recipients of European research but should be active contributors to the advancement of classical archaeology. It was natural that the new American archaeological organization would begin fieldwork in the German manner with an architecturally oriented, big site excavation, and that the effort would be focused somewhere in the Greek world.

The site selected for these initial American excavations was Assos, a Greek city located on the Turkish coast not far from Troy.[30] Norton and others who provided the initial organizational and financial backing for the enterprise felt that Assos, a Greek urban center without a long post-Hellenic occupation history, would provide an ideal laboratory to study key phases in the development of Greek architecture and urban life. These goals fit nicely into the ideology of Greek perfection advanced by scholars like Norton. The underlying values that supported the Assos expedition were captured in the long eulogy of Greek civilization and the Greek spirit presumably written by Norton that was included in the discussion of the Assos project in the AIA'a fifth annual report: "The superiority of the Greeks had its source in their moral discipline and was the result of adherence to principles of universal application and validity, and is therefore of perpetual service, alike as an example for emulation and as a criterion of conduct" *Annual Report AIA* 1884: 28).

The Assos excavation had other potential scholarly benefits as well. The sponsors felt that the research would provide useful information on the development of Greek building forms for the contemporary architectural community. The site might also produce objects that could be exported back to the United States. In Turkey the export rules were still more flexible than those in Greece or Italy, although that was to change shortly.

The acropolis site of Assos has a spectacular setting overlooking the

29. C. H. Young 1895, Lord 1947: 69–71, 85.
30. *EHCA* s.v. "Assos"; Freely 1990: 22–25.

Mediterranean. The location, however, posed a range of logistical problems for the inexperienced American excavators. Even today the area offers relatively little for the comfort of the tourist, and in 1881 the isolation must have been overwhelming. The excavations started in 1881 and continued through the spring of 1883. They were under the direction of Joseph Thacher Clarke, assisted by Francis Bacon and the young German student of architecture and archaeology Robert Koldeway (1855–1925).[31]

The aims of the excavation reflected the scholarly, architectural and artistic values of scholars of the period.[32] The Boston Society of Architects contributed to the excavations, hoping that the archaeological findings would contribute to a greater understanding of the history of the Doric order. These architectural historical but also ideological concerns were expressed well in a letter which the Boston architect Edward C. Cabot published in the first report of the excavation in 1898. He stated that the support of the Boston Society of Architects

was intended as an expression of its desire to know more of the principles underlying the development of Greek architectural forms; for to those principles in the midst of the complications and sophistications which inevitably beset all modern works of design, we must continually repair for correction, inspiration and reflection. (*Annual Report AIA* 1898: vii)

The sponsors of the project also saw the Assos excavations as making an important contribution to the emerging "scientific" discipline of classical archaeology. In the words of the 1884 AIA *Annual Report,*

The methods of archaeological investigation are constantly becoming more thorough and intelligent. They have passed the empirical stage, and archaeology may now claim its place among the exact sciences. It is not by the brilliant, haphazard discoveries of speculative excavators that progress is secured, but by carefully considered and deliberately executed investigations. (*Annual Report AIA* 1884: 30)

Assos was to answer the needs both of those who saw in classical archaeology a major instrument in ongoing humanistic battles, and those who sought its ultimate justification by claiming its place in the increasingly dominant intellectual world of the pure sciences.

The excavations themselves focused on the public buildings within the city and the cemeteries just outside the city gates. The acropolis provided the ruins of a fine temple in the Doric order. These were cleared, measured, and drawn. There were an Agora with associated civic buildings, city walls, and an extensive cemetery outside the city gates with monumental architecture and portable objects. These were all explored. The

31. *EHCA* s.v. "Koldeway, Robert (1855–1925)." On the later career of Koldeway, cf. Kuklick 1996: 144–45.
32. C. Gates 1996: 49.

architectural emphases of the Assos excavations should not mask certain interdisciplinary aspects of this pioneering project. The search for new inscriptions was naturally a major focus of the investigations: their study was undertaken by John Sterrett. The project also employed a geologist, Joseph Diller, and a dig photographer, John Henry Haynes, who took pictures not only of the sites and the antiquities but also "of picturesque features of the city and its vicinity which lent themselves to this manner of representation."[33] Since a considerable part of the excavations were to be focused on the cemetery areas, interest was expressed in research on physical anthropology. Clarke in an *AJA* 1885 review of the German Rudolph Virchow's books on burials in the Troad had stressed the importance of studying human remains especially skulls to understand changing populations.[34]

The newly founded Boston Museum of Fine Arts was one of the major sponsors of the Assos excavations, and it hoped that the excavations would add to its collections. As has already been noted, one of the reasons for selecting Turkey over Greece for the site of the dig was that Ottoman Turkey still allowed the exportation of excavated antiquities. A Turkish law of 1874 provided that one-third of the finds would go to the landowner, one-third to the Turkish government, and one-third to the excavators. In the case of the Assos project, two-thirds were to go to the Turkish government and one-third to the Museum of Fine Arts. The Boston Museum also received casts of architectural and sculptural items found during the excavations made at the site. Efforts to buy more of the finds from the Turkish government were blocked.[35]

The rapid export of these finds to the American museum was important, since the era of foreign looting in Turkey was ending. In 1884 the Turkish government had changed its excavations laws and "had resolved thenceforth to grant no further permission to excavate, and even to forbid the sale and exportation of all antiquites discovered in the Turkish dominions."[36] Some archaeological projects could still operate under grandfather clauses. Clarke used this impending change as a lever to extract more excavation funds from the AIA while the Assos permit was still valid. The editors of the *AJA* reacted strongly to these proposed changes on the part of the Turkish government, warning direly that "If these regulations are strictly adhered to, the result will be a complete

33. J. T. Clarke 1898: 4. Haynes reappeared as the AIA representative when W. J. Stillman undertook archaeological investigations in Crete (Stillman 1901: 630–45) and as an excavator in Mesopotamia (Kuklick 1996: 32, 55–57, 65–77, 82–91, 143–46).

34. J. T. Clarke 1885. Virchow's works were *Alttrojanische Graber under Schadel.* (1882) and *Uber alte Schadel von Assos und Cypern* (1884).

35. J. T. Clarke 1898: 6; Sheftel 1979: 7–8.

36. J. T. Clarke 1898: 22.

cessation of the enterprising activity which has led to such magnificent discoveries at Pergamon, Halicarnassus, Assos."[37] Unfortunately, the presence of the Pergamene sculptures in Berlin and the Halicarnassus sculptures in London was spurring Turkish cultural nationalism.[38] By 1884 the Assos excavations were winding down. The final cost of the whole project to the Institute from 1880 to 1884 was $19,121.16.[39] Some of this support had come from other Boston cultural and professional institutions; the rest was raised through private subscriptions. The range and level of this individual support was impressive. Assos hence set a pattern of fundraising that continues to dominate American excavations in the present.

The history of publication also established a less fortunate pattern for American archaeological projects. Clarke was placed in charge of producing the final reports and proved to be a painfully slow author. Laments and complaints about delays in the Assos publications filled the pages of the AIA's reports and official correspondence for decades. By 1916 the generous patron of classical archaeology James Loeb was asking that advances he had made toward publication of the Assos excavations be returned, since publication had not been completed.[40] In late 1918 the acting secretary of the Institute wrote that: "this long delayed and troublesome enterprise will be a serious reflection on American scholarship if this report is not published very soon" (AIA Archives Box 20: Acting Sec. to W. F. Harris 7 Dec. 1918).

By this time Clarke had disappeared from the archaeological scene. Francis Bacon, who had left field archaeology for the family furniture business, was still trying to push ahead with the publication. However, the AIA was unable to provide much financial help. Bacon noted piteously that he himself would be willing to finance the publication, but his own economic position had been undermined by the war. He ultimately shouldered the responsibility and through his own work and money brought the essential volumes to completion. Finally, in 1921, Mitchell Carroll, secretary of the AIA, was able to report to President James Egbert that the Assos publication was completed.[41]

In historical perspective the Assos excavations must get mixed reviews. The goals were not those of archaeology today, and the sad history of slow publication was regrettable. Still it must be remembered that this was a project launched in an isolated area a bare two years after the AIA was founded by a country that had no classical archaeology tradition, no

37. *AJA* 1 (1885): 225.
38. Marchand 1996: 201–2.
39. J. T. Clarke 1898: 38.
40. AIA Archives Box 20.
41. AIA Archives Box 20: Carroll to Egbert 2 May, 1921.

trained field workers, and no support structure. For their day, Clarke, Bacon, and their colleagues showed competence and imagination.

AIA Excavations: The Post-Assos Experience

The Assos excavations had whetted the archaeological appetites of the ruling elite of the AIA but also had revealed serious financial and organizational problems in the support community. The Americans did not have the state-sponsored institutional base for archaeology that the Germans used to maintain an excavation like Olympia, and they were not likely to have that.[42] The increasing restrictions on the export of antiquities from countries in the Mediterranean limited the interests of both private collectors and the newly developing museums. Significantly, both collectors and museums turned to Egypt for archaeological field research, since in Egypt the antiquities laws of the British administration made the exportation of artifacts much easier.

Still, the AIA pushed ahead with the effort to find a new classical site. Epidaurus and Orchomenus were considered.[43] Crete appeared as a tempting possibility. The institute had a contact in Crete: the former consul W. J. Stillman. Stillman and John Henry Haynes were commissioned to explore archaeological possibilities there. Stillman was especially impressed by the site of Knossos, where wall remains were visible on the surface. Unfortunately for the Institute, Stillman was perceived by the Ottoman government as having been too sympathetic to the anti-Turkish agitation on the island, and permission to excavate was refused.[44]

Interest in Cretan archaeology continued nonetheless. In 1893 the AIA provided funds to support the research of the Italian archaeologist Frederico Halbherr (1857–1930).[45] Halbherr was doing pioneering archaeological research in Crete and started the island's long tradition of distinguished Italian archaeology.[46] The confused political situation on the island limited Halbherr's activities and the AIA support soon ended. Historically the association proved ironic, since Halbherr was later accused of playing a major role in the collapse of the AIA-sponsored Cyrene project in 1911.

The major lost opportunity for the AIA and for the American classical

42. *EHCA* s.v. "Olympia, Greece"; Stoneman 1987: 256–64.

43. *EHCA* s.v. "Epidauros," "Orchomenos" Norton had mention Orchomenos along with Samos as a possible AIA site at the May 10, 1879 foundation meeting (AIA Archives Box 1).

44. Stillman 1901: 630–45.

45. *EHCA* s.v. "Halbherr, Federico (1857–1930).

46. At the 13 May, 1893 meeting of the executive committee, $3,000 was appropriated for the research of Halbherr (AIA Archives; La Rosa 1986).

archaeologists of this first generation came at Delphi, the great Greek sanctuary site. Delphi is today considered a quintessential French archaeological excavation, for French scholars have been working there for a century.[47] However, it came very close to becoming an American project. With its wild, haunting beauty and its deep historical and cultural associations with the very essence of Greek civilization, Delphi was very attractive to the early generations of foreign archaeologists. The problems of work at the site were daunting, though. Earthquakes and other natural phenomena had deeply buried many of the remains. The modern Greek village of Kastri had developed over the sanctuary site and would have to be removed. This meant expensive land purchases and compensations for destroyed structures.[48]

Americans had shown early interest in the site. An earthquake in 1873 had destroyed much of Kastri and made excavation more feasible. In 1876, even before the AIA was founded, the American minister in Athens, General John Meredith Read, was asked to sound out the Greek government on the possibility of American excavations at Delphi. The reply was favorable, but funds could not be found.[49] By the 1880s the French had requested a permit from the Greek government to excavate at the site. But the granting of permission was connected to the ratification of certain commercial treaties between France and Greece.[50]

When the French government did not move on that diplomatic front, the Greeks were offended, and the Americans decided to try their luck at gaining the Delphi concession. In 1887 the AIA led by Charles Eliot Norton and the newly founded American School of Classical Studies began joint efforts to make Delphi an American excavation. A fundraising appeal was launched in the United States and a considerable sum collected.[51] Diplomatic support was elicited from the American State Department, and long and complicated negotiations among the Greeks, Americans, and French ensued.[52] For a while it looked as though the Americans would win.

In the end, the French diplomatic efforts were successful. France had a much longer history of cultural and archaeological involvement in Greece and was certainly seen by the Greeks as a more important nation than the raw, emerging power from across the Atlantic. The final decisions revolved around connections between lowering tariffs on Greek

---

47. *EHCA* s.v. "Delphi, Greece"; Amandry 1992.

48. *EHCA* s.v. "Delphi, Greece."

49. *Annual Report AIA* 1891.

50. Lord 1947: 59–60.

51. The Delphi fundraising campaign, among other things, stimulated the formation of the Chicago AIA chapter (Guralnick 1990: 1–2).

52. Lord 1947: 58–62, Amandry 1992.

currants being imported into France and conceding excavation rights at
Delphi.[53] In 1891 the permit for Delphi was granted to France. As Louis
Lord noted in his history of the American School, it was probably for the
best. Even if the money could have been raised for the initial program of
excavations, it is not clear that such support could have been sustained,
nor that the Americans had the technical expertise to carry out an excavation of this magnitude with a competence even approximate to that
shown by the Germans at Olympia. The record of the early French excavations at Delphi was certainly uneven, even though they always enjoyed impressive government support.[54]

In contrast to the American's efficient efforts in connection with the
Delphi concession, the abortive AIA project at Croton in southern Italy
was somewhat farcical. It again highlighted the problems foreign archaeologists faced in the changing world of Mediterranean nationalism. The
AIA executive committee, with special support from the Baltimore society, decided that Magna Graecia would be a good area for archaeological
investigation.[55] At that time the Greek cities of southern Italy had been
relatively little explored. The Greek ruins of Sicily and southern Italy
were among the best preserved in the Hellenic Mediterranean. The areas
where they were located were often desolate and the conditions primitive, but not daunting to archaeologists willing to work in Turkey and
Crete.

Two young AIA archaeologists, Joseph Clarke, former director of the
Assos excavations, and Alfred Emerson, were sent out in 1886 to explore
the possibilities for an American excavation in Magna Graecia. After
examining a number of sites in the region, they decided that the late
archaic temple and sanctuary of Hera Lakinia at Croton in southwest
Italy offered the best prospects for another architecturally oriented archaeological project.[56]

The land where the temple was located was owned by Baron Luigi
Berlingieri, who was also the mayor of the modern village. He was very
willing to grant permission for the excavations, and as a great southern
Italian landowner he felt free to do what he wanted with his feudal domain. The hopes of the excavation rapidly came to grief in the complicated interaction between local and national authority in newly unified
Italy, however. The diverse rules of the often indulgent governments of
the earlier nineteenth century were being replaced by the centralized
regulations of a nationalistic state. In an 1887 *AJA* newsletter from Rome,

53. Lord 1947: 62.
54. *EHCA* s.v. "Delphi, Greece."
55. *Annual Report of the AIA* 1885–86: 40–43.
56. For the remains at the site itself, cf. Greco 1981: 108–12.

the archaeologist A. L. Frothingham Jr. commented on the current antiquities laws of Italy with the AIA experience very much in mind:

It is a general feeling that the laws regulating archaeological investigations and
excavations in Italy should be changed. Firstly, they are too restrictive and unen-
lightened, and, secondly, each province has preserved its antiquated laws, so
there is no uniformity throughout the land. Owing to the confusion and uncertainty reigning in this question, there are endless law-suits and violations of the
law: such an amount of red-tape officialism is required as effectually to discourage
scientific work in many cases, and notwithstanding the most benevolent of intentions, the letter of the law is made to kill the spirit. (*AJA* 1881: 388)

The developments in Italy relating to the archaeological work of foreigners paralleled the Americans' experience elsewhere, as the Assos
events demonstrated. Now, however, foreigners could not export antiquities legally, nor could they conduct excavations within Italian national
territory.[57] Topographical investigations and survey of standing remains
were possible. However, as field archaeology became more complex,
it became more difficult to distinguish between excavations and topographical research that involved clearing and cleaning of the site the
Americans proposed to undertake.

Clarke began initial field investigations at Croton in 1887. Almost immediately he ran into problems created by the Italian legal and bureau-
cratic world and the regional rivalries in a newly unified country. Following procedures learned in Greece and Turkey, Clarke wanted to notify
the authorities at Rome about his intended project, but Baron Berlingieri
protested. Members of the south Italian nobility had little affection or respect for the Piedmontese-dominated government in Rome. The baron
argued that the territory of Croton was ruled not by the decrees of the
new Italian government but by privileges granted to Calabria under Bour-
bon decrees of 1823. Since the baron was sponsoring the excavations on
his private property, he felt it was up to him to decide what the Americans
could and could not do in the way of archaeological research at Croton.

The Italian government authorities did not share his views. They shut
the American project down and sequestered the excavated artifacts. Local legal challenges were mounted against what was considered an abu-
sive exercise of authority by the national government. Given the glacial
qualities of the Italian judicial system, it was not surprising that nothing
was heard again of the Croton project.[58] Italian-American archaeological
relations had gotten off to a rocky start. The problems were exacerbated
with the Cyrene expedition.

57. Arrias 1995.
58. *Annual Report AIA* 1887: 40–47.

The Cyrene Excavation

The last major Mediterranean archaeological effort of the AIA, that at Cyrene in what is today Libya, fell victim to even more complicated (and deadly) diplomatic intrigues than at Croton. As far back as the early 1880s Charles Eliot Norton had expressed an interest in excavating at Cyrene.[59] Like Assos and Croton, Cyrene represented a Greek urban outpost that might yield important evidence on the classical phases of civilization.[60] Moreover, Cyrene was located at the fringes of the crumbling Ottoman Empire and was of only marginal interest to Turkish authorities. This raised the possibility of a more flexible approach to the excavations and even possibly to the disposition of finds than at Assos. In 1910 the Americans were able to persuade the Ottoman authorities to grant a permit to excavate Cyrene. Fund-raising was undertaken and a staff appointed.[61]

The AIA Cyrene excavation committee consisted of the American businessman and philanthropist Allison Armour (1863–1941), Arthur Fairbanks (1864–1944) of the Boston Museum of Fine Arts, and, as an adviser, the English archaeologist and sometime intelligence operative David G. Hogarth (1862–1927).[62] Armour had already explored Cyrene in 1904 with Hogarth.[63] Armour put his three-masted yacht the *Utowana* at the disposition of the project to explore the area and transport staff and equipment. The Boston Museum of Fine Arts joined the AIA in funding the excavation. As at Assos, the MFA was to receive any archaeological objects that might be exported from Cyrene. The ever supportive James Loeb (1867–1933) and Gardiner Lane (1859–1914), a prominent Boston philanthropist, son of Harvard Latin professor George Martin Lane and son-in-law of the Johns Hopkins classicist Basil Gildersleeve, provided major private funding, which was supplemented by a range of private subscriptions from Boston, Washington, and Chicago.[64]

Richard Norton (1872–1918), a son of Charles Eliot Norton, was appointed director of the project. Educated at Harvard and in Germany, young Norton had been a student at the American School, an excavator at Assos and the Argive Heraeum, and director of the American School of Classical Studies in Rome (1899–1907). Most recently he had been operating as an agent for American art collectors in Europe. World War I-era

59. Vanderbilt 1959: 80.

60. *EHCA* s.v. "Cyrenaica."

61. R. Norton (1910–11a).

62. For Armour, cf. *WWW America* 30. For Hogarth, cf. *EHCA* s.v. "Hogarth, David George"; Sayce 1927; Lock 1990.

63. Hogarth 1910: 123–24.

64. On Lane, *WWW America* 702 s.v. "Lane, Gardiner Martin"; Briggs 1987: 372.

photos show a thin, crisp-mustached individual resembling a British officer more than his benign New England intellectual father.[65]

Richard Norton was a man of strong opinions. His negative views of Arabs and Turks read painfully even given the many stereotypes present in the literature of the period. He had already aroused the anger of the Italians with his observations to the London *Times* about their mismanagement of the new archaeological sites and materials that were being discovered during a period of frenetic building at Rome.[66] Even as he prepared for excavations at Cyrene, he asserted in a report to the AIA "that the Italians had spread false reports about my intentions was certain and the question was how much the Arabs believed."[67]

Norton's history of stormy relations with the Italians soon took on additional meaning and consequences. The distinguished Italian archaeologist Frederico Halbherr had long been interested in starting an Italian archaeological project in North Africa, and especially at Cyrene.[68] This coincided with Italy's growing colonial ambitions. The relatively new Italian state desired to become an imperial power. Its initial forays into East Africa and Ethiopia had proved disastrous. Now the lands of the disintegrating Ottoman Empire in eastern North Africa seemed tempting to imperialists who dreamed of restoring the Roman Empire in Mare Nostrum.[69]

The arrival of an American archaeological expedition, whose opulent headquarters on a yacht indicated elite support, increased Italian anxiety. Rumors spread that the Americans were not after just artifacts, but also Libya's mineral resources. The Italians reacted energetically on the diplomatic front, even reminding the officials at Constantinople of the looting of artifacts from Turkish Cyprus by the American consul Cesnola decades before. In the view of the Italian diplomats, "ognuno di essi, sotto lo scienziato, celi, e male, il saccheggiatore" (the Americans, each of them behind the scientist hides and badly, the looter).[70]

The confused, tragic ending of the Cyrene expedition has obscured its definite, if limited, accomplishments and its innovative potential. Norton was assisted by such experienced American School excavators as H. Fletcher DeCou, G. D. Curtis, and Joseph Hoppin. Although at the core it was a late nineteenth-century, architecturally oriented excavation, efforts were made to develop its wider research possibilities. Richard Norton in his typical trenchant style stated that "There is no possible justification for treating an excavation as though it were a South African diamond

65. Kelsey 1919.
66. Lanciani 1988: 241–47.
67. R. Norton 1910–11.
68. Di Vita 1986; Petricioli 1990: 104–49.
69. Bosworth 1979: 127–64.
70. Petricioli 1990: 114–16.

mine."[71] Scholars like the physical anthropologist Alec Hrdlicka of the Smithsonian and Francis Kelsey of Michigan lamented that skeletal material on excavations was being discarded rather than studied.[72] In a letter to Norton, Kelsey urged that the skeletons and especially the skulls be saved

because they have bearing on the problem of the races inhabiting this part of Africa. In this regard, the excavators in Greek lands have been indescribably careless. If, for example, the human bones found at Corinth and other places had been saved with an exact notation of the period to which the accompanying finds belonged we should already be well along on the way toward a solution of the vexed question of the physical relations of the Greeks in the classical period. (AIA Archives)

This was an oldfashioned, even racist physical anthropology, but it represented the dominant approach of a period when scholars often closely connected race and culture. Still, these were archaeologists who considered the study of human remains a worthy research enterprise. Sadly, only recently have classical archaeologists followed Hrdlicka and Kelsey's advice and given the human skeletal material the attention it deserves. Human remains were recovered from the tombs at Cyrene, but like so many other aspects of that expedition, concern for them soon became secondary as more dramatic events unfolded.

The American excavations got underway in early 1911 but were soon disrupted by tragedy. On the morning of 11 March 1911, one of the assistants, H. Fletcher DeCou, was shot and killed on the site by local Arabs. DeCou had graduated from the University of Michigan in 1889 and had long been associated with the American Schools of Classical Studies in both Athens and Rome and with various American field projects in the Mediterranean (Figure 3). His career was representative of the "wandering scholars" in the first generation of classical archaeologists. Francis Kelsey summarized DeCou's distinctive archaeological life in his obituary:

From the fall of 1890 . . . until his death Mr. DeCou spent the greater part of his time abroad, first as a student upon fellowships at Athens or in Germany, then as secretary and lecturer in the American Schools in Athens and Rome. He twice returned to the University of Michigan to fill vacancies in the classical department; an offer of a permanent position, starting with the rank of Junior Professor, he declined because of his devotion to the School in Rome. The year 1909–1910 he spent in Munich, working upon collections for Mr. James Loeb. (1910–11: 113)

Richard Norton eulogized him in rather more florid terms:

71. R. Norton 1910–11a: 142.
72. AIA Archives Box 19: Sept. 1911 Kelsey-Hrdlicka correspondence.

Figure 3. Reproduction of the memorial erected to the American archaeologist Herbert Fletcher DeCou after his murder by Arabs on March 10, 1911 at the Libyan site of Cyrene during excavations conducted there by the Archaeological Institute of America. Photo courtesy of the Kelsey Museum Archives of the University of Michigan.

To the chivalry of a medieval knight he added the deep learning and broad outlook of a true scholar. Words cannot picture him to those who knew him not, and give but a sad satisfaction to us who loved and admired him. But though his sweet and gentle presence no longer is with us to cheer and to inspire, his blood has added a new grace to the asphodel where it blows across the sleeping ruins of Cyrene, and his spirit has entered into our efforts to bring the work to such conclusion that he would himself have said "Well done." (1910–11a: 143)

A variety of motives for the attack were proposed at the time, including DeCou's involvement with local Arab women and a case of mistaken identity on the part of the Arabs, who had meant to kill Norton.[73] However, Richard Norton early persuaded himself that the real instigators were the Italians and that the ultimate agent responsible for the murder may have been Frederico Halbherr, who like the Englishman Hogarth had a long history of combining archaeology and colonial politics. Norton claimed that Armour himself had been warned by both the Turks and the German emperor about Italian intentions in the North Africa area.[74]

The Italians were certainly preparing to move on Cyrene, and they may well have wanted the Americans out of the way. The local Italian consul, Vincenzo Bernabei, was in constant contact with Rome about the Americans and had asked about the advisability of some "occulta ma efficace azione" (hidden but effective action).[75] Halbherr had even remarked darkly about the possibility of resorting to obstructionary tactics "per mezze delle tribù del luogo anche a costo di qualche serio incidente" (by means of the local tribes even at the cost of some serious incident).[76]

DeCou's murder provoked American imperialistic reactions typical of the period. Communications flew back and forth between the AIA, the State Department, Norton, and Armour, who used his yacht as a floating command post. AIA officials made appropriately high-level visits to the State Department and rallied their contacts in the government, the Senate, and the American establishment. A destroyer, the USS *Chester*, was sent to the waters off Cyrene to provide a suitably admonitory presence as the Turks prepared to try the individuals they claimed were associated with the murder.

The situation became even more complicated when the Italians decided to invade Cyrene in late September 1911. Richard Norton further inflamed matters by writing to various British publications, denouncing as fraudulent the Italian claims that justified their attack on Ottoman territory. He supported his actions by stating that he was one of the few people in London who knew the country directly, and that "there is a

73. Goodchild 1976: 290–97; Petricioli 1990: 129.
74. Petricioli 1990: 130–31.
75. Petricioli 1990: 121.
76. Petricioli 1991: 126.

moral question involved which seems to be of more importance than archaeological discoveries."[77] American officials were concerned that Norton would further complicate the situation by undertaking a provocatory visit to Cyrene. In the words of an Italian diplomatic communication of the period: "Italian government greatly regrets his visiting Tripoli at this moment, fearing some regrettable incident because of extreme and general indignation felt against Norton by all Italians, because of prejudicial articles by Norton in London TIMES and GRAPHIC" (17 Oct. 1911 telegram from Secretary of State Knox to American Consul, Malta — copy in AIA archives).

The plans for Norton's visit were canceled, the destroyer *Chester* stayed well clear of the more powerful Italian fleet, and no major Italian-American diplomatic crisis developed. The fate of the Cyrene expedition was sealed, however. Although the AIA claimed that "the Italian government, through its authorized representatives, promised to the Chairman that the excavations could be continued after the war under Italian protection,"[78] this permission was never granted. Norton reminded his colleagues of the hostility of "Italy's attitude toward foreign archaeologists in her own country" and observed that he saw "no reason for the Italian leopard to change its spots."[79]

Norton's pessimism proved to be well founded. The Italian war in Cyrene was longer and more bitter than expected. When the area was finally secured, it was designated Italian national territory and closed to foreign excavations. Halbherr used his considerable influence to oppose renewal of the American concession.[80] He felt strongly that "la nostra parola d'ordine dev'essere che gli scavi della nuova colonia devono essere, d'ora in avanti, soggetti alle leggi italiane ed eseguiti dall'Amministrazione Italiana" (our watchword needs to be that the excavations of the new colony from now onwards subject to Italian laws and executed by the Italian administration).[81] In the end the Italian government paid $25,000 in compensation for the lost American archaeological investment.[82] Halbherr saw this as another confirmation of the American character. He cynically observed that the Americans had abandoned "quegli scavi dietro un compenso pecuniario. Sono dei mercanti e coi soldi ai mandano via" (had abandoned the excavations in return for a monetary compensation. They are merchants and with money they sent away).[83] American

77. Letter to London *Times* 3 Oct. 1911.
78. *Annual Report AIA* 1922: 107.
79. AIA Archives: Richard Norton to AIA, 4 November 1911.
80. Bosworth 1979: 127–66; Petricioli 1990: 144–45.
81. Di Vita 1986: 84.
82. *Annual Report AIA* 1922: 107–8.
83. Petricioli 1990: 149.

archaeologists only returned to the region only after World War II with the University of Michigan's excavations at Apollonia, the port of Cyrene, from 1965 to 1967.[84]

Richard Norton hoped that the goodwill he had gained with the Turks for his anti-Italian stand in regard to the attack on Cyrene would gain him a permit elsewhere in Ottoman territory. Projects at Colophon in Turkey and Siwhah in Egypt were considered, but no new expedition came to pass. In 1914 World War I broke out and American attention was directed elsewhere. Norton died in 1918 as a consequence of his service in the ambulance corps in Italy. With him died his father's hopes that the AIA would become an independent research force.

One of the AIA's stated aims, proclaimed at its foundation, was the sponsorship of expeditions and explorers. The institute's activities in the New World are outside the scope of this study, although in its early years the AIA made significant contributions to the development of American archaeology.[85] It is fair to say that the core leadership of the AIA saw an involvement in New World archaeology as a tactical measure, which as Thomas Day Seymour put it, would relate to "an increasing interest in American archaeology among affiliated societies of the Institute."[86]

The results in the Old World during the thirty years between Assos and Cyrene could hardly have been considered spectacularly successful, despite the energy, goodwill, and financial support of the AIA ruling elite. Part of the failure can be blamed on the increasingly severe limitations placed on field archaeology by the new, rather sensitive national governments that controlled most of the classical lands. But the failure also related to the changing nature of archaeological research. Classical archaeology was becoming less a world of expeditions and explorers and more one of long-term research projects requiring stronger institutional bases. State-supported foreign schools and long-term government investment in archaeology made the successes of the Germans at Olympia and the French at Delphi possible. Significantly, it was the American School of Classical Studies in Athens that created and shaped the American classical field archaeology tradition in the Mediterranean.

Early Excavations by the American School of Classical Studies in Athens

The guiding powers of the American School saw almost immediately that they could fulfill their mission only by engaging in field research. However, for financial and logistical reasons, the American School's early

84. Goodchild, Pedley, and White 1976.
85. Hinsley 1986.
86. *Annual Bulletin AIA* 1905: 170; Hinsley 1986: 121–24.

excavation experiments were launched in a small and hesitant manner. Louis Lord, the school's first official historian, described this as a period "when the School could spread devastation over the face of the land by attacking theaters and ruined Byzantine churches in seven different sites in one season"[87] (Lord 1947: 85). This was not a totally fair judgment. It is true that during the 1880s and early 1890s, the school undertook a number of short excavations at Sparta, Eretria, Phlius, and Plataea.[88] However, at that point the school had limited resources and limited archaeological expertise. The small scale of the excavations suited both student and faculty background and needs. Nor was this totally random activity. Certain research foci such as the investigation of the physical remains of representative Greek theaters represented important classical research topics at the time. Even those modest excavations gave the Americans considerable scholarly visibility and earned them growing respect.

As the archaeological representatives in Greece of a growing international power, the management of the American School felt that the institution needed a major excavation. This was also Charles Waldstein's view. As director (1888–92) and later as professor of ancient art at the school (1892–97), he promoted an active excavation program. He had pushed very hard to obtain the Delphi concession for the Americans. When that failed, he turned to the excavation of the Argive Heraeum in the Peloponnesus. It was an important site, housing one of the oldest and most important temples and sanctuary complexes in Greece.[89] The joint AIA-ASCS excavations conducted there between 1892 and 1895 were in many ways the most successful undertaken during the early period of the school.[90] The scale of work was much greater than the small theater projects of earlier years. At its high point the size and complexity of the school work at Argos approached that of the great European projects. Starting off the 1892 season with sixty-three workers, Waldstein rapidly expanded the number to two hundred and forty. The central focus of the work was the temple and its associated buildings.[91]

At the Argive Heraeum a generation of young American classical archaeologists matured as field archaeologists. The names listed on the title page of the Argive Heraeum publication include George H. Chase, H. Fletcher DeCou, Theodore W. Heermance, Joseph Hoppin, Albert Lythgoe, Richard Norton, Rufus Richardson, Edward Tilton, Henry S. Washington, and James R. Wheeler. They represented the best of an emerging

87. Lord 1947: 85.
88. Lord 1947: 75–86. The American School returned to Phlius in the 1920s (Lord 1947: 173–4).
89. *EHCA* s.v. "Argive Heraion (Heraeum)."
90. Lord 1947: 86–88.
91. *Annual Report ASCS* 1891: 29–30.

second generation of American professional classical archaeologists. In the preface of volume one, Waldstein was very candid about the initial limitations of his field crew: The young men who acted as my assistants at the excavations,

who one and all stood by me loyally in all difficulties and ultimately became so efficient in their work came to me, with hardly an exception, as novices who, in those days, had not even been able to pursue a complete course in archaeology in any of their home universities.In most cases, when they had thus become really efficient, they were called away by the offer of some appointment at home and by some other inducement. (1902: ix)

Their recruitment, field development and later prestigious careers say very positive things about Waldstein's sometimes maligned archaeological leadership.

Waldstein praised Richard Norton, Henry Washington, and Joseph Hoppin as assistants of special importance. Henry S. Washington (1867–1934) was educated at Yale and in Germany, at Leipzig. His training was strongly geological, and he finished his career as a petrologist at the geophysical laboratory of the Carnegie Institution in Washington, D.C. He had excavated at several other sites in Greece such as Phlius and Plataea before joining Waldstein as his second in command. Waldstein noted that "owing to the experience which for several years past he has acquired in such work, as well as to his enthusiasm and unselfish devotion, his services were such that I can hardly realize how the undertaking could have been carried out as it has been done without his cooperation."[92]

Joseph Hoppin (1870–1925) became one of the first artifact specialists in American classical archaeology. Educated at Harvard, Berlin, and Munich, Hoppin undertook the analysis and publication of the Greek pottery excavated at the Argive Heraeum. He went on to a pioneering career in vase painting studies, publishing such works as *Euthymides and His Followers* (1917), *A Handbook of Red-Figured Attic Vases* (1919), and *A Handbook of Greek Black Figured Vases* (1924).[93] Hoppin started the long and distinguished tradition of Greek ceramics studies in the United States.

The two volumes of the Argive Heraeum report, in spite of the delays (short compared with the Assos volumes) and the limitations characteristic of archaeological publications of the era, display an impressively holistic approach to excavation publication.[94] Geological studies were juxtaposed with those in architectural archaeology, while bronzes and

92. *Annual Report ASCS* 1891–2: 27–8. For Washington, cf. *WWW America* 1304 s.v. "Washinton, Henry Stephen."
93. *WWW* 587 s.v. "Hoppin, Jospeh Clark."
94. Waldstein 1902, 1905.

terra-cotta figurines received attention along with the Greek vases. Waldstein showed himself knowledgeable in such newly emerging fields as Aegean prehistory. The whole history of Waldstein's excavation and publication of the Argive Heraeum represented a vast improvement on Assos and showed the increased professionalism of American classical archaeology that had emerged in less than two decades.

Corinth

The Argive Heraeum proved to be a useful project for the American School, yet it did not provide a suitable setting for a long-term excavation that would present the best face of American archaeology in Greece to the scholarly world. It was not an ancient center on the scale and complexity of a Delos, Delphi, or Olympia. A proper foreign academy of a great nation still had to have a major archaeological concession. The most desired of the Hellenic sites had been taken by the Germans and the French or reserved for the Greeks. After a series of abortive project proposals, the American School in collaboration with the Archaeological Institute of America in 1895 selected the ancient Greek city of Corinth as their long-term excavation project.[95]

Ancient Corinth had a long and important history.[96] We now know that occupation of the site extended back to the Neolithic period. Corinth was one of the greatest cities of archaic, classical, and Hellenistic Greece. Destroyed by the Romans in 146 B.C., it was refounded by Julius Caesar in 44 B.C. and became an important urban center in Roman and Byzantine Greece. At a time when the Christian religion and Christian studies still played a central role in American cultural life, Corinth's association with St. Paul's mission and the development of early Christianity provided another major incentive for raising financial support for what the School hoped would be long-term excavations.

Corinth had other technical and logistical advantages for the American School archaeologists. The site was relatively clear of recent settlement; the small village of Old Corinth occupied a limited part of the ancient city. As the school's supporters of Corinth noted, it provided the first opportunity for the systematic excavation of a Greek urban site. It had a splendid location, with the great rock of Acrocorinth and its medieval walls overlooking the plain with its buried city and the blue Mediterranean. Compared to Assos or even the Argive Heraeum, Corinth was relatively accessible to the archaeological base of the American School at Athens.

95. Fowler and Stillwell 1932: vii.
96. *EHCA* s.v. "Corinth (Korinthos)"; Salmon 1984.

The school's decision to undertake a complicated, multi-season excavation at Corinth did not meet with universal approval. The elderly
Charles Eliot Norton still felt that such major field projects were more
suitably the work of the AIA, which had after all been founded as America's major research institution, and that a single large excavation would
distract the school from its other functions in the areas of teaching,
research, and publication.[97] The AIA did cosponsor Corinth until 1898
and contributed significantly to funding the first phase of excavations.
However, the school's extended commitment to Corinth as their lone
major excavation meant that American classical field archaeology in the
Mediterranean would be increasingly focused on one site and one type of
field archaeology.

The school started excavations at Corinth in the spring of 1896 and
pursued them for almost every season until 1916.[98] Although there have
been several breaks, they continue today. Corinth has remained the base
for archaeological training at the American School, the primary breeding ground of classical archaeologists in the United States for nearly a
century. A complex of excavation buildings in the manner of European
archaeological projects in the Near East has been constructed at the site,
and the excavations have acquired their distinctive patriarchal traditions
and rituals. More Americans have trained at Corinth than at any other
archaeological site in the Mediterranean, and the names of the greats of
the past are inscribed in the various field notebooks and records stored
neatly on the workroom shelves and cabinets. These documents not only
provide information for the researcher on decades of excavation but also
instill a strong sense of conservative intellectual tradition. This cult of the
ancestors has helped ensure quality, but also stiffles intellectual innovation. Time spent at the American excavations at Corinth is more likely to
encourage the development of an archaeological Confucius devoted to
the word of the ancestors rather than a classical Lewis Binford, willing
to challenge received tradition.

Archaeologically Corinth proved to be a complex site with occupation
extending from the Turkish period back to the Neolithic. Much of the
early excavation focused on the central part of the city, especially the
areas around the agora and the archaic temple of Apollo, one of the few
classical structures that had survived the Roman sack. This emphasis on
the archaeology of temples and government and public structures was
normal for Greek archaeology in the late nineteenth and early twentieth
centuries. The continued concentration on the public monuments over

---

97. AIA Archives Box 2: Norton to Marquand, 4 Feb. 1896.
98. Lord 1947: 89–105; reports on the excavations of those years appeared in the *American Journal of Archaeology.*

much of the history of the excavations has meant that a distorted picture of Corinth's ancient urban history has emerged. Only a limited part of the large known urban area has been investigated, and topics like housing at Corinth have received relatively little attention. After one hundred years, it is still easier to use Corint's vast excavation record to write architectural history than socio-economic history.[99]

Given the almost total destruction of 146 B.C. and the massive Caesarean and post-Caesarean rebuilding, the Corinth excavations turned out to be as much of an exercise in Roman as Greek archaeology. Almost reluctantly, the American archaeologists made important, pioneering contributions to our understanding of Roman architectural developments in Greece. As was normal for the early period of excavation, post-Roman remains were largely ignored. The Turks were still despised as the cruel conquerors recently removed from the Greek landscape and the Byzantines as a sad aftermath to Greek classical glory. Later pioneering research like that of Charles Morgan on Byzantine pottery helped correct some of this imbalance, but until very recently the long archaeological record of Byzantine, Frankish, and Turkish Corinth has received relatively little attention.[100]

Early excavations were not costly. H. N. Fowler calculated the total cost of the excavations from 1896 to 1916 as $35,000.[101] However, as at Assos, publication lagged. By the end of World War I, little except preliminary reports had appeared. It took the energetic intervention of a dynamic chair of the managing committee and the defenestration of the school's director to get the publication program moving in the interwar period.

Women and Archaeological Field Research at the ASCS

Throughout its history, the ASCA's influence in Greece has extended well beyond its own formal research undertakings. As the process of excavation formalized, the school fought hard to ensure that all research permits for Americans went through its hands. Initially this posed few problems, for almost all American archaeologists working in Greece were products of the school and shared its intellectual ideology. Gradually other individuals and organizations sought to work in Greece outside the direct school framework. This world of American archaeology tied to the school yet outside it created tensions, but also fostered creativity and provided a safety valve for those whose ambitions could not be met by the often conservative world of the institution on Souidas Street.

This outsider framework was most important for the small pioneering

99. Engels 1990.
100. Morgan 1942; Williams and Zervos 1996.
101. Fowler and Stillwell 1932: 3.

band of American women classical field archaeologists. During the early years women were admitted into the school's regular programs in impressive numbers but were excluded from its excavations. It was felt that women might be up to the archaeological tours around Greece, but not to the prolonged field projects. Moreover, the powers that controlled the school probably considered the archaeological excavations special exercises in the formalities of male bonding, and the presence of women would only provide unwelcome distractions. The first woman allowed on the Corinth excavations, Elizabeth Gardiner, a Radcliffe and Wellesley graduate and a specialist in Greek sculpture, was assigned there as an assistant only in 1908, more than a decade after the excavations started. Ironically, with a speed uncommon among Corinth excavators, she published some of the sculptures found at Corinth.[102]

Most of the women who attended the school accepted the restrictions, since they were directing their careers toward teaching in undergraduate college and secondary school programs that had limited research expectations. However, as one would have expected from a group of strong, independent-minded women, who had demonstrated the intellectual ability and force of personality to make it to the school, not all accepted the archaeological status quo. Although they were not initially ready to challenge the fundamentals of the system and demand places on the official excavations, some were ready to strike out on their own.

Among the first of these women was Harriet Boyd Hawes (1871–1945) (Figure 4).[103] A New Englander, Boyd Hawes graduated from Smith College in 1892. She became fluent in modern Greek through Red Cross work in the 1897 Greco-Turkish war. Although she had won an official fellowship at the School in 1898–99, Boyd Hawes soon discovered that as a woman she was denied access to regular archaeological field projects. This meant that she could not participate in the newly started excavations at Corinth.[104]

Little daunted, she struck out on her own, undertaking strenuous archaeological explorations in the still wild and relatively uninvestigated world of Crete. Not only was Crete in the 1890s one of the most backward parts of Greece, but its Bronze Age archaeology was still very poorly known. Frederico Halbherr had done important researches on the island, but his most important discoveries related to the archaic and classical periods.[105] When Harriet Boyd Hawes first rode around the island in 1899, Arthur Evans's excavations at Knossos were just about to begin.[106]

102. Fowler and Stillwell 1932: 10; Lord 1947: 107, 114, 377; Gardiner 1909.
103. Allesbrook 1992; Bolger 1994.
104. Irwin-Williams 1990: 7–8; Bolger 1994: 44.
105. La Rosa 1986.
106. A. Brown 1983.

Figure 4. Harriet Boyd Hawes sorting sherds at Herakleion, 1902. Courtesy of Smith College Archives.

Boyd Hawes systematically toured the island and identified a number of important prehistoric sites during her travels. She then wanted to turn from survey to excavation. The problem was funding, since the school and its patrons would not look overly sympathetically at an excavation conducted by a woman in faraway Crete. For support, Boyd turned to the American Exploration Society of Philadelphia, one of whose founders was another pioneering female archaeologist, Sara Yorke Stevenson (1847–1921).

Stevenson represented an even earlier generation of American women in archaeology, when higher educational opportunities were almost non-existent, and women had to make their way in the intellectual world through social networking and institution building.[107] Stevenson was born in Paris. In 1870 she married a prominent Philadelphia lawyer and settled in that city. Over the years she had developed a strong interest in Mediterranean archaeology. In 1889 she became associated with Dr. William Pepper in founding the Department of Archaeology at the University of Pennsylvania and joined him in creating the American Exploration Society. She went to Rome and Egypt on special archaeological missions, acquired Etruscan material for the University of Pennsylvania, served as president of the Pennsylvania branch of the AIA, and presented a number of papers and articles in scholarly meetings and journals.[108] Hers was an impressively energetic and productive academic career for someone who had not attended college. It was natural that Stevenson would look with favor on the ambitious field proposals of the young Harriet Boyd Hawes.

With the financial backing of the American Exploration Society, Harriet Boyd Hawes undertook her pioneering Cretan excavations, first with a short season at Kavousi and then for three campaigns at the Minoan village site of Gournia (1901–4).[109] She was the first woman of any nationality to have charge of an excavation and then publish the results.[110] In the excavation and publication Boyd Hawes was greatly assisted by Richard Seager (1882–1925), an American who had settled in Crete for health reasons and spent the rest of his life exploring the island's history and archaeology, excavating such important sites as Vasilike, Pseira, and Mochlos.[111] Other women were involved in the Gournia research too. The final report on the excavations that appeared in 1908 contained

107. *NCAB* 13.83.

108. Kucklick 1996.

109. *EHCA* s.v. "Gournia." For more recent American work at Kavousi and Gournia, cf. Soles 1979, 1991, 1992.

110. FDé. Sherman 1981: 32–33.

111. *EHCA* s.v. "Seager, Richard Berry (1882–1925)"; Kenna 1970; Becker and Betancourt 1997.

chapters on aspects of the work undertaken by three other female archaeologists: Blanche Wheeler Williams, Jean Patten, and Edith Hall.[112]

Of the three women, Hall (her married name was Edith Hall Dohan) had the most distinguished archaeological career.[113] Like Boyd Hawes, Hall graduated from Smith College, in 1899. She was selected as the final Hoppin fellow at the American School. In 1908, after her years of excavation at Gournia, she earned the first Ph.D. in classical archaeology from Bryn Mawr with a dissertation titled *The Decorative Art of Crete in the Bronze Age.* She taught briefly at Mount Holyoke College and excavated on her own in Crete. She then spent many years as a curator at the University of Pennsylvania Museum. She also served as book review editor of the *American Journal of Archaeology* and as a lecturer at Bryn Mawr College. In her later years Hall became one of the first American experts on Etruscan archaeology, publishing the Italian material that had been collected by A. R. Frothingham for the University of Pennsylvania collection.[114]

Boyd Hawes worked during the period when the excavations of Sir Arthur Evans at Knossos were restoring Minoan civilization to its rightful place in Mediterranean Bronze Age archaeology. Very little was known of preclassical Cretan archaeology, and Evans's research was largely focused on Knossos. In 1909 Harriet Boyd Hawes, together with her husband, C. H. Hawes, undertook an equally pioneering work, publishing a synthetic work on Minoan archaeology titled *Crete: The Forerunner of Greece*, aimed at a general educated audience in the Harper Library of Living Thought.[115] Arthur Evans wrote the preface. He observed of the Haweses that:

> They have the great advantage of writing "not as the scribes" but as actors working in the field that they describe. Mrs Hawes, as Miss Harriet Boyd, had indeed herself carried out, in a manner which has won the approval of all competent judges, the excavation of an extensive Minoan settlement at Gournia, the results of which have been presented to the world in a scientific form in an admirably illustrated volume. (Hawes and Hawes 1909: viii)

Although the number of sites explored in Crete was very small, the book did provide an overview of the island's archaeology, covering not only Knossos and Gournia but also the early Italian research at Phaistos and that of Seager at Vasilike and Mochlos. Individual chapters dealt with such topics as houses, art, industry and commerce. C. H. Hawes was very interested in physical anthropology, although at that period such studies took on a racial tone. Indeed, the book ended with a picture of classical

112. Hawes et al. 1908.
113. *EHCA* s.v. "Dohan, Edith Hayward Hall (1877–1943)"; Bolger 1994.
114. Dohan 1942; Hanfmann 1944.
115. Hawes and Hawes 1909.

Greece as the product of two racial strains, one from the Mediterranean and one coming out of the north:

In time the wounds of warfare were healed and in classical Greece we see the results of the mingling of two unusually gifted races-one autochthonous, the other immigrant-the former contributing the traditions and skills of a highly advanced nature especially rich in art, the latter its heritage of Aryan institutions, power of an all conquering language. (142)

Gournia was the last major archaeological project undertaken by Boyd Hawes. For much of the rest of her life, academic career played a secondary role to family concerns and charity work. She did not leave the field totally: she taught for many years at Wellesley College. However, it was at Gournia at the turn of the century where she did her pioneering work for Aegean prehistory and served as a role model for later generations of women who would do fieldwork in classical archaeology.

Outstanding among a slightly younger group of ambitious women academics and field archaeologists was Hetty Goldman (1881–1972).[116] Goldman was a 1903 graduate of Bryn Mawr, where she had studied with Joseph Hoppin. She did graduate work at Columbia (M.A. 1910) and Radcliffe College (Ph.D. 1916), where her mentor was George Chase. She went to the American School on a Harvard Norton fellowship. There she began the most extended and impressive field career of any American woman classical archaeologist. In 1911 she and Alice Walker were among the first women to excavate at Corinth.[117] Goldman's field work took a more independent turn in 1911, when she and Walker started excavations at Halae, a small seaport site on the east coast of Greece.[118] According to Goldman, one of the reasons for selecting the site was its distance from Athens, removing the women from the environs of the male dominated School.[119] Their four seasons of work concentrated on the cemetery and on the acropolis.

Goldman's education, ability, and energy contributed to a very successful field career during the interwar period. This was aided by key research-oriented appointments. In 1920 she was appointed Fellow of the Fogg Museum for Research in Greek Lands. In 1921 she started Fogg Museum-sponsored excavations at the Ionian Greek city of Colophon in Turkey (Figure 5).[120] Among her staff was the young American prehistorian Carl Blegen, who may well have stimulated her interest in the problems of early Greece. The Fogg connection also allowed Goldman to

116. *EHCA* s.v. "Goldman, Hetty (1881–1972)"; Vermeule 1987: 168–69; Wren 1995.
117. Fowler and Stillwell 1932: 12.
118. Walker and Goldman 1915; Sherman 1981: 33.
119. Thompson 1974a: viii; Sherman 1981: 35.
120. *Art and Archaeology* 1933: 256–60.

Figure 5. Staff photo at the short-lived excavations at the Greek city site of Colophon in Turkey, 1922. Hetty Goldman is on the right, lower row. Courtesy of the American School of Classical Studies in Athens.

cultivate contacts at Harvard's Peabody Museum and to bring a greater anthropological perspective to her work.[121] The early promise of the Colophon project ended with the outbreak of the Greek-Turkish war in 1922, which not only terminated the excavations but resulted in the destruction of most of the finds.

Goldman was undeterred. She looked for new excavation sites that would answer research questions that grew out of her increasing interest in Greek and Balkan prehistory. From 1924 to 1927 she excavated at Eutresis and in 1932, at the prehistoric site of Starcevo in Yugoslavia.[122]

121. Hanfmann 1974: 15–18.
122. Ehrich 1974.

The Eutresis excavations provided field experience for a new generation of women archaeologists, including Hazel Hanson (1899–1962), long time professor of classical archaeology at Stanford, Dorothy Burr (later Dorothy Burr Thompson), Barbara McCarthy, and the archaeological architect Dorothy Cox.[123] The final report on Eutresis, which appeared in 1931, an impressively short time after the completion of the excavations, presented the results and finds in commendable detail.[124]

Hetty Goldman's last major field project was the excavation in 1934–39 and 1947–48 of Tarsus in southeast Turkey. Tarsus's occupation extended from the prehistoric through the Roman periods. The city is best known as the birthplace of St. Paul. It was located geographically and culturally at the juncture of the classical and Near Eastern worlds. Goldman now found herself dealing not only with early Neolithic settlements but also with Hittite-Mycenaean interactions. Among the Hittite finds was a seal of the Hittite Queen Puduhepe. The artifact associated with this strong-willed Hittite sovereign struck a responsive cord not only with Goldman but also with the archaeologists at Bryn Mawr College, who had been major supporters of the Tarsus project. Mary Hamilton Swindler wrote in the March 1938 issue of the *Bryn Mawr Alumnae Bulletin*: "The seal of no more interesting historical figure could have been unearthed for feminist Bryn Mawr than Puduhepe."[125] Again the excavations provided significant roles for women archaeologist like Dorothy Cox, Virginia Grace, and Frances Follitt Jones. The results of the Tarsus excavations were published in three austere, detailed volumes which appeared between 1950 and 1963.[126]

The Tarsus expedition was funded jointly by the Fogg Museum, Byrn Mawr, and the AIA. It was the AIA's last venture into direct field support, and a stormy finale to a rather checkered history. The United States was in the middle of the Great Depression, and AIA President Louis Lord of Oberlin succeeded only with difficulty in balancing the institute's budget after a period of serious deficit.[127] Support for Tarsus was an additional, unwelcome burden. By 1936 Lord felt that without special outside funding the institute could no longer provide such support. A long and complicated battle ensued during which Hetty Goldman temporarily resigned as field director, and increasingly polemical charges and countercharges were traded between Lord and the Goldman camp. In the end the Tarsus group resorted to stealth to ensure continued AIA support. Goldman's

123. For Hanson, cf. Mylonas 1963. Dorothy Burr Thompson became a distinguished expert in the field of Greek terracottas. McCarthy taught Classics for many years at Wellesley.
    124. Goldman 1931.
    125. Mellink 1974.
    126. Goldman et al. 1950–63.
    127. AIA Archives Box 31.

supporters waited until Louis Lord was out of the country and then called a meeting at Boston to make the final decision on funding. Present were a representative of Bryn Mawr, Paul Sachs of the Fogg Museum, who was also Hetty Goldman's uncle, and the amiable, pliant George Chase of Harvard, who had also been Goldman's teacher. Not surprisingly, Goldman received her AIA allotment.[128]

In 1936 Hetty Goldman was appointed research professor at the Institute for Advanced Study in Princeton. She was the first woman scholar in any discipline to enter the august research institution. The professorship provided her with more time for research, even if it limited her long-term impact as a teacher. Still, through her excavations, Goldman was a very visible role model for women entering the profession. Her range as an archaeologist was impressive, as was her ability to think independently. This quality came across well in a speech that she gave at Bryn Mawr in 1955:

No, the field archaeologist must have the courage to collect and to interpret wisely and boldly, better a theory if the data at all allows, which may eventually be proven inadequate or false, for it will stimulate the imagination and awake speculation in others who may well reach more acceptable results. (Goldman 1955)

In a classical archaeology world where both men and women were increasingly characterized by intellectual narrowness and timidity, Hetty Goldman was a breath of fresh air.

Goldman's colleague at Corinth in 1911 and codirector at Halae was Alice Leslie Walker (Kosmopoulos). Walker took a B.A. and an M.A. from Vassar and was a student at the American School from 1909 to 1914. She earned a Ph.D. from the University of California in 1917 and after World War I returned to Greece to work on the prehistoric pottery of the Corinthia.[129] Walker married a Greek and settled in the Peloponessus.[130]

Classical Archaeology and the Universities

By the 1880s Charles Eliot Norton had popularized art history and archaeology as undergraduate subjects at Harvard. Other undergraduate institutions, inspired by Norton's Norton's success, began to make these disciplines part of their academic programs. However, in classical archaeology, as in most other humanistic fields, promising young scholars still had to go to Germany for formal advanced education. A period of study at the American School at Athens did provide direct, intensive contact with the monuments and increasingly archaeological field experience. It

128. The documents related to this controversy are in the AIA archives.
129. Lord 1947: 138–39.
130. Wren 1995.

could not substitute for the graduate seminars and the specialized library resources and museums of the German universities, however.

Despite the large number of Americans who studied in Germany, there was still a complicated, ambivalent attitude toward graduate education in the university and its relevance to the undergraduate teaching enterprise, especially in the humanities. A B.A. and broad-based humanistic culture had been sufficient for Norton to teach art history at Harvard. Many would have argued that Norton's successes in the classroom were evidence against the need for German-style professional education. In fact, some feared that introducing German inspired scientific art criticism would destroy the spiritual, aesthetic essence of Norton's teaching. Norton himself was highly suspicious of German scholarship.[131] Edmund von Mach, a Norton student, dedicated his *A Handbook of Greek and Roman Sculpture* (1905) to the master with the following words:

The author finally wishes to record his deep sense of gratitude to the man, whose name by permission appears on the dedication pages and who for many years has boldly fought the battle of the spirit against matter. Recently, some have dared to affirm that even art should be studied "scientifically" with the spirit left out. The name of Charles Eliot Norton preserves the reader from this folly (1905: x–xi)

Americans who looked to England for their values could also point out that the dons at Oxford and Cambridge still felt that a rigorous B.A. program was sufficient to prepare effective teachers of undergraduates. However, more and more universities and even colleges felt that their instructors should have an M.A. and even a Ph.D., and that research and publication, as well as teaching, should be part of the ideal academic lifestyle. Increasingly, universities instituted some graduate education, although in areas like classics the ideals of undergraduate education dominated, especially at such bastions of tradition as the Ivy League universities. In that they remained closer to Oxbridge than to Berlin or Munich.

The Johns Hopkins University was founded in Baltimore in 1876 to meet the increasingly felt need for a German-style graduate university in the United States.[132] Its first president, Daniel C. Gilman, wanted Johns Hopkins to become an institution very different from the run of American universities.[133] It was to be a graduate center, where Americans could be trained in academic specializations in the German manner. The focus of its educational enterprise was to be the advanced seminar. Such an ambitious institution, modeled after the research universities of Germany,

131. Vanderbilt 1959: 181–82.
132. French 1946; Cordasco 1960: 54–81.
133. Gilman 1906.

had to have a strong graduate classics program. In fact, the classics department initiated graduate work at Johns Hopkins.[134]

Among the first appointments at the new university was that of the classical philologist Basil Gildersleeve.[135] Like Charles Eliot Norton, Gildersleeve believed that American scholars should be prepared to make their own distinctive research contributions to the field of classics. Unlike Norton, he was the product of formal German graduate education.[136] Although Gildersleeve's own research interests were focused on a rather technical brand of classical philology, as a scholar trained in the German *Altertumswissenschaft* tradition, he stressed the importance of studying the monuments and inscriptions as well as the Greek and Latin texts to his students.

An archaeological seminar was soon established at Johns Hopkins. The philosophy that guided this seminar was articulated in a 1910 circular prepared to advertise the department's program. The brochure noted that the archaeological seminar was "designed to furnish to students who are already well grounded in classical literature and philology the same kind of assistance and training as the students of the natural sciences receive in the laboratories." Each student was to be assigned a definite research project oriented toward materials in local museums. The corollary institutions necessary to sustain such a program were soon created: in 1888 the Baltimore chapter of the AIA was organized, a small museum collection was assembled, and in 1885 the *AJA* began to be published in Baltimore.[137]

Fellowships were central to the new universiity's graduate program of the new university were the fellowships program, for they provided young scholars the opportunity to advance their research free from the pressures of teaching. The Johns Hopkins fellowships soon attracted bright, budding archaeology students. Two of the second generation of founding figures in American classical archaeology, Arthur Frothingham Jr. and Alfred Emerson, were fellows in archaeology and Greek in the early 1880s. So was Allan Marquand, who with Frothingham established the Princeton art and archaeology department as well as the *American Journal of Archaeology*. Later, T. L. Shear, another former Hopkins fellow and Ph.D., joined the Princeton department. Certainly the appreciation for research rigor acquired at Johns Hopkins helped guide the powerful Princeton department during the first third of the twentieth century.

It is interesting to observe that this dynamic group of young archaeolo-

134. Briggs and Benario 1986.
135. Briggs 1987: 52–88.
136. Briggs and Benario 1986.
137. Williams 1984: 3–5.

gists developed in a program that did not have an especially strong archaeology faculty. Mitchell Carroll, educated at Hopkins, in Germany, and at Athens, briefly held the position of reader in classical archaeology. But in 1898 he left for George Washington University and the secretaryship of the AIA.[138] Harry Langford Wilson (1867–1913), who received his Ph.D. from Hopkins in 1896, served as professor of Roman archaeology and epigraphy from 1906 to 1913. At the time of his death he had been engaged to write a book on Roman archaeology. However, most of his training and publications were in Latin literature and Latin epigraphy.[139]

Not until 1905, when the young David Robinson joined the newly constituted department of art and archaeology, did a new archaeological era began at Johns Hopkins. By 1910 the department had developed what would today be considered a real archaeology curriculum. Undergraduate offerings included "Outline of Classical Archaeology" and courses on the private lives of the Greeks and the Romans. The graduate program had courses such as "Topography of Rome," "Introduction to Latin Epigraphy," "Greek and Roman Theatre," "Greek Inscriptions," and "Greek Vase Paintings." Robinson made Johns Hopkins into one of the major centers of American classical archaeology in the pre-World War II period.

Bryn Mawr and Women's Education

The presence of women during the early years of the American School in Athens shows the appeal that classical archaeology had for students regardless of their gender. It also demonstrated the quality and rigor of their education. Some of the women were graduates of the public and private institutions of the Midwest, where classical studies already had an honorable tradition, and coeducation was more readily accepted than in the male academic bastions of the East. Others came out of the women's colleges founded in the Northeast during the later nineteenth century.

At colleges like Mount Holyoke, Smith, Vassar, and Wellesley, classics was an important part of the curriculum. As art history gained respectability as an academic subject, it too found a special place there, for it was seen as a particularly appropriate subject for a woman's education.[140] Not only did art history have a quality of gentility that made it suitable for women, but it provided a useful cultural background for students who would become the elite married women of American society and play an increasingly important role in collecting and taste-making in the late nineteenth and early twentieth centuries.

138. Kelsey 1926c; Hiss and Fansler 1934: 101.

139. *NCAB* 31:482; Briggs 1987: 239 n. 12.

140. Hiss and Fansler 1934: 115–17 (Mt. Holyoke), 150–52 (Smith), 158–60 (Vassar), 163–66 (Wellesley).

Women's colleges also offered female academic professionals employment opportunities not found in other countries. Almost none of the women's colleges had positions just devoted to classical archaeology during this era, but archaeology figured in many aspects of their curriculum. By 1911 Louise F. Randolph of Mount Holyoke could describe herself as teaching archaeology and art history, and her colleague Edith Hall as teaching archaeology.[141] Since a number of these pioneering faculty members had studied at the American School of Classical Studies, they could bring their personal experiences of the Greek sites and the latest archaeological discoveries directly into the classroom.

One major problem women academics faced was obtaining the rigorous graduate education that would allow them to compete in the changing world of American academia. It was not easy for them to undertake formal studies in Germany, although figures like M. Carey Thomas, the founder of Bryn Mawr, had demonstrated that persistent, strong-minded women could succeed at the German universities.[142] American universities, especially along the East Coast, were ambivalent or hostile to women students seeking to do advanced degrees, as Thomas herself found out when she attempted to enroll for graduate study at the new, supposedly progressive Johns Hopkins University.[143]

A potential resolution of the problem of women's graduate education came with the founding of Bryn Mawr College in 1885. This movement was led by a group of Quakers who had close ties with the ruling elite at Johns Hopkins.[144] Bryn Mawr soon developed into an institution that provided both undergraduate and graduate education for women in a rigorous and supportive environment. Much of its success as a major force in American graduate education was owed to M. Carey Thomas.

Thomas, who served first as dean and then as president from 1894 to 1922, had studied philology in German and Switzerland and supported the classics at Bryn Mawr. She had a strong touch of Helleno-romanticism as is seen in an early statement she made on Greece's virtues:

It makes us proud to belong to the human race to be able to feel that just once in the history of the world a highly gifted people, living in a wholly lovely country washed on all sides by the most beautiful seas we know, speaking the most perfect of languages wonderfully expressive of the loftiest thought, attained to absolute perfection in poetry, prose, temples and statues. (quoted in Horowitz 1994: 428)

Thomas also had a strong interest in classical archaeology and encouraged its academic development at her college. By 1887 A. L. Frothingham

141. Sterrett 1911: 173.
142. Horowitz 1994: 109–65.
143. Horowitz 1994: 71–75.
144. Horowitz 1994: 182–224.

Jr. of Johns Hopkins was teaching the monuments of Rome at Bryn Mawr, and Herbert Weir Smyth, later a distinguished philologist at Harvard, was teaching Greek art and archaeology.[145] In 1895–96, Richard Norton organized one of the first independent departments of art and archaeology in the United States at Bryn Mawr.[146] In 1908 Edith Hall (1877–1943) received the first Ph.D. in archaeology awarded by Bryn Mawr.[147] Mary Hamilton Swindler (1884–1967), who had her earlier education at Indiana University and studied at Berlin, received a Bryn Mawr Ph.D. in 1912. In 1913 President Thomas entrusted a newly hired faculty member, Rhys Carpenter, with the further development of classical archaeology.

The Universities of Michigan and Missouri

The early development of classical archaeology in the United States was geographically diverse. Many important figures came out of the Midwest, and midwestern undergraduate and graduate institutions, especially the Universities of Michigan and Missouri, played a major role in shaping the new discipline.

Interest in classical archaeology at the University of Michigan had begun before the Civil War. In 1854 Henry S. Frieze (1817–1889), who had a B.A. from Brown, was appointed professor of Latin. He immediately used a leave of absence in 1855 to purchase "illustrations of Greek art for the university's museum." In 1857 the museum was founded, and in 1858 Frieze published a *Descriptive Catalogue of the Museum of Art and Antiquities in the University of Michigan*. His research in classical archaeology continued and in 1888 he published *Classical Antiquities and Art in the Latin Text of Pliny the Elder*.[148] Lectures on Greek art were offered for seniors by 1872 and by 1879 Professors Martin D'Ooge and Frieze were lecturing regularly on classical archaeology. The first seminar in Roman archaeology was offered in 1891 by Kelsey and the first in Greek archaeology in 1892 by D'Ooge.[149]

In 1892 John Pickard (1858–1937) came to teach at the University of Missouri at Columbia. He had grown up in New Hampshire and had both his M.A. and Ph.D. from Dartmouth College. Like so many of his generation he went to study in Germany, obtained a Ph.D. from Munich in 1892, and then spent time at the American School in Athens. There he partici-

145. E. Vermeule 1987: 167.

146. Hiss and Fansler 1934: 69; E. Vermeule 1987: 168.

147. *EHCA* s.v. "Dohan, Edith Hayward Hall (1877–1943)"; Sherman 1981: 33.

148. *NCAB* 1: 250; Kelsey 1910–11; Hiss and Fansler 1934: 8. Frieze's enthusiasm for things classical extended to his tomb, which was modeled on the monument of Scipio in Rome.

149. Hiss and Fansler 1934: 105–6.

pated in Charles Waldstein's Eretria excavations. At Missouri Pickard was designated professor of classical archaeology and assistant professor of Greek. He proceeded to develop a range of courses in classical art and archaeology.[150] Although Pickard had had practical experience in Greece, his view of ancient art's cultural role was very close to that of Charles Eliot Norton. Appropriately enough he was known as "Missouri's Apostle of the Beautiful."[151]

Pickard felt that an ambitious archaeology program needed a museum and all other aids available for teaching the subject. The university supported his endeavors, and by 1896 he could identify significant acomplishments:

During the past year an excellent beginning has been made in equipping a laboratory for the study of Classical Archaeology. For this purpose the third floor of the west wing of Academic Hall, a room 110 x 36 ft., is fitted up. It is now supplied with models of temples, illustrating the three orders of Greek architecture, and with fifty plaster casts of the most famous specimens of Greek and Roman Art. These are arranged chronologically, and with them are hung one hundred and fifty framed photographs of other works of classic art. Besides these, the museum possesses some six hundred photographs, and a fine collection of lantern slides. (Weller 1992: 11)

Indicative of classical archaeology's complex self perception in the late nineteenth century is the fact that even an apostle of beauty must describe his museum as a scientific laboratory.

Pickard was also active in the early development of the College Art Association. Often regarded today as an elitist East Coast entity, the organization grew out of a group of midwestern primary and secondary school teachers, the Western Drawing and Manual Training Association. The College Art Association was officially established in 1912, and Pickard served as president from 1915 to 1919.[152] His successor was the Johns Hopkins archaeologist David Moore Robinson, and a number of the art historically oriented classical archaeologists were involved at an early date.

Pickard's colleague at Missouri for many years was a redoubtable alumnus of the American School Walter Miller. Miller had been educated at the University of Michigan and at Leipzig, where he studied with Johannes Overbeck.[153] Miller's long career at Missouri was broken by periods of teaching at Stanford and Tulane, but he returned to Missouri in 1911 and stayed there until his death. Not only was Miller renowned as a teacher,

---

150. Weller 1992.
151. Weller 1992: 10.
152. H. Smith 1913; Pickard 1919; Weller 1992: 14–18.
153. Luce 1950; Weller 1992: 27–34. For Overbeck, cf. *EHCA* s.v. "Overbeck, Johannes (1826–95)."

but he was also extremely active in the University Travel Bureau, an organization that pioneered guided tours for academics and educated laypeople.[154]

Profile of an Emerging Profession in the Later Nineteenth Century

During the last years of the nineteenth century, complex, even contradictory trends were operating in the American colleges and universities where classical archaeology was taught. Despite the creation of new American graduate opportunities for both men and women, many ambitious scholars still looked to Germany for their advanced education. After all, German universities still led the world in the number of archaeology chairs, the size of their archaeological collections, and the diversity of their library resources.[155] Furthermore, despite the creation of Johns Hopkins and the growing strength of several midwestern public universities, the Ivy League elite still dominated the profession with generally rather mediocre classical archaeology programs. Of thirty-eight individuals holding non-sex-specific fellowships at the American School before World War I, twenty-one were from Ivy League schools and only six were from public universities.

The unifying professional experience for this emerging professorial generation of the 1880s and the 1890s was time spent at the American School of Classical Studies in Athens. Ivy Leaguers and German Ph.D.s, public and private graduates, men and women, most of those who rose to any distinction at the college and university level had studied at the school in Athens. They had taken the same field trips and often participated in the same excavations. A lifelong bond that unified American classical archaeology in a way that no other institution was able to accomplish was established.

In a 1952 obituary of the Yale classical archaeologist Paul Baur, David Robinson of Johns Hopkins identified Baur, Frank Tarbell, Harold Fowler, and George Chase as part of an older generation of scholars to whom "is due much credit for the emphasis in Classical Archaeology as a separate field of study and its great growth in America."[156] A look at the careers of these four pioneering figures reveals the potential and limitations of classical archaeology at the end of this period.

Paul V. Baur (1872–1951) took his B.A. at the University of Cincinnati and his Ph.D. at Heidelberg. He attended the American School of Classi-

154. Luce 1950.
155. Clarke 1902: 99–100, 102.
156. Robinson 1951–52: 26.

cal Studies. After holding short-term positions at the Universities of Cincinnati and Missouri, he was appointed to Yale, where he taught classical archaeology from 1902 to 1940. By all accounts Baur was a devoted if not terribly inspiring teacher and a pedestrian scholar. His publications are mainly of a cataloging nature. His impact on the development of the Yale graduate program in classical archaeology appears to have been limited.[157] Yale did not become a graduate force in ancient history and classical archaeology until the arrival of Michael Rostovtzeff after World War I.

George Chase's academic career (1875–1952) was centered at Harvard, where he was educated and taught for almost his entire career.[158] He had attended the American School and had excavated with Waldstein at the Argive Heraeum. Besides Harvard, Chase devoted considerable time to two other Boston archaeological instititions: the Boston chapter of the AIA, of which he was president for twenty-seven years, and the Boston Museum of Fine Arts, where he, along with Lacey Caskey, was responsible for developing one of the two major classical collections in the United States.

Chase's publications focused on sculpture and ceramic studies and displayed solid scholarship, if limited synthetic imagination.[159] Yet he was one of the few American scholars open to new developments in the scholarship of Roman art, writing an appreciative essay on the highly innovative scholarship of the Austrian art historian Franz Wickhoff (1853–1909).[160] A sympathetic picture of Chase appears in a brief personal aside in Walter Muir Whitehill's history of the Boston Museum of Fine Arts:

He was a minute little man full of learning and human kindness; as a graduate student I took a reading course with him on Greek vases, simply for the pleasure of seeing him once a week. (1970: 374)

Frank Bigelow Tarbell (1853–1920) was educated at Yale. He taught first at Yale and then at the University of Chicago, where he continued on the faculty from 1893 to 1920. He was closely associated with the American School, serving as first annual professor (1888–89) and secretary (1892–93).[161] His *History of Greek Art* (1896) was one of the early efforts to provide an archaeology text for the growing college and university audience. Although the book employed new technology like photographic illustration, the message was Norton's:

157. Luce 1952b; His major publications were Baur 1912, 1922, 1947.
158. Luce 1952b.
159. G. H. Chase 1916, 1924, 1950.
160. G. H. Chase 1912. For Wickhoff, cf. *EHCA* s.v. "Wickhoff, Franz (1853–1909)."
161. Hiss and Fansler 1934: 71–72; Lord 1947: 50–55, 78–79.

This book has been written in the conviction that the greatest of all nature for studying art, the nature which is and ought to be strongest in most people, is the desire to become acquainted with beautiful and noble things, the things that "soothe the cares and lift the thoughts of men." (Tarbell 1896: iii)

Tarbell was also interested in getting the classical art message out in the variety of new media. He was one of the first to use printed photographs, writing the commentaries for a catalog of carbon prints of classical monuments prepared by A. W. Elson in Boston in 1897. In 1909 he published a catalog of copies of bronzes in the Chicago Field Museum, which were exact reproductions of originals from Pompeii and Herculaneum in the Naples Museum.[162]

Harold North Fowler (1859–1955) spent most of his teaching career at Western Reserve College in Cleveland. He was originally an easterner, born in Westfield, Massachusetts. Before attending Harvard, he was sent to study in Dresden at the age of fifteen. At Harvard his mentors were Charles Eliot Norton and William Watson Goodwin. One of Fowler's tasks as Norton's student had been to address the brochures for the organizational meeting of the AIA.[163] Goodwin encouraged Fowler to become the first student to enroll at the newly founded American School of Classical Studies at Athens in 1882. Fowler also studied at Berlin and in 1885 earned a Ph.D. from Bonn. There "he thus acquired the German habit of thoroughness without German pedantry."[164]

Fowler had a more energetic professional career than either Baur or Chase. His teaching career centered on the undergraduate world of the midwestern college. In 1893 he joined the faculty of Western Reserve. He found there a tradition of teaching Greek archaeology that went back to 1886. Fowler taught there until his retirement in 1923.[165] He pioneered in demonstrating that a pedagogical career focused on undergraduate teaching could be combined with vigorous research and a professional career. From 1906 to 1916 he edited the *American Journal of Archaeology*.[166] His 1909 book *A Handbook of Greek Archaeology*, written with James Rignall Wheeler of Columbia, was one of the first general American textbooks to deal with Greek archaeology as a subject distinct from Greek art.

Fowler outlived all his contemporaries. In 1954 he spoke at the seventy-fifth anniversary of the AIA, representing a last link with the founders of the profession. An obituary writer summed up Fowler's career:

162. Tarbell 1909.
163. Dort 1954: 195–96.
164. Gulick 1956: 16.
165. Hiss and Fansler 1934: 166; Gulick 1956.
166. Donahue 1985: 13–15.

His life span of nearly a century was coincident with amazing changes taking place within the United States. He saw the retreating frontier of the West finally vanish as the railroad, the automobile and the airplane overcame barriers of space and time, while learning and culture followed in the wake with increasing impetus from their long established seats on the eastern seaboard. (Sanborn 1956)

Although not included in David Robinson's list of founding fathers, James Wheeler (1859–1918) should also be honored in this group of pioneers. He received his B.A. from the University of Vermont, but afterward followed the emerging elite *cursus honorum* in classical archaeology with graduate work at Harvard, study in Europe, a fellowship among the first group of students at the American School of Classical Studies in Athens, and a readership at Johns Hopkins. His teaching career was from 1895 centered on Columbia, where in 1906 he became professor of Greek art and archaeology. He served as chairman of the American School managing committee from 1901 to 1918.[167] His publication record was relatively slim, but his influence as a teacher and administrator was extensive.[168]

Creating a Curriculum

Tarbell's *History of Greek Art* and Fowler and Wheeler's *Handbook of Greek Archaeology* serve as reminders that the new classical archaeology classroom of the late nineteenth century required more than just Charles Eliot Norton ruminating on the beauty of Greek art and fulminating against contemporary Harvard architecture. An academic subject that claimed to be part of the sciences as well as the humanities needed more than just inspired teachers. Courses had to be designed, textbooks produced, and in the case of classical archaeology visual materials had to be developed.

In 1909 Professors Fowler and Wheeler in collaboration with Gorham Phillips Stevens produced *A Handbook of Greek Archaeology*. It was part of the Greek Series for Colleges and Schools edited by Professor Herbert Smyth of Harvard[169] and the first classical archaeology textbook aimed at an American college audience. The definition of archaeology that opens the first chapter is interesting:

Greek archaeology may be defined as the scientific study of the arts of construction and design as they were developed by the Greeks; but since much important information concerning art is derived from inscriptions, and the identification of works of art, especially of architecture, is often affected by topographical considerations, epigraphy and topography are frequently included in the definition of archaeology. (11)

167. Lord 1947: 99–129; Briggs 1987: 181 n. 8.
168. Fowler 1918.
169. Fowler and Wheeler 1909.

Architectural study's centrality to teaching classical archaeology was
made clear throughout the text. Topography and epigraphy were not
even covered. After a historical introduction concerned with the development of Greek archaeology as a field of study and a now quaintly
outdated chapter on Greek prehistory, the volume was divided into topi-
cal chapters on subjects such as architecture, sculpture, and coins.

Although Fowler and Wheeler's work was the first American textbook
on Greek archaeology, it was not the first general American text on ancient art. That honor belongs to a work titled *A History of Ancient Sculpture*,
which appeared in 1883 and was written by Lucy Mitchell. It was an
impressive two-volume study that examined ancient sculpture from its
Egyptian origins to the end of antiquity, with a companion volume of
plates, *Selections from Ancient Sculpture*. The project was not just the work of
a Boston lady using the Athenaeum's resources. Lucy Wright Mitchell
(1845–1888) had been raised in a missionary family in Persia and had
studied at Mount Holyoke Seminary. Her brother was the classicist John
Henry Wright of Harvard, one of the early editors of *AJA*. After her
marriage to an artist, Mitchell spent much of her time in Europe and
the Mediterranean, using both the museum and library resources to be
found there. While in Rome during 1876–78, she "gave popular lectures
to ladies on Greek and Roman sculpture, accompanied by visits to the
Roman collections."[170] In her preface, she thanks distinguished European archaeologists such as Friedrich Von Duhn, Adolf Furtwängler, and
Charles Newton for their assistance. In 1884 Mitchell was elected an
active member of the Imperial Archaeological Institute of Germany.
Clearly this was a woman who struck out on her own ay an early stage,
creating an impressive work of scholarship. Sadly she died at a relatively
young age.

American books were increasingly supplemented by translations of
important European works on classical archaeology. A translation of
Winckelmann's *History of Ancient Art* had been published in Boston in
1849. Schliemann's accounts of his discoveries at Mycenae, Troy, and
Tiryns soon appeared in American editions. The more technical *Manuel
d'archéologie grecque* by Leon-Maxime Collignon was translated by John
Henry Wright and published in 1886. Translations of Perrot and Chi-
piez's *Histoire de l'art dans l'antiquité* (1882–90) began to appear soon after
its publication.[171]

Fowler and Wheeler noted that one of archaeology's most important recent innovations of archaeology had been the introduction of
photography:

170. *NCAB* 6: 147–48 s.v. "Mitchell, Lucy."
171. Hiss and Fansler 1934: 51.

Perhaps no single agency has done more to facilitate archaeological work in the field, the publication of new discoveries, the intensive study of monuments already known and the giving of systematic instruction than the development of photography and the allied methods of accurate and inexpensive reproduction. By the aid of photography the archaeologist of today commands a more accurate acquaintance with the entire field than was attainable without its aid when the entire field was vastly less extensive than it now is. (1909: 26)

It is hard to imagine what teaching art history must have been like in the early days, when one had no slides, illustrated books, or files of photographs. Edward Forbes of Harvard described taking art history with Norton:

I took his classical course in 1892–1893 and was deeply interested. The only visual impression that I remember having received (since Professor Norton used practically no illustrations) was from a visit to the Museum of Fine Arts in Boston, where I went one day obeying his instructions. All that sticks in my mind is a long dismal row of plaster casts of Greek and Roman heads. (Forbes as cited in Vermeule 1990: 11)

Casts filled the gap up to a certain point. When Alfred Emerson was appointed to teach archaeology at Cornell, one of his first responsibilities was developing the cast collection, a resource in which Cornell took great pride.[172] Pickard did the same at Missouri. But casts were cumbersome to display and use and most colleges had neither the money nor the space for a comprehensive collection.

We have already seen how photography pioneers like W. J. Stillman created collections of photographs of classical monuments. By the 1880s firms in Greece and Italy made a range of images of the most important monuments available to tourists and scholars.[173] These were expanded to include major museum collections. For the first time, detailed comparisons of large numbers of buildings, pieces of sculpture, and vases became possible. Increasingly large collections of photographs became part of the resources of art history and classical archaeology seminars. Scholars like Oxford's Greek vase painting expert, John Beazley, would not have emerged without the vast files of images of ancient art that photography made possible.

Photographs were fine for small classroom teaching, but they were not suited for large lecture situations. There the introduction of the lantern slide transformed the teaching of art history. Vivid and at times opinionated descriptions by dynamic professors in sunlit classrooms were succeeded by photographic images projected on a screens in darkened classrooms. The history of the lantern slide in American art history and its

172. Hiss and Fansler 1934: 82–83; Briggs 1987: 180 n. 2.
173. Miraglia 1996; Weber and Malandrini 1996.

impact of teaching and learning is just beginning to be written. Lantern slides were already appearing by the 1850s, but they did not become popular until the 1870s. Allan Marquand used slides in his Princeton lectures as early as 1882, and James Hoppin introduced them into his Yale classes about the same time.[174] The cumbersome, glass-mounted, black-and-white lantern slides of that era seem dreadfully old-fashioned in these days of laser disks, but they must have seemed absolute wonders to undergraduates of the late nineteenth century.

Another improvement in the visual arts was the illustrated art book. It was one thing to create a portfolio of art photographs or to run through a series of slides accompanied by ephemeral verbal texts; it was another to craft a closely reasoned text or a carefully researched catalog and then illustrate it with accurate reproductions of the works discussed. By the late 1880s rotary photogravure and halftones were coming into use. College and university libraries began to fill with these new works of visual scholarship.[175]

Cast collecting has already been mentioned, and a full discussion of the role of casts in American museums is provided in the next chapter. Casts were an important part of the last instrument of college art historical and archaeological pedagogy, the college and university museum. By the end of the nineteenth century, most colleges and universities had some type of museum. Many were bizarre combinations of geological specimens, stuffed Pacific Island war clubs, mummies, and Assyrian reliefs sent back by missionaries. However, others had higher cultural aspirations. Casts were complemented by coin collections, originals or copies, sherds and vases, figurines, squeezes of inscriptions, and occasional pieces of sculpture. Many of these teaching collections were stored in the classics department. Others began to become real museums in both facilities and collection size. In 1886 the *American Journal of Archaeology* published a notice that a donor had provided $100,000 for a new art museum at Wellesley College.[176] By any standards, and especially by those of women's education for that era, it was a princely sum to invest in culture. Other college art museums also grew by private benefactions. The Fogg Museum at Harvard, which opened in 1895, owed much of its early classical collection to Edward Forbes, a Norton student, and to various members of the Norton family.[177] The museum at Bowdoin College benefited from donations by the leading American agent for the acquisition of ancient art for American collections, E. P. Warren.[178] In other instances,

---

174. H. Leighton 1984.
175. Fawcett 1986.
176. *AJA* 1886, Hiss and Fansler 1934: 165–66.
177. Vermeule and Brauer 1990: 11–14.
178. Herbert 1964: 1–10.

museums were built largely around cast collections. This was true at the University of Illinois, where an English critic defined the collection and its usefulness in the following manner:

The fact that this university is not within easy reach of a large museum has conditioned the character of the collections. I noticed a very fine series of Minoan replicas from Athens, other important reproductions including complete casts of the old and new Ludovisi, sculptures which are nowhere else (I think) juxtaposed. (Browne 1917: 268–69)

In later years, these campus collections and museums had different fates as art historical and archaeological teaching moved toward a more self-contained classroom experience, and the concept of what was appropriate for display in a museum altered with the rise of the cult of the genuine object and the growing disdain for casts and reproductions.[179] Some college and university museums, like those at Smith, Oberlin, Wellesley, the University of Pennsylvania, Michigan, Harvard, and Yale, developed into strong art historical and archaeological institutions. Others withered and saw their collections sold or moved into storage. Still, in 1932 among the 1400 museums in the United States, 600 were related to universities, colleges, and schools.[180]

One of the most unusual and important college art museums is that of the Rhode Island School of Design. RISD itself was founded by a group of local women who were displeased by the quality of American design exhibited at the Philadelphia Centennial Exposition of 1876. Looking to the example of the South Kensington Museum in London and its practical, educational message, they decided to found a school that would provide instruction in the various arts and also promote the "general advancement of public art education by the exhibition of works of art."[181] The very fine RISD collection developed as a "laboratory" for art students. This was a reversal of the general pattern in America, where the major art museums often sponsored their own art schools.[182]

The Formation and Early Years of the American Academy in Rome

The last American archaeological institution created in the impressively dynamic period before World War I was the American School of Classical Studies at Rome, the institution that later became the classical division of

179. Sloan and Swinburne 1981.
180. Hiss and Fansler 1934: 109–10, 124–25, 151–52, 159–60, 171–73; Sloan and Swinburne 1981: 10.
181. Brinkerhoff 1958: 150.
182. For the School of the Museum of Fine Arts, cf. Whitehill 1970: 431–34, 493–97.

the American Academy in Rome (AAR).[183] The American School of Classical Studies in Rome opened in 1895. The late date of its foundation indicates the secondary role that Roman art and archaeology and even Roman literature had come to occupy in American classics and classical archaeology. Despite the long traditions of foreign academies in Rome and the fundamental role that contact with Italy had played in developing interest in ancient civilization in the United States, Charles Eliot Norton and his contemporaries in the American cultural elite felt strongly that archaeological research in Greece deserved primary attention. Hellas had come to be regarded as the wellspring of Western civilization.

The limited opportunities foreign archaeologists had for field research in Italy also contributed to the delay in founding an American archaeology school in Rome. The somewhat absurd outcome of the Croton expedition highlighted larger problems related to the position of non-Italian scholars working in Italy. In the years before the 1870 capture of Rome by Piedmontese forces, a small Anglo-Saxon archaeological community in Rome centered around the activities of the British and American Archaeological Society had emerged. Founded by the English antiquarian and pioneer photographer John Henry Parker (1806–1884) in 1868,[184] the society met regularly to hear lectures on the latest archaeological discoveries and to visit important sites. The participants were Rome residents or long-term visitors. The society enjoyed official patronage at the ambassadorial level; at the opening session in January 1885, the American ambassador William Waldorf Astor spoke of the combination of romantic and practical motives that led men like himself to become patrons:

Besides its historical value and its association with the men and the times we like to read about, Archaeology has the practical use, that from the teachings and traditions of the Past we gather ideals and inspirations for the Present. In this aim its pursuit is as valuable to my countrymen as to any of the nationalities that frequent the familiar ruins about us. (British and American Archaeological Society of Rome Session 1884–85: 1)

Many of the presentations were by educated amateur members, but others were by leading Italian and Anglo-Saxon scholars. The group also undertook limited excavations in and around Rome in the days before the new national laws discouraged such activities.

Such an antiquarian organization was not an adequate replacement for foreign schools modeled on the American School in Athens. By the early 1890s, sufficient cultural momentum had developed to ensure that America would have a teaching and research center in Rome. This was due in part to the fact that the cultural pendulum was swinging back in

183. Valentine and Valentine 1973: 22–24, 49–51.
184. Einaudi 1979: 9–12.

the direction of ancient Rome. The Great Chicago Exposition of 1893 had reinforced the interest in eclectic neoclassical architecture with a strong Roman emphasis.[185] Strong pressure to create an American academy in Rome came from prominent architects in such prestigious, historically oriented firms as McKim, Mead, and White in New York and Daniel Burnham in Chicago.[186] Many of these architects had studied in France, where they came to appreciate the Beaux Arts training, with its emphasis on the production of elegant, detailed drawings that reconstructed important ancient Roman monuments, as well as the long tradition of art and architectural study in Rome represented by the French Prix de Rome.[187] They were busy designing public and private buildings that reflected the influences of the Renaissance and ancient Rome more than those of the classical Greece beloved by Norton and the pre-Civil War American builders. As has been observed of Daniel Burnham, "His love of pomp, ceremony, and architectural magnitude made his interest in Rome and things Roman quite natural if not inevitable."[188]

In 1894 the *American Journal of Archaeology* published a notice announcing the establishment of an American School of Architecture in Rome. The school's main mission was to provide a base of operation for winners of traveling scholarships in architecture. Support for the venture came from such major architectural, artistic, and cultural figures as Richard Morris Hunt, Charles Follen McKim, Augustus St. Gaudens, Henry G. Marquand, Martin Brimmer, and, of course, Charles Eliot Norton. The school promised to maintain workrooms and a library "which may prove serviceable to the students of archaeology and antiquities."[189] It was natural that such a group of neoclassical architects would seek a close identity with the emerging discipline of American classical archaeology. The American School of Architecture opened in rented rooms in the Palazzo Torlonia. In 1895 John Russell Pope arrived as the first American Rome prizewinner. He was to become the last great figure in American neoclassical architecture, designing such monuments as the Jefferson Memorial and the National Gallery.[190]

The classicists were also attempting to establish their own program in Rome. Even if the field archaeologists found limited research opportunities in Italy, the ancient art historians as well as the Latinists and

185. LaFarge 1925; Valentine and Valentine 1973: 1–11; Hines 1974: 218.

186. Andrews 1964: 170–76, 184–97; Granger 1972: 86–102; Hines 1974: 218–25; Roth 1983: 135–38, 320–21.

187. Watkin 1983: 34; *Roma Antiqua* 1992. Rome's importance for an American architect of the period is captured well in J. H. Clark 1974.

188. Hines 1974: 224–25; Moore 1929: 273–77.

189. *AJA* (1894): 9.

190. Duncan 1995: 88, 97.

Roman historians needed to have a base for their research. Many of them had studied in Germany, where they had come to appreciate the innovative scholarship of archaeologists like Adolf Furtwängler, who were providing new interpretations of the history of Greek sculpture based on comprehensive study of Roman copies of Greek originals. The public and private collections of ancient sculpture in Rome were a major resource for this type of research.[191] The U.S. visits of Italian archaeologists like Rodolfo Lanciani also made American scholars aware of the potential for original research in Roman topographical studies at a time when the new discoveries made almost daily forced radical rethinking about many aspects of ancient Rome and its history.[192]

More strictly pedagogical concerns also drove those who pressed for the establishment of an American school in Rome. Latin had far surpassed Greek as the preferred ancient language in the U.S. secondary schools, colleges, and universities. However, even Latin teachers felt their position threatened in the practical, even philistine, educational environment of the late nineteenth century. They argued that classical studies needed revitalization and that one of the ways of accomplishing that was to bring more Latin teachers directly into contact with the physical environment of the ancient authors they were studying and teaching. This meant a center for organized educational programs in Rome.[193] In 1894 Professors Samuel Platner of Western Reserve College in Cleveland and E. T. Merrill of Wesleyan University in Connecticut proposed establishing an American school at Rome. Significantly both these scholars came from quality undergraduate institutions. The American School of Classical Studies in Rome opened in 1895, occupying rented space in the Villa Aurora on the Pincio.[194]

Among the first faculty appointments made at the school was that of Richard Norton, the son of Charles Eliot Norton and later the director of the ill-fated Cyrene expedition.[195] He served as assistant director of the School of Classical Studies from 1897–89 and director from 1899 to 1907. Although his classical training was almost completely in Greek archaeology and he appears to have shown little interest in the new approaches to Roman art and archaeology being produced by such scholars as the Viennese Franz Wickhoff, Norton's study with Furtwängler had certainly impressed upon him the importance of the copies in the great Roman collections for understanding the development of Greek art. His appointment to the Classical School in Rome indicated how the academic

191. *EHCA* s.v. "Furtwangler, Adolf (1853–1907)."
192. Lanciani 1894, 1901.
193. West 1917.
194. *EHCA* s.v. "American Academy in Rome."
195. Kelsey 1919.

founders wanted the city's archaeological resources used. Norton lectured regularly on Greek art, using the great variety of Roman copies in the galleries and museums of Rome as illustrations. He combined the scientific art historical analysis he had learned in Germany with the aesthetic approach of his father and his American School mentor Charles Waldstein. Like Waldstein, Norton stressed the importance of the "seeing eye" for interpreting art.[196]

Richard Norton was also a man of broad general culture with a very good knowledge of Italian art and a well-developed sense of connoisseurship. He acted as an art purchasing agent for institutions such as the Boston Museum of Fine Arts and for members of the Boston elite, like Isabella Stewart Gardner.[197] These activites brought him into the orbit of another ambitious and strong-minded Boston connoisseur, Bernard Berenson. Berenson's initial reaction to Norton was favorable. In a 1900 letter to Isabella Stewart Gardner, he described Norton as "a splendid fellow, firm, incisive and with a fine dry sense of humor."[198] However, the relationship soon soured, and the Berensons came to see Norton as an enemy who used every opportunity to attack Bernard Berenson's art critical judgment and professional ethics.[199]

As has already been made clear in the description of the Cyrene disaster, Richard Norton bore little physical or temperamental resemblance to his mild-mannered, diplomatic father. Almost immediately he got himself into difficulty with the Italian authorities by criticizing the government's excavation and antiquities policies. Expressive of that attitude was a stinging letter he wrote to the London *Times* of London of 9 January, 1899.[200] The letter's tone is captured by these final sentences:

When one sees such things as these done, one can only be delighted whenever marbles and pictures leave the country. Until the Italians show some proper respect for the treasures of their past, one is glad when they fall into the possession of others who will treat them as they ought to be treated." (Lanciani 1988: 247)

Whatever the merits of Norton's position on the Italian government's failure to prevent the destruction of archaeological remains in rapidly changing nineteenth-century Rome (and he was not alone in such criticisms), this was hardly the restrained language one would expect from a recently appointed official at a small, newly founded foreign school. The Italians were clearly sensitive about their ability to carry out their ambitious archaeological programs, and Anglo-American criticism was most

196. Kelsey 1919: 335.
197. Samuels 1979: 414–16; Hadley 1987: 195, 211–12, 328–29, 616–67.
198. Hadley 1987: 212.
199. Hadley 1987: 467–68, 596–97.
200. Lanciani 1988: 241–47.

unwelcome. Norton's position was made more ambivalent by the fact that
he was involved in collecting for foreign individuals and institutions. His
argument that the locals were incapable of caring for their own antiquities would be used by generations of American collectors down to the
present day. Certainly the Italians remembered these outbursts when the
Cyrene affair developed. By the time the Cyrene crisis ended A. L. Frothingham Jr. of Princeton, a man who knew Italy's cultural and academic
scene in Italy very well, could observe in a letter to Francis Kelsey that

It is such a pity that Norton has "queered" himself for any work in Italy and North
Africa. The feeling is so strong against him among the Italians. Silence is golden.
(AIA Archives: Frothingham to Kelsey)

During its early years, the Classical School was housed in temporary
quarters in the center of the city. As in Athens there developed a rhythm
of activities, which included conducted tours of major monuments and
research.[201] However, an increasing number of key individuals in both
the classical and the artistic communities felt that a combined art and
classical institution not only would be more efficient but also would promote intellectual interaction from which both communities would benefit. Complex negotiations ensued. By the end of 1912 the decision had
been made to merge the American School of Classical Studies at Rome
with the art and architecture school to form the American Academy in
Rome.[202]

The newly founded academy moved into a complex of buildings located on the Janiculum Hill overlooking the city.[203] The property included the Renaissance structure known as the Villa Aurelia, given to the
academy in 1909 by a wealthy American widow living in Rome. The Villa
Aurelia, which had a most impressive view over the city, had served as
Garibaldi's headquarters during the 1849 siege of Rome.[204] The central
building of the academy was a new structure designed by McKim, Mead,
and White in the form of a Florentine Renaissance palazzo. One entered
through the rusticated facade, up broad stairs into the central courtyard
around which were arranged bedrooms, studios, the library, and common rooms. The start of the academy, which opened in 1914, was not
totally auspicious for the first director, Francis Davis Millet (1846–1912)
went down on the *Titanic*.[205]

Much of the early success of this new venture was owed to the directorial skills of Jesse Benedict Carter (1872–1917). He was a graduate of

201. Valentine and Valentine 1973: 49–51.
202. Valentine and Valentine 1973: 51–65.
203. Rand 1914–15; Valentine and Valentine 1973: 51–68.
204. Valentine and Valentine 1973: 39, 51–53.
205. *DAB* VI.644–66 s.v. "Millet, Francis Davis"; Valentine and Valentine 1973: 54–63.

Princeton and had studied at several German universities, obtaining a Ph.D. at Halle. He taught mainly at Princeton before going to Rome. Carter had been professor of the American School of Classical Studies in Rome during 1904–7 and director from 1907 to 1912. Following Millet's death, he was appointed director of the combined schools, a post he held until his own death while on World War I Red Cross duty.[206] Carter was an elegant man of broad general culture, who combined archaeological and historical interests. His area of special expertise was Roman religion, which allowed him to range over the whole field of classical studies.[207] In the words of one of his obituary writers, Carter "was through and through a humanist."[208] He also had the diplomatic skills Norton lacked.

The new institution combined classical and archaeological studies with the pursuit of the fine arts, especially architecture, painting, and sculpture. It tried to foster the type of art-oriented humanistic education that Charles Eliot Norton had so long advocated, and whose roots went back to Ruskin and Morris. The architect William Rutherford Mead, one of the academy's founding figures, captured the school's intended spirit when he stated "We can say though that it should mean a long step toward renewing, what our life of today has so sadly lost, the influence of that element for which no better name has ever been found than 'The Humanities'."[209] In this humanistically centered institution, special emphasis was placed on historical architectural studies in the Beaux Arts tradition. Academy architects in later years undertook projects like design reconstructions of buildings at Hadrian's villa, activities that were often more archaeological in orientation than the research of classical scholars.[210] In the beginning these fitted nicely into a world of architectural values still dominated by a Roman-centered neoclassicism. The conflicts this orthodoxy produced in an architectural discipline that increasingly had to come to grips with modernism will be discussed later.

The severe limitations placed on foreign excavations in Italy meant that archaeological research was limited to architectural, topographical, epigraphical, and museum studies. Still, each offered impressive scholarly opportunities at a time when so much was being discovered in and around Rome. The academy initially hoped to play a major role in Italian archaeology, but fate destined that not all these hopes were to bear fruit.

206. *DAB* II.539 s.v. "Carter, Jesse Benedict"; Valentine and Valentine 1973: 61–75.

207. Carter 1906. In 1906 he also translated Christian Hülsen's study of the Roman Forum into English.

208. *Annual Report ASCS* 1916–17: 67. It was appropriate that in 1916 the French Minister of Public Instruction asked Carter to lecture at the Sorbonne on the growth of the humanities in the United States.

209. Quoted in Rand 1914–15: 20.

210. Frazer 1932; Johnson 1932; Price 1932; Mirick 1933; Reichardt 1933.

Figure 6. Ester Van Deman in front of one of her beloved Roman cement ruins at a site near Rome. Courtesy of the Fototeca of the American Academy in Rome.

The scholarly potential and frustrations of this era can be seen in the careers of three early academy archaeologists: Ester Van Deman, Samuel Platner, and C. Desmond Curtis.

The forced emphasis on above-ground archaeology very much shaped the career of Ester Boise Van Deman (1862–1937), who in 1901 became one of the first women to enter the Classical School of the American Academy (Figure 6).[211] Van Deman was raised and educated in the Midwest, where she took a B.A. and an M.A. at the University of Michigan under Francis Kelsey and a Ph.D. from the recently founded University of Chicago.[212] Her education was philological and historical, but her dissertation research on the cult of Vesta forced her to consider physical remains.

211. *EHCA* s.v. "Van Deman, Esther Boise (1862–1937)"; Sherman 1981: 33–34; Geffcken 1991.
212. Geffcken 1991.

Van Deman went to Rome in 1901 to revise her dissertation. There she was brought in contact with the remains in the Roman forum related to the temple of Vesta and the house of the vestals, which had recently been uncovered by Italian archaeologists.[213] Her monograph on the subject, which appeared in 1909, contained an introduction by the great German archaeologist and topographer of ancient Rome, Christian Hülsen, who especially praised Van Deman's use of changes in the technique of brick-work to define and date various constructions.[214] Indeed, in Rome Van Deman's interests had turned to more strictly archaeological problems. She became involved in the architectural and topographical researchs of the Englishman Thomas Ashby and made herself a formidable expert on Roman construction. Financing from the Carnegie Institution beginning in 1906 allowed her to pursue a lifelong career as a researcher, focusing on the technical aspects of Roman architecture and construction, and to spend much of her life in Rome.[215]

Van Deman became one of the legendary American academics in Rome, famous among other things for her ability to date Roman cement by its distinctive taste. Her sometimes acerbic personality and her pains-taking, pedantic approach to scholarship limited her impact on the field somewhat. In Katherine Geffcken's words,

in 1925, a confidential memorandum of the Carnegie Institute of Washington relying heavily on Kelsey's knowledge comments on Van Deman's "inadequate sense of humor" and her excessive, almost morbid "conscientiousness in ac-cumulating detail." Although such perfectionism meant her final conclusions would stand the test of time, she was extremely slow in bringing projects to completion. (1991: 10)

This slowness in completing scholarly projects was demonstrated by her publication record. Her major book, *The Building of the Roman Aqueducts*, which drew heavily on her friendship and collaboration with Thomas Ashby, was not published until 1934.[216] Research on her works dealing with the evolution of Roman construction techniques went even slower. The manuscripts were left incomplete on Van Deman's death in 1937. Her voluminous notes and observations on the history of Roman con-struction techniques in the early empire were pulled together, updated, and published by Marion Blake.[217] In her obituary of Van Deman Blake vividly describes the way Van Deman selected her as the continuator of

213. For a discussion of those remains, cf. Lanciani 1897, 1967: 221–31.
214. Van Deman 1909. For Hülsen and his research in the Forum, cf. *EHCA* s.v. "Hülsen, Christian Karl Friedrich (1858–1935)."
215. Colini 1938.
216. For Thomas Ashby cf. *EHCA* s.v. "Ashby, Thomas (1874–1931)."
217. Blake 1947.

her work and shaped much of her scholarly career from beyond the grave.[218] It was left to a third archaeologist, Doris Taylor Bishop, to complete the cycle by finishing the last of Blake's volumes after the latter's death in 1961.[219]

Van Deman represented the emergence of a new type of American classical archaeologist, who was to become very common in the new century. A formidable concentration of research energy and the increased availability of archaeological data made such individuals into world-class specialists on arcane but important archaeological subjects. This expertise often led them into positions as research associates, appointments that tended to isolate them from the American academic mainstream, especially the world of teaching (where Van Deman displayed little talent or interest) and student mentoring. Yet this expertise provided them with impressive power, as they controlled access to essential material and information. Van Deman was an early version of scholars like the amphora expert Virginia Grace, who played an important role in the Athenian Agora excavations.

It is often forgotten that the first name on the title page of the standard handbook *The Dictionary of Roman Topography* was not that of the Englishman Thomas Ashby but that of the American Samuel Ball Platner, and that the work had been preceded by two editions of a more general handbook, written by Platner alone. Platner (1863–1921) had received a philological education at Yale and had only gradually been drawn into questions of Roman history and hence of topography and archaeology.[220] In 1904 he produced the first edition of his *Topography and Monuments of Ancient Rome*, dedicated to the dean of Roman topography, Christian Hülsen.[221] The work relied heavily on the latest German topographical scholarship and represented the first handbook of this type available in English. Platner then turned to a more comprehensive archaeological dictionary of the monuments of ancient Rome. For this project he joined forces with Thomas Ashby, the director of the British School at Rome. The friendship and scholarly collaboration that developed with Ashby, the leading topographer of his day, indicated the seriousness of Platner's research interests and the respect with which he was treated by distinguished archaeologists in Rome.

The project for the topographical dictionary was well underway when World War I broke out. Ashby was forced to withdraw from the project

218. Blake 1958.
219. Blake 1973.
220. Fowler 1921; *WWW America* 1897–1942: 977 s.v. "Platner, Samuel Ball"; *DAB* VII: 648.
221. Platner 1904, 2nd ed. 1911.

owing to war service, and it was left to Platner to finish the work. Sadly, Platner died on shipboard 20 August, 1921 while sailing to Italy. He had been planning to spend the winter in Rome completing the dictionary. By an ironic turn of fate, it fell to Ashby to bring the volume to completion. With Platner, the academy lost a scholar who was clearly capable of bringing major projects to conclusion.

C. Densmore Curtis (1875–1925) was born in Augusta, Maine, but sought his education in the west, first at Pomona College in California and then at the University of Colorado. He studied at both the American Academy (1901–5) and the American School in Athens (1905–6); his major field experiences were at Cyrene and at Sardis, where he published the jewelry from the American excavations.[222] In 1912 he went back to Rome, where he served first as assistant and then as associate professor of archaeology at the American Academy. If Van Deman was a "construction material" archaeologist and Platner a topographical archaeologist, Curtis was a museum archaeologist. He realized that the rapidly expanding storerooms of museums, like those of the newly opened Villa Giulia museum of Etruscan archaeology, held much more archaeological material than Italian scholars could ever hope to study and publish. His scholarly credentials and engaging personality won the confidence of his Italian colleagues. He was entrusted with the publication of such important finds as the seventh century B.C. Bernardini and the Barberini tombs from Praeneste with their rich finds of gold jewelry and imported objects. Both of these appeared in the *Memoirs of the American Academy in Rome*.[223]

Curtis was more than just a connoisseur of flashy gold objects. Albert Van Buren, in an obituary of his American Academy colleague, highlighted Curtis's more scientific side, describing him as "prone to describe things as they exist rather than to develop theories of their formal significance were of a sort which is perhaps more frequently met in the sphere of the natural sciences than in classical archaeology" (1926). He encouraged students at the academy to range widely intellectually and to use prehistoric as well as classical material to investigate the early cultural developments around Rome. Both W. R. Bryan in his *Italic Hut Urns and Hut Urn Cemeteries* (1925) and Louise Adams in her *The Faliscans in Prehistoric Times* (1925) acknowledged Curtis's strong influence in shaping their thinking. In fact, Adams dedicated her work to Curtis, "A patient helper, a merry comrade, a well-loved friend." He died even younger than Platner and left archaeology at the American Academy to the much more restricted scholarly mentalities of Ester Van Deman and Albert Van Buren.

222. *WWW America* 1897–1942: 286 s.v. "Curtis, C(harles) Densmore"; C. D. Curtis 1925.
223. C. D. Curtis 1919, 1925.

A Backward Glance

As American classical archaeology entered the new century it was already showing signs of the complex interaction of self-confidence, insecurity, and paranoia that were to characterize it throughout much of its history. Two works captured these conflicting tendencies. The Carnegie Institution in its yearbook of 1903 published a report prepared by Professor Thomas Seymour of Yale on a recent Carnegie-sponsored trip he had undertaken in the Mediterranean to investigate the state of archaeological research there and the potential for American involvement.[224] His observations on the American and foreign archaeological scene are very illuminating. Naturally, he spoke well of the Corinth excavations, noting that the excavations had produced good results for a cost he estimated at $15,000, one-fifth of that expended at Ephesus and much less than the $200,000 the Germans had spent on the excavations at Olympia between 1875 and 1881.[225] He had special praise for the research of Harriet Boyd Hawes and John Sterrett. Of the possible sites for American research, Thebes in Greece and Antioch on the Orontes in Syria held special appeal for him. In conclusion, Seymour stressed the importance of the classical heritage for American values. Classical archaeology had scientific importance for him, though he considered it a discipline subordinate to philology and ancient history. At the same time, Seymour expressed concern about the fact that although two hundred classical teachers had been brought into contact with Greek and Roman antiquity through the Schools in Athens and Rome, only four to five archaeologists whose attainments were up to European standards had been produced.

These complex and contradictory feelings about the position of classical archaeology at the turn of the century were also captured in a 1902 essay written written by Joseph Thacher Clarke for a volume entitled *Methods of Teaching History*. In the years since Assos, Clarke had gone from a bright young hopeful to a marginal figure remembered mainly for his failures in finishing the Assos publications. His own frustrations with the development of American classical archaeology and his failure to attain a significant place in it, as well as a continuing confidence in its potential as a field for research are clear throughout the essay.

Clarke's vision of archaeology remained the blend of science and Helleno-romanticism that had inspired most of the classical archaeologists educated since the Civil War. He expressed his sense of himself as a scientist when he wrote

224. Seymour 1903.
225. Seymour 1903: 224, 230.

we have to-day in archaeology a new science, which, in perfection of apparatus and results, may be proudly ranked with comparative anatomy: that branch of research which practical archaeology most closely resembles in point of method. (1902: 97)

Yet he closed his essay with an affirmation of more humanistic classical values:

It has first become possible to the younger generation of today to enter into full possession of the land of milk and honey of Greek perfection. And this possibility is almost wholly due to the investigation of practical workers upon classic soil, and to those archaeological scholars who have taught the world the true values of the materials thus obtained. (1902: 103)

There also appears in Clarke's text a resentment against those who were privileging the philological approach in the development of the field. Clarke asserted that as classics faced new challenges in a utilitarian age, "improvement can only proceed from a rejuvenation of philological studies by that living knowledge of antiquity gained by practical archaeology."[226] Yet he saw the discipline being held back by nonarchaeological interests:

This inability to recognize and enter into the actual life of the ancient led to the appearance of that great and yet deplorable race of scholars who, Cyclop-like, lacked the eye of practical acquaintance with the material remains of those civilizations to whose literary vestiges they devoted an erudition not yet surpassed. (1902: 91)

The first American classical field archaeologist was clearly a sad and embittered man. He identified some of the strengths of his still protean discipline but also recognized the structural problems faced by American classical archaeologists, especially those with a more unorthodox educational background, that would continue to haunt the profession down to the present day.

226. J. T. Clarke 1902: 90.

4. The Formation of the Museum Tradition

The modern museum has its ultimate origins in the growth of the collecting mentality during the Renaissance. Popes, princes, and other potentates sought to accumulate the works of both man and nature for prestige, study, and contemplation.[1] Initially private collections were the focus of such endeavors, but the notion of collections that were at least partly open to the public also goes back to the Renaissance. One of the principal and most publicly proclaimed aims of the museum throughout history has been the collection and conservation of objects. However, through their accessibility policies and modes of displaying their collections, museums have developed an ideological dimension that gives them an important social as well as cultural role.[2]

The popes and leading ecclesiastical figures of Italy led the way in creating large collections of ancient art. Part of their aim was to preserve as much as possible of the fragments of sculpture, painting, architecture, and inscriptions that were constantly being found in the soil of Rome and other parts of Italy. They also sought to create a visual cultural context for their beloved authors from antiquity. To surround oneself with busts of emperors and Roman copies of Greek originals was to proclaim oneself a person of culture and taste with a close self-identity with antiquity. Within this complex world of collecting, the museums of the Capitoline and the Vatican assumed a special role, in part owing to the exalted status of patronage and their identity with more than just private concerns.[3]

This approach to collecting and displaying of ancient art remained dominant throughout the seventeenth and eighteenth centuries, spreading to the secular royal families and even to the nobility in other parts of Europe.[4] The Grand Tour and the discoveries at Pompeii and Herculaneum in the eighteenth century accelerated this process but also changed

1. Wittlin 1970: 13–74; Haskell and Penny 1981: 1–15.
2. The ideology of the modern museum has been the object of considerable study and debate in recent years. Cf. Wittlin 1970; Duncan 1995.
3. Haskell and Penny 1981: 7–15; Bober and Rubinstein 1986.
4. Wittlin 1970: 31–6; Haskell and Penny 1981: 23–89.

it in fundamental ways. The major players in the Grand Tour were sons of the English nobility and their purchases, often made through British agents in Rome like Gavin Hamilton (1723–1798) and Thomas Jenkins (1722–1798) spurred classical collection where it had previously been relatively underdeveloped.[5] The arrival of the German aesthete and antiquarian J. J. Winckelmann in Rome and his appointment as curator of Cardinal Albani's collections linked innovative archaeological scholarship, neoclassical aesthetic ideology, and one of the great holdings in antique art in a new way. The era also saw some of the first ideological debates on the political and cultural roles of the museum in papal Italy.[6]

The nature and purpose of the art and archaeology museum changed even more dramatically during the nineteenth century. Collecting became associated with nationalism and imperialism as Napoleon looted the private collections of Europe, and especially Italy to enhance the Louvre's already rich holdings.[7] The approach toward acquiring ancient objects changed from gathering limited numbers of art works on the Grand Tour to the systematic plundering and exportation of large collections of ancient materials from Greece and Turkey. Lord Elgin brought back the sculptures of the Parthenon from Athens, and Charles Thomas Newton carted off the marbles of Cnidus and Halicarnassus in Turkey.[8] In 1815 Ludwig of Bavaria steered the Germans in the same direction by acquiring the Aegina sculptures for Munich.[9] The last great classical acquisition of this sort were the Pergamene marbles, which went on display in Berlin in 1880.[10]

Significantly, all these major importations of ancient art into Europe were associated with a new type of museum, which had a much more public role than the older cabinets and private collections. The Elgin marbles were rather grudgingly taken into the British Museum, an institution established by a combination of private and public efforts: the same institution received the Halicarnassus and Knidos material. The Aegina marbles made their way into the Glyptothek at Munich. The Pergamene marbles ultimately received their own gallery in the Berlin Museum complex.[11]

As museum collections became more public, and in some cases the mu-

5. Haskell and Penny 1981: 62–79; B. Cook 1985. For the role of Gavin Hamilton, cf. *EHCA* s.v. "Hamilton, Gavin Inglis (1723–98)." For Thomas Jenkins, cf. *EHCA* s.v. "Jenkins, Thomas (1722–98)."

6. Springer 1987: 21–63; Potts 1994.

7. Wittlin 1970: 15–16; Burt 1977: 23–26; Hudson 1987: 4–6.

8. *EHCA* s.v. "Elgin, Lord (Thomas Bruce; 1766–1841)," "Halikarnassos (Halicarnassus)," "Newton, Sir Charles Thomas (1816–94)"; Jenkins 1992: 171–95.

9. *EHCA* s.v. "Aigina (Aegina)," "Ludwig I (1786–1868)"; Stoneman 1987: 192–98.

10. Stoneman 1987: 284–91; Marchand 1996: 92–103.

11. *EHCA* s.v. "British Museum, London," "Glyptothek, Munich"; Marchand 1996: 188–294.

seums derived increasing financial support from the state, debate intensified over the social and cultural roles of museums like the British Museum
and the best way to display their collections.[12] Debates over the museum's
purpose, so vigorous in Europe today originated in the nineteenth century. This in turn led to the development of new types of museums like the
Basel Museum in Switzerland (1849) and the South Kensington (later
Victoria and Albert) Museum in London, which were founded specifically
to use the arts for public improvement.[13] The American art museum was
born when these debates and developments, especially those related to
the South Kensington Museum, were at their height.

A few words must be said about the historical relationship between the
art museum and academic classical archaeology in the United States,
since certain events and circumstances have tended to separate those two
spheres of classical archaeological studies in recent years. Reflections on
the origins and development of museum classical archaeology have to be
part of any study of the evolution of classical archaeology in the United
States, since classical archaeology in the colleges and universities and in
the museums have historically had a symbiotic relationship. Both have a
common ancestry in Charles Eliot Norton's aesthetic archaeology movement and early enjoyed an ideological affiliation that led Norton himself
to play a major role in founding both the Archaeological Institute of
America and the Boston Museum of Fine Arts. Both owed much of their
financial support to a shared base of wealthy, interested amateurs.

Art museums have also since the 1870s played a major role in introducing the public to, and educating them about, classical archaeology. Before the advent of television they were the only media for mass education
about art and archaeology. Unquestionably, the first visit to a museum
stimulated the desire in many to become archaeologists. At the same
time, college and university courses in archaeology have helped fill museum corridors of museums and ensure long-term museum patronage by
the educated class.

This chapter has a wider chronological range than the others. I feel
that the basic approach to collecting and display in American classical
archaeological museum collections has a continuum from the founding
of the first significant museum collections after the Civil War to the intensified debate on the importation of antiquities in the 1970s and early
1980s. Hence this chapter bridges the World War I and II divisions and
ends with the start of the antiquities-collecting debate and the early development of the Getty Classical Collection.

12. Hudson 1987: 22–25.
13. Burt 1977; Hudson 1987: 10–13, 47–54; C. S. Smith 1989: 8–9; Goodwin 1990.

The origins of the museum in the United States can be traced back to a natural history museum founded at Charleston in 1773.[14] and to the collection of curiosities that Charles Willson Peale established in the early nineteenth century.[15] Interestingly, although the Peale collection contained assorted archaeological and ethnographic objects, it does not appear to have exhibited any classical archaeological objects. P. T. Barnum continued certain aspects of the Peale tradition later in the nineteenth century, but his "museums" and those of his imitators were a potpourri of objects appealing to a range of popular tastes.[16] Moses Kemball's Boston Museum, founded in 1841, displayed paintings by artists of Sully's and Peale's quality along with Chinese curiosities, stuffed animals, and mermaids.[17] In 1844 the Wadsworth Athenaeum, generally credited as being the first art museum in the United States, opened in Hartford, Connecticut.[18]

More refined and focused cultural institutions like the Boston Athenaeum began to acquire small collections of casts and original artifacts by the 1820s.[19] These objects were purchased to improve taste and provide suitable ancient models for aspiring artists. Although the increasing numbers of Americans traveling to Italy had the opportunity to purchase original works of ancient art, very few availed themselves of that opportunity. Pre-Civil War private American collections of classical artifacts seem to have been relatively few and very small. Italian tourism was becoming much more of a middle-class phenomenon, and most Americans who traveled did not have the wealth to purchase antiquities in significant quantities. Morever, few had the English-style stately homes suitable for decoration in the classical manner. Those who did have financial resources and cultural interests tended to collect such things as "Old Master" or Barbizon paintings and European and oriental ceramics.[20]

By mid-century, cultural, ideological, and practical foundations were being laid for the creation of different types of museums in the United States. In 1860 Ralph Waldo Emerson expressed some thoughts in his essay *The Conduct of Life* on the role great art and its accessible display should play in cultivating public taste. He agreed with the ancient Greeks that it was "profane that any person should pretend a property in a work of art, which belonged to all who could behold it." He advocated public

14. Coleman 1939: 6–7; L. B. Miller 1966: 121–28; Burt 1977: 26.
15. Burt 1977: 26–33; L. Levine 1988: 146–49.
16. Harris 1990: 18, 147.
17. Dimaggio 1982a: 34.
18. Burt 1977: 45–46.
19. Whitehill 1970: 22.
20. Hiss and Fansler 1934: 10–12; L. B. Miller 1966: 144–59; Burt 1977: 80–85.

ownership for art properties that could "provide this culture and inspira-tion for the citizens."[21] Emerson was not alone in arguing that a culti-vated public could be created only by public institutions of taste. James Jackson Jarves, the pioneer collector of Italian primitives in America, had argued strongly for the creation of distinctly American art museums.[22] Although the development of public art museums in pre-Civil War Amer-ica had been a very limited, the need for such institutions was increas-ingly felt.

Americans were also aware of changes in the museum world of Europe, especially England. While the British Museum of the mid-nineteenth century seemed overwhelmed by the massiveness of its collections, the in-adequacies of its buildings, and the debates about its future mission and its accessibility to an increasingly diverse British public, new types of museums were being established in London and in the expanding cities of The Midlands.[23] The South Kensington Museum, founded in the after-math of the Great Exhibition of 1851, advocated a more practical mission than the British Museum, involving the improvement of popular taste and industrial design, which would in turn improve the competitiveness of English products. This new museum proved to be extremely popular, with fifteen million visitors between 1857 and 1883.[24] The South Kensing-ton Museum particularly influenced early American museum planners.[25]

This growing interest in creating a new type of museum in the United States was articulated clearly in an 1870 article that the Boston art histo-rian Charles Callahan Perkins (1823–1886) published in the influential *North American Review*.[26] Perkins, who was certainly the leading American art historian of his day, argued that America needed museums modeled on the South Kensington Museum not only to raise the general level of taste, but also to improve the quality of industrial products. He stated:

This can only be done by the organization of comprehensive museums, which will raise the standards of taste, furnish materials for study to artists and archaeolo-gists, affect industry, and provide places of resort for the general public where amusement and unconscious instruction will be combined. (1870: 5)

Perkins cautioned that the lack of public patronage and the small number of large fortunes (an ironic assertion at the dawn of the Gilded Age) would limit fledgling American museums' ability to acquire large

21. L. B. Miller 1966: 87.
22. Hiss and Fansler 1934: 10–12; N. Harris 1962: 555–61.
23. Jenkins 1992: 196–210; T. Bennett 1995: 70.
24. T. Bennett 1995: 70–73.
25. N. Harris 1962: 555–58; Whitehill 1970: 9–10.
26. C. Perkins 1870; Dimaggio 1982a: 41.

numbers of original artworks. For this and for more general educational reasons, he argued for the creation of museums based on comprehensive cast collections, which could be arranged in chronological order and used for various instructional purposes. Although not all the casts in Perkins's proposed museum would be Greek and Roman, the great majority would, and their systematic arrangement would allow the viewer to trace the rise, peak, and decline of classical art. Athenian art of the age of Pericles stood at the center of Perkins's ideal museum, much as it did in Charles Eliot Norton's Harvard teaching. Perkins was interested in the development of art museums as part of a wider program of expanding the role of the arts in American education. He lectured on Greek and Roman art to Boston schoolteachers and in general tried to promote art as a subject in the Boston and Massachusetts schools.[27]

The moment was opportune for the founding of public museums in the major American cities in other ways. The period between the end of the Civil War and the beginning of World War I saw a combination of increased philanthropy and the institutionalization of many aspects of American life. This extended from professional societies to symphony orchestras. In Edith Wharton's words, "The best class of New Yorkers had shaken off the strange apathy following on the Civil War, and begun to develop a municipal conscience, and all the men I have mentioned were active in administering the new museums, libraries and charities of New York."[28] Marxist-oriented social and institutional historians have placed a slightly more sinister spin on these developments. For them, the creation of institutions like museums and symphony orchestras represented the effort of an elite that was losing political power to maintain other types of power by defining and appropriating the realm of high culture.[29] Not unexpectedly, this development started in Boston.

The origins of Boston's Museum of Fine Arts reflect most of these trends. Its foundation was an outgrowth of changes at another venerable cultural institution, the Boston Athenaeum. The Athenaeum's primary mission was to provide a high-quality library for educated Bostonians. However, as the name implies, the Athenaeum was also intended to be a broad-based cultural center; its mission included building an art collection. By the 1850s the Athenaeum had acquired a substantial collection of casts of European sculptures, including classical pieces, and also numberous works by American neoclassical sculptors like Thomas Crawford and Hiram Powers. A woodcut published in 1855 shows the Athenaeum

27. Hiss and Fansler 1934: 15–17; Whitehill 1970: 8–9.
28. Wharton 1934: 95.
29. Dimaggio 1982a, b.

Sculpture Gallery lined with casts of such familiar classical works as the Dying Gaul and the Apollo Belvedere.[30] In the years before Charles Eliot Norton began teaching at Harvard and the Museum of Fine Arts opened its doors, Boston's cultural elite owed much of its local aesthetic education to afternoons spent contemplating that collection.

Expanding the Athenaeum's art holdings raised its own problems. Walter Muir Whitehill, long-time director of the Athenaeum and eloquent narrater of Boston's cultural history, summarized the dilemma faced by the Athenaeum by the 1860s with the succinct statement "Institutions outgrow their buildings with remarkable regularity."[31] By 1866 the competition for space at the Athenaeum between art and books had become acute. The 1869 bequest of a major collection of arms and armor made the Boston brahmins realize that the Athenaeum would soon be overwhelmed by an increasing flow of private art donations.[32] Since the maintaining of the library was the Athenaeum's principal mission, an alternative institution had to be developed for the display of works of art.

Boston's leading cultural figures in Boston began to push for the establishment of an art museum. Charles Callahan Perkins was a major driving force in the Boston museum movement. With nearly ten years of art historical and musical studies in Europe and the publication of works like *Tuscan Sculptors*, he probably had the best art historical credentials to be found in America at that time.[33] Another founding father was Martin Brimmer (1829–1896).[34] He had excelled at Harvard in Greek and Latin studies, but initially turned to the study of law. Brimmer's interest in law waned, for "although admitted to the Massachusetts bar, he found European travel and the study of art more congenial than the practise of law."[35] Brimmer perceived that the art museum in America would have a complex role; it would acquire the best art objects, yet at the same time "the museums of today open their doors to all of the world and the scope of their collections has broadened to meet the public needs."[36]

The new Boston Museum of Fine Arts was incorporated by the Massachusetts state legislature in 1870 and opened in Copley Square in 1876. The first president was Charles Loring, a much decorated Civil War general and an early American enthusiast of Egyptian archaeology.[37] Al-

30. Whitehill 1970: 4.

31. Whitehill 1970: 5.

32. N. Harris 1962: 548–49; Whitehill 1970: 1–8.

33. Brooks 1958: 109; Burt 1977: 107–9.

34. N. Harris 1962: 550–51; Whitehill 1970: 11–12.

35. Whitehill 1970: 11.

36. Brimmer's article in the 30 Oct. 1880 *American Architect and Building News* quoted in Whitehill 1970: 12–13.

37. Whithill 1970: 21–22; Burt 1977: 107.

though the initial impulse to found the museum came from the Boston elite, it soon enjoyed a broad base of public support. The amount of $261, 425 was collected for the initial building fund, including one thousand gifts of less than $2,000. Attendance was equally impressive. In 1877, the first full year of operation, there were seventeen thousand paid visitors and one hundred forty thousand free visitors, the latter all coming on Saturdays and Sundays, when no fee was charged.[38] By the late 1890s attendance had risen to two to three hundred thousand per year.[39] Visitors saw a potpourri, which included original art and a large number of casts and reproductions. This did not bother the first generation of museum organizers and patrons, for they conceived the museum's principal role as education and not collecting.[40]

New York was always very sensitive to cultural developments in Boston and sought to rival and surpass what they saw as a declining New England center. If Boston had a museum, New York would have to have a bigger and better one. The movement to found what became the Metropolitan Museum started in 1869 with a group of wealthy and cultivated New Yorkers associated with the Union League Club, an important elite power center in many cities of post-Civil War America.[41] These men were obviously interested in competing with Boston, but they too were inspired by the educational goals of London's South Kensington Museum. The charter granted by New York state's legislature defined the museum's mission as that of "a Museum and library of art, for encouraging and developing the study of the fine arts, and the application of arts to manufactures and practical life, of advancing the general knowledge of kindred subjects and to that end of furnishing popular instruction and recreation."[42] Such sentiments were echoed by Joseph Choate at the opening of the new Metropolitan Museum building in 1880:

[The founders] believed that the diffusion of a knowledge of art in its higher forms of beauty would tend directly to humanize, to educate, and refine a practical and laborious people . . . but should also show to the students and artisans of every branch of industry . . . what the past had accomplished for them to imitate and excel. (quoted in Howe 1946: xi)

Both museums faced formidable obstacles. Not only were there no real collections, but there was no tradition in America of either professional museum curatorships or directorships. This can be appreciated by con-

38. N. Harris 1962: 557.
39. N. Harris 1962: 557.
40. L. Levine 1988: 151–52.
41. Lerman 1969: 11–18; Tomkins 1970: 15–59; Burt 1977: 91–92; Hudson 1987: 54–60.
42. Tomkins 1970.

sidering the lives and careers of the first leading administrators at Boston and New York museums: Luigi Palma di Cesnola and Edward Robinson.

Luigi (Louis) Palma di Cesnola (1832–1904) was certainly one of the more colorful individuals ever to grace the American museum world (Figure 7). Of Piedmont Italian origins, he served in brave if somewhat stormy fashion in the American Civil War.[43] In 1865 he was appointed American consul in Cyprus.[44] Cesnola used that diplomatic position (as well as the associated position of Russian consul) to acquire a large collection of Cypriote antiquities, especially sculptures, through informal excavation. Thousands of tombs were opened and looted. This pillaging can be excused in part by the standards of the time, although Cesnola's activities were criticized by his contemporaries.[45] His book *Cyprus: Its Ancient Cities, Tombs and Temples* (1878) was a partial response to criticism of his methods.[46] Perhaps the fairest judgment in the end is that of Professor John L. Myres of Oxford, who first published the Metropolitan Cesnola collection in 1914:

> In 1865, therefore, the archaeological position was this. Preliminary explorations had begun; the attention of scholars was aroused; and a start was being made with interpretation. The moment was near when Cyprus must be won for archaeology, and "digging" be tranformed from a mischievous pastime into a weapon of historical science. With Cesnola's opportunities, an archaeological genius had the chance to anticipate modern work by a generation; it was a pity — but no fault of Cesnola — that the United States Consul in Cyprus was not an archaeological genius. (1914: xv)

Cesnola was not satisfied to leave his collection in Cyprus. He used his American and Russian consular positions to move most of the objects from Cyprus onto the international art market. Efforts to sell the collection in England failed and in the end the bulk of the material came to the United States.[47] Here again Cesnola's efforts were not without controversy as he was accused of excessive restorations and the recombination of totally different pieces. Press controversy and legal action swirled around the collection.

The artifacts acquired by Cesnola formed an odd first stage for the history of American classical collecting. Growing interest in the cultural interactions between Greece and the Near East would later make Cyprus a fashionable area for American archaeological research, and there is

43. *EHCA* s.v. "Cesnola, Luigi Palma di (1832–1904)"; McFadden 1971: 27–77.
44. Cesnola 1878.
45. Goring 1988: 13.
46. Cesnola 1991, reissued with a preface by Stuart Swiney.
47. Adelson 1958: 85–87; Loring 1988: 11–13.

Figure 7. Louis Palma di Cesnola, one of the most colorful and controversial figures to grace the American archaeological scene. Courtesy of
the Metropolitan Museum of Art.

now an American archaeological research center in Cyprus.[48] That was not the case during the Cesnola era. The scholarly community reacted with ambivalence to the often strange-looking Cypriote objects, which seemed to blend the art styles of the Greek and Near Eastern worlds. Such bastard pieces could not rival Athenian vases and Greek statues and did not represent the pure Greek culture that interested later nineteenth-century archaeologists; they still arouse negative reactions in more Western art-oriented connoisseurs.[49]

In the end, the newly founded Metropolitan Museum acquired the bulk of the Cesnola collection of Cypriote antiquities.[50] A few items formed the nucleus of the Boston MFA classical collection.[51] These Cypriote pieces represented the first and indeed only major collection of non-Egyptian or Near Eastern ancient Mediterranean material from a single area ever to come to a U.S. museum. They were also along with the Pergamon sculptures exported to Berlin, the last example of classical looting in the Elgin-Newton tradition. After the Cesnola acquisitions, classical art collecting in America and art collecting in general moved toward the more piecemeal, furtive acquisition of individual pieces that would characterize museum practices down to the present day.

The Cesnola collection itself aroused other major controversies after it arrived in the United States. A French art dealer, Gaston Feuardent (1843–1893), argued in public that Cesnola had falsified information on where objects had been found, and that some of the statues were pastiches. Feuardent had good art historical credentials had done his homework, and had impressive support in both the United States and Europe. The learned art critic and journalist W. J. Stillman backed Feuardent, and Charles Newton of the British Museum testified to his credentials. Cesnola, supported by the power elite at the Metropolitan Museum, counterattacked fiercely. Feuardent felt sufficiently aggrieved to sue Cesnola for libel. The jury produced an ambivalent decision that Cesnola and the Metropolitan interpreted as a victory.[52]

Cesnola returned to the United States with the collection and became a major shaper of the fledgling Metropolitan Museum of Art. He first served as a board member, then as secretary, and finally as director from 1879 until his death on 21 November, 1904. His was an autocratic regime with unseemly fights over such issues as whether to open the museum on Sundays, making it more accessible to ordinary New Yorkers, but lower-

48. Davis 1989.
49. Hoving 1997: 209–10.
50. Myres 1914: xviii–xx; Tomkins 1970: 55–68.
51. Whitehill 1970: 19–20.
52. Tomkins 1970: 62–68.

ing the tone of the place.[53] Cesnola was equally highhanded in his collections development policy. Without consulting staff, he acquired the Roman wall paintings from Boscoreale near Pompeii and the Etruscan chariot from the Monteleone tomb in Italy at auction in Paris.[54] Still, his vigorous personality gave the Metropolitan a dynamic early life. Cesnola's spirit certainly smiled down benignly on such later successors as Thomas Hoving.

Edward Robinson (1858–1931) was a very different and historically more important figure in this fledgling museum world (Figure 8). In her memoirs, Edith Wharton described him thus:

Edward Robinson, tall, spare and pale, with his blond hair cut short "en brosse," bore the physical imprint of his German University formation, and might almost have sat for a portrait of a Teutonic *Gelehrter* but for the quiet twinkle perceptible behind his eyeglasses. (1934: 156)

Robinson was educated at Harvard, where he learned the gospel of the aesthetes from Charles Eliot Norton, and then spent five years studying in Europe.[55] German education impressed him both physically and intellectually. He had seen the role archaeology played in German university life, as well as the role museum collections played in public life.[56] Robinson was one of the emerging classical archaeologists, who excavated at Assos in 1881.[57] He began his museum career as assistant curator in the Classical Collection of the Museum of Fine Arts in 1885.[58] In 1902 he succeeded the founding president, General Charles Loring, as head of the MFA. Disputes over policy issues, including the fate of the cast collection, gradually alienated him from the ruling elite.[59] In 1905 Robinson moved to the Metropolitan Museum in New York to head the classical department. He brought the acquisitions connections of the Englishman John Marshall with him. Robinson became director of the Metropolitan in 1910 but remained curator of the classical collection until 1925.[60] His combined qualities as an art scholar and educator were summed up in one obituary:

Always he stood consistently for a high standard of taste and performance, while giving sympathetic aid to popular education in art. (*NCAB* 23: 9)

53. E. McFadden 1971: 235–36.
54. Von Bothmer 1991.
55. Dimaggio 1982b: 305–7.
56. Hoffman 1994.
57. Congdon 1974: 84.
58. Whitehill 1970: 146–47.
59. Whitehill 1970: 172–217.
60. *Bulletin of the Metropolitan Museum of Art* 26 (1931): 111–12; Tomkins 1970: 103–15.

Figure 8. Edward Robinson, a leading figure in the early development of both the Boston Museum of Fine Arts and the Metropolitan
Museum of Art. Courtesy of the Metropolitan Museum of Art.

The MFA and the Metropolitan were the first two major art museums
in the United States, but they were leaders in a much wider museum
movement that spread not only along the east coast, but into the Midwest.
In 1885 the *AJA* reported a series of substantial donations to the Cincinnati Art Museum to provide for the museum, its building, and an associated art school. Museum culture in Cincinnati went back to 1820, when

the city had become a major steamboat port and was aiming to become the Athens of the Midwest. By 1822 some Greek and Roman antiquities had made their way there.[61] In 1879 the American art museum officially crossed the Mississippi with the creation of Washington University art gallery that would grow into the St. Louis Museum of Art.[62] Although the importance of classical art to the Western cultural tradition was emphasized in museums like the Chicago Institute of Fine Arts, which placed the cast of the Winged Victory of Samothrace at the entrance, no midwestern museum would soon equal the classical collections of the Met and the MFA.[63]

The Museum of Fine Arts, the Metropolitan Museum, and the other emerging museums in the United States faced major problems in developing classical collections, concerns that continue to haunt and shape museum policy toward the acquisition of Greek and Roman art down to the present day. The great days of collecting through approved excavations in Greece and Italy were over. The Ottoman Empire offered better possibilities for obtaining antiquities, as Cesnola had demonstrated. The MFA sponsors of Assos had hoped to use those excavations to build their collection. However, the United States did not yet have the scholarly prestige and diplomatic muscle that allowed the Germans in particular to built collections by massive exports from Ottoman territory.[64] Moreover, even the Ottomans were tightening their antiquities regulations, as the Assos excavators were annoyed to discover.

The Museum of Fine Arts inherited some ancient material from the old Athenaeum collection. It purchased a relatively small group of objects from the Cesnola collection.[65] A few antiquities came into the museum through the excavations at Assos. Various Bostonians like Thomas Appleby lent their personal collections of Greek vases and other works of ancient art to the fledgling institution.[66] Still, until E. P. Warren arrived on the scene, the MFA had a rather paltry assemblage of Greek and Roman originals.

European options were available to the ambitious American museum offical. Some antiquities were acquired from Americans who had settled in Florence and Rome.[67] Others came directly from European collections, as noble families, especially in Italy, needed cash and sold off parts or all their art treasures. This process accelerated in the aftermath of the

61. Tucker 1967.
62. Sox 1987: 73.
63. Duncan 1995: 49–53, 61.
64. Kuklick 1996: 118.
65. Whitehill 1970: 20.
66. Whitehill 1970: 33–34.
67. Von Bothmer 1991.

world wars and the Russian Revolution. These recirculated ancient art-works were supplemented by material from new clandestine excavations, especially from Rome and its environs. The city's expansion after Italian unification and the construction of both public and private buildings on the grounds of the great noble villas on its outskirts yielded numerous finds, many of which made their way onto the art market. The production of fakes, an industry with a long history in Europe, continued to flourish in Italy.

In this era the museums also found themselves competing increasingly with private collectors. It is significant that in the 1880s the Parisian art dealer Feuardent, who specialized in ancient art, thought it worthwhile to establish a branch office in New York.[68] Both museums and private collectors were served by a new breed of professional art agents who lived in Europe and kept their eye on the art market in the interest of various clients. Such transactions were certainly not limited to ancient art, for this was the era when megapatrons like Isabella Stewart Gardner were building their Renaissance art collections.[69] This growing art market attracted entrepreneurial scholars like Richard Norton and Bernard Berenson.

For Boston and the MFA the most important antiquities agent was Edward Perry Warren (1860–1928). Warren was the son of a wealthy New England paper manufacturer and had studied at Harvard and Oxford.[70] His brother Samuel, who continued to manage the family business, was one of the most prominent supporters of the MFA in its early years. Sam Perry was a quintessential culturally oriented Boston businessman of the later nineteenth century.[71] He served as its president until he was replaced by the Board in Trustees in 1908, an event which contributed to his suicide in 1910.

Ned Warren, as Edward was generally known to his friends and associates, was very different from his brother. Whereas Sam had the beefy appearance of a late nineteenth-century American industrialist, Ned Warren had the smooth, handsome features of an aesthete. Sam was a vintage Victorian family man; Ned was gay. Ned wrote poems to a fellow student, comparing him with Hadrian's youthful lover Antinous and welcomed Oscar Wilde's visit to Boston.[72] The Warrens' mother had been a collector of the French paintings and Chinese pottery popular in Boston before the Civil War, and their Boston house had its breakfast room decorated in imitation of Pompeian painting.[73] Ned had been strongly

68. Adelson 1958: 85–86.
69. Hadley 1987.
70. Burdett and Goddard 1941; Green 1989.
71. Whitehill 1970: 173–217; Green 1989: 196–212.
72. Burdett and Goddard 1941: 18, 44; Whitehill 1970: 142–71.
73. Burdett and Goddard 1941: 3.

influenced by the aesthetic-oriented education promoted by Charles Eliot Norton at Harvard.[74] He read Shelley and Swinburne. At Harvard he also befriended the young Bernard Berenson. Warren, who enjoyed access to substantial independent means, through timely grants played a key role in advancing Berenson's career.[75]

Ned Warren became a great enthusiast of the English genteel culture of the era and spent much of his life near Oxford. He attended the university at a time when Romantic phil-Hellenism blended in complex ways with an aesthetic and gay culture.[76] He purchased a house at Lewes in Sussex, which became the focus of an aesthete, homosexual community.[77] There he was assisted in his art acquisition enterprises by a series of handsome young secretaries and restorers, and especially by John Marshall, who later became the chief European purchasing agent for the Metropolitan Museum.

In his aestheticism Warren was closer to William Morris than to Oscar Wilde. He identified with the more vigorous Greek culture of the Homeric-Pindaric period rather than with the Periclean epoch beloved by Norton or the decadent world of later fifth-century Athens that appealed to Wilde.[78] Life at Lewes House revolved around horseback riding and swimming, as well as the caring and feeding of the antiquities business.[79]

Ned Warren played the major role in developing the MFA's classical collection. His efforts were aided by a $95,000 gift made by Mrs. Catherine P. Perkins to support the purchase of classical art; in 1900 Frank Bartlett contributed $100,000 to the same cause.[80] The English classical archaeologist John Beazley, whose career Warren was instrumental in advancing, noted that of the 134 ancient sculptures added to the MFA's collection before 1925, 108 were acquired through Warren.[81] Warren had first refusal of most good examples of ancient art on the European market and expected to receive 30 percent above original cost from the museum.[82] Charles Eliot Norton wrote in 1900 that "There is not and never has been in America or in Europe a man with such capacities, will and circumstances for collecting and the Museum must be entirely dependent upon him."[83]

---

74. Shand-Tucci 1995: 219–22.
75. Samuels 1979: 28, 48, 60–61, 78, 128, 166, 277; Green 1989: 72–76.
76. Burdett and Goddard 1941: 51–61; Dowling 1994.
77. Sox 1991.
78. Green 1989: 86–87.
79. Sox 1991: 38–49.
80. *Annual Report MFA* 1895: 18; Whitehill 1970: 84, 162–65.
81. Green 1989: 136.
82. Samuels 1979: 328.
83. Green 1989: 173.

At Lewes House Warren displayed his own sizable collection of ancient art and carried on his antiquities acquisition activities.[84] Like his friend and protégé Bernard Berenson, Warren developed a network of European, especially Italian dealers, who brought to his attention objects that might be of interest to the MFA or other individuals and institutions he represented. He and Marshall maintained an apartment in Rome to facilitate their business and both had a wide acquaintance with the dealers and collectors of that city and elsewhere in Europe.[85]

Ned Warren had more than one agenda in building the MFA collection. A biographer described it thus:

When asked whether he gave Greek antiquities to American museums for the sake of the hundredth person who might appreciate them or whether the ideas for which the antiquities stood were a fundamental challenge to American conceptions, he replied "For both, but especially for the latter." (Burdett and Goddard 1941: 132–33)

Warren also regarded his activities as a collector and purchasing agent, as propaganda for the gay lifestyle and its associated values. This was especially reflected in his acquisitions of nude Greek male sculptures. He described that work as a subversive activity, "my plea against that in Boston which contradicted my (pagan) love."[86] At that time Warren's literary efforts were focused on a never completed study of Uranian love, a fashionable effort of the era to blend Plato and homosexuality.[87] Not accidentally he donated his collection of obscene art as well as his vases and gems to a somewhat embarassed MFA.[88]

Warren pioneered in developing the American collectors' appreciation of both Greek vases and ancient gems.[89] The German archaeologist and antiquities operative Wolfgang Helbig (1839–1915) started Warren on collecting Greek pottery while he was in Rome.[90] He saw ancient vases and gems as the most practical way for American museums to obtain representative collections in important areas of ancient art.[91] Warren's insight, at least in the area of vases, has proven correct, for that field of ancient art has dominated American museum-based classical archaeology.

In stimulating American interest in vase collecting, Warren also helped

84. Beazley 1941: 331–56.
85. Ashmole 1994: 42–43; Pollock 1994: 232–33.
86. Whitehill 1970: 142.
87. Green 1989: 87–89, 226–30; Dowling 1994: 114–16, 134–37.
88. *EHCA* s.v. "Museum of Fine Arts, Boston."
89. Green 1989: 125.
90. Burdett and Goddard 1941: 117–18. On Helbig cf. *EHCA* s.v. "Helbig, Wolfgang (1839–1915)"; Hoving 1997: 257–78.
91. Burdett & Goddard 1941: 151–52.

advance the career of the greatest twentieth-century scholar of Greek vase painting, the Englishman John Beazley (1885–1970).[92] Beazley is known to the current generation of scholars as the learned, detail-dominated student of Greek vase attribution.[93] However, his youthful persona related very much to the *fin de siècle* aesthetes of Oxford and Lewes House. It was young Beazley who translated the poems of A. E. Housman into Latin elegaics.[94] At Lewes House Beazley found his life's work as an intellectual organizer of Greek art, especially Greek vases.[95] Warren arranged for Beazley to do some of his first catalogs of American collections and helped him spread the gospel of the Morellian method of detailed stylistic analysis Beazley had applied to Greek pottery. Beazley dedicated his *Attic Red-Figured Vases in America* to Warren and Marshall, and in 1920 published the Lewes House collection of ancient gems.[96]

Sam Warren, Ned Warren, and Edward Robinson were at the center of much Bostonian acrimony and controversy during the last years of the nineteenth century. The Warrens fought over the distribution of the family fortune.[97] They also fought over the relative degree to which the MFA's limited resources should be spent on the new museum building that was rising on the Fenway, as opposed to expanding the classical collection at a time when Ned Warren knew that an immense amount of quality material was available on the European art market.[98] All were embroiled in a heated debate over the future of the MFA's cast collection. This last saga provides interesting insight into the changing world of American classical collecting.

Even with the efforts of agents like Warren and Marshall, the ancient holdings of the two major American museums remained a mixed bag of good and mediocre objects, with a fair number of fakes, before World War I. Moreover, only a scattering of ancient art was to be found in smaller institutions. If American museums were to achieve their self-proclaimed goals of educating the public in the arts and improving taste in general, they had to rely on other materials and approaches to bring classical art to their audiences. The most important of these alternatives was the cast. The Germans had led the way in demonstrating that representative casts of great works of sculpture and architecture could substitute for originals. By the late nineteenth century the cast business had become both institutionalized and commercialized. Through an active

92. Sox 1991: 96–98.
93. *EHCA* s.v. "Beazley, Sir John Davidson (1885–1970)"; Robertson 1985.
94. Ashmole 1985: 58–60; Green 1989: 184–85.
95. Green 1989: 184–85.
96. Beazley 1918; 1920.
97. Green 1989: 159–98.
98. Green 1989: 167–77.

network of purchase and exchange, a museum could acquire casts of most great works of Greek and Roman sculpture.[99]

Both the Boston and New York museums went vigorously into cast acquisition. The MFA had inherited a collection of casts from the Boston Athenaeum. This was soon supplemented by new purchases. By 1890 casts filled the first floor of the old Copley Square Museum, and Boston could boast that its cast collection was more than double that of the South Kensington Museum and surpassed only by those in two German museums.[100] One of the early controversies at the museum related to the provision of fig leaves for these plaster reproductions.[101]

The Met was equally active in expanding its cast holdings. The Met did have the Cesnola collection of antique originals, but as noted above, the Cypriote objects were not regarded as representing the best of classical art. Casts of great Greek and Roman works were needed to fill that void, and the Met moved quickly to acquire a representative collection. The 1888–89 guide to the museum shows that the cast collection was exhibited just beyond the main entrance. In 1891 a special committee was appointed to develop a cast acquisition program for the Met. By 1908 a cast catalog listed 2,607 objects.[102] More than 900 were classical. One of the first two curatorial positions created at the Met was curator of casts.

Such collections did not have to be limited to the great museums. In fact, the flexibility of the cast allowed it to become the major instrument in promoting taste and higher aesthetic values. As has already been mentioned, early college museums like those at Cornell, Missouri, and Illinois moved heavily into casts. By 1876 the University of Illinois had two hundred fifty casts.[103] Small urban museums, such as the modest Slater Museum attached to the Norwich Free Academy in Connecticut, did the same thing. There the collections of casts and other art objects and artifacts are still displayed in a late nineteenth-century setting.

The Slater Museum's background reveals much about the importance of cast collections in the later nineteenth century and their central role in public education. The museum was attached to an elite public secondary school in an industrial area of New England; its group of casts was acquired in consultation with Edward Robinson of the Museum of Fine Arts. The opening ceremony held on 22 November 1888 drew not only Robinson but also Charles Eliot Norton and Daniel Gilman, the first president of Johns Hopkins University and one of the day's leading educators. Gilman gave the keynote speech, entitled "Greek Art in a Man-

99. Whitehill 1970: 45–46; Marchand 1996: 67–68.
100. Whitehill 1970: 75–76.
101. Whitehill 1970: 31, 45–46.
102. E. Robinson 1908; Noble 1959–60.
103. Browne 1917: 268–69; Burt 1977: 166.

ufacturing Town in New England." In it he laid out what he saw as the ideological bases for the study of classical art in America.[104] These ranged from the Ruskinian idealist's promotion of refined taste to the practical argument that America needed to produce goods of higher aesthetic quality to compete in an increasingly demanding international business environment. Winckelmann, Lessing, Ruskin, and Pater were evoked by President Gilman. So was Colbert, the seventeenth-century French minister whose policy of promoting culture to stimulate economic development was presented as a model for blending artistic and economic development in the United States.

Although limited representative cast collections could play a very important role in small museums, massive accumulations like those of the Met and the MFA raised curatorial and space problems. Moreover, as the opportunity for acquiring original works increased, the debate over devoting large areas of floor space to often crumbling plaster reproductions became more heated. The conflict between those who favored a major role for casts in major American museums and those who only wanted genuine objects on display came to a head in Boston, as plans were being made for the new MFA building on the Fenway.[105]

In 1901 Sam Warren was elected president of the Boston museum, and in 1902 Edward Robinson was made director. Robinson had done much to develop the antiquities collection, but he also favored a continuing major role for casts in American public museums. His arguments focused on the educational importance of comprehensive cast collections for a museum like the MFA.[106] His chief opponent on the issue was an Englishman named M. S. Prichard. Prichard was part of the Lewes House group and echoed Ned Warren's elitist aesthetic values.[107] In 1902 he was appointed secretary at the MFA. Prichard proved to be a great social success in Boston, winning the approval of the prominent art collector Isabella Stewart Gardner among others, and looked to have a very promising career at the MFA.[108] Prichard despised the cast collection and was indifferent to the public educational they served. He stated contemptuously that casts were "engines of education and should not be shown near objects of inspiration."[109] As a proper *fin de siècle* aesthete he talked about inspiration, not education as the museum's primary goal. That required original works of ancient art, not copies.

The complex battle in Boston over the casts' future was acrimonious

104. Gilman 1906: 318–25.
105. Whitehill 1970: 172–217.
106. Dimaggio 1982b: 306–8; L. Levine 1988: 152–54.
107. Whitehill 1970: 176–89, 198–210; Sox 1991: 167–208.
108. Shand-Tucci 1995: 221–28.
109. Whitehill 1970: 202.

and produced no clear personal victors. Prichard saw less and less of a future for himself in Boston and decided to return to England. Robinson felt increasingly dissatisfied with his role as director and in 1905 resigned. Within a few weeks he started a new career at the Metropolitan Museum. In 1907 Samuel Warren was ousted as president of the museum. On 19 February 1910 he shot himself at his suburban Boston estate.[110]

In the long run the aesthetes gained the ideological victory and were able to promote attitudes that shaped American museums' classical collections for generations. The cult of the original object came to dominate museum ideology, and the inflow of new financial resources and the expansion of the art market made the acquisition of many such objects realizable. Benjamin Ives Gilman, who succeeded Robinson as director at the Boston Museum of Fine Arts, had a very different view of art appreciation and education from his predecessor. He stated bluntly that "in an exhibition of fine art, instruction becomes a means, the end being appreciation" and he advised his docents at the museum that "the essential office of the docent is to get the object thoroughly perceived by the disciple. Hence draw attention to the object first; talk about it afterwards, and only if the occasion offers."[111] The museum was changing from a place of general aesthetic education to a temple of the beautiful in which only those of already refined sensitivity would feel comfortable.[112] A cast gallery was planned for the MFA's new Huntington Avenue building, but it was never built. Gradually the casts were displaced from the exhibitions and even from the collections. A notice that the Boston Museum of Fine Arts had followed the Metropolitan's lead and dispersed its cast collection to schools and other groups better able to use them appeared in a 1933 issue of *Art and Archaeology*.

The same sequence of events took place at the Metropolitan Museum in New York. Edward Robinson had published a catalog of the Met cast collection as one of his first tasks in New York.[113] However, as the collection of original pieces of ancient art expanded, an attack was launched on the casts and the space they occupied. An effort was made in 1924 to remove them from exhibition, but public demands led to restoration of some of the casts.[114] In 1938 the casts began to be moved systematically

110. Whitehill 1970: 210–17; Green 1989: 196–212.

111. Dimaggio 1982b: 307. For the development of the docent program at the MFA, cf. Whitehill 1970: 293–301.

112. Benjamin Gilman used the expression "a museum of art is in essence a temple." L. Levine 1988: 155; Duncan 1995: 16–17.

113. E. Robinson 1908.

114. *Bulletin of the Metropolitan Museum of Art* 21 (1926): 278.

into storage. By that time the collection of real (or presumed real) objects dominated the activities of the Met's classical archaeologists.

The marginalization of the casts coincided with a period of spectacular growth in the Met's classical collection. The Met was involved in major antiquities purchases before Robinson and Marshall arrived on the scene. In 1903 General Cesnola obtained two major classical acquisitions for the museum. The first was the so-called Monteleone Etruscan tomb group, which included a finely decorated bronze Etruscan chariot, other Etruscan bronze vessels, and Attic black-figure vessels. The objects had been found in a tomb near Monteleone on the Via Cassia and passed through several hands before they were acquired by the Metropolitan.[115]

The other early purchase was a set of Roman frescoes identified as coming from a Roman villa excavated at Boscoreale near Pompeii. Other paintings apparently from the same villa made their way to the Field Museum of Chicago.[116] They had been found in 1900, removed from the site, and sold at auction in Paris in 1903.[117] The transactions related to their exportation from Italy were complicated, but apparently legal, for the dealer had in essence traded the frescoes for other objects desired by the Naples Museum. These first Met frescoes were joined in 1920 by a second set from another Roman villa at Boscotrecase near Pompeii. The villa had been found during the construction of a railroad in 1902 and excavated by the landowner between 1903 and 1905. The site was covered again by an eruption of Vesuvius in 1906. After long and complicated negotiations with the landowner and the Italian government, the bulk of the paintings were permitted to be exported to the Metropolitan Museum.[118]

These first examples of classical art had been random acquisitions, made largely outside Italy. Now the Met, using Marshall's services, began buying more directly in Italy. The Italian antiquities market of the late nineteenth and early twentieth centuries was a complicated, bizarre, and treacherous world.[119] Complex and often rigorous Italian laws forced much of the trade into gray areas. The material on the market came mostly from illegal excavations or the sale of family collections. Relatively few objects available had solid, visible pedigrees. The world of the dealer in legitimate objects shaded off into that of illicit objects, then into the world of the restorer, and then into that of the forger. Objects were doctored to make them appear less important than they were to customs

115. Richter 1915: 17–29, 177–180; 1940: 26–27.
116. DeCou 1912.
117. P. W. Lehmann 1953: 1–12.
118. M. Anderson 1987: 5; Von Blanckenhagen and Alexander 1990: 1, 4–5.
119. Pollak 1994.

officials.[120] "Respected" scholars like the German archaeologist Wolfgang Helbig apparently worked in close collaboration not only with dealers but also with forgers and customs smugglers.[121]

In 1917 the classical department of the Metropolitan Museum of Art spent $45,000 on ancient art. By 1926 this had risen to $185,000.[122] Edward Robinson's arrival as curator of the classical collection and his elevation to director in 1910 meant that John Marshall's activities as art purchasing agent now shifted from Boston to New York.[123] Marshall had been E. P. Warren's housemate (and lover) at Lewes. The two met at Oxford in 1884. According to one version of their early relationship, Warren had turned Marshall from a life of aesthete decadence toward a serious interest in classical studies and collecting.[124] However, Marshall's academic career at Oxford had been more disciplined and successful than Warren's, and Warren tended to admire, even envy, the type of academic success attained by Marshall and especially by John Beazley.[125] Warren and Marshall collaborated closely on the acquisition program at the MFA.[126] After the turn of the century, they drew apart. Warren's collection activities declined dramatically after 1902. Marshall's strong Met contacts made him the most important American museum agent on the European antiquities scene. He had a special base in Rome and until his death occupied an elegant apartment near the Spanish Steps, which became an important artistic and cultural gathering place.[127]

Marshall acquired many striking objects for the Met, although usually pieces without clear provenance. Even though he was regarded as having a good eye for fakes, he purchased some impressive forgeries for the Met.[128] Chief among these were the life-sized or larger terra-cotta statues of Etruscan warriors, which for decades occupied a place of pride in the museum's display collections.[129] The group consisted of two six-and-a-half-foot statues and a four-and-a-half-foot head. They were supposedly found at a site located between Orvieto and Bolsena, although efforts to identify the exact spot proved elusive. Marshall acquired the fragments of the Etruscan warriors over a several years and shipped them to the Met

120. Burdett and Goddard 1941: 170.

121. *EHCA* s.v. "Helbig, Wolfgang (1839–1915)"; Burdett and Goddard 1940: 170; Moltesen 1987; Hoving 1997: 258–78.

122. Tomkins 1970: 124.

123. Sox 1991: 107–32.

124. Green 1989: 96.

125. Sox 1991: 26, 97.

126. Burdett and Goddard 1940: 151–85.

127. Ashmole 1994: 42–43.

128. Sox 1991: 64–67.

129. Sox 1987: 97–111; 1991: 116–23; Hoving 1997: 90–100.

Figure 9. Gisela Richter, the most distinguished American museum curator of classical art of her generation, 1952. Courtesy of the Metropolitan Museum of Art.

between 1915 and 1921.[130] From the beginning, rumors circulated in Italy that the pieces were fakes. Marshall early developed his own reservations about them and advised delays in their exhibition and publication.[131] However, Gisela Richter (1882–1972), the distinguished scholar who from 1925 to 1948 served as curator of Greek and Roman art at the Metropolitan Museum and one of the world's leading classical art authorities gave her imprimatur to their authenticity (Figure 9).[132] In 1933 they were put on display and for decades were considered one of the jewels of the Met's classical collection. Yet concerns about their authenticity con-

130. Von Bothmer and Noble 1961: 7–8.
131. Von Bothmer and Noble 1961: 8.
132. Richter 1937.

tinued. Massimo Pallottino, the foremost Italian Etruscologist of the era, denounced them as fakes, but the Met officials and curators chose to follow what was regarded as the superior, positive judgment of German scholars about their authenticity.[133]

Not until 1961 did the Met and Miss Richter finally admit that the Etruscan warriors were indeed fakes. The final admission owed much to the persistent challenges to their authenticity made by a Rome-based art dealer named Harold Parsons, another veteran of the Lewes House set. Key documentation came from scientific tests, which proved that the glazes used in the statues were modern. In the end, it even proved possible to trace the forgery to a specific group of Italian terra-cotta workers.[134]

Ironically, it was the growing cult of the genuine ancient object that fueled this frenetic pursuit of the uncertain and the false in the murky world of the international art market. Belief in the ineffable beauty of Greek art had become a dominant theme in Anglo-Saxon art history. Richter herself articulated this ideology in the 1917 catalogue to the Met Classical Collection:

The chief value of Greek art . . . lies in its inherent beauty. The Greek were the most artistic people the world has known, and there is no better way for the training of eye and taste than to spend some time in their company. (Richter 1917: xv)

The company in this case was the genuine object. In this value scheme even battered fragments of ancient marble or Roman copies of Greek originals that had little or no known archaeological context and had been heavily restored in the Renaissance were preferred to the now often dirty and decrepit casts. Since Greek art was supposed to carry the essence of beauty within itself archaelogical context and historical background mattered little.

Richter's attitudes and values were very representative of those of museum archaeologists of the period.[135] Richter's father was the noted British-German art connoisseur Jean Paul Richter (1847–1937), who was a major intellectual propagandist for the scientific stylistic analysis of his close friend, the Italian art historian Giovanni Morelli.[136] Morelli's best-known disciple in the United States was Bernard Berenson; the senior Richter brought the two men together.[137] Gisela Richter grew up in the

133. Von Bothmer and Noble 1961: 11–12.
134. Tomkins 1970: 125–29; Green 1989: 218; Sox 1987: 97–113; 1991: 245–47.
135. *EHCA* s.v. "Richter, Gisela M. A. (1882–1972)"; Richter 1971; Edlund, McCann, and Sherman 1981.
136. *WWW* 3: 1143 s.v. "Richer, Jean Paul."
137. Richter 1972: 2, 72–73, 87, 90, 94–95.

cosmopolitan world of pre-World War I Europe. She traveled widely and at the age of fourteen attended the lectures of Professor Emanuel Loewry, the distinguished German archaeologist then teaching at the University of Rome.[138] She studied at Girton College, Cambridge, and in 1904–5 she was a student at the British School in Athens. There she established a lifelong friendship with Harriet Boyd Hawes and through her was introduced to Edward Robinson and the world of the Metropolitan Museum of Art. Robinson hired Gisela Richter in 1905 as part of his campaign to turn the Met into a more professional museum.

For nearly forty-seven years, Richter was centrally involved in creating the Met's impressive classical collections. In 1906, when she arrived there, the collection consisted mainly of the Cesnola purchases, a potpourri of individual acquisitions, and a limited number of choice objects like the Roman frescoes from Boscoreale and the Etruscan chariot from Monteleone.[139] The combined interests and talents of Edward Robinson, John Marshall, and Gisela Richter changed that. In her account of the development of the classical collection at the Met during these years Richter captured the feeling of excitement as new purchases arrived from Europe.[140] Her writings also expressed the rituals and often ethically ambiguous expectations of that world. A short article published by Richter in the January 1929 *Bulletin of the Metropolitan Museum of Art* provides insight into the world of art dealing between the wars.

The Met had recently been offered two life-size archaic Greek sculptures by a European dealer. They were sent to New York for close inspection and final decision on acquisition. The Met experts decided that they were fakes and had them shipped back to Europe. In the meantime, John Marshall had been conducting his own investigations in the demimonde of the antiquities business and had come to the conclusion that these items were forgeries by Alceo Dossena's atelier.[141] However, the statues continued to circulate on the antiquities market without the Met making public its strong suspicion about their authenticity. According to Richter, "Since they had been sponsored by prominent European archaeologists and were still for sale, we could not, according to professional etiquette, mention the reasons for declining them unless specifically asked to do so, which we were not."[142]

Other purchases, like the extremely well preserved archaic male figure now known as the New York kouros, provoked debate about their authen-

138. Richter 1972: 7.
139. Richter 1917; Edlund, McCann, and Sherman 1981: 284.
140. Richter 1970.
141. Sox 1991: 124–26.
142. Richter 1929: 4.

ticity. Richter was able to convince almost all of her scholarly colleagues that the New York kouros was genuine.[143] She was also able to easily dismiss any ethical doubts about what was very likely a piece illegally exported from Greece. A passage in her memoirs makes clear the attitudes of that era:

With regard to the second question [How was it exported from Greece or Italy] which was asked by some Greek archaeologists about the kouros, we could assure them that we had nothing whatever to do with its export, but had bought the statue from a Swiss dealer. And when I shortly afterwards went to Greece, I took the opportunity of telling this to my friends there, especially to Mr. Oikonomos, the director of the National Museum of Athens and to Mr. Kourooniotes, ephor of Eleusis. Each of them gave me the same answer: "And if you had not bought the statue some other museum would have." (1972: 26)

The reason Gisela Richter and the Met were so sensitive to the danger of acquiring fakes was the recent revelations about the Italian forger Alceo Dossena (1878–1937).[144] Dossena was active in forging not only antiquities, but also sculptures attributed to later periods. Several American museums had been tricked by the creations of this artful Italian. Richter was well aware of Dossena's activities. and in 1928 she visited his studio, where he talked about his methods. Richter noted that he was very proud of the fact that

he does not (like forgers of old) copy a known work of art with slight variations, but . . . he really creates in the manner of the antique. What differentiates him, however, from other clever modern imitators is that he has the courage to make large, monumental pieces for which high prices can be charged. (1929: 4)

Not surprisingly, much of Gisela Richter's long scholarly career was devoted to typological and stylistic analyses, designed to place floating pieces of art market sculpture in a more definite chronological and artistic context. Richter was concerned with stylistic analysis and the creation of evolutionary sequences, and about the attribution of works within those frameworks. She admitted that her highly regarded book on the Greek kouros grew out of her experience proving the authenticity of the New York example.[145] Her article on the Dossena fakes contained a defense of her approach to Greek archaeology, which combined connoisseurship with a strong belief in the cult of the genuine object and the inherent superiority of Greek art:

143. Richter 1970: 85–88; Edlund, McCann, and Sherman 1981: 288; Hoving 1997.
144. Sox 1987.
145. Richter 1942, 1960, 1970: 88.

About the beauty and intrinsic value of Dossena's imitations there will inevitably be differences of opinion. An editorial in the Times advised museum curators to apply the simple tests of "archaeology" as against the uncertain ones of "connoisseurship." But since a large number of leading archaeologists, backed by chemists and mineralogists, had pronounced the pieces genuine, the case is clearly not so simple. In the last analysis it must always be quality and style that serve as infallible guides. It is quality — and probably quality only — that cannot be successfully imitated by even a gifted modern forger. This is especially the case where Greek works of a good period are attempted. Therefore, the higher the aim of the forger, the more inevitable the final detection; for there is still a long step between a Greek archaic artist and a Dossena. (1929: 5)

Richter was also very much interested in the technical aspect of ancient art production. She took care to educate herself in the ways in which modern artists and artisans worked, and that was reflected in studies like her *Craft of Athenian Pottery*.[146] In spite of this interest in the working artisan, her many publications and the galleries that she organized at the Metropolitan showed relatively little interest in the socio-cultural background of the classical artifacts that she brought to New York. Contemplation of pure ancient beauty in an environment that recalled worship in a cathedral counted most.[147] Richter came out of the elite world of Europe and had little identity with the democratic, educative mission that had shaped the American museum movement in the nineteenth century.

The historical and social aspects of ancient art were mainly relegated to a corridor exhibition space that focused on the daily life of the Greeks and the Romans. Helen McClees of the museum staff prepared a full handbook, *The Daily Life of the Greeks and Romans as Illustrated in the Classical Collections* (1924), to accompany the exhibition. This new exhibition was introduced to the Met membership by a short article in the museum bulletin.[148] McClees opened both her article and her handbook with short statements in which several complementary and even contradictory themes were aired. She lamented that

at the time when interest in the classical literatures is slight and their honorable place in education has generally been allotted to other subjects, knowledge of the people who produced them, of their racial affinities, their appearance, their art, and their customs, is increasing almost day by day. (1924a: 18)

The objects of daily life were seen as providing a vivid sense of the past. However, such a historical-anthropological approach had to be controlled, for "imaginings of this kind can be carried so far so as to obscure

146. Richter 1923.
147. Richter 1917: xv.
148. McClees 1924a.

the real reason for studying ancient art—its beauty." In the catalog's preface what was stressed was the use these ordinary objects had for understanding ancient texts.[149] They were also expressions of honest ancient craftsmanship, which had a lesson for the present day. Nevertheless, all this was marginal to the main purpose of the Metropolitan classical galleries.

Not everyone was pleased with the direction being taken by classical exhibitions in major museums. In 1913 Oliver Tonks published a trenchant essay in which he stated his case for a more education oriented museum archaeology:

The time has passed when we felt that we had employed to the best purpose an object of archaeological or artistic interest the moment we derived from it an aesthetic titillation or a momentary wonderment at the unusual character of the object seen. (1913: 97)

Tonks still believed in the old South Kensington mission of using past art to improve current artisan production. Rather than allowing archaeology to serve as a handmaiden to philological activity, he asserted that archaeological objects must be used to counter the inherent dullness of much philological pedagogy, "Homer by the Yard" as he described it. Archaeology should make students realize that "We have, in fact, in the monuments a more intense record of ancient life than can be found in the literature alone"[150] and "it is by the employment of these monuments that you are going to be able to illuminate your literature and your history and make them live."[151] Tonks did not represent attitudes that were going to shape the future of American museum archaeology. Ironically what triumphed in the classical galleries of the Met and elsewhere was not the original educational vision of Tonks or of the young Boston curator Edward Robinson, but the aesthete obsessions of Robinson's hated rival Matt Prichard. As a recent critic of classical archaeological display observed, the objects "are presented entirely out of their historical and cultural context, with only the dreaded yellowed label to assist the uninformed visitor. The objects, shrouded in quasi-religious mystery, seem to peer down on the visitors and say, 'You will never understand us unless you have a Ph.D.; we belong to the domain of scholars, not real people.' "[152]

It should also be remembered that during these years the classical sections of both the Met and the MFA were overshadowed by the activities of their Egyptian departments. Not only were excavations easier and

149. McClees 1924: xv–xvi.
150. Tonks 1913: 100–10.
151. Tonks 1913: 137–38.
152. Cole 1997. On this subject, see also the observations of Duncan 1995: 48–71.

cheaper to conduct in Egypt than in Greece or Italy, but it was possible to bring back large numbers of fine objects to grace museum collections. This was the heroic era of George Reisner's excavations at Gizah for the MFA,[153] and Herbert Winlock's at Deir al-Bahri for the Met.[154] It is hardly surprising that the classical collections, whose expansion was only possible on limited and dubious terms, fell to second-class status as numerous packing cases full of Egyptian sculpture began to arrive from Cairo.

Nevertheless, the holdings of classical art in American increased enormously during those decades. George Chase of Harvard delivered a set of lectures at the Lowell Institute of Boston which were later published as *Greek and Roman Sculpture in American Collections* (1924). He honestly admitted his initial fears and subsequent satisfaction as he undertook the task:

The subject of these lectures "Greek and Roman Sculpture in American Collections" may seem, at first sight, to invite comparison with the familiar topic of "Snakes in Ireland" or to suggest the theme once proposed in jest for an address to the American School in Athens "The Influence of the Discovery of America on the Development of Greek Art"; and I must confess that after I proposed it, I had moments of wonder, whether I had not been rash. I was not, however, quite prepared for what I actually found when I began a more careful study of the matter, namely, that there is so much material available that I shall be obliged to omit some less important examples, if I am am going to treat the more important monuments with any fullness. (1924: 3)

As a good Bostonian, Chase concentrated almost totally on the MFA and the Met collections, with most other examples drawn from New England museums. Such an exclusive focus on New England and New York was at that moment largely justified, although the foundations of other collections were being laid in different parts of the United States. In Baltimore, the railroad magnate Henry Walters (1848–1931) was creating a comprehensive private art collection that included several thousand works of ancient art. These now form one of the best collections in the gallery that bears his name. The centerpiece was the Massarenti collection, formerly housed in the Accoramboni Palace in Rome, which Walters acquired in 1902.[155] Cleveland, Toledo, St. Louis, Kansas City, and other city museums across the country acquired classical art as part of their comprehensive collections.[156] The ideological bases for the creation of those collections and the methods used to build them were not very different from those employed at the Met and the MFA. Education yielded to

153. Whitehill 1970: 248–76.
154. Tomkins 1970: 135–48.
155. *EHCA* s.v. "Walters, Henry (1848–1931)"; Hill 1949, 1974.
156. Vermeule 1981.

aesthetics, the casts to a small number of supposedly genuine pieces, with the odd fake making it past the curator's eyes.[157]

By 1940 the classical collections of most American museums were exquisite expressions of elite values. The emphasis was on the tasteful display of the genuine, or what the experts judged to be genuine. The casts were largely gone. Most of the museum's educational mission had been relegated to the education department. The associated art schools, which had often been founded at the same time as the museums and had a closely associated mission, assumed more of a secondary role in the life of the museum or disappeared altogether.

Both change and continuity characterized the development of American classical museums after World War II. They became even more isolated from the world of field archaeology. In Egypt and the Near East, new national governments ended the former colonial policy of allowing selected objects excavated by foreign archaeological projects to be exported. This did not mean that the availability of antiquities diminished. Rather, the reverse occurred. The parlous economic situation of many noble families in postwar Germany, France, and England meant that classical collections continued to be broken up and put on the international art market. Land reform, urban expansion, and general economic development in the Mediterranean produced major disruptions in the landscape, resulting in a marked increase in random archaeological finds. The demands of public and private collectors provided major incentives for clandestine excavations. Americans became extremely prosperous after World War II, and the cultural elite showed great willingness to spend money on their private collections and on those of the museums they patronized.

The two major classical curatorial figures who emerged during this period, Dietrich von Bothmer of the Metropolitan Museum of Art and Cornelius Vermeule of the Boston Museum of Fine Arts, mirrored the attitudes of the era. Von Bothmer, born in Germany in 1918, started his university education at Berlin. He was a German Rhodes scholar to Oxford, where he studied under John Beazley, and discovered his lifelong vocation in the study of Greek vases. His family fled to the United States at the outbreak of the war, and von Bothmer served with distinction in the American army.[158]

After his discharge from the military, von Bothmer went to Berkeley to work on his Ph.D. under H. R. W. Smith. Smith had completed his under-

157. Sox 1987: 73–78. For the problem of forgeries and American museums, cf. Cohon 1996.
158. Von Bothmer 1985; Hoving 1993: 69–70.

graduate studies at Oxford and had fallen totally under the spell of Beazley. Dietrich von Bothmer described Smith's reaction to Beazley:

To be accepted by Beazley, not to disappoint him and to maintain the standards, sometimes only divine, became the guiding principles of Smith's life and work. (1985: 7).

By the time von Bothmer arrived, Smith, with a string of pottery publications including that of the Hearst collection of vases in the *Corpus Vasorum Antiquorum*, was establishing Berkeley as the major Beazley beachhead in North America.[159]

Upon the completing his doctorate, von Bothmer went to the Metropolitan Museum, where in 1959 he succeeded Christine Alexander as the chief curator of the classical collection.[160] Unlike Richter, whose wide-ranging interests in the field of classical art were reflected in the broad-based collection she did so much to build, von Bothmer was almost totally concerned with expanding the Metropolitan's Greek vase collection.[161] As a devoted disciple of John Beazley, he took over at the Met when the venerable vase scholar's influence was at its height in America. Several factors contributed to the Beazley phenomenon. German universities and cultural institutions were in shambles as a result of the war; many aspects of German scholarship had been discredited. Americans turned increasingly to English classics, but in the area of classical archaeology, Britain had relatively little to contribute to America's flourishing archaeological culture. The Beazley school of Greek vase painting analysis represented the exception, since it blended inductive research and an appreciation for artistic individualism that appealed to the values of American academics.

The inductive appeal grew out of the fact that Beazley was the ultimate gatherer and classifier of obscure data. He recorded in his files and carried in his head details on thousands of Greek vases. He used this to reconstruct the artistic personalities of hundreds of vase painters and trace their interconnections. His approach appealed very much to a generation of American classical archaeologists who strongly believed that truth is revealed through the systematic accumulation and ordering of factual information.

The best expression of this value system in the field of Greek vase studies is the *Corpus Vasorum Antiquorum* (*CVA*), an international project devoted to the systematic collection of all the ancient (mainly Greek and

159. Smith 1936.
160. Hess 1974: 141–42.
161. Hoving 1993: 69.

Roman) vases in the world. *CVA*-related research flourished in the United States both before and after World War II. The first volume in the American series drew together two pioneers in American vase studies, Joseph Hoppin and Albert Gallatin, each cataloging his own collection.[162] It was followed by fascicles of the vases in the Rhode Island School of Design Museum,[163] the University of Michigan,[164] the David Robinson collection in Baltimore,[165] and the Hearst collection in California[166] in the years before the outbreak of World War II.

The individualizing aspect of Beazley's research was represented by his technique of creating profiles of artistic personalities from the attributes found on vases he had grouped under a single hand. Euphronios and the Berlin painter became artists with the status of Botticelli or Degas. Greek vases were to be regarded as artworks created by artists and not as craft pieces produced by ignorant artisans.[167] Archaeologists in other areas of ceramic studies adopted this approach, hypothesizing Mycenaean and even Cycladic artistic personalities.[168] This suited an era when artistic individualism became rampant and class divisions had increased between artists and their rich patrons who collected art and the craftsmen increasingly marginalized by an industrial society.

Von Bothmer's curatorship at the Met was highlighted by two events. The first was his revelation in 1961 that the Etruscan terra-cotta warriors were as fakes.[169] The second, the purchase of the million-dollar Euphronios vase, is considered in detail in chapter 6. Von Bothmer served as classical curator during one of the most dynamic periods in the Met's history. Although his focus on Greek pots could, as occurred with the Euphronios vase, bring significant publicity to classics, the narrowness of his vision prevented the classical department from playing a significant role in the museum's development during a high-stakes era.

In 1957 a young Cornelius Vermeule III (1925–) was made curator of the classical collection at the Boston Museum of Fine Arts. He took over a department that had seen dynamic growth during the era of Robinson and Warren but had, like much of the museum during the first half of this century, declined into a sleepy Bostonian gentility.[170] As Walter Muir Whitehill put it,

162. Hoppin and Gallatin 1926.
163. Luce 1933.
164. Van Ingen 1939.
165. Robinson 1934–38.
166. Smith 1936.
167. M. Robertson 1985; Vickers 1987.
168. Getz-Preziosi 1987: 57–70; Cherry 1992; Gill and Chippindale 1993.
169. Von Bothmer 1961; Sox 1987: 97–113.
170. Burt 1977: 307–8.

In Boston and Cambridge in the nineteen twenties classical studies were shrouded in a dignified but melancholy twilight. With the abrogation of compulsory requirements for the study of ancient languages in schools and colleges, most classical scholars, feeling that the world no longer appreciated what they had to offer, became increasingly withdrawn. (1970: 650)

The principal curators of the previous era, Lacey Davis Caskey (1880–1944) and Arthur Fairbanks (1864–1944), were respectable archaeological scholars. Caskey, a Yale Ph.D., was made assistant curator in 1908 and remained with the department until his death. He did pioneering research on the use of proportions in Greek vases.[171] Fairbanks, who had completed his doctorate in Germany, came to the MFA in 1907 as director and classical curator. He served as director until 1925.[172] Caskey and Fairbanks both specialized in Greek pottery and Fairbanks did an early study of Athenian white ground lekythoi.[173] Fairbanks had considerable intellectual range, producing an early work on sociology and a number of popular books on classical civilization, including his 1933 *Greek Art: The Basis of Later European Art*.[174]

After the massive acquisition program of the Warren era, when $676,904 from a total acquisitions budget of $1,202,894 was spent on classical art and more than four thousand objects were acquired, the opportunity to acquire new objects was limited.[175] E. P. Warren was no longer closely associated with the museum and John Marshall had gone to New York. Gradually the MFA fell behind the more opulent and active Metropolitan Museum in the acquisitions game that flourished between the wars. Curatorial activity declined. With Caskey's death in 1944, the department survived for a number of years on the acting curatorial services of George Chase. When Chase died in 1952, low-level curators maintained the department until Vermeule was appointed.

Vermeule proved to be a curator similar to Gisela Richter, a museum administrator who looked back to the golden age of E. P. Warren for his model.[176] Educated at Harvard and the University of London, Vermeule represented another example of the replacement of Germany by England as a center for the advanced education of American classical archaeologists. He brought both curatorial dynamism and distinguished scholarship to the MFA. His publication record is probably the best of any museum archaeologist of his generation.[177]

171. L. B. Holland 1944; Whitehill 1970: 374–75.
172. G. H. Chase 1944; Whitehill 1970: 399.
173. Fairbanks 1907.
174. Fairbanks 1910, 1933.
175. *Annual Reports MFA* 1895–1904; Chase 1950: 1.
176. *Annual Report MFA* 1957: 27–30; 1958: 29–34; Whitehill 1970: 649–78.
177. Major publications include C. Vermeule 1964, 1968, 1981, 1987.

Vermeule's purchasing policy revived the traditions of Warren, Marshall, and Robinson at the MFA. His interests in classical art were much broader than von Bothmer's had been. However, he worked with more limited resources than the Met. Vermeule's main interest was in adding impressive new pieces to the museum's classical collection, and he showed little concern about the ultimate sources of the objects he purchased on the international art market. The MFA did not share the growing international concern about clandestine excavations and the destruction of sites. Vermeule dismissed the efforts of museums like that at the University of Pennsylvania to abstain from purchasing artifacts of uncertain origins.[178] This attitude led increasingly to controversy and criticism. In 1968 the MFA purchased a large hoard of Aegean Bronze Age gold jewelry, which it acknowledged was probably made from gold of Turkish origin. The 1972 issue of the *Boston Museum Bulletin* displayed a picture of an attractive young woman wearing the jewelry and little else.[179] The MFA was initially coy about the identifying the source of the jewelry; however, the Turkish government claimed that the material had been illegally exported from their country.[180]

Even in the aftermath of the Turkish gold controversy, Vermeule and the MFA displayed relatively little sensitivity to the growing concern about archaeological looting and the trade in illegal antiquities. In 1988 Vermeule published a catalog that described stone and bronze sculptures that had been added to the MFA collection since 1971.[181] The catalog contained 132 entries. Only about twenty of these had a clear provenance from an identified private collection, whose origins went back before the rise of concern about illegally exported and imported ancient art. Vermeule himself had joked about manufacturing a fictional Polish family to provide a seemingly more legitimate source for objects acquired in the more general antiquities market.[182] The MFA continued to cultivate collectors and play the international art market with attitudes little changed from the days of the robber barons.[183]

When Gisela Richter died in Rome in 1972, the attitudes and approaches of the American classical museum world had changed little from the most active days of her curatorship between the world wars. The early battle over casts had been key in determining the course of museum archaeology. For the winners it had meant the triumph of pure and genuine beauty over imitations and second-rate works. Although the days

178. Meyer 1973: 76, 90–91.
179. W. Young 1972; Burt 1977: 405–6.
180. Meyer 1973: 61–64.
181. Vermeule and Comstock 1988.
182. Meyer 1973: 76, 90–91.
183. Brandt 1990.

of acquisition through formal research excavations were over for classical archaeologists, the massive increase in clandestine archaeological looting provided unparalleled opportunities for the acquisition of ancient art objects. While the prices of these works on the international market were rising, American patrons had the money and the willingness to spend it on developing ancient art holdings. Museum curators could look forward to a golden age of collecting.

For the losers in the cast battle, the popular educational mission that had been one of the justifications for the creation of classical archaeology collections in American art museums had ended. The affluent cultural elite of New York, Boston, and Malibu, who admired the latest museum purchases at chic cocktail parties and wandered through galleries whose layout and labeling assumed certain educational levels, were far from those who created American museums in the spirit of South Kensington and saw public education and the improvement of honest workers' tastes as principal aims of the American museum movement.

5. The Triumph of the Establishment
Classical Archaeology Between the Wars

The United States emerged largely unscathed from the slaughter of World War I. The country had not suffered the horrid losses in life and fortune that crippled Britain, France, Italy, and Germany during the 1920s and 1930s. But America was not immune to the social and cultural changes that the cataclysmic events of 1914–18 wrought on Western society. The 1920s, as in Europe were a decade of change. In education, art, and literature as well in social mores, the old values were being challenged.

In this changing American society, classics and classical archaeology increasingly became a bulwark for those defending traditional values against revolutionary assaults from a variety of cultural and political directions. Fairfax Harrison, president of the Southern Railway Company, stressed the role of classics in educating leadership, and expressed fears that such subjects would be neglected in a period of social democracy in a short book, *The School of Hellas*, published in 1914. In 1917 Dean Andrew West of Princeton published the proceedings of a conference on Classical Studies in Liberal Education held at Princeton. The book, entitled *Value of the Classics*, included not only academic presentations and statistics on the state of classical studies, but also testimonials on the value of classics from leaders in business, law, and medicine.

In some respects the postwar situation recalled that of Charles Eliot Norton's generation. However, this new appreciation of antiquity was not a call for salvation from a grim industrial world through radical aesthetics but an affirmation of the existing order and its cultural traditions, against Bolshevism and the Bauhaus. It was based on the cultivation of a benign, nonthreatening traditional humanism, which sought a return to the secure roots of Western civilization. Indeed, this has remained a primary role and foundation for the study of classics up until the present day.

The perceived threat to the established intellectual and social order was expressed by James Egbert in his 1919 presidential address to the Archaeological Institute of America:

Those who are attacking in government and in society all that we hold most dear, are entirely opposed to a study of the past or anything that has to do with history or the records of the past. Therefore, beyond the ordinary reason for interest in archaeological study as of cultural importance and as a hand-maid of history, the encouragement of the study of archaeology will have great power in thwarting the destructive influences that desire entirely to ignore the past.[1]

The same theme resurfaces with a call to meet the "challenge to accept the gage of battle against encroaching materialism" in the Institute's 1925 annual report.

Classical archaeology was no longer considered a humanistic science, meeting the late nineteenth-century challenge of modernism with a combination of socially improving aestheticism and inductive scientific rationalism. Rather, it was seen as a conservative discipline providing support for the traditional order, and hence playing an essential role in preserving intellectual and social stability. The central importance of this need for humanists, especially architects, art historians, and archaeologists, to identify with traditional values is considered below in the important role conservative architects played in scholarly policy formation at both the American Academy in Rome and the American School of Classical Studies in Athens. At both institutions, the ruling elite saw preparing a new generation of archaeologists and architects to uphold the classical tradition in the face of threatening modernism as an important part of their mission.

The period between the Civil War and World War I had been one of great cultural creativity for American classical archaeology. By 1914 the pleasant, broadly educated amateurs of the early era had been transformed into commendable professionals. Graduate programs at places like Princeton, Johns Hopkins, and Bryn Mawr, overseas research institutions like the American School of Classical Studies and the American Academy in Rome, and museums of international stature like the Metropolitan and Boston Museum of Fine Arts, had helped achieve Charles Eliot Norton's goal of making American archaeological scholarship rival that of Europe. Indeed, American academics and curators had become important scholarly contributors on the international scene.

In the years between the world wars, American classical scholars lost their sense of confidence to a certain degree, as academics feared that social, economic, and cultural changes were making them increasingly irrelevant. These decades also saw the growing separation between classical archaeology and the broader disciplines of archaeology and art history. There had been a longstanding internal dispute regarding the mis-

1. *Annual Report AIA* 1925: 7.

sion of the Archaeological Institute of America between those individuals who wanted a more inclusive vision of AIA archaeology and those who promoted a narrower European and Mediterranean focus. Initially the broader vision had triumphed, but gradually the agenda of the more parochial classical archaeologists came to dominate.

Some still adhered to the founding concept of the AIA as a broad-based archaeological organization. Francis Kelsey of the University of Michigan argued for the continuation of this mission in 1919 at the opening of the School of American Archaeology's new headquarters in Santa Fe, the last separate archaeological institute founded by the AIA:[2]

The earlier humanism felt no necessity of passing beyond the domain of the languages and literatures of ancient Greece and Rome. The new humanism must be broader, taking account of a half-millennium of progress since the earlier movement. Upon a foundation of the ancient classics, it will base a superstructure of knowledge concerning man in the Orient, in the Occident, in those phases of development and activity that shall best reveal the capabilities of man as man and fit youth to live in accordance with ideals in a world of humankind. (*Annual Bulletin AIA* 1919: 41)

This position was very similar to that advanced by Francis Parkman at the organizational meetings in 1879. It was a vision that no longer reflected the reality of an institute whose members now thought largely in Mediterranean terms. The change was reflected in the programs of the annual meetings. In 1920 the program still listed papers on Gothic, Mayan, and European prehistoric art and archaeology. By 1939 these nonclassical subjects had largely disappeared. The same trends developed in the pages of the *American Journal of Archaeology* during the 1920s and 1930s, where articles on topics outside the Mediterranean and the Near East became rarer and rarer.

The direction taken by the AIA during those years grew partly out of a narrower, professionalized concept of classical archaeology as a discipline that was closely linked, even subservient to, classical philology and ancient history. James Egbert in his 1919 presidential address had used the term handmaid in describing the relation of classical archaeology to other classical disciplines, a designation that would have made many in the generation of Charles Eliot Norton cringe. The classical philologists, while facing their own crisis of identity on the American educational scene, moved gradually away from the all-embracing vision of German *Altertumswissenschaft*, in which all branches of the discipline had equally honored places, to a disciplinary position that stressed the superiority of those who studied literary texts over those who focused on stones and bones.

2. Hinsley 1986.

The AIA archaeologists were increasingly thrown back upon the philologists, as archaeologists and art historians working in other fields sought their own disciplinary independence. The College Art Association was founded in 1913. Although it had its origins in certain midwestern professors' desire to link art historians and practicing artists, the association soon attracted art history-oriented archaeologists working in a variety of periods including the classical.[3] The classical archaeologist David M. Robinson of Johns Hopkins was a driving force in the development of both the College Art Association and its journal, *The Art Bulletin*.[4] The loss of the diachronic, art-historical component meant that many classical archaeologists became increasingly cut off from developments in other art-historical fields, and more and more focused on an increasingly narrow methodological, geographical and temporal frame of reference. In his *AJA* annual report of 1924, the editor George Elderkin noted that articles on medieval and Renaissance art and archaeology now tended to be published in *Medieval and Renaissance Art*. He regretted the fact that "the fields of antique culture, other than Greek and Roman, are so little exploited by contributers to the journal."[5]

Elderkin noted that "the lack of articles on American Archaeology is also conspicuous" in the pages of *AJA*. Although the AIA had played a major role in founding the School of American Archaeology in Santa Fe, the glory days for the AIA-sponsorship of research in the Americas were over.[6] The results of this research tended more and more to be presented and published in an anthropological context. This process culminated in the founding of the Society for American Archaeology in 1936 and the creation of *American Antiquity* as the major place of publication for research in Americanist archaeology.[7]

It would be a grave mistake to classify all the classical archaeologists of the interwar period as timid conservatives, isolated and slightly paranoiac about contemporary trends in related fields. This was an era of major scholarly achievement both in the field and in the library. Such important, innovative, and productive American excavations as the Athenian Agora, Dura Europos, and Antioch were products of that time. Some classical archaeologists tried during this period to move beyond blind defense of a traditional cultural education to affirmation of the American tradition of bringing the achievements of archaeological research to as wide an audience as possible. Expressions of this populist identifica-

3. Panofsky 1955: 324–25.

4. *EHCA* s.v. "Robinson, David Moore (1880–1958)."

5. *Annual Report AJA* 1924.

6. Hinsley 1986.

7. Griffin 1985; Meltzer, Fowler, and Sabloff 1986: 7–8.

tion were the foundation of a new popular archaeology magazine, *Art and Archaeology*, and the creation of summer programs at both the American Academy and the American School of Classical Studies. *Art and Archaeology* sought to bring new research discoveries in archaeology to an educated lay audience. The summer schools were aimed especially at secondary school teachers and sought to promote using a combination of texts and monuments to revive interest in classical languages and classical culture in the nation's schools.

American classical archaeology before World War I had been characterized by a high level of openness and fluidity. Although certain institutions such as the American School of Classical Studies in Athens had established dominant positions, no graduate program held an overwhelming position in prestige and resources. Undergraduate colleges like Western Reserve produced eminent figures like Harold Fowler and Samuel Platner. Independent scholars like Harriet Boyd Hawes made important contributions. This pattern did change in the 1920s and 1930s. An establishment emerged, and it was increasingly eastern-centered. Within the eastern establishment, Princeton became the dominant force in American classical archaeology both as a university and as a research center.

The Four Pillars of Domination

The 1920s and the 1930s saw an increasing concentration of professional power within a group of four interlocking classical archaeology-oriented institutions centered in Princeton, New Jersey. They were the Princeton art and archaeology program, the American School of Classical Studies, the Athenian Agora excavations, and the Institute for Advanced Study. All had physical connections with the town, and all were shaped by Princeton faculty. They were identified with a community and university characterized by wealth, conservatism, and elite status in an era when America was going through some of the greatest social, economic, and political changes in its history.

The Princeton Art and Archaeology Program

As early as 1832 a course on Roman antiquities had been part of the Princeton college curriculum.[8] However, James McCosh, Princeton president from 1868 to 1888, pushed strongly for the establishment of a "School of Historic Art" for "the purpose of educating the aesthetic faculty of the student body." McCosh argued that "If students are re-

8. Morey 1925.

quired to know the literature of Greece, England, Germany, and France, why should they not have the means of becoming acquainted with the painting, sculpture, and architecture, which have an equally refining and elevating character?"[9]

The Princeton art and archaeology program traces its formal origins to the 1882 appointment of Allan Marquand (1853–1924) as instructor in art and archaeology (Figure 10).[10] Marquand's father was the wealthy collector Henry G. Marquand (1819–1902), president of the Metropolitan Museum of Art from 1889 to 1902 and a major force in its development.[11] The younger Marquand had initially studied philosophy and theology at Johns Hopkins, but eventually turned to his real love, art and archaeology.[12] He shared with Charles Eliot Norton what would be considered today a cultured amateur's education in art history and archaeology, as well as a deep belief in the redeeming qualities of art and beauty. With Norton he played a major role in bringing art history into the American curriculum. Even more than Norton Marquand focused on developing art history as a formal, professional field of study, helping to create a discipline where, even at the turn of the century, none existed.[13]

Whereas Norton cultivated a range of cultural institutions, Marquand built an academic program, staffed by talented faculty with diverse but interconnecting scholarly interests. Arthur Frothingham Jr. was recruited in 1886, Howard Crosby Butler in 1902, and Charles Rufus Morey in 1906. A younger generation of classical archaeologists was later represented by George W. Elderkin, who arrived in 1911 from Johns Hopkins, E. Baldwin Smith, who came in 1915, and T. L. Shear, who joined the faculty in 1922.[14]

Marquand himself was the type of scholar with elite connections and large personal income (he had lived in a private hotel while at Johns Hopkins) who has played a dominant role in classical archaeology throughout much of its recent history. He contributed generously to the development of Princeton's art and archaeology program, supporting both a professorship and the publication of its scholarly outlet, the *Princeton Monographs in Art and Archaeology*, out of his own funds. With his main research interest focused on Italian Renaissance sculpture, Marquand linked the world of classical archaeology with that of later European art

9. Lavin 1983: 8; Thorp, Myers, and Finch 1978: 14–43.
10. Morey 1925; Thorp, Myers, and Finch 1978: 35–36.
11. *DAB* VI.292–93 s.v. "Marquand, Henry Gordon"; Tomkins 1970: 73–83; Duncan 1995: 60.
12. Lavin 1983: 7–8.
13. Panofsky 1956: 482.
14. Panofsky 1956.

Figure 10. Allan Marquand, the scholar most responsible for the development of Princeton as the major center for art and archaeological research in the period between the World Wars. Courtesy of the Special Collections, Princeton University Libraries.

history. His first independent book was, in fact, *Greek Architecture*, published in 1909. The success of his endeavors in program development was shown by the fact that Princeton granted more doctorates in art history than any American graduate program before World War I. Princeton's dominance accelerated during the interwar period.[15]

Arthur Frothingham Jr. has already been profiled as the energetic first editor of the *American Journal of Archaeology*. Like Marquand, he came out

15. Sherman 1981: 29.

of a world of elite American culture.[16] His father had a strong interest in artistic culture and aesthetic theory and contributed a long and sensitive piece on the state of philosophy of art studies to an early issue of *AJA*.[17] The younger Frothingham spent his early years in Italy before completing his Ph.D. at Leipzig and becoming fellow and instructor at Johns Hopkins.[18]

Frothingham's scholarly interests ranged from the Near East to the Middle Ages. In 1886 he gave the first art history graduate course at Princeton. Both he and Marquand were more art historians and connoisseurs than dirt archaeologists, even as that was defined in the early twentieth century. However, Frothingham published a series of very important pieces on Roman and Christian architecture in Italy, demonstrating that creative archaeological scholarship could still be done, even within the limits of Italian excavation policy.[19] He was a collector of art as well, and arranged the purchase of important Etruscan and Roman objects from recently excavated Italian tombs for American museums.[20] Frothingham's later years at Princeton were clouded by disputes with Marquand. He ended his teaching career with a course on Christian antiquities in 1903–4 and then retired to live out the rest of his life as an independent scholar.[21]

Howard Crosby Butler (1872–1922) most clearly established the archaeological field tradition at Princeton.[22] He received his B.A. and M.A from Princeton, studied architecture at Columbia, and in 1897 was resident at the American School of Classical Studies at Rome. Butler devoted much of his relatively short research career to studying the classical and early Christian architectural monuments of the eastern Mediterranean, an endeavor that satisfied his wide-ranging scholarly interests. His first archaeological expedition to Syria was undertaken in 1899 and was followed by others in 1904 and 1909. They represented the type of Mediterranean architectural and epigraphical field survey started in America by John Sterrett. The published volumes were impressive in both the detail of their presentation and the time range of the buildings studied. The emphasis on early Christian churches helped establish the Princeton art and archaeology tradition of bridging antiquity and the early Middle Ages.[23]

---

16. *DAB* IV.42–3 s.v. "Frothingham, Arthur Lincoln"; *EHCA* s.v. "Frothingham, Arthur Lincoln, Jr. (1859–1923)."
17. A. L. Frothingham Sr. 1894.
18. Hawkins 1960: 152.
19. A. L. Frothingham, Jr. 1905, 1910.
20. Dohan 1942; DePuma 1986.
21. Lavin 1983: 16–18.
22. Morey 1925; Thorp, Myers, and Finch 1978: 93–94; Lavin 1983: 17–18.
23. *DAB* II.361 s.v. "Butler, Howard Crosby."

From these topographical investigations Butler moved to the excavation of Turkish Sardis, the city of the fabled Lydian king Croesus.[24] Charles Eliot Norton had dreamed of digging there; his dreams of Norton were being realized. As the *Dictionary of American Biography* observed:

> It was the sterling integrity, as well as the consummate skill of Butler's work there which led to the highest distinction ever offered to an American and Christian explorer by a Mohommedan government, namely, the unsolicited invitation to enter and take command of the excavation of Sardis. The Turks knew they could trust Butler; they knew he was absolutely honorable.

When Butler and his colleagues arrived at the site, only the tops of the columns of the great temple of Artemis lay above the silt from the Pactolus River that had collected at the foot of the Sardis acropolis. The rest of the once great city was deeply buried. In campaigns in 1910–14 and 1922, Butler cleared much of the Artemis temple and prepared a scholarly publication of its architecture. He also established a long-standing American link with the site that was continued by Harvard after World War II. However, war, ill health, and untimely death aborted Butler's project. The main initial legacy of the first American excavations at Sardis was the elegant publication series, and a generous donation of Sardis artifacts by the Turkish government to the Metropolitan Museum of Art.[25]

With Charles Rufus Morey (1877–1955), the Princeton art history program gained a scholar who established an international scholarly reputation researching at the juncture of classical archaeology and early medieval art history. Morey had been educated at the University of Michigan and came to Princeton in 1906.[26] He succeeded Marquand as chair of the program in 1924 and helped make Princeton into a major center for the study of early Christian and medieval art and archaeology.

Princeton's strong early interest in Roman archaeology and the art and archaeology of late antiquity and the early Middle Ages is worth emphasizing, for these fields have often been perceived as marginal to the real concerns of classical archaeology. The liminal status always accorded Christian archaeology and the poor reception given in recent years to the emerging discipline of medieval archaeology in the United States would seem to confirm that. Yet American classical archaeology grew in a society that had a strong religious faith and regarded classical culture as important in part because of its role in nurturing Christianity's early development. The pioneers showed considerable interest in Christian archaeology. In early editions of its newsletter, the *American Journal of*

24. *EHCA* s.v. "Sardis"; Hanfmann 1983c.
25. H. C. Butler 1922; Richter 1970: 91.
26. Panofsky 1955: 324–25; Sjoqvist 1956; Lavin 1983: 19–25.

Archaeology published a special section devoted to Christian archaeology at Rome, and for a number of years the American Academy in Rome offered a fellowship in Christian archaeology.[27] However, the increasingly Hellenic-oriented American classical archaeologists, who found even the monuments of ancient Roman civilization decadent, showed less and less interest in the transition period from antiquity to the Middle Ages. The articles published by James Whitehead of Vassar on early church excavations in Rome were rare exceptions.[28] Christian archaeology became the preserve of early medieval art historians.

Charles Rufus Morey was a scholar oriented toward monuments, museums, and libraries, not an explorer of exotic corners of the Mediterranean like Howard Crosby Butler. Under Morey the Princeton ancient and medieval art history program assumed an identity closer to art-historical than field-oriented archaeological research. Morey was also a leader in creating the institutions necessary to support that type of research. In 1913 he was one of the founders of the College Art Association, and later he helped establish *The Art Bulletin*. In 1917 he started his greatest scholarly work and one of America's greatest scholarly enterprises, the *Index of Christian Art*. This index of iconographical themes and representations in Christian art had grown to five hundred thousand entries and one hundred thousand photographs by the time Morey retired in 1955.[29]

One major Princeton archaeological project of the 1930s did reflect the department's scholarly focus on Roman and early Christian art and archaeology: the expedition organized by Princeton together with the Baltimore Museum of Art and the Worcester Art Museum in Massachusetts to excavate the Hellenistic and Roman city of Antioch on the Orontes in Syria.[30] Antioch had been founded by one of Alexander the Great's successors, and developed into the third greatest city in the Roman Mediterranean.[31] Unlike the two greatest Roman urban centers, Rome and Alexandria, it had not been buried by medieval and modern cities. The Princeton archaeologists hoped that the site would produce important evidence for Hellenistic and Roman urbanism and the complex interaction of Mediterranean and Near Eastern art in the late Roman Empire, as well as major archaeological treasures.[32] Since Syria was part of the post-World War I French territorial mandate, the exportation of some antiquities from the excavations to the United States was possible. For this reason, museums joined the project in the hope of enriching their collec-

27. Sjoqvist 1956: 6.
28. Whitehead 1927b.
29. Lavin 1983: 23.
30. *EHCA* s.v. "Antioch-on-the-Orontes"; Morey 1938: v–vi, 3–17.
31. Downey 1961.
32. Morey 1934: 7.

tions. The Worcester Hunt mosaic from Antioch, one of the museum's treasures, shows that their expectations were indeed fulfilled.[33]

Excavations started at Antioch in 1932 and continued through 1939. They were under the direction first of George Elderkin and then of Clarence Fischer and William Campbell.[34] What the archaeologists had not calculated on was the great depth to which the silt brought down by the Orontes River had buried the ruins of the ancient city. In the days before extensive use of mechanized earth-moving equipment in that part of the world and the development of remote sensing as an archaeological tool, this geological problem proved overwhelming. Little in the way of structural remains relating to the Hellenistic and early Roman city were unearthed, and hopes of studying urban development in a great Hellenistic and Roman center were largely frustrated.

A superb group of mosaics was uncovered at Antioch and in its ancient suburb of Daphnae, however. These provided important insight into the evolution of Roman pictorial style from the second to the sixth century A.D.[35] The project's disparate results are made clear by comparing the splendid publications of the mosaics and the exiguous reports on the other remains. The outbreak of World War II suspended the project. The creation of a Syrian national government after the war ended the policy of antiquities exports, and a new generation of postwar Princeton archaeologists had other agendas. American excavations never resumed at Antioch.

The strength of the Princeton department was obviously based first and foremost on the intellectual range and productivity of its scholars. Although Princeton later developed a reputation for academic inbreeding, the founders of the art and archaeology department came from diverse academic backgrounds and the program drew heavily on the new professionals coming out of Hopkins. Princeton also had unmatched financial resources. This allowed the development of excellent libraries, visual aids, fellowship programs, and the creation of a very good art history museum. From 1924 to 1931, George Elderkin edited the *American Journal of Archaeology* out of Princeton.[36] Finally, the Princeton classical archaeologists intersected closely with several other classically oriented institutions that added strength to their program.

The American School of Classical Studies at Athens

Princeton classicists and classical archaeologists held dominant positions at the American School of Classical Studies at Athens. The key link was

33. Morey 1938: 40–42.
34. Elderkin 1934; Stillwell 1938, 1941.
35. Morey 1938; Levi 1947; Campbell 1988.
36. Donahue 1985: 18–22.

Princeton classics professor Edward Capps (1866–1950), who served as chairman of the American School managing committee from 1919 to 1939.[37] Capps was born in Jacksonville, Illinois and received his B.A. from Illinois College in 1887. He earned his Ph.D. from Yale in 1891 and in 1892 joined the faculty of the newly founded University of Chicago. In 1907 he was lured to Princeton and became strongly identified with that university and the eastern establishment. Using the connections he developed through such cultural and philanthropic positions as director of humanities for the Rockefeller Foundation, he advanced the Princeton cause, especially at the American School of Classical Studies. In the words of one historian of classical scholarship "he secured Princetonian hegemony over the School for some fifty years."[38]

Capps was a man of strong will and tremendous energy. As one obituary writer put it, "If, as his parents intended, he had been Sales Manager for the Capps Mills, we should all now be wearing Capps Woolens."[39] Capps was not really an archaeologist but a wide-ranging classicist with a special scholarly interest in the development of the Greek theater. He had participated in the early school theater excavations at Eretria. He was a superb, if forceful administrator, made evident in the way he engineered the firing of the long-serving and highly respected director of the American School Bert Hodge Hill in 1926, for failing to advance the publication of the American School excavations at Corinth.[40]

All aspects of the school flourished under the Capps hegemony. In 1922 he secured the library of the Greek diplomat, scholar, and bibliophile Joannes Gennadius, providing the school with a superb research resource for Byzantine studies.[41] He helped start the journal *Hesperia* for the publication of research done at the American School. The first issue appeared in 1932, featuring articles on the recently started school excavations in the Athenian Agora.[42]

If Capps was the major external force shaping the school during these years, Bert Hodge Hill (1874–1958) was the dominant scholarly figure in Athens. Educated at the University of Vermont and Columbia, Hill went to the school as a fellow in 1900 and, except for three years as an assistant curator at the Boston Museum of Fine Arts, spent most of the rest of his life in Greece. He served as director from 1906 to 1926 and remained a familiar figure in Athens until his death.[43] Hill had a broad, deep knowl-

37. Lord 1947: 130–270; 1949–50; Meritt 1950.
38. Calder 1984: 45.
39. Lord 1949–50: 14.
40. Lord 1947: 190–93; Calder 1984: 45.
41. Lord 1947: 150–62.
42. Lord 1947: 67, 209–10, 218–20.
43. *EHCA* s.v. "Hill, Bert Hodge (1874–1958)"; Blegen 1958.

edge of Greek archaeology and a passion for accuracy and precision, which kept him from completing major publications. He brought higher professional standards to the school excavations at Corinth, while reinforcing the architectural emphasis of the school's archaeology program.

The archaeologically based study of Greek architecture had been central to the mission of the school since its foundation. During that era, debates about entasis and the origins of the Doric order aroused great excitement not only in the scholarly but also in the general architectural community. The school's earliest excavations had focused on the recovery of evidence for the the architectural development of the Greek theater. Starting in 1882, members of the school had undertaken detailed architectural studies of the Erechtheum, the Propylaea, and other Acropolis structures.[44]

By the 1920s the proponents of the neoclassical-Beaux Arts school within American architecture found themselves under increasing assault from advocates of modernism as represented by such movements as the German Bauhaus.[45] Both the American Academy in Rome and the American School of Classical Studies in Athens were drawn into the struggle as defenders of honored architectural traditions against the new barbarians. At the American Academy in Rome, study of the antique by archaeologists combined with the carefully monitored education of a new generation of architects designed to perpetuate the Beaux Arts tradition. Deviation by academy architects was severely punished.[46] At the American School, where there was no formal program in architectural education, the focus was still on the perpetuation of classical artistic values and the precise archaeological reconstruction of the glories of Greek architecture.

The major advocate of these classical architectural values at both schools was Gorham Phillips Stevens (1876–1963) (Figure 11).[47] Educated at MIT and the Ecole Nationale Supérieure des Beaux Arts in Paris, Stevens was appointed Resident Architect of the Athens School in 1903. The presence of a professional architect on the small staff of a foreign institution without an architectural training program indicated the centrality of that approach to archaeology at the Athens School. In 1904 the importance of architectural archaeology at the American School was enhanced by a Carnegie grant of five years to establish a fellowship in architecture. Stevens was the first to hold that fellowship.[48]

44. D'Ooge 1908; *Art and Archaeology* 1922: 234–44; Fowler 1924; Lord 1947: 111, 118, 122–24, 165–66.
45. Andrews 1964: 232–87.
46. Yegul 1991.
47. *NCAB* 52: 71–72; *EHCA* s.v. "Stevens, Gorham Phillips (1876–1963)."
48. Lord 1947: 102–3.

Figure 11. Gorham Phillips Stevens, architect, classical archaeologist, and administrator. Courtesy of American School of Classical Studies, Athens.

Stevens remained a lover of classical architecture and the classical orders throughout his life. In 1955 a volume of his architectural drawings was published by the American School. Accoridng to the dedication,

Believing that their scholarly correctness and exquisite technique are characteristic of their author, a group of his associates and former students have subscribed the necessary funds to publish them as a tribute to him, hoping thereby to share with a larger public their esteem for the artist and the man. (5)

As late as 1956, when modernism and the international style were dominant, he published in the *Memoirs of the American Academy in Rome* a report on the invention of a machine that would facilitate the drawing of volutes of Ionic columns. Stevens acknowledged that "The Ionic order is out of date today. In modern architecture, even in buildings which are expected to last for centuries, there is little, if any, demand for Ionic columns," but the article was "written in the hope that some day architects will revert to the use of classical orders, particularly in the design of public buildings."[49]

Stevens returned to the United States in 1905 and joined the prestigious traditionalist architectural firm of McKim, Mead, and White. However, his heart remained very much in the Mediterranean, and his combination of scholarly concerns, practical architectural experience, and administrative ability made him a logical candidate for the directorial position at one of the American schools. In 1917 he was appointed director of the American Academy in Rome, a position he held until 1932. During his years in Rome, he did much to promote architectural archaeology at the academy. But Stevens found that even his traditional aesthetic values could not satisfy the ultraconservative artistic views of the academy trustees.[50] Replaced as director, he retired to Athens, where he ran the American School during the difficult war years. After the war, he was one of the major forces behind the reconstruction of the Stoa of Attalus in the Athenian Agora, a massive reaffirmation of archaeological neoclassicism built in an era when architecture was dominated by the ultramodern International School. Stevens died in 1963, three years before the American architect Robert Venturi published *Complexity and Contradiction in Architecture*, the bible of the postmodern movement.[51]

It would be unfair to conclude this account of Stevens without stressing his many positive, inspiring qualities. These is is well summarized by the Valentines in their history of the American Academy in Rome:

He had a scholar's love for history, particularly as expressed in architecture, and when he took students on field trips, they found themselves spellbound by his re-creation of the places they visited, which he peopled and brought to life for his audience. His care for the beauty of the past and his championship of the artist in man won him the affection of the fellows even when they clashed with him over details of Academy management. (1973: 91–92)

The second archaeological architect closely associated with the American School was William Bell Dinsmoor (1886–1973). The son of a New England architect, Dinsmoor graduated from the Harvard School of Architecture in 1906 and was engaged for a while in private architectural practice.[52] Inspired by a period of study at the American School, he turned to architectural archaeology and was fellow in architecture in Athens from 1908 to 1912 and architect of the school from 1912 to 1919. His early research focused on the buildings of the Acropolis. On a more

49. Stevens 1956; Yegul 1991: 100.
50. Valentine and Valentine 1973: 80–81; Yegul 1991: 98–100.
51. Yegul 1991: 100.
52. *EHCA* s.v. "Dinsmoor, William Bell (1886–1973)"; Thompson 1974b.

practical level, he was involved from 1920 to 1931 in the reconstruction of the Parthenon in Nashville, Tennessee. Most of his academic career was spent at Columbia University, where he was appointed to the faculty in 1920. During his long tenure at Columbia Dinsmoor was associated with both the School of Architecture and the Department of Fine Arts. His own lifelong research, centered on the monuments of Greece, especially those of the Acropolis, culminated in the 1950 publication of his *Architecture of Ancient Greece*.

Dinsmoor operated extensively on the national archaeological scene. From 1936 to 1945 he was president of the Archaeological Institute of America, leading the organization through the last years of the Great Depression and World War II. During World War II he was chair of the Committee for the Protection of Cultural Treasures in War Areas and worked hard to protect art historical monuments from the ravages of combat.[53]

Dinsmoor was a strongly conservative force in American classical archaeology. In an obituary notice Homer Thompson summed up Dinsmoor's qualities in relation to his career at Columbia:

Perhaps too there was some incompatibility of temperament when a man of New England origin with a natural inclination to be conservative, frugal, and reserved found himself in a New York milieu that favored a more open-handed, dynamic, and egalitarian way of academic life. (1974b: 157)

The American School maintained its dominant position in U.S. field archaeology in Greece and much of the classical Mediterranean throughout this period. Part of this power resulted from the reassertion of the school's role as the sole conduit through which all American excavation permit requests in Greece had to pass. In 1928 the Greek government tried to limit the school's monopolistic position in the permit process. Vigorous protests were lodged by the school's board and by its forceful American director, Rhys Carpenter. The Greek government yielded and affirmed the American school's status as arbiter of American archaeology in Greece. At the December 1928 meeting of the managing committee, Professor Capps read a letter from Mr. Kourouniotis, chief of the Greek Archaeological Division of the Ministry of Education, which reasserted the position that "no permission would be granted to an American Archaeologist to excavate in Greece in conjunction with a Greek, independent of the American School at Athens."[54] This meant that American

53. *EHCA* s.v. "Dinsmoor, William Bell (1886–1973)."
54. Lord 1947: 205.

archaeology in Greece continued to be American School archaeology, reflecting the attitudes and outlook of the institution's power brokers.

But the American School's archaeological house was not totally in order. The legacy of decades of unpublished Corinth excavation results hung like an albatross over the research program. Although Hill had improved the archaeological field methods employed at Corinth, he did not speed up the publications of past excavations. The 1920–21 annual report of the American School stated the situation trenchantly:

No report so definite or encouraging can be made on Dr. Hill's Bulletin on the excavation at Corinth. The Committee does not forget that the piecemeal method of excavation which has necessarily been followed at Corinth owing to scanty and uncertain provision of funds, the great length of time that has elapsed since the excavation was first undertaken, and the retirement of Dr. Richardson and the death of his successor Dr. Heermance before any systematic account of the undertaking had been prepared, laid upon Dr. Hill a task of exceptional delicacy and difficulty. It would have been better policy to discontinue the excavations when Dr. Hill became the Director, until he should have published the work of his predecessors [a footnote states that with the exception of 1906, 1912, and 1913 work had been continuous from 1896–1917.] As it is, the difficulties have increased with each year of active digging. The war brought a stop to this vicious cycle and fortunately there is now an opportunity to make amends for it. (34–35)

The report was prepared by Edward Capps and marked the intensification of his campaign for the proper publication of the Corinth excavations, which led to Hill's dismissal as director in 1926.

In spite of these warnings and assertions that the publication of previous research had to precede any new excavations, the American School returned to dig at Corinth in 1925. The justification for this violation of often proclaimed policy was the fact that Professor T. Leslie Shear of Princeton offered to finance the new excavations out of his own resources.[55] With that initiative began one of the most productive periods in the history of the American excavations at Corinth. Between 1925 and 1939, many of the most important ancient public buildings at Corinth were unearthed. These included the theater with its Roman paintings of gladiatorial combats and quantities of sculpture, and a Roman villa with impressive mosaics.[56] The publication program was also advanced with typical Capps vigor, aided by the work of the young Princeton architectural archaeologist Richard Stillwell. Twelve final reports on different aspects of the archaeology of Corinth appeared between 1929 and 1941,

55. *EHCA* s.v. "Shear. Theodore Leslie (1880–1945)"; Lord 1947: 172.
56. *EHCA* s.v. "Corinth (Korinthos)"; Shear 1927; Lord 1947: 183–84, 186–90, 195–97, 208, 212–13, 215–17, 220–21, 248–50, 254–55, 264–65.

nine between 1929 and 1932.[57] In 1927 the first general guide to the Corinth excavations, long promised by Hill but never produced, was rapidly brought to completion by Rhys Carpenter.[58] The excavation program at Corinth acquired a further sense of permanence with the construction of an excavation house and a museum.[59]

Toward the end of the interwar period, another young scholar who continued the Hill tradition of the benign, influential, though not overly productive father figure for students and visiting academics came to the school. Eugene Vanderpool (1906–1989) arrived as a student from Princeton in 1929 and joined the Agora staff in 1932.[60] For the rest of his life (including most of the war years) he remained in Greece. From 1949 until his retirement in 1971, he served as professor of archaeology at the school. He published no book, but a number of articles.[61] This lack of a substantial bibliography might lead a historian of archaeology to underestimate Vanderpool's influence in American classical archaeology. In fact, Vanderpool shaped a generation of American classical archaeologists at a time when most of the best and the brightest passed through the Athens school.

Vanderpool was in this respect rather like his contemporary Albert Van Buren at the American Academy in Rome. However, much more than Van Buren, Vanderpool represented the tradition of vigorous topographical investigations that went back to such nineteenth-century explorers as Edward Dodwell, William Gell, and William Leake.[62] He was an energetic walker and displayed feats of physical stamina that established his reputation for archaeological macho among his contemporaries. Vanderpool was also famous for his broad knowledge of Greek archaeology, history, topography, and even the flora and fauna of the Hellenic countryside. He identified totally with Hellas in the Romantic manner that has maintained ancient Greece's centrality in the American classical value scheme. Generations of students at the American School learned topography and love of Greece from Eugene Vanderpool. As one of his obituary writers expressed it, "With the death of Eugene Vanderpool we mark the passing of the greatest Philhellene America has produced in this or any century."[63]

The last archaeologist who shaped the American School's archaeological program during the interwar years was Carl W. Blegen (1887–1971)

57. *EHCA* s.v. "Corinth (Korinthos)"; Lord 1947: 188–90, 332.
58. Lord 1947: 200.
59. Lord 1947: 193.
60. Camp 1990b.
61. Vanderpool 1982: vii–xii.
62. *EHCA* "Dodwell, Edward (1767–1832)," "Gell, Sir William (1777–1836)," "Leake, William Martin (1777–1860)"; Stoneman 1987: 147–62.
63. Camp 1990b: 292.

Figure 12. Carl W. Blegen played a major role in creating the discipline of Greek prehistoric archaeology. Courtesy of the Department
of Classics, University of Cincinnati.

(Figure 12).[64] Blegen obtained his first degree from Augsburg Seminary
in Minnesota and his Ph.D. from Yale. He arrived at the American School
in 1910 and remained in residence until 1927, when he left to become a
professor at the University of Cincinnati. It was under Hill that Blegen,
whose previous classical education had focused on philology, learned to
appreciate the role archaeology could play in understanding antiquity.
He stayed closely connected with the school until his death. A quiet, au-

64. *EHCA* s.v. "Blegen, Carl William (1887–1971)"; J. L. Caskey 1972; McDonald and
Thomas 1990: 197–243.

stere man, he became through his excavations and publications one of the most creative forces in Greek prehistoric archaeology between the wars.

Blegen's independent fieldwork began at the mound of Korakou near Corinth in 1915–16.[65] At the time there was little detailed knowledge about the prehistory of mainland Greece before the Mycenaean period. At Korakou, Blegen identified stratified deposits with a methodological precision rare for that era. That helped define the prehistory of the Corinthia and to a certain degree the general prehistory of Greece[66] Blegen also established his reputation for rapid yet careful publication. Despite of the disruptions caused by the war, the final publication of Korakou, which had been Blegen's Ph.D. dissertation at Yale, appeared by 1921.[67] Blegen resumed his prehistoric researches after World War I. In 1920 he excavated a series of settlements of the early and middle Helladic periods at Zygouries,[68] and in 1925–28 he excavated Mycenaean tombs at the Argive Heraieum.[69]

Hill's firing as director of the American School weakened Blegen's position in Athens. In 1927 he accepted the position of professor of classical archaeology at the University of Cincinnati. Blegen's patron at the university was Professor William Taft Semple. Not only was Professor Semple a respected classicist, but he and his wife, Louise, generously donated personal resources to finance classical archaeology at Cincinnati.[70] Their support, both moral and financial, allowed Blegen to undertake his most important field projects before and after World War II.

In 1932 Blegen and the University of Cincinnati took on the greatest of the classical-prehistoric sites, Troy. Schliemann's earlier depredations there had given way to an increasingly professional approach, especially as the influence of German archaeologists like Wilhelm Dörpfeld came into play. Dörpfeld (1853–1940) had continued Schliemann's excavations, employing highly professional standards for the times, and provided a much more plausible reconstruction of the site's evolution and its place in the prehistory of the eastern Mediterranean.[71]

Major new perspectives had opened up on Aegean prehistory in the 1920s, owing to Blegen's research of Blegen and that of other archaeologists at the American School. Excavation techniques, and especially strat-

65. McDonald and Thomas 1990: 204–8.

66. Lord 1947: 106–7.

67. Blegen 1921.

68. Blegen 1928; Lord 1947: 140–41; McDonald and Thomas 1990: 208–10.

69. Blegen 1937; McDonald and Thomas 1990: 210–17.

70. Bradeen 1967: vii–viii.

71. *EHCA* s.v. "Dörpfeld (Doerpfeld), Wilhelm (1853–1940)," "Troy (Ilion)"; Dörpfeld 1904; Goessler 1951: 49–52, 65–74; Döhl 1981: 55–61; McDonald and Thomas 1990: 14–46, 84–86, 218–20.

igraphic investigation, were improved. Since knowledge of Aegean material culture and prehistoric development was now so much greater, Troy needed a major reexamination. It was time to dig the site again.

Blegen's principal interest in returning to Troy was to redefine the chronology of its occupation and relate that new information to historical and archaeological questions connected with the Trojan War. The excavations, conducted from 1932 to 1938, again demonstrated Blegen's qualities of meticulous fieldwork and recording. In his skilled hands the history of the Hissarlik mound was revealed as even more complicated than Dörpfeld had realized. Schliemann's and Dörpfeld's nine major phases expanded into some forty-nine archaeological subphases. These same detailed analyses allowed Blegen to associate the Troy of Homer with the major phase Troy VIIA, dated to c. 1250 B.C.[72]

Blegen also continued his habit of full and rapid publication of his excavation results.[73] Despite the interruptions caused by a major World War and the start of another large excavation project at Pylos, Blegen and his colleagues completed the Troy final publications by 1958.[74] These are specialists' works in the new archaeological mode, not the Schliemann narratives that appealed to a popular audience. Blegen did write a more popular book on the excavations and their results, his *Troy and the Trojans*, which appeared in 1963 as the first volume in the influential Peoples and Places series, edited by the English archaeologist Glynn Daniel.[75]

Blegen's final and perhaps most important excavation was started in the western Messenia on the eve of World War II. Archaeologists and topographers had long sought the site of Pylos, the palace home of Homeric Nestor along the coast of the southwest Peloponnesus. After conducting precise and thoughtful topographical investigations in the area, Blegen decided that the palace site must be located at the Bronze Age site of Epano Englianos.[76] An initial season of excavations in 1939 proved him correct. In addition to remains of the Mycenaean palace, he unearthed a large hoard of clay tablets, written in a then undeciphered language designated by Arthur Evans, the excavator of Minoan Knossos, as Linear B. The Pylos tablets played a major role in the decipherment of Linear B by the young English architect and cryptographer Michael Ventris (1922–1956), who demonstrated in 1952 that Linear B was the oldest known dialect of ancient Greek.[77] Blegen continued the excavations at Pylos

---

72. *EHCA* s.v. "Troy (Ilion)"; Blegen 1963; Fitton 1996: 158–61.

73. McDonald and Thomas 1990: 220–29.

74. Blegen, Caskey, Rawson, and Sperling 1950–58.

75. McDonald and Thomas 1990: 221.

76. *EHCA* s.v. "Pylos, Messenia"; McDonald and Thomas 1990: 229–43.

77. *EHCA* s.v. "Ventris, Michael George Francis (1922–56)"; Ventris and Chadwick 1956; Chadwick 1958.

after World War II, meticulously uncovering one of the best preserved Mycenaean palaces and making yet another important American contribution to Aegean prehistoric archaeology.[78]

The Athenian Agora

The most momentous decision that the American School in Athens made in its history was to begin excavations in the Athenian Agora in the center of the modern city. Although the school had continued to use Corinth for its archaeological field training, there was increasing interest in finding a site that would make an even greater impact on the archaeological world and provide a higher level of visibility for American archaeology than was possible at isolated Corinth.

The decision to undertake this bold venture in the heart of Athens was to a large degree that of Edward Capps. Indicative of his shrewd organizational skills was the way that he carefully and methodically tested the waters for the project. He noted in the 1924–25 annual report of the American School that

Guided by this unqualified expression of opinion [i.e., support of the board], the Chairman endeavored at the beginning of summer to test out public sentiment on the project by means of a cautious and carefully prepared communique to the press. If one can judge by the space and position which our leading newspapers gave to the subject (to say nothing of the imaginative and sensational details with which some papers saw fit to embroider a matter-of-fact statement), there would be no lack of general interest in so notable an undertaking. (1924–25: 55)

Capps had a world of useful connections that could be tapped in developing the project. They ranged from Eleutherios Venizelos, the dominant Greek politician to Abraham Flexner of the Rockefeller Foundation. The former helped provide the political support necessary to obtain the excavation permits, while the latter helped obtain the enormous financial resources needed to launch such a bold undertaking. American was in the grips of the Great Depression by the time the Agora excavations got underway in 1931. Yet solid financial support continued for the work until the outbreak of World War II, demonstrating the strength of support that Capps and the school had within the philanthropic establishment of the United States. Funding over those years came from the likes of John D. Rockefeller Jr., the Rockefeller Brothers Fund, the Andrew W. Mellon Foundation, and the S. H. Kress Foundation.[79]

From the beginning, the Agora excavations acquired a special ideological status in American classical archaeology. In his foreword to the first

78. Blegen and Rawson 1966–73.
79. Thompson 1954: 25–27; A. Flexner 1960: 218–20; Camp 1986: 12.

"Agora" edition of *Hesperia*, the American School's new journal, Capps wrote:

Indeed, all who are interested in the history of the city whose civilization has so profoundly influenced the rest of the world are entitled, in the opinion of the American School, to learn from year to year, whatever the soil of the Agora yields up that throws new light upon the history, institutions, topography, architecture, art, religion and, in general, the culture, of the ancient Athenians. (1933: 89)

Supporters argued that the Agora was the original seat of Greek democracy. As Europe moved increasingly toward dictatorship, propaganda benefits would be gained from supporting this key archaeological research project of America, the greatest modern Western democracy, on the site where ancient Greek democracy was born.

Getting an excavation permit to operate in the heart of classical Athens was a major coup for the Americans. Some excavation had already been undertaken in the Agora.[80] The site of the Stoa of Attalus had been cleared as early as 1859–62, and the German Archaeological Institute had done some work in the agora area.[81] However, Athenian topographers had only a vague and often rather inaccurate picture of the location of the major buildings.[82] Nothing on the scale and complexity of the American project had been undertaken anywhere in modern urban Athens.

The chain of events that led to the start of the Agora excavations began with the 1922 defeat of the invading Greek army in Turkey and the subsequent forced repatriation of large numbers of Asian Greeks to the homeland.[83] This new influx placed enormous housing pressures on the increasingly crowded urban core of Athens, where most of the ancient monuments were located. The Greek government had long restricted new building on what was assumed to be the site of the Agora, for they hoped to conduct their own excavations there. Now pressure mounted to either excavate or turn the land over to development. The Greek government's decision to respond favorably to the American approach in 1924 was based on the fact that only the United States had the resources to undertake such an extensive and expensive project. This represented a significant change in the perception of American academic prestige and international power from the 1880s, when the French easily outmaneuvered the Americans for the excavation rights to Delphi.

The Americans were granted preliminary permission to start excavations in 1925. However, the complex politics surrounding the project and

---

80. *EHCA* s.v. "Agora, Athens."
81. *EHCA* s.v. "Stoa of Attalus, Athens."
82. Camp 1986: 12–13.
83. Capps 1933: 90–94; Lord 1947: 177–79.

especially pressure from the residents, who would be displaced by the excavations, delayed the final agreements until August 1928. The law authorizing the American excavations was not made official until 1930. In January 1931 the residents in the first blocks of houses in areas designated for excavation received ninety days notice to move. In mid-May their houses were destroyed and excavations began.[84]

The decision was made to clear the site down to the classical levels with an emphasis on careful study of structures and areas that represented the ideological heart of ancient Greek democracy. The Plaka, the picturesque Turkish quarter of Athens, had developed over the ruins of the ancient agora. Large sections of this historic district were confiscated and leveled. Descriptions of this process in the American reports of the time reflect a colonial insensitivity to the needs and concerns of the locals and a cavalier attitude toward the demolition of urban fabric and postclassical urban history. Some ten thousand Athenian residents were displaced from homes, where they had dwelt for years, and dispatched into an ever tighter and more costly Athenian housing market.[85] A compact, functioning urban community was disrupted. But the Americans involved in the negotiations could only express annoyance at the litigious ways of the modern Athenians, who were impeding the progress of scientific archaeology.

The destruction of a physical and social urban center that had developed over centuries to allow for an excavation and, ultimately, for an open archaeological park was viewed by the Americans as an unmitigated good. In the words of American School historian Louis Lord:

The excavations had cleared about sixteen acres. Three hundred and sixty-five undesireable buildings had been removed. These unsightly structures will be replaced by an archaeological area beautified by appropriate planting. (1947: 244)

After the disastrous urban renewal projects that were conducted in the historic districts of U.S. and European cities in the post-World War II period, students of urbanism might question the priorities that destroyed appealing areas of the Plaka to create the summer dust bowl that the Agora has become.

The approach to urban archaeology used by the Americans was not that different from that being practiced in Fascist Rome at the same time. There, Benito Mussolini's urban planners and archaeologists were destroying whole quarters of the medieval city to expose the remains of an ideologically approved past.[86] For Mussolini, it was the Rome of the Caesars. For the Americans, it was the Athens of Pericles. Members of the

---

84. Capps 1933: 92; Lord 1947: 200–202; 231–32.
85. Lord 1947: 201.
86. Manacorda and Tamassia 1985.

American social and cultural elite on the whole approved of Mussolini's actions and were not expected to object to their application in Athens.

The Agora excavations were placed under the direction of Dr. Theodore Leslie Shear of Princeton (1880–1945), a Capps protégé, who had studied at New York University, Johns Hopkins, and Bonn, dug at Knidos and Sardis, and proved himself an energetic excavator and archaeological publisher at Corinth (Figure 13).[87]

The major difference between the Agora and the contemporary Fascist excavations in Rome was the quality of the American organization, recording, and, ultimately, publication. While the Fascist excavations became notorious for their wretched record keeping and the destruction of archaeological information lost in the pursuit of propagandistic goals, the Athenian Agora excavators from the beginning took pains to document carefully, and their accounts remain even today a model of meticulous archaeological recording.[88] Whereas most of the Fascist excavations have not been and probably never will be published, the Athenian Agora researchers have produced a range of publications from preliminary field reports, starting in the first issue of *Hesperia*, through the long series of blue-covered final reports, to general guides[89] and the attractive Agora picture books such as *Pots and Pans of Classical Athens*, *The Athenian Citizen*, and *Socrates in the Agora*.

The Agora excavations soon developed an operating sociology that represented a complex blend of American corporate efficiency, European hierarchy, and Mediterranean clientship. The directorship, an office of tremendous power rather like the CEO of a major American corporation, became a career appointment. Between 1928 and 1992, there have been only three directors of the Agora, two of them father and son. The director was supported by an expanding technical staff and a cadre of loyal Greek workmen and supervisors, many of whom spent their whole working lives with the Agora excavations. The most mobile groups were the trench supervisors, positions held by the school's best field-oriented students, who often went on to distinguished careers in the profession. Through these trench supervisors the methodology and ideology of the Agora excavations were diffused throughout North American classical archaeology.

The development of the Agora technical bureaucracy highlighted the changing role of women in American classical archaeology. Women graduate students continued to attend the school in considerable numbers

87. *EHCA* s.v. "Shear, Theodore Leslie (1880–1945)"; Stillwell 1945; Thompson 1945.

88. Riggs 1931; Lord 1947: 231–32; MacKendrick 1962: 386–92.

89. For various editions of the general Agora guide, see Thompson 1954, 1976; Camp 1990a.

Figure 13. Theodore Leslie Shear Sr. of Princeton, one of the most active classical archaeologists of his generation. Courtesy of American School of Classical Studies, Athens.

and then to go on to academic positions, especially at women's colleges. However, for American women archaeologists the possibility of challenging men's domination of the profession was largely over. Hetty Goldman became the only important American woman field director of a classical excavation during this epoch. Women archaeologists increasingly became defined as catalogers and material culture specialists. In 1933, the top three positions at the Agora (director, supervising architect, and epigrapher) were held by men, whereas special areas like coins, records, and photography were more often represented by women. In 1957–58 the same hierarchy remained with the posts of director, assistant director, architect, and assistant architect filled by men, while records, photography, amphorae, figurines, lamps, terra-cottas, and coins were the responsibility of women. These specialist posts, though heavily compartmentalized by gender, were sought by women attracted by annual trips and long-term residence in Athens.

Specialist posts at the Agora often meant considerable scholarly power, for those individuals controlled access to, and information about, some of the most extensive and best-documented collections of material culture in classical archaeology. Representative of this type of Agora expert was Virginia Grace (1901–1994), who devoted her entire scholarly career to studying the Greek amphorae of the Mediterranean, and especially those of the Athenian Agora.[90] Educated at Bryn Mawr, where she received her Ph.D. in 1934 with a dissertation on stamped transport amphorae, Grace spent the rest of her life cataloging and dating amphora stamps. She lived in Athens and worked in the Agora laboratories, where she cataloged, recorded, and dated thousands of examples of Greek amphorae. Her publications were numerous, although she never produced her planned synthetic work on the development of the Greek amphora. Today computers and scanners would undertake much of the drudge work archaeologists of Grace's generation did by hand. However, without the research of scholars like Grace, the intellectual framework from which the new technological analysis begins would not exist.

The Institute for Advanced Study

The final instrument in Princeton's domination of classical archaeology during the interwar period was the Institute for Advanced Study. Founded in 1930, the institute was designed to be a research center, where internationally renowned scholars could pursue their investigations with minimal interruptions and maximal support. The foundation of the institute owed much to the personal philanthropy of Louis Bamberger and his sister, Mrs. Felix Fuld. The educational godfather was again Abraham Flexner (1866–1959) of the Rockefeller Foundation, better known as an expert in the fields of education, science, and medicine, but also a classicist who had taught Greek and Latin until the age of thirty-nine.[91]

90. Koehler 1996.
91. *DAB* supp. 6: 207–9; A. Flexner 1940: 52–92, 356–97.

Although the institute is best known to the general public for its scientists and mathematicians, the humanities, especially classical history and archaeology, played a major role in its development from the earliest days.[92] In 1935 the School of Humanistic Studies was established and the Greek epigrapher Benjamin Meritt (1899–1989) joined the faculty as professor of Greek epigraphy, followed the next year by the archaeologist Hetty Goldman. Homer Thompson, the director of the Agora, became a professor there in 1947. Meritt worked at the juncture of epigraphy, history, and archaeology (he was deeply involved in the publication of the Agora inscriptions) and used his strong position at the institute to develop classics there.[93] Over the years, the institute become one of classical archaeology's most visible research centers. Although the institute is not part of Princeton University, there have been close relations from the beginning between the two institutions located in the same small town. Much of the scholarship at the institute, both ancient historical and archaeological, has been Athens-Agora oriented. Both the regular faculty and visiting scholars have been closely involved with the American School of Classical Studies and the Agora excavations.

Other Graduate Programs in the Interwar Era

Princeton, with the interconnected institutional power bases just described, dominated American classical archaeology during the 1920s and 1930s. Its program had a large and distinguished art and archaeology faculty, superb libraries, a major research institute at its doorstep, lavish financing, and a dominant position in the management of the American School. Furthermore, with American classical archaeological research focused intellectually and ideologically on Greece of the seventh through fourth centuries B.C., Princeton, through its position in Athens and the Agora, could lay dominant claim to that symbolic landscape. No other Ivy League school could challenge Princeton's supremacy. Despite Norton's role in pioneering the teaching of art and archaeology in the United States, Harvard did not develop a graduate classical archaeology program of distinction until George Hanfmann's arrival after World War II. Yale became an important graduate center in the late 1920s and 1930s under Michael Rostovtzeff, but without Princeton's depth and web of connections.

Michigan

The most important midwestern university classical archaeology program in this period was at Michigan. It owed its distinction in part to the

92. A. Flexner 1940: 330–32.
93. Traill 1990.

school's early development as a major state university. In the years immediately after World War I it also benefited greatly from the energetic
leadership of Francis W. Kelsey.[94] A visiting English scholar observed in
1917 that "No one has done more than Professor Kelsey for promoting in
America a classical revival on rational lines."[95] Kelsey modeled himself on
the tough, aggressive robber barons who were transforming American
industry during that period. Photographs show a man with a strong face
and close-cropped beard looking rather like a Roman soldier emperor
of the mid-third century A.D. Kelsey was also a strong regionalist who
wanted to promote the development of classical archaeology in America's heartland.[96]

As a collector, Kelsey brought what became the largest collection of
Latin inscriptions and one of the largest collections of brick stamps in
North America to Michigan. Most of the inscriptions were acquired
around the Bay of Naples area by Walter Dennison (1869–1917). Dennison was a Michigan alumnus and faculty member as well as one of the
first fellows of the American School of Classical Studies in Rome.[97] The
brick stamps were purchased mainly by Kelsey himself.[98] Appreciating
the growing importance of photography for archaeological research, Kelsey obtained thousands of archaeological photographs with a special
focus on Rome and the Naples area for Michigan. One of his last acts for
the department was to obtain in 1925 a set of more than three thousand
photographs of Rome and Italy taken by the pioneering nineteenth-
century English photographer John Henry Parker.[99]

Kelsey published widely in both Latin studies and archaeology. His archaeological publications included a translation of August Mau's highly
influential *Pompeii: Its Life and Art*.[100] He served as president of the Archaeological Institute of America from 1907 to 1912. During his presidency the AIA took its final step toward broader horizons with the foundation of the American School of Oriental Research in Santa Fe.[101]

Kelsey was also active in promoting classical archaeological fieldwork at
Michigan. In 1920 he led the first Michigan expedition to the Near East,
which secured important photographs, archaeological objects, manuscripts, and papyri for the university.[102] In 1925 he headed the joint

94. *EHCA* s.v. "Kelsey, Francis Willey (1858–1927)"; Riggs 1927.
95. Browne 1917: 268.
96. Riggs 1927.
97. E. Bace in Baldwin and Torelli 1979: xvii–xviii, 1–5.
98. Bodel 1983: 5.
99. Keller and Breisch 1980.
100. Mau 1902.
101. Hinsley 1986: 222–31.
102. Kelsey 1920; Sanders 1927.

Michigan-Washington Society of the AIA, University of Rochester excavation at Carthage, where the tophet, the site of burial of hundred of infant sacrifices, was excavated (Figure 14).[103] In spite of initial successes, the Carthage project did not seem to offer good long-term prospects for the University of Michigan, and Kelsey looked elsewhere.

Kelsey's final archaeological project was launching the Michigan excavations at Karanis in Egypt, to which he had devoted major fund-raising efforts and where he had just completed the first season at the time of his death.[104] The Michigan research at Karanis continued until 1935 and represented the most important archaeological project undertaken by that university, until its return to Carthage in the 1970s. Karanis was a Greco-Roman village in the Fayoum area of western Egypt. In the words of his colleague, the ancient historian A. E. R. Boak, Kelsey planned that "the work would be carried on for a sufficient number of years to obtain a reasonably complete picture of the various aspects of life in an Egyptian country town under the rule of the Ptolemies and the Roman Emperors."[105]

Much of the excavation did focus on the residential quarter of Karanis.[106] This archaeological emphasis on the daily life of ordinary villagers was unusual for American classical archaeology during that period, where much more effort was focused on the study of religious and public monuments. Along with the excavations at Olynthos and Dura, Karanis represented a brief emphasis of the archaeology of ordinary people that was largely forgotten in the monument-oriented research of the postwar period. His publication history was uneven.[107] The early reports did contain some innovative research, including one of the first analyses of seed and animal bone material from a classical site.[108] The excavations produced quantities of papyri and various types of artifacts, which the generous export laws of the period allowed to reach Ann Arbor.

Closely associated with Kelsey and the University of Michigan during this era was the amateur historian and archaeologist Thomas Spencer Jerome. Jerome was a successful Detroit lawyer who retired early to the island of Capri, where he built a splendid villa with his friend the Washington art collector Charles Freer.[109] There Jerome pursued his research which centered on Roman moral history and the vindication of the Emperor Tiberius, who had also lived on Capri in his old age.[110] Jerome is

103. Kelsey 1926a, b.
104. Sanders 1927: 308.
105. Boak 1931: v.
106. Boak and Peterson 1931.
107. Gazda 1978: 5–10.
108. Boak 1933.
109. Gazda 1983.
110. Jerome 1923.

Figure 14. Francis Kelsey photographed at the site of the tophet, the infant sacrificial area at Carthage, in 1925. Pictured with various French and America archaeologists including Père Hugenot and Père Delattre of the White Fathers, the religious order responsible for much of the early French excavation at Carthage. Photograph by George R. Swain. Courtesy of the Kelsey Museum of Archaeology of the University of Michigan.

depicted as the withdrawn, antiquarian character in Compton MacKenzie's 1927 novel of Capri expatriate life *Vestal Fire*.[111] Jerome's main legacy to the University of Michigan was the endowment of the classics lecture series, shared with the American Academy in Rome, that still bears his name.

At the time of Kelsey's relatively early death in 1927, Michigan had a classical archaeology program of considerable strength that could compete with the best. There was a well-established tradition of classical archaeological studies, good library resources and a useful museum. Excavations continued at Karanis. In 1927 Michigan started excavations at Seleucia, a Hellenistic and Parthian site just south of Baghdad.[112] The excavations, which continued down to 1937, were under the auspices of Michigan, the Toledo Museum of Art and the Cleveland Museum of Art. Since Iraq at that time was under effective British control, antiquities could be exported, and the two museums hoped to add to their collections.

The excavations at Seleucia, directed first by Leroy Waterman and then by Clark Hopkins, revealed a city with a history rather rather like Dura Europos in Syria which was being excavated by Yale at the same time. Seleucia developed from an Hellenistic urban foundation into a Parthian city.[113] Although the excavations provided considerable evidence for city planning and domestic housing, and small finds related to trade and daily life, they did not yield anything like the wealth of dramatic objects that came out of Dura. Again the outbreak of World War II stopped work and scattered the staff. Publication in many cases was seriously delayed.[114]

In spite of all this field activity, no classical archaeologist in the Michigan classics department during the interwar years could match Kelsey's dynamism and leadership. There was an Institute of Archaeological Research at Michigan, but it was dominated by ancient historians and papyrologists like A. E. R. Boak, C. Bonner, and John Winter. Clark Hopkins (1895–1976), who joined the department in 1935, had a great range of field experience in the Near East, but was not a creative intellectual force like Rostovtzeff or a major professional presence like Capps or Kelsey.[115] In that era, Michigan was not a serious competitor to Princeton or even Johns Hopkins in the field of classical archaeology.

111. Gazda 1983.
112. Hopkins 1972.
113. Savage 1977.
114. Van Ingen 1939; Hopkins 1972.
115. Hopkins 1979.

Bryn Mawr

The Bryn Mawr classical archaeology program was dominated by two very different scholarly personalities who reflected two very different traditions in American classical archaeological scholarship. Rhys Carpenter (1889–1980) came to Bryn Mawr from Columbia in 1913 and, except for spells at the American School in Athens and the American Academy in Rome, spent his entire teaching career there.[116] He had been educated at Columbia and Oxford, where he was strongly influenced by the same culture of aesthetes that had helped shape the attitudes of E. P. Warren and John Beazley. His early interests in questions related to aesthetics and the philosophy of art were reflected in scholarly works such as *The Aesthetic Basis of Greek Art of the Fifth and Fourth Centuries B.C.* and *The Humanistic Value of Archaeology.*[117]

The circumstances of Carpenter's initial Bryn Mawr appointment were unusual and informal, reflecting the rather amateur nature of classical archaeological studies during this period. Edith Finch, a biographer of Bryn Mawr president M. Carey Thomas, describes it thus:

Years afterwards, when Bryn Mawr needed a classical archaeologist and none suitable appeared to be available, Carey Thomas, then president, discovered a young Rhodes scholar teaching Greek at Columbia who impressed her as possessing to a distinguished degree the qualifications needed. He himself had never contemplated entering the archaeological field. After an interview in which she put to him that he could, if he would, change the direction of his work, he found himself so fired by her words and enthusiasm that he accepted her appointment and plunged into archaeology, reaching in a few years a position of marked eminence in the field. (1947: 227)

Carpenter's scholarly research ranged widely, and he approached the field of classical archaeology with great imagination and a high degree of iconoclasm. One of his first publications was concerned with the early impact of Greek trade and colonization on Spain.[118] One of his last dealt with the controversial question of the role of climate in the collapse of Greek Bronze Age civilization.[119] As the disparate topics of his research suggest, there was always a restless quality about Carpenter's scholarship. Traditional questions and expected responses seldom satisfied him. His distinctive intellectual character was captured well in a memorial poem ("Elegy for Rhys Carpenter") written by his Bryn Mawr colleague Richmond Lattimore:

116. *EHCA* s.v. "Carpenter, Rhys (1889–1980)"; Lang 1980.
117. Carpenter 1921, 1933.
118. Carpenter 1925.
119. Carpenter 1966.

You wanted to slip away
quietly and did. Ours
to remember today
what had been yours.
The bold mind setting sail
on uncharted exciting
seas. Artist's eye for detail.
The sculptured writing.
Love for all growing grace,
flowers, wild creatures.
Full-lived adventurous days
in all that is Nature's.
The huge walks on the Greek
hills, and the climb
in the crack of the bleak
cliff, in your strong prime.
Now light comes in the trees.
The world turns green.
Fortunate he who sees
them as you would have seen. (1980)

Balancing Carpenter in the Bryn Mawr archaeology program during
these years was Mary Hamilton Swindler (1884–1967).[120] A product of
the educational opportunities provided by the public universities of the
Midwest, Swindler joined the faculty with her fresh Bryn Mawr Ph.D in
1912. Her entire teaching career was spent at the college, where she
trained several generations of archaeology students. The excavators of
Tarsus gratefully acknowledged her enthusiastic support for the first classical excavation sponsored by a women's college.[121] The high respect with
which she was held in the profession was demonstrated by the fact that
she served as editor of the *American Journal of Archaeology* from 1932 to
1946, one of the longest tenures in the journal's history. She assumed the
editorship in the midst of the Great Depression and continued through
the dark days of World War II.[122]

In contrast to Carpenter, Swindler "was an outstanding instance of
long devotion to a single dominant interest in a field of scholarship
whose fruits she was ever ready to share with all who came to her for
encouragement or instruction or professional advice."[123] The major
product of that focused scholarship was her book *Ancient Painting*.[124] The
book's chronological range, which takes the reader from the cave paint-

120. *EHCA* s.v. "Swindler, Mary Hamilton (1884–1967)."
121. E. Vermeule 1987: 168.
122. Carpenter 1967; Donahue 1985: 22–27.
123. Carpenter 1967: 14.
124. Swindler 1929.

ings of Altamira to the art of the high Roman Empire, remains striking. It reflected the cultural, geographical, and chronological range of the Bryn Mawr art and archaeology program. Students studied Mediterranean prehistory as well as classical archaeology and considered the interactions of Near Eastern and Greek civilizations as much as the internal developments of Greece and Rome.[125]

This departmental interest in the archaeological intersection of classical and Near Eastern civilizations was evidenced in the appointment of Valentin Müller (1889–1945) to the department. With Müller's arrival, Bryn Mawr added the traditions of Germanic archaeological scholarship of Göttingen, Bonn, and Berlin to its British and American roots. Müller was a rare early example of a common postwar phenomenon, the imported foreign scholar. His expertise linked the archaeologies of the Near East and Greece.[126] Yet Müller's impact was limited. Although he published some important research during his years at Bryn Mawr, Müller found himself in an America where classical archaeology was increasingly dominated by currents different from the strong late-nineteenth-century German influences that he reflected.

Mention should also be made of Tenney Frank (1876–1939), who served on the Bryn Mawr faculty from 1904 to 1913, when he moved to Johns Hopkins. Although principally an ancient historian, Frank, like Michael Rostovtzeff of Yale, realized the importance of interconnecting archaeology and ancient history.[127] His B.A. work at the University of Kansas had been in both classics and geological studies. These research interests were combined in his pioneering studies of the use of tufa building materials as a key to date Roman construction phases and identify quarry sources and their relation to Roman imperial expansion in Latium. Professor Shear of Princeton summarized Frank's interdisciplinary quality thus:

> To him the disciplines of philology, history and archaeology were never in isolation. As a result he developed a method peculiarly his own which enabled him to cross the ordinary barriers of scholarship and make bold and original combinations. (*Annual Report AIA* 1939: 25)

Shear goes on to describe the way Frank also related those combinations to his literary studies.[128] It was through Frank's influence at Bryn Mawr that Louise Adams Holland became interested in the problems of Central Italy's early Iron Age and began her research on land, settlement, and trade in early Roman history.[129]

125. Vermeule 1987: 168–69.
126. Hanfmann 1983a: 20–22; Broughton 1988.
127. Broughton 1990b.
128. *Annual Report AIA* 1939: 25–26.
129. L. Adams 1925; Holland and Holland 1950; Broughton 1990a.

Johns Hopkins

Johns Hopkins University continued to play an important role in research and graduate education in American classical archaeology during the interwar period. The German refugee scholar George Hanfmann, who completed a second Ph.D. at Hopkins after his arrival in America from Germany, described it as the leading training school for classical archaeology in the the United States during the 1930s.[130] Hopkins did not have the depth of faculty or the combination of research resources underpinning Princeton's preeminence. However it was certainly an important place for advanced study and in many respects the most open and democratic of the major graduate institutions. Hopkins had the largest graduate program in classical archaeology in the United States at that time. Between 1908 and 1947 David Robinson alone advised seventy-four dissertations. Indeed, the program became somewhat an academic factory, where M.A.s and Ph.D.s were ground out and the dissertations published in the Hopkins monographs series.

But it would be unfair to designate Hopkins as a place of mass-produced scholarly mediocrity. The program graduated a number of classical archaeologists who went on to careers of distinction in the pre- and post-World War II period. These included Hanfmann of Harvard and the Greek refugee George Mylonas (1898–1988) of George Washington University.[131] Hopkins was also one of the few American graduate programs in classical archaeology where women were welcomed. Thirty-one of the students who completed Ph.D.'s with Robinson were women.

It is impossible to appreciate the strengths and weaknesses of the Johns Hopkins program during the interwar period without discussing its most prominent and controversial classical archaeologist. David Moore Robinson (1880–1958) was born in 1880 in Auburn, New York and received his American undergraduate and graduate education at the young University of Chicago. He went on to additional studies in Germany at universities in Halle, Berlin, and Bonn and at the American School of Classical Studies in Athens.[132] He was recruited by Hopkins in 1905 to help found the classical archaeology program and served as chair of the Department of Art and Archaeology from 1913 to 1947. Robinson was the first editor (1914–18) of *Art and Archaeology* and founder and first editor-in-chief (1919–21) of the scholarly art history journal *The Art Bulletin*. Robinson was a discerning collector of Greek vases, and published his own collection in three fascicles of the *Corpus Vasorum Antiquorum*.[133]

130. Hanfmann 1983a: 25.
131. Iakovidis 1989.
132. *EHCA* s.v. "Robinson, David Moore (1880–1958)"; Mylonas 1951, 1957–58.
133. D. M. Robinson 1934–38.

Robinson obtained his basic archaeological training on American excavations at Corinth and Sardis. He also conducted excavations at Pisidian Antioch.[134] Since it was important that an ambitious graduate program like that at Hopkins should have its own excavation, Robinson organized the expedition to the northern Greek city of Olynthos, one of the most important American excavations of the interwar period (1928–38). Olynthos was a colony founded around 432 B.C. close to the border with Macedon. It was a planned city, which prospered from trade in the region. As part of his campaign to expand Macedonian power in the northern Aegean Philip II attacked and destroyed Olynthos in 348 B.C. Olynthos's relatively short period of habitation, sudden destruction, and apparent lack of major reoccupation gave the site the quality of a classical Greek Pompeii. It allowed detailed and relatively uncomplicated study of city planning, urban development, and daily life at an important center of the Greek classical period.[135]

Robinson first visited Olynthos in 1902, when he was a student at the American School in Athens. Only after he had established his position in the profession at Johns Hopkins did an excavation there became feasible, however. Again, as at Athens, the project was advanced considerably by the traumatic developments following the Turkish defeat of the Greeks in 1922. The need to provide land for new refugees threatened the archaeological site of Olynthos. At the same time the desperate transplants provided an abundant and cheap source of archaeological labor. Robinson started digging at Olynthos in 1928 and continued with seasons in 1931, 1934, and 1938.[136]

The Hopkins excavations at Olynthos, like almost everything else in David Robinson's long career, remain controversial. His combination of a massive Greek workforce and a relatively small supervisory staff and the supposedly slapdash field methods he used have often been contrasted negatively with the more careful, scientific Agora excavations of the same period. Sometimes employing more than two hundred workmen, Robinson and his small team moved tons of earth each season. This was done with slender financial resources, for Hopkins could not provide anything like the financial support available at Princeton.[137]

Needless to say, it was impossible to recover and record archaeological materials and information in a manner that would be acceptable today. Robinson did learn from his initial errors. In 1931 a Hopkins graduate student, James Walter Graham (1906–1991), introduced new recording

134. D. M. Robinson 1924.
135. *EHCA* s.v. "Olynthos."
136. Lord 1947: 205–6, 250–52, 260–61; D. M. Robinson 1952; Cahill 1991: 115–30.
137. The total cost for four campaigns was $50,000, of which Robinson himself contributed $20,000 (Lord 1947: 261).

systems that dramatically improved the quality of archaeological information recovered. Graham went on to a distinguished career in architectural archaeology, culminating in a professorship at the University of
Toronto.[138] Robinson was always an energetic publisher, and the speed
and completeness of the Olynthos reports compares favorably with many
American projects. In recent years, there has been revived interest in,
and appreciation for, the Olynthos excavations. With increased interest
in the archaeology of domestic space and the common man, Olynthos is
once again coming into its own. Archaeologists have been returning to
the dig records and discovering that much valuable new information can
be extracted from those archives.[139]

Given the archaeological culture of the period, with its emphasis on
the study of temples and public buildings, Robinson deserves credit for
investigating a site that yielded much information on the domestic architecture and material culture of the ordinary Greek, rather than the structures of religious or political culture. The one hundred or more houses
excavated by the Johns Hopkins archaeologists at Olynthos still represent
our largest sample of Greek urban domestic architecture and associated
material culture.[140] In contrast, we know very little about the domestic
archaeology of the ancient Corinthian, even though American School
archaeologists have been working at the site for a century.

Although David Robinson's energies and productivities remained formidable, he was in many respects alone in the department. Tenney Frank
had arrived at Hopkins in 1913 and was a very distinguished classicist
with a strong interest in archaeology. But his main responsibility was
to teach ancient history. Furthermore, money was always short. Johns
Hopkins as a university moved increasingly toward big science, and the
humanities, including classics and classical archaeology, gradually declined into second-class.

Yale

Until the mid-1920s, the classical archaeology program at Yale was hardly
a major force in the discipline. Its main professor was Paul Baur (1872–
1951), described as a "modest, retiring professor, but an excellent teacher
of sterling qualities, a painstaking, accurate and thorough scholar, a wise
and sound counsellor."[141] These were decent human and academic qualities, but hardly the profile of a dynamic program developer in the mode of
Capps at Princeton or Robinson at Johns Hopkins. Yale classical archaeol-

138. Thompson 1991; J. Shaw 1992.
139. Cahill 1991.
140. MacKendrick 1962: 306–8.
141. D. M. Robinson 1951–52: 26–27.

ogy seemed destined to a perpetual genteel mediocrity. All that changed with the arrival of Michael Rostovtzeff (1870–1952) in 1925.

Michael Rostovtzeff's career closely mirrored the changing fortunes of many European academic intellectuals during the first half of this century.[142] Rostovtzeff's father had been the principal of a Russian classical gymnasium and a czarist education ministry official. Rostovtzeff received his university education in St. Petersburg.[143] As a student, he traveled and studied in both Greece and Italy. He developed an early interest in the archaeology of Pompeii, a site he first visited in 1892 and about which he wrote his Russian university thesis. This was the start of a lifelong fascination with Pompeii and the ways archaeological information could illuminate aspects of the ancient experience not covered by written sources.[144]

By 1914 Rostovtzeff had established an important position for himself among the academic intellectuals of prerevolutionary Russia.[145] He did pioneering research on Greek-Scythian interactions in the Black Sea region, demonstrating his ability to work at the juncture of ancient history and archaeology and to view archaeological remains as an important and neglected type of historical document.[146] He summarized his views on the relation between historical and archaeological evidence in his 1922 book *Iranians and Greeks in South Russia*:

> But I should like to call for a more rational use of archaeological material than has been usual hitherto. For me archaeology is not a source of illustrations for written texts, but an independent source of historical information, no less valuable and important, sometimes more important, than the written sources. We must learn, and we are gradually learning, how to write history with the help of archaeology. (quoted A. H. M. Jones 1952)

As a member of the liberal bourgeoisie, Rostovtzeff was ultimately forced to flee Russia in 1918. Neither the universities of France nor those of England were willing to provide him with an academic home, but in 1920 he was finally able to put down roots at the University of Wisconsin. From there he moved to Yale in 1925. Rostovtzeff's scholarship had impressive range, both in the time periods covered and in the variety of sources employed. He also brought the European intellectual's tradition of relating classical scholarship to wider cultural issues. He was by no

---

142. *EHCA* s.v. "Rostovtzeff, Michael Ivanovitch (Rostovzev, Michail Ivanovich; 1870–1952)"; Reinhold 1946, A. H. M. Jones 1952; Momigliano 1966; Christ 1972; B. Shaw 1992.
143. Wes 1990.
144. Rostovtzeff 1927, 1933.
145. Wes 1990; B. Shaw 1992.
146. Rostovtzeff 1922; Ascherson 1996: 115–16, 122–23.

means an intellectual radical, but he did feel the importance of combining specific research with general ideas at a time when empiricism dominated Anglo-American scholarship.[147]

Rostovtzeff's depth and range can be best appreciated in the two great works of his Yale period: *The Social and Economic History of the Roman Empire* (1926) and *The Social and Economic History of the Hellenistic Age* (1941). In these works Rostovtzeff displayed a vast knowledge of European scholars and scholarship, archaeological sites, and museum collections. He had a prodigious memory and an impressive capacity for work. He also synthesized these diverse types of evidence in a way that few American scholars could. This was due in part to the fact that he operated from general intellectual and cultural models in the tradition of nineteenth century European scholars. That Rostovtzeff and his work have become the object of study and analysis by intellectual historians more often than any other ancient historian and archaeologist is indicative of their scholarly complexity and sophistication.

When Rostovtzeff transferred from Wisconsin to Yale, he almost immediately began to explore the possibility of Yale's undertaking its own major excavation. Yale classics had historically been stronger in philology than either archaeology or ancient history, and the university had no classical excavation tradition. Rostovtzeff soon decided that Yale's best archaeological prospect was a joint French-American excavation at Dura Europos on the Euphrates border of Syria. Dura Europos had been founded on the left bank of the upper Euphrates River in the wake of Alexander the Great's conquest of the Persian Empire and the dynastic wars that followed his death. As a Hellenistic city that had successively come under Parthian and Roman control, it provided the type of complex cultural interaction and change that fascinated Rostovtzeff.[148] Furthermore, Dura's dry climate and its permanent abandonment soon after a Sassanian Persian siege in the mid-third century A.D. meant preservation of archaeological materials would be excellent. Rostovtzeff dubbed Dura the "Pompeii of the East," and the recovery of wall painting, leather, textiles, and papyrus at the site justified his claim.[149] Finally, since Syria was under French control, the exportation of some portion of the archaeological materials to America was possible.

Dura Europos had been discovered during post-World War I military operations. The American Egyptologist James Breasted made a hurried visit to the site and published a preliminary report on the first discoveries

147. Momigliano 1966.
148. *EHCA* s.v. "Dura-Europos"; Rostovtzeff 1938; A. Perkins 1973; Hopkins 1979.
149. Pfister and Bellinger 1945; Welles, Fink, and Gilliam 1959.

Figure 15. Michael Rostovtzeff with French and American archaeologists at the excavations of the Roman frontier site of Dura. Courtesy of the Yale University Art Gallery, Dura-Europos Archive.

made there.[150] At the end of the war, the French began a program of systematic excavations at Dura. Initially they were directed by the Belgian historian of ancient religion Franz Cumont. Yale University archaeologists joined the French in 1924 and then continued on their own from 1926 to 1939.[151] Clark Hopkins was the first American field director, succeeded in the last years by Frank Brown. Rostovtzeff followed the excavations closely, regularly visiting the site and energetically publicizing the importance of the finds (Figure 15). The excavations yielded abundant evidence about life in a beleaguered Roman garrison town in the mid-third century A.D. They also allowed researchers to reconstruct

150. J. Breasted 1924; C. Breasted 1943.
151. Hopkins 1979.

the changing urban framework of Dura as it passed from Greek to Parthian to Roman control and to document the diverse ethnic, social, and religious groups found in a border town along Rome's eastern frontier.

The meeting of diverse religious cultures at Dura was dramatically illustrated by the discovery of a Mithraic temple, a synagogue, and a Christian chapel, all buried by the Roman countersiege works of the mid-third century.[152] The chapel was the oldest Christian building yet found.[153] The synagogue was especially interesting, for its walls were extensively decorated with scenes from the Old Testament, showing that some sects within Roman Judaism had no reservations about displaying images in their places of worship.[154] All the sculpture and wall painting reflected a combination of Greek, Roman, and Parthian influences that not only demonstrated the complex cultural interactions of the mid-third century A.D. but also provided insight into the process of transition from antiquity into the medieval and Byzantine periods.[155]

The combination of Michael Rostovtzeff's intellectual energy and originality and the exciting discoveries at Dura had the potential of making Yale into one of the most creative graduate centers for ancient history and classical archaeology in North America. The Yale Art Gallery was enriched by some of the choice finds at Dura such as the Mithraeum and the Christian chapel. During the 1930s Rostovtzeff attracted very promising graduate students of the era like Frank Brown (1908–1988), C. Bradford Welles (1901–1969) and Alfred Bellinger (1893–1978), who made major contributions in both ancient history and archaeology during the postwar era.[156]

The outbreak of World War II destroyed much of this hope and promise. Rostovtzeff's health broke down, spurred by his again being witness to the barbarous collapse of the European civilization he so admired. By 1944 his scholarly career was effectively at an end. The French mandate in Syria and the possibility of continued exportation of objects from the area ceased shortly after the war. Dura and Antioch were the last two American classical excavations that legally enriched U.S. museums. Although many Rostovtzeff students, including Bellinger, Brown, and Welles, remained in the Yale classics department after the war, and the

152. Hopkins 1979: 89–117; 123–77; 193–212.

153. Kraeling 1967; Frend 1996: 198–99.

154. Kraeling 1956; Gutman 1973.

155. Breasted from the very beginning stressed the connections with Byzantine art (J. Breasted 1924). Rostovtzeff 1935 and 1938 both deal with the complex associations of the Dura paintings.

156. For Brown cf. *EHCA* s.v. "Brown, Frank Edward (1908–88)"; Scott 1988. For Bellinger, cf. *WWW* 10.25 s.v. "Bellinger, Alfred"; *AJA* 82 (1978): 427.

American Academy excavations at Cosa in Italy were closely associated with Yale, the graduate archaeology program there never again achieved the strength and dynamism to challenge Princeton's hegemony.

The AIA Between the Wars

The years between World War I and World War II saw the center of power and influence in American classical archaeology shift toward the American School of Classical Studies and a limited number of graduate institutions, especially Princeton University. These developments further undermined the Archaeological Institute of America's position as the center of American classical archaeology. No longer was it a leader in sponsoring research, and the individual schools it had spawned went their own way. The AIA faced marginalization in the profession that it had done so much to create. Membership growth stagnated. Between 1917 and 1930, AIA membership increased only slightly, from 3,215 to 3,460. With the onset of the depression, it declined dramatically. Between 1932 and 1933 it dropped from 3,008 to 2,679. By 1935 it hit a low point of 1,489. Clearly the AIA had to reflect on its mission and try to strengthen its base. Some argued that the organization should focus on a relatively conservative research base. Ralph Magoffin of NYU, who was soon accused of being an uncontrolled populist, made the case for the central role of serious research in the AIA mission in 1926:

The forty-eight years of educational and scientific service rendered by the Archaeological Institute of America in an honest and creditable way seem to mark out the Institute as the logical and proper clearing house for archaeological enterprises undertaken by Americans. Archaeology at the moment is almost too popular. There is a distinct danger that the scientific aims of archaeology may be hindered, yes even frustrated, by the sensational amateur who digs for fun, or by the acquisitive opportunist who digs for profit. Either one may easily bring international discredit upon us. (*Annual Bulletin AIA* 1926)

The AIA's recovery from the problems of the war years was complicated by power and personality clashes centered on Mitchell Carroll (1870–1925), the major administrative figure associated with the AIA in the pre- and postwar years.[157] Carroll's early academic profile was typical of the new emerging American professionals. He had a Ph.D. from Hopkins, a brief period of study in Germany, and then a year at the American School of Classical Studies in Athens. After a year of teaching at Hopkins, he went to George Washington University, an appointment that provided good contacts on the Washington scene. Carroll was very much involved in the development of the Washington society into one of the strongest

157. Kelsey 1926c.

AIA chapters. He became associate secretary of the AIA in 1904, helped obtain its charter from Congress in 1906, and in 1908 became secretary of the AIA, a position he held until 1918. During his administration, the AIA flourished and Carroll built a strong political base both in Washington and in the membership at large. He won the support of another populist academic, Francis Kelsey, and even the grudging respect of his enemies. As one admirer-critic observed, "the spread of the Institute is his religion . . . I came to have a tremendous amount of sympathy for the tenacity of a man who could hold so many volunteer workers with divergent opinions together at all" (AIA Archives Box 21: Currelly to Egbert 3 July 1918).

The 1917 election of James Egbert (1859–1948) to the AIA presidency seems to have changed the mood. Egbert was a conservative Romanist with a career spent totally in the Ivy League preserve of Columbia.[158] From correspondence in the AIA archives, it is clear that he was not a Carroll enthusiast; in that, he represented the views of a conservative Ivy League group. However, Egbert had to move cautiously for fear of offending Kelsey and the powerful Washington society, which threatened to secede from the AIA if Carroll were dismissed.[159] Intersociety rivalries also fueled the tensions. Boston and New York resented Washington's rise, and St. Louis hoped to benefit from Washington's discomfiture. In the end a compromise solution was reached in which the Washington society assumed financial responsibility for *Art and Archaeology* and Carroll devoted the bulk of his energies to Washington and *Art and Archaeology*.

The AIA's scholarly activity during this era was focused mainly on disseminating of the results of research done by other organizations and individuals. Its two organs of outreach were the scholarly meeting and the *American Journal of Archaeology*. The annual meeting continued to grow in importance; attendance rose and the number of presentations increased. Quaint customs from the Victorian Age still survived. At the 1921 AIA meeting in Ann Arbor there was still a male smoker at the University Club and a reception for women at a private residence. But the topics of presentations became ever more narrowly focused. The program of the 1926 meeting held at Harvard still reflected to a certain degree the broader archaeological vision of the AIA's founders. Although the bulk of the papers were on subjects related to classical archaeology, there were several presentations on early Christian and medieval art. By

158. Luce 1950a.
159. AIA Archives Box 20: Correspondence of James Egbert 1918. The Currelly-Egbert letter of 3 July 1918 makes clear that losing the Washington society would be a disaster for the AIA.

the 1940 meeting, the New World was represented by one general paper; all the other presentations related to the ancient Mediterranean. Almost all of those were classical, and within classical archaeology the great majority were on Greek topics.

The course of the *AJA* held steady during those decades. From 1920–23 the editor was William Nickerson Bates (1867–1949) of the University of Pennsylvania. His was a holding operation, which suited a person conservative in temperament and without a strong background in archaeology. According to his obituary "A man of New England upbringing, and naturally conservative, he relinquished the editorship, when a more expansive policy was sought than he thought wise at the time."[160] The unhappy period of Bates's editorship saw financial problems, dispute about editorial policy, and a disastrous fire at the printing house where *AJA* was produced.[161] In 1924 George Elderkin of Princeton assumed the editorship and held it until 1931. Elderkin created a regular book review department and tried to raise endowment. Otherwise, the journal continued on its classical archaeology course under both Elderkin and his successor, Mary Hamilton Swindler.[162]

The Lecture Program

The lecture program continued to be a major unifying force for the institute and an important bridge between the worlds of the amateur and the professional. The number of local societies continued to increase. Scholars crisscrossed the country, bringing news of the latest archaeological discoveries to larger and more diverse audiences. The lecture program peaked in 1930 with 219 lectures given before fifty-four societies by fifty-one different lecturers. Then the effects of the Great Depression began to be felt, as AIA membership declined and the revenues available to support traveling lecturers shrank. By 1931–32 the number of lectures sponsored by the AIA was down to 144. By 1933 it had decreased to 105 and in 1936 to 102. Although this decline was arrested in the last years before the war, it was not until conditions of peace and prosperity returned that the lecture program resumed its old vitality.

The centerpiece of the lecturer program remained the Norton lecture series, which James Loeb (1867–1933) had endowed in 1909. Between the wars such distinguished European scholars as E. A. Gardner, Michael Rostovtzeff, Alan Wace, Thomas Ashby, and John Garstang were Norton lecturers. The same year that Hitler seized power in Germany, Loeb died in Munich. It was a great loss for classical studies and in many ways the

160. Luce 1949; Donahue 1985: 15.
161. Donahue 1985: 15–18.
162. Donahue 1985: 18–27.

end of an era. Loeb came from a successful New York banking family, and after Harvard he planned to pursue a business career. However, ill health intervened, and in 1901 he retired to pursue a variety of personal interests including classics and classical archaeology. Most of his later years were passed in Munich, where he built up a substantial personal collection of antiquities.[163]

Loeb strongly felt the need to support a "wide cultivation of the humanities, which are suffering neglect in the stress of modern life."[164] He is best known in classical circles for his endowment of the widely used Loeb classical text series with facing pages of Greek and Latin texts and translations. His aim in supporting this ambitious venture was to stimulate interest in the classics at a time when decline in the study of Greek and Latin in schools and colleges was cutting off many interested people from literary works regarded as part of the foundations of Western civilization. Loeb also encouraged teaching classical archaeology by endowing a professorship at Harvard.[165]

Art and Archaeology Magazine

In the period between the wars archaeology was clearly becoming a very popular subject for educated lay audiences. It was to meet the challenge of providing a journal for these people that the magazine *Art and Archaeology* was founded in 1914. The magazine's mission statement made clear the goals of the new publication:

> The purpose of *Art and Archaeology* is to give people in an interesting and attractive way the information they all want and ought to have in the wide realm embraced by its name from the first stirrings of the artistic consciousness among the cave dwellers of prehistoric ages through the period of the rise, culmination, and decline of the great civilizations of former times down to the living present. (AIA Archives)

Art and Archaeology was the brainchild of people in the AIA's Washington society, one of the organization's most dynamic chapters. David Moore Robinson of Johns Hopkins was appointed the first editor. The magazine was aimed at the growing audience of educated, interested amateurs who also subscribed to magazines like *National Geographic*. Each monthly issue contained articles, reviews, and news items on archaeology and the arts. The geographical and chronological range of the articles was great. A distinctive feature was the special issue devoted to archaeology and art in a single country like Germany and Spain, with articles on

163. *EHCA* s.v. "Loeb, James (1867–1933)."
164. *NCAB* 100:73 s.v. "Loeb, James."
165. *EHCA* s.v. "Loeb, James (1867–1933)."

the latest archaeological discoveries written by distinguished local scholars. The initial goal of 10,000 subscribers proved ambitious, but by 1923 there were 4,755 subscribers and the balance sheets were healthy.

The early years were characterized by personal tensions on the editorial board and especially between the ever prickly David Robinson and Mitchell Carroll. In 1918 Robinson was forced out of the editorship in a bitter power and policy struggle. He was replaced by Carroll and then by the less controversial Arthur Stanley Riggs (1879–1976), whose background was more editorial than archaeological.[166] Robinson and his supporters did not leave the scene gracefully. Robinson peppered the long-suffering AIA president James Egbert with letters, reminding him of his own positive qualities and noting his successors' inefficiencies and lack of concern for quality.[167] Still, the magazine remained very popular with the lay membership.

The depression hit the magazine very hard. While *AJA* had a solid scholarly base of subscribers among both individuals and institutions, *Art and Archaeology* was an intellectual luxury that could be abandoned in hard times. Its 1932 annual report succinctly stated "Circulation decreased materially during the year and advertising dwindled to the vanishing point."[168] Severe cost-cutting measures had to be taken. By 1932 the journal had been reduced from a monthly to a bimonthly.

The magazine also came increasingly under ideological attack from conservative forces within the AIA. These were led by Louis Lord of Oberlin College and William Dinsmoor of Columbia. Dinsmoor's conservative stance was to be expected. Lord (1876–1957) was more of a teacher and popular educator who spent his retirement years heading up the Bureau of University Travel. However, as president of AIA during the depression years of 1932–37, he had to be deeply concerned with the financial implications of any AIA action.[169]

Lord and Dinsmoor's position on *Art and Archaeology* was summarized in the 1933 AIA annual report:

President Lord presented the view of a faction of the Institute which feels it will be better without *Art and Archaeology*. Professor Dinsmoor endorsed the view, on the two grounds that the Institute does not wish to be represented at all by a magazine of popular character, and then to use his own words, "*Art and Archaeology* has ceased to be what the Institute expected. It has become largely an art magazine. To keep up the interests of the Institute it should be limited to archaeology." (*Annual Report AIA* 1933)

166. *WWW America* 6: 345.
167. AIA Archives Box 20: Egbert-Robinson correspondence.
168. *Annual Report Art & Archaeology* 1932.
169. I owe the material on Louis Lord to Dr. Richard Bauman, archive librarian of Oberlin College.

Beset by financial problems and undermined by this strong faction within the AIA establishment, *Art and Archaeology* ceased publication in 1934. The negative results of this termination were obvious almost immediately. Clarence Ward, the AIA secretary, noted, in his 1935 report, that there had been a significant drop in sustaining members and that it "is probable that a good many of those members could be regained should we offer them a journal which supplemented the *AJA* in a satisfactory manner."[170] The journal's legacy would be taken up after the war with the foundation of *Archaeology* in 1948.

The attacks on *Art and Archaeology* were part of a greater philosophical and ideological struggle that sharply divided the Archaeological Institute of America during the late 1920s and early 1930s. These hostilities came to a head in 1931, when a very serious effort was mounted by conservatives to bring a no-confidence motion against AIA president and NYU professor Ralph Magoffin, and thus remove him from office. Since Magoffin had served as AIA president since 1921, such an attack represented a serious political revolt.

The issues that provoked these actions were intricate and convoluted. Many of the arguments derived from complex financial charges and countercharges. But the core debate centered on the degree to which AIA should be a popular organization as opposed to a strictly scholarly one. One petition for Magoffin's removal prepared by William Dinsmoor and George Elderkin put the case bluntly in a statement which ended with a short quote from a negative review that Magoffin's book had received in *Antiquity*:

His attitude and his entire financial policy are directed toward propaganda and popularization. It is an attitude which has exposed his writing to the criticism that "it conveys a wholly wrong impression of what archaeology is." (AIA Archives Box 29.3)

The key issue was framed as popularization versus serious scholarship and research. The petition for Magoffin's removal quoted with approval Magoffin's 1919 report:

The direct object of the Institute's existence is the encouragement of archaeological research and study. . . . To this object all else should be subsidiary and the means of supplying funds for the attainment of the purpose for which the Institute exists. (*Annual Report* AIA 1919)

To substantiate their claims of creeping popularization, Dinsmoor and Elderkin noted that in the days of Charles Eliot Norton 81 percent of the AIA budget had gone for research and only 6 percent for administration,

170. *Annual Bulletin AIA* 1935: 13–14.

whereas under Magoffin only 12 percent went for research (and that mainly to AIA-associated institutions, not AIA-sponsored research) and 30 percent for administration.[171]

Magoffin's attackers had complex motivations. The petitioners were genuinely concerned about an AIA policy that seemed to favor support for *Art and Archaeology* over the *American Journal of Archaeology* at a time when funds were very limited. There was a Boston-New York-Philadelphia area jealousy about the power of the Washington society that sponsored *Art and Archaeology*. The movement probably reflected a certain amount of academic snobbism with Harvard, Yale, Princeton, and Columbia lined up against New York University and the world of more popular education. The list of conspirators included George Chase and Stephen Lucas of Harvard; Mary Swindler and Edith Dohan of Philadelphia; Rufus Morey, Emerson Swift, and Baldwin Smith of Princeton; and William Dinsmoor, Edward Robinson, Edward Newell, and Gisela Richter of New York.

Ralph Magoffin (1874–1942) had perfectly solid scholarly credentials, although they were not always those of the eastern elite.[172] He had received his B.A. from Michigan and his Ph.D. from Johns Hopkins and had been a fellow at the American Academy in Rome in 1907. He taught at Johns Hopkins from 1908 to 1923 and then went to NYU as chair of department in 1923. He served as president of the AIA from 1921 to 1931. In 1922 he was professor in charge of the School of Classical Studies at the American Academy.[173] Magoffin did solid scholarship but also realized the need for classical archaeologists to reach out to a wider audience. He served as president of the American Classical League and wrote a guide to the forum for Latin teachers titled *The Roman Forum: the Greatest Small Spot on Earth* (1927). He also pioneered the popular archaeology book with his *Magic Spades* (1923). His *The Romance of Archaeology* (1930), coauthored with Emily Davis, received a short review of vintage snobbish British condensation in *Antiquity*: "This is an unnecessary book; but it is worse than that—it conveys a wholly wrong impression of what archaeology is. The style is commonplace and occasionally lapses into vulgarity, especially in the titles of illustrations" (*Antiquity* 1930: 503). The AIA conservatives and the editor of *Antiquity* might sniff at such productions, but they helped create and sustain a popular interest in archaeology at the start of the Great Depression, when the field needed all the help and support it could get.

Magoffin was a vigorous personality, and he soon counterattacked

171. AIA Archives Box 29.3.
172. *EHCA* s.v. "Magoffin, Ralph Van Deman (1874–1942)"; Luce 1942.
173. Luce 1942; Valentine and Valentine 1973: 184.

against his enemies. In a memo of 30 April 1931, he placed himself solidly in the populist academic tradition of Francis Kelsey. He noted that ideological tensions within the AIA had a long history and traced them back to the presidency of Thomas Seymour of Yale:

> During the presidency of T. D. Seymour of Yale there began a cleavage between those who wished to keep the Institute a small professional and research organization and those who believed that it should grow into a large national body which recognized an obligation to the cultured public which was beginning to take an absorbing interest in archaeology. (AIA Archives Box 29.6)

Magoffin expressed no surprise at the fact that *Art and Archaeology* was going to be more popular than *AJA* among this new membership drawn from the "cultured public." He regarded both publications and the two activities that they represented as necessary for a healthy institute.

In the end the direct assault on Magoffin failed. However, his presidency was crippled, and he refused to stand for reelection. He cited as his precedent the fact that even the great Charles Eliot Norton had served for only ten years. He then thanked those who had helped him "revive the Institute from a post war torpidity and put it on the road to the success it deserves."[174] Stephen Luce grudgingly acknowledged that under Magoffin's presidency "the Institute underwent a period of great expansion and growth."[175] Magoffin's successor as president was his archenemy Louis Lord. The conservatives now turned on *Art and Archaeology*, and in 1934 they had the satisfaction of seeing that enterprise fail. The institute could then devote all its slender, depression-era publication resources to *AJA*. Lord cleared the institute's debt, but its general financial position and membership base continued to decline. The Tarsus funding fiasco with Hetty Goldman and her supporters indicated how far the AIA had descended from the dynamic days of Norton and Magoffin.

Summer Schools in Rome and Athens

Ralph Magoffin was not alone in arguing that popular, pedagogical approaches were necessary if classics was going to maintain its position in the world of American education and cultured society. Special concern was expressed for the fate of the classical languages, which had stood at the heart of American elite education since the seventeenth century. Enrollments in Greek and Latin were declining, and it was felt that this was in part the result of failed educational imagination. An increasing number of enlightened teachers felt that the prevailing emphasis on grammar review and often rote translation was not sufficient to sustain

174. *Annual Report AIA* 1931: 8–9.
175. Luce 1942: 412–13.

classics in changing times. New approaches were needed. Some hoped that through intensive exposure to the ancient monuments and to the latest archaeological discoveries in both Greece and Italy teachers at both the secondary and college levels would be able to make classics in the classroom a more interesting experience. This concern led to the foundation of schools for teachers at both the American Academy in Rome and the American School of Classical Studies in Athens.

These summer schools cooperated with and built on the tours developed by the Bureau of University Travel. The Bureau had conducted high-quality classical tours and provided funds for archaeological research for several years. Its leaders were enthusiastic and successful teachers who strongly believed in the redeeming power of ancient art and civilization, especially that of Greece. One president of the organization, H. H. Powers, laid out clearly his vision of Greece in his book *The Message of Greek Art*, first printed in 1913 and reprinted twice in the 1920s. He opened his introductory chapter by stating, "By common consent the Greek civilization is the most remarkable that the world has ever known."[176] He then went on to describe the development of Greek art with an idealizing enthusiasm that would have pleased Charles Eliot Norton.

The American Academy in Rome conducted its first official summer school in 1923. The trustees had approached the concept cautiously and had initially insisted that the summer session be sponsored "not under the name of the Academy" but by "an interested group of Trustees."[177] Professor Grant Showerman (1870–1935) of the University of Wisconsin conducted the first session and continued to teach the summer program until 1932. Like Ralph Magoffin, Showerman was a great believer in the popularization of the classics. He possessed a deep knowledge and love for Rome in all its periods and aspects which he clearly conveyed to his summer school students.[178] While the course was considered superficial and brief by the standards of the American Academy's year-long program, it was felt that "every one of [Showerman's] students returns to America prepared to resume teaching of the classics with increased enthusiasm and with clearer understanding of Roman life.[179]

Most of those who attended were high school teachers. By 1927, the summer school's fifth year, 208 classicists had participated in the program. Given the fact that the bulk of those attending were secondary school teachers in an era when women dominated that profession, it is

176. Powers 1928: 1.

177. Valentine and Valentine 1973: 89.

178. *NCAB* 27: 318; Showerman received his degrees and did all his teaching at the University of Wisconsin. For his role as a teacher and proponent of classical humanism, cf. Allen, Beatty, Goodnight, and Laird 1935; Oldfather 1936.

179. *Annual Report AAR* 1922: 24–25.

not surprising that women represented the great majority of those in most summer school programs, often outnumbering men by three or four to one. These Rome summers helped to create a sense of common identity among educators working to promote classical culture in an era of philistine values. They also served to increase awareness of the growing contribution archaeology was making to understanding the classical past. While most teaching of Greek and Latin retained its strong grammatical emphasis, the presence of photos of Rome or plaster reproductions of the Prima Porta Augustus in the classroom conveyed some sense of an ancient world beyond the gerundive.

The academy summer programs focused on the principal sites and monuments in and around Rome with short visits to places like Pompeii. This was an exciting time for such archaeological tours, since Fascist building and excavation programs were transforming Rome, clearing and reconstructing monuments like the Forum of Augustus and the Ara Pacis. The American teachers saw in Fascist education, especially in the secondary schools, a world in which classical languages and civilization were still central to the teaching mission.[180]

The first Greek summer school at the American School of Classical Studies was held in 1925. The initial part of the program was linked to a regular tour of the Bureau of University Travel and consisted of lectures delivered on board ship and in England, France, and Italy. The second part focused on site visits in Greece. Only six people participated.[181] The intellectual and ideological purpose of the Athens summer program was summarized by the director and old Athens hand Walter Miller of the University of Missouri:

> The main purpose of the Summer Session has been to give the members an opportunity to see as much of Greece as is practicable in a few weeks of midsummer and to take in as much as possible of the spirit of the great days of Hellas by intimate association with her peerless monuments and by reading and reviewing some of the great literature associated with the scenes visited. (*Annual Report ASCS* 1925)

Since teaching Greek was no longer a significant enterprise in American secondary education, the language-culture connection was not so strong in Athens as in Rome. However, since Greece was a still primitive place for the average traveler, the summer program's organized tours made sites and ruins accessible to a greater range of classicists who were not hard core archaeologists. In the period before World War II, the Athens summer school became an important program.

---

180. The educational activities of the Fascists led by the philosopher Giovanni Gentile were very well received in many American educational circles. Cf. Diggins 1972: 252–55.

181. *Annual Report ASCS* 1924–25: 51.

Within a few years, the basic pattern of both summer schools had been established. Most of the site visits were the same from year to year. The directors rotated, exposing the participants to a variety of the better archaeology teachers from the United States. The schools also served to reaffirm the centrality of the schools' programs and values to American classical archaeology. Program participants met the resident archaeologists, observed the ongoing excavations, and learned the history and traditions of the sponsoring institutions. Both summer schools proved to be very successful ventures; both were restarted soon after the war and continue in full vigor today. Hundreds of teachers, graduate students, and even undergraduates have obtained their first direct contact with classical antiquity through these programs. Probably no other institutions have done more to keep classics alive at the grassroots level in America.

Archaeology and the American Academy in Rome Between the Wars

The creation of the summer school was the main programmatic innovation at the American Academy during the interwar period. Otherwise, inherent conservatism and external circumstances allowed for little change. Tradition reigned supreme and innovation was discouraged. This view was summarized in the director's report for 1934–35:

A proper appraisal of the tendencies shown in the work of our Fellows in architecture, sculpture, painting, and landscape architecture involves a careful comparison of the work of several successive years, years during which the influence of a movement summarized generally under the term "modernism" — highly destructive of the students' appreciation of classical precedent and classic example, has been evident in our schools at home. The most difficult problem for the Academy today is to determine the wisest method for bringing back the students' enthusiasm and reverence for the basic tradition which underlies all the greatest art of twenty centuries. (*Annual Report AAR* 1933–34: 23)

No group of artists experienced these tensions more than more than the architects. The ruling architectural elite of the academy, centered mainly in New York, wanted a virtually unchanged Beaux Arts program to remain in force. They tended to enforce their wishes with a heavy hand directly from New York. Director G. P. Stevens was caught in the middle of this dispute and by 1932 was eased out of his position.[182]

Stevens's years as director of the academy had not been without archaeological accomplishments. His love for architectural archaeology provided the basis for a fruitful research program centered on Roman architectural reconstruction. Several of the architectural fellows worked

182. Valentine and Valentine 1973: 92–93; Yegul 1991.

on hypothetical reconstructions of ancient monuments at Ostia, Horace's Sabine Villa, Hadrian's Villa at Tivoli, and structures at Pompeii. By the early 1930s the Italian government showed slightly more flexibility toward foreign excavations. Stevens took advantage of this to conduct excavations at Horace's Sabine Farm and at Hadrian's Villa at Tivoli.[183] Interestingly enough, the architects, not the classicists, were in charge, and the digs were focused on the recovery of building plans.[184]

The only other American institution to take advantage of the slight relaxation of Italian excavation rules for foreigners was the University of Pennsylvania, which conducted a short-lived (1931–34) but nevertheless productive excavation at the Roman Republican port city of Minturnae in southern Italy. The director was Jotham Johnson (1905–1967), later the first editor of *Archaeology* magazine.[185] The Penn archaeologists uncovered public buildings in the forum area along with important inscriptions.[186]

During these years other scholars associated with the academy felt that the institution should have an expanded research mission. In 1919–20 Professor G. L. Hendrickson of Yale proposed that the School of Classical Studies be expanded into a School of Historical Studies that would include "students of medieval or modern history, of economic and social life, of art, or of modern and especially romance literature and philology."[187] The idea died stillborn. Gorham Stevens suggested as early as 1920–21 that the academy begin a program of long-term topographical research on the ancient towns in Latium and Etruria. This would have involved study of standing remains and antiquarian records in the tradition of such Campagna researchers as Rodolfo Lanciani and Thomas Ashby.[188] Stevens already had a model in the topographical study of Lanuvium undertaken by Guy B. Colburn, a fellow in 1910.[189]

Aiding this positive research environment was the general support in the United States for Mussolini and the Fascists.[190] The American economic and cultural elite, including the classical community, was on the whole very sympathetic to the Fascist movement and the academy administration and associated American academics enjoyed good relations with influential fascist political and cultural figures. In his first report on the Fascist coup Gorham Stevens stated that:

183. Valentine and Valentine 1973: 89.

184. *Annual Report AAR* 1929–30: 37; 1930–31: 25; 1931–32: 22–23.

185. *EHCA* s.v. "Johnson, Jotham (1905–67)."

186. J. Johnson 1932, 1933, 1935.

187. *Annual Report AAR* 1919: 20.

188. For the tradition represented by Lanciani and Ashby, cf. *EHCA* s.v. "Ashby, Thomas (1874–1931)," "Lanciani, Rodolfo (1847–1929)"; Barker, Hodges, and Ferrari 1989.

189. Colburn 1914.

190. Diggins 1972: 144–286.

The leadership of Benito Mussolini is producing important results. A feeling of nationalism is noticeable among the Italian youth. Thus far Mussolini has devoted his efforts chiefly against disorder and toward governmental reforms. (*Annual Report AAR* 1922–23: 19)

Grant Showerman, the director of the summer school during much of that period, was even more enthusiastic. In an essay entitled "Darkness and Light in the Old World" he observed:

In the last days of the month the Fascisti executed the famous March on Rome, and for a few days there was barbed wire at the city gates. With the Revolution of October 28 began the new life of Italy—no more strikes, no more political parties, no more legislative deadlocks, no more superfluous officeholders, no more wordiness, and everybody to work for the good of the state. (1924: 243)

The American Academy's annual report for 1928–29 had as its frontispiece a painting by fellow Deane Keller titled *Fascismo* which echoed the pictorial imagery of the regime, including a muscular youth giving the Fascist salute toward a symbol that blended the cross and the fasces. In February 1934 Mussolini paid an official visit to the academy.[191] Esther Van Deman was especially enthusiastic toward Mussolini and his policies. The Fascist archaeologist A. M. Colini emphasized that in his obituary of her:

La Van Deman era non solo romana, ma anche italiana di elezione e grande ammiratrice dell'opera rinnovatrice del Fascismo. E questa devozione alla nostra Patria dimostro in uno dei momenti politici piu difficili, quello della guerra di Abissinia. Ella che allora si trovava per un ciclo di conferenze in America, chiedeva di poter aggiungere al suo tema dieci minuti per parlare dell'Italia; e prima di partire aveva offerto il suo oro piu caro al Fascio di Monteverde. (Colini 1938: 324)

[Van Deman was not only a Roman, but also an Italian by choice and a great admirer of the renewal activities of Fascism. This devotion to our country she demonstrated in one of the most difficult political moments, that of the Ethiopian War. She, while she was in America for a lecture tour, asked to be able to add to her topic ten minutes to speak of Italy, and before leaving had offered her most precious gold to the Fascist shrine of Monteverde.]

A major problem Stevens faced in trying to develop an archaeology program at the academy was the lack of vigorous leadership in the resident AAR archaeological community. The deaths of Samuel Ball Platner in 1921 and Densmore Curtis in 1925 had left a vacuum only partially filled by Albert Van Buren (1878–1968). Van Buren became the central archaeological figure at the academy during the interwar period. He had been trained as a paleographer at Yale and came to Rome with little

191. *Annual Report AAR* 1933–34: 22; Valentine and Valentine 1973: 90.

academic archaeological training. Compared to his counterparts at the American School in Athens, he was not a professional. Yet from his arrival as librarian and instructor of archaeology at the Academy in 1908 to his retirement in 1946, he largely represented archaeology at the American Academy.[192]

Van Buren was described by an Italian colleague as "archeologo di straordinaria erudizione, dotato di un senso di concretezza ammirevole, piu topografo ed antiquario che storico dell'arte" (an archaeologist of exceptional erudition, endowed with an admirable sense of detail, more of a topographer and antiquarian than an art historian).[193] He became in some ways the Eugene Vanderpool of the American Academy. Both were individuals with vast knowledge of the classical archaeology of the respective countries where they lived. Both shaped a generation of students at their school through their teaching of archaeology. Van Buren even resembled Vanderpool in that he remained in enemy Italy during World War II.[194]

Like Vanderpool, Van Buren's scholarship was generally expressed in short articles, with no major works to his credit. But Van Buren the outdoor dynamism that made his Greek counterpart beloved by field-oriented students and colleagues. Van Buren did not have the concentrated research energy of his older English contemporary Thomas Ashby. He was satisfied to enjoy the peace and quiet of the academy library, flavor the exciting classical and archaeological world of Fascist Rome, conduct the academy archaeological tours, and give an occasional lecture or write a short article.

Following Curtis's death, no major archaeological figure stepped in to supplement Van Buren. Stevens's interests in academy archaeology seem to have been largely frustrated. Rhys Carpenter of Bryn Mawr served a brief but dynamic term as professor in charge for 1926–27 and again in 1939–40.[195] Tenney Frank was professor in charge for 1916–17 and 1922–25.[196] Frank's role as an ancient historian who appreciated the importance of archaeology for understanding ancient history, especially social and economic, that the literary texts did not illuminate has already been considered. This approach influenced several of the fellows resident at the academy during his professorship.

These young scholars sought to combine topographical research, epigraphical studies, museum work, and even excavation. Three of the most active were women. It is ironic that during these years the American

192. F. E. Brown 1969: 70; Valentine and Valentine 1973: 202.
193. Susini 1970.
194. Valentine and Valentine 1973: 106.
195. Valentine and Valentine 1973: 161.
196. Valentine and Valentine 1973: 169.

School in Athens, with its dynamic archaeological research program, increasingly moved women into subordinate, intellectually routine roles, while the sleepier American Academy produced a group of highly innovative, dynamic women working at the juncture of archaeology and ancient history.

Lily Ross Taylor (1886–1969) first came to the academy as Bryn Mawr Scholar in 1909–10 and was fellow in archaeology there from 1917 to 1922. She early developed a strong interest in the topographical and epigraphical aspects of archaeology and remained a vigorous topographical surveyor into old age.[197] Her early research focused on Italian, including studies of the cults of Ostia and Etruria and the location of the sanctuary site of Lucus Feronia.[198]

Another founder of the AAR historical-archaeological tradition was Louise Adams (later Louise Adams Holland) (1893–1990). She received a Ph.D. from Bryn Mawr and was a fellow at the academy in 1922–23.[199] Her research reflected the influence of both Densmore Curtis and Tenney Frank. In her two important monographs of the period, *A Study of the Commerce of Latium from the Early Iron Age Through the Sixth Century* (1921) and *The Faliscans in Prehistoric Times* (1925), she demonstrated an impressive ability to combine literary sources, excavated archaeological material and vigorous topographical investigation.[200] These research interests continued throughout her life and culminated in her important monograph *Janus and the Bridge* (1961).

The third member of that early group was Inez Scott (later Inez Scott Ryberg) (1901–1980). She was a classical philology student out of Minnesota and Wisconsin, who was introduced to archaeology by Tenney Frank as an important tool for reconstructing the early centuries of Roman history.[201] This interdisciplinary approach shaped her pioneering study *The Early Roman Traditions in the Light of Archaeology* (1929), in which she undertook a complex and sophisticated investigation of the relationship between literary texts and the archaeological remains for reconstructing early Roman history.[202] Her second monograph also dealt with Rome's early archaeological record.[203]

After Frank's professorship but continuing his tradition of research were Elizabeth Evans (1905–1977) and Agnes Kirsopp Lake (1909–

197. Valentine and Valentine 1973: 50–51, 76, 82, 89; Susini 1969–70.
198. Taylor 1912, 1920, 1923.
199. Valentine and Valentine 1973: 175.
200. Broughton 1990a.
201. Broughton 1983.
202. Scott 1929.
203. Ryberg 1940.

1993). Elizabeth Evans, graduate of Radcliffe and fellow in 1932, even took part in a temple excavation in the Abruzzi as part of her research on the cults of the Sabine country.[204] Lake (later Agnes Michaels), who was a fellow in 1933, did archaeological research on the Tuscan temple and excavated with the University of Pennsylvania group at Minturnae.[205] Although the field activities of this group of women scholars were limited, their publications and teaching were highly influential in shaping the next generation that would take advantage of expanded archaeological opportunities in Italy.

Prelude to War

In 1939, barely twenty years after the war to end all wars, Europe once again prepared for combat. As had happened before World War I, Americans had divided emotions about what was happening in Europe, especially in Germany. Germany had been the fountainhead of American classical archaeology and even in the 1930s still represented the best of classical scholarship. But the Nazi regime that seized power in 1933 rapidly demonstrated a level of brutality and intolerance that alienated most American intellectuals.

The complexities of these reactions can be appreciated through a small but significant series of actions taken by Americans just as the war started. In December of 1940, a year before the United States entered the conflict, Professor William Dinsmoor of Columbia severed his twenty-six-year relationship with the German Archaeological Institute. Among the events that precipitated Dinsmoor's action was the receipt of "a personal letter signed by thirty-six well known archaeologists and classical scholars, describing themselves as 'former Austrians' and protesting against any criticism of the Nazi annexation of their ex-country." Dinsmoor went on to observe sadly that "One cannot but wonder if scholarship is worth serious consideration, when it can bend so easily and stultify its voice in the service of political aggression."[206]

That not all American scholars subscribed to Dinsmoor's views about how to react to current developments in Germany can be seen in the actions of B. H. Hill of the American School of Athens. As a consequence of Dinsmoor's open letter of resignation to the German Archaeological Institute, German scholars in Athens were prohibited from accepting invitations from the American School. Hill moved quickly to placate the Germans by going to the institute and explaining that "the American

204. *Annual Report AAR* 1931–32: 22–23; Evans 1939: 127–32.
205. Kohl 1995: 214–15.
206. *Annual Bulletin AIA* 1940: 7.

School is not a department of the AIA" and that he wanted the long-established relations between the two schools maintained.[207]

As war enveloped Europe, American schools and expeditions began to close down and most scholars and students made their way home. With their departure, an era came to an end. Never again would there be a project like Dura or Antioch, with archaeologists bringing home great collections of mosaics and wall paintings to grace their museums. The interwar generation could look back on their accomplishments with pride. Although the field of classics, including classical archaeology, had lost ground in the American schools and universities, it had not been been totally buried under a wave of crude practicality as some had feared. The discipline retained strong relationships with many segments of American society, especially the economic elite. While popular enterprises like the Archaeological Institute of America's lecture program and *Art and Archaeology* magazine had felt the impact of the Great Depression severely, favored projects like the Athenian Agora continued to operate with no indication that America was in the midst of the greatest economic crisis in its history.

If 1879–1914 had been an era of archaeological institutional and professional creativity, 1918–1939 were years of consolidation. During this period, graduate student training, overseas schools, and major excavations assumed the basic forms they retain today. Although the era lacked the innovation and excitement of Norton's times, tradition and hierarchy came to dominate.

207. Meritt 1984: 194.

6. World War II and Its Aftermath

The twenty-five years following World War II represented the most active, though not necessarily the most creative, period in American classical archaeology. The American economy flourished, providing the economic elite with surplus wealth that could be spent on archaeological research. For the first time, the government became significantly involved in funding archaeological research. Archaeological costs of doing archaeology in the Mediterranean remained low, allowing more institutions than ever before to undertake major excavations.

This was a period of dynamic growth at American universities, spurred on by the pentup demand produced by the war and by the increased interest in higher education that followed the war. Scholarships provided first by the GI Bill and later by the National Defense Act allowed more students to undertake undergraduate and graduate education. Research was stimulated by new government agencies like the National Science Foundation (NSF) and the National Endowment for the Humanities (NEH). Classical archaeology benefited from the enrichment of old graduate programs, the development of new programs, and the sponsorship of an increasing array of field activities. American classical archaeology also profited from an unparalleled influx of European scholars, first as refugees from the Nazis and Fascists and then as honored invitees, as universities sought to enhance their prestige by appointing foreign faculty. Public interest in archaeology increased greatly, stimulated by popular publications such as *Archaeology* and *National Geographic,* and by the exploitation of new media such as the University of Pennsylvania's archaeological television quiz show, *What in the World.* Established visual media like movies were put to new purposes. In 1954, an archaeological film show was the most popular event at the annual meeting of the Archaeological Institute of America.

The years immediately after the war saw classical scholars rethinking and rebuilding values and associations. The horrible events of those years traumatized all. The barbaric behavior of the Germans, who had long represented the pinnacle of civilization, especially shocked Americans. The legacy of Goethe, Mommsen, and Wilamowitz seemed to have ended at Dachau and Auschwitz. The devastation and discrediting of Germany had severe practical consequences for American classical archaeologists. The great scholarly support structures of German classical archaeology represented by their universities, libraries, and museums lay in ruins. The country itself was divided into two hostile segments with many of the surviving resources in East Germany. Great German archaeological publications on which scholars had depended for the dissemination of research had suspended operation.

England, in contrast, emerged from the war with a glorious reputation as the country that defended western democracy in its darkest hour. Anglophilia reached new heights; Oxford and Cambridge became the meccas of American classicists in the years immediately after the war. This growing identification with Britain contributed to a subtle but important shift in the relation between classical archaeology and philology in American classical scholarship. The German concept of *Altertumswissenschaft*, which had shaped American classics in its formative years, had stressed the need for researchers to integrate all approaches to the ancient world. Philology, archaeology, and ancient history were partners in the common enterprise of reconstructing the classical past. In England, classical archaeology had never enjoyed the level of support it had in Germany. Moreover, the Oxford and Cambridge undergraduate classics programs of Greats and the Tripos privileged philology over archaeology. As American classicists educated in England attained key positions in important departments and English scholars began taking up posts in America, an increased sense of archaeology's subordination to philology developed at American universities.

The Italian classicists and classical archaeologists received more benign treatment for their nation's role in World War II. They had not been taken as seriously intellectually as the Germans, and their government had not committed the same level of wartime atrocities. The American elite was happy to forget and have forgotten its identity with Il Duce's policies, archaeological and otherwise. Italy was still Italy with its sunny climate, friendly people, wonderful monuments, and low cost of living. Less familiar to the American academic elite of the immediate postwar period was the new generation of Italian intellectuals who traced their roots to the Resistance and the writings of Antonio Gramsci and who were casting in their lot with the emerging Italian communist party. They were young, generally Marxist, and included a number of bright emerging classical archaeologists. Their intellectual mentor was the aristocratic Tuscan Communist archaeologist and art historian Ranuccio Bianchi

Bandinelli.[1] Unfortunately, American classicists and especially classical archaeologists were generally conservative, and the country's strong anti-communist attitudes did not encourage contacts with this emerging intellectual group. Italian scholars closely identified with the Italian Communist Party could not travel to the United States. Increasingly important in Italy, this emerging group of Italian classical archaeologists only slowly impressed themselves on the American classical consciousness.[2]

In contrast, the heroic resistance of the Greeks, first against the Italians and then against the Germans, reaffirmed the faith earlier generations of Americans had placed in the freedom-loving Greek spirit. This was captured by William Dinsmoor in the same report in which he announced his resignation from the German Archaeological Institute. He stated that "Ancient Greece was the creator of the ideals of democracy and freedom, and hand in hand with these went an intellectual development which has never been equalled. Among all occidental lands the only surviving inheritors of those ideals are modern Greece, Britain and the American continent."[3] For the new groups of students arriving at the American School after World War II, the Greek resistance assumed its place beside the wars of independence against the Turks as part of the mythology of modern Greek struggles for freedom. The political complexities and ambiguities of that period were largely ignored and the brutalities forgotten.[4]

Americans rightly felt the greatest pride in themselves. American democratic self-confidence had been reaffirmed by the war experience. In spite of mistakes and shortcomings, America had fought a good fight for democracy, and that democracy had its roots in Athens. A reinvigorated United States emerged from World War II much as it had emerged from the Civil War. Nor did the U.S. role as the leader of democratic society end with the European peace of April 1945. All the European powers were prostrate, and the United States had to lead the way in economic reconstruction and democratic restoration. American archaeologists and art historians had been very active in preserving cultural resources during the war, and in restoring them to their rightful owners afterward. Grateful allies and even former enemies were ready to make concessions

1. Carandini 1979: 121–62.

2. The first American classical archaeologist to work closely with Bianchi Bandinelli was Kyle Phillips (DePuma and Small 1994: xxv–xxviii).

3. *Annual Bulletin AIA* 1940: 7.

4. For the period of the Nazi occupation of Greece, cf. now Mazower 1993. For the political and military events of the immediate postwar period, cf. Tsoucalas 1969; Iatrides and Wrigley 1995.

to the victors, including cultural ones. American classical archaeologists were well placed to take advantage of those opportunities.

Classics and classical archaeology faced a complex future in 1945. On one hand, Americans were always known as pragmatic, and after a world war and the Great Depression they had other things to do besides think about Pericles and Phidias. Educational trends, especially in the secondary schools, still tended to favor practical subjects like science over old-fashioned areas of learning like Greek and Latin. On the other hand, idealist assertions of eternal Western values were very much in the air, as the United States not only savored its victories over the Nazis and the Fascists but prepared to do battle with totalitarian Communists. A still powerful American elite learned to appreciate the classics at their prep schools and universities. A new generation of classicists at universities like Harvard and Princeton made the ancient world, especially Greece, relevant and exciting for a new generation.[5] Periclean Athens acquired new meaning for Americans who saw themselves as the new defenders of democracy.

The importance of this classical outreach to a generation that had been cut off from Europe by the war was emphasized with the rapid revival of the summer schools in Rome and Athens. In 1947 Professor Henry Rowell of Johns Hopkins conducted a group of nineteen American Academy students around the monuments of Rome and Latium.[6] The reopening of the summer school of the American School in Athens followed in 1948 despite concerns about Greek guerrilla activities and the fact that many museums were still closed.[7]

Summer programs reached an important but limited audience. Classical archaeology needed greater outreach if it was to develop the support necessary to sustain its new and ongoing education missions. Some museums enhanced their education programs and expanded cooperation with local schools. Theodore Low of the Walters Art Gallery in Baltimore noted that four thousand schoolchildren had attended archaeological programs at the museum and that "each child probably derived as much information and inspiration from attending those activities as did the approximately two hundred and fifty adults who constituted the total attendance at meetings of the local society of the Archaeological Institute of America."[8]

Many remembered with fondness *Art and Archaeology*, the sophisticated popular journal killed by the depression and the professional conserva-

---

5. Whitehill 1970: 650.
6. Valentine and Valentine 1973: 109–10.
7. Meritt 1984: 37.
8. Low 1948.

tives within the AIA. A process of reevaluation was set in motion that led to the creation of a new general interest archaeology magazine in 1948. By 1946, AIA President Sterling Dow (1903–1995) of Harvard had been considering several types of new publications that would bring the discoveries of classical archaeology to a wider audience than that served by *AJA*.[9] Dow, who had heard *Art and Archaeology* criticized by his colleagues in the Eastern establishment, was initially skeptical about recreating a popular magazine. However, his attitude changed as he read through back issues. As he admitted in a memo, "From time to time during these last months, we here in the office have been sorting masses of old numbers of *Art and Archaeology*. Rather to my surprise, my admiration for it has grown steadily" (AIA Archives Box 37.1: 1 August 1946).

Several publication alternatives were considered. In the end, launching a magazine in the tradition of *Art and Archaeology* seemed the best solution. At the December 1946 annual meeting of the Archaeological Institute of America, Professor and Mrs. William Semple of the University of Cincinnati, longtime patrons of American classical archaeology, agreed to provide $11,600 as seed money for a popular magazine that would replace *Art and Archaeology*.[10] The first issue of *Archaeology* appeared in March 1948. Ironically, the cover photograph featured the large terracotta warriors from the Metropolitan Museum, then thought to be masterpieces of Etruscan art but shortly to be branded as fakes.

Unlike the increasingly narrow classical perspectives of the postwar *AJA*, *Archaeology* was to be a magazine of world archaeology. Its initial resources were modest. The first editor, Jotham Johnson of New York University, had considerable experience as an editor of classical publications but was an amateur in the world of semipopular publication.[11] The first issue featured a humorous foreword by Sterling Dow, introducing the new periodical and placing it in the lineage of *Art and Archaeology*. It contained articles on the early medieval ship burial at Sutton Hoo, the Mayan site at Bonampak, and Roman Ostia. The magazine proved to be highly successful. Readership rose steadily over the years, gradually reaching its 1997 level of more than two hundred thousand copies sold.

Launching the magazine was a bold venture for the Archaeological Institute of America, since it had not yet recovered from the financial and membership losses produced by the depression and World War II. Membership that had stood at 3,460 in 1930 had shrunk to 1,121 in 1945. This extremely parlous financial situation hindered AIA activities. When the distinguished Italian Pompeian scholar Matteo della Corte asked for a

9. AIA Archives Box 37.
10. Johnson 1957.
11. For Johnson, cf. *EHCA* s.v. "Johnson, Jotham (1905–67)."

small subsidy to continue his research, President Dow was forced to say that the AIA could not help. The AIA found it difficult to support new international ventures such as the worldwide Association of Classical Archaeology.[12]

The AIA was fortunate to have Sterling Dow as its new leader.[13] With his strong research interest in epigraphy, Dow was more ancient historian than archaeologist, but he was, as the start of *Archaeology* magazine showed, open-minded to new approaches in bringing archaeology to the public. He was a person of great energy, well connected through his impeccable Harvard background to the eastern establishment, and well aware of the problems faced by the AIA.[14] Realistic, but also idealistic, Dow moved to energize all aspects of the AIA operation.

The *American Journal of Archaeology* faced especially serious editorial and financial pressures. Its endowment was small, and it had been seriously hurt by the retrenchments forced by the depression.[15] The new editor, Joseph Daniel of the University of Pennsylvania, had to deal with the many new problems created by the war. The demise of established archaeological news sources like the German *Archaeologische Anzeiger* made features like *AJA*'s Archaeological News even more important. The death or curtailment of many European archaeological journals meant that *AJA* was at risk of being flooded by manuscripts from overseas. This could have resulted in the loss of access for American scholars. Daniel stated his position clearly, giving first priority to publications by American authors and then to foreign articles that reported on major new discoveries.[16] Daniel seemed to be very much the young, dynamic figure needed to revive *AJA*. Tragically, he died young.[17]

Financial pressures continued to build on *AJA* and with it pressures for further retrenchments. Another editor, Glanville Downey, was in fact forced to cancel one venerable feature, Archaeological News, in 1952. This action produced a vehement reaction from William Dinsmoor and a group of like-minded associates such as Mary Swindler, recalling the controversies surrounding *Art and Archaeology* during the early 1930s. In a letter to then AIA President Kenneth Conant, Dinsmoor lamented *AJA*'s small size (only 244 pages in 1952) and asked rhetorically, "Can we not get back to the ideal set up by Mary Swindler, who forced the budget

12. AIA Archives Box 39.

13. E. Vermeule 1995.

14. These concerns were summarized well in Dow's 1946 and 1947 annual reports. Cf. *Annual Bulletin AIA* 1946: 5–19 and 1947: 7–28.

15. *Annual Report AIA* 1947: 15–16.

16. Donahue 1985: 27–28.

17. For Daniel's short but impressive career, cf. Swindler 1948.

makers year by year to concede that the Journal is the most important single activity and responsibility of the Institute?" (AIA Archives Box: W. Dinsmoor to K. Conant, 1 October 1952).

In this moment of financial constraint, some of the same popular versus scholarly publication issues of the 1930s resurfaced. In a 5 December 1952 letter to Sterling Dow, Downey noted that Swindler was supporting Dinsmoor because "She loves her journal and hates to see 'Arky' competing with it." 1952 was in fact the low point for postwar *AJA*. That year the editorship passed to the elderly Cyrus Ashton Sanborn at the Boston Museum of Fine Arts for what was to be a short, interim editorship.[18] However, positive change for the journal was soon to come. In 1954 Richard Stillwell of Princeton began what was to be the longest (1954–1973) editorship in *AJA* history.[19] Page numbers increased and the journal gradually moved into postwar prosperity.

The Rise of Refugee Scholars

The years immediately before, during, and after the war witnessed a new phenomenon in American classical archaeology: the arrival of a large number of distinguished European scholars fleeing the terrible events in the Old World. They contributed to a strong re-Europeanization of American classical archaeology. American classical archaeologists of the first generations had very often studied in Germany. However, between the wars most professionals were products of American graduate programs. Now a group of native European scholars moved into key positions in America.

Hitler's rise to power in Germany in 1933 precipitated this migration. Anti-Semitic policies were quickly instituted, and by mid-1933 Jews were being dismissed from university posts. These were accompanied by other assaults on legal rights and intellectual freedoms. Classical archaeology, like so many other aspects of the great German academic tradition, was deeply affected.[20] Many distinguished scholars fled. A good number were Jewish, but others were non-Jewish intellectuals who felt that they could not live and work under the Nazi and Fascist systems.[21]

If one considers only the later distinguished postwar careers of great archaeological scholars like Margarete Bieber, Otto Brendel, George

18. Whitehill 1970: 408–9.

19. Shear Jr. 1983; Donahue 1985: 29–30.

20. Marchand 1996: 341–54.

21. Eisler 1969; Krohn 1993. Certain Italian scholars fled to the United States, but the only distinguished classical archaeologist was Dori Levi (1898–1991), who was in exile at Princeton (*EHCA* s.v. "Levi, Doro [1898–1991]"). Levi returned soon after the war and in 1947 was made director of the Italian School of Archaeology in Athens.

Hanfmann, and Richard Krautheimer, one tends to forget the disruption, danger, and despair they faced when they left what had once been secure and honored positions in Europe and entered into the new and unknown. Most arrived in the United States during the depression of the 1930s, seeking work in an academic world that was financially strapped and still harbored a high level of aristocratic anti-Semitism. Some struggled in secondary academic positions until after World War II, when they were called to more important posts. Once established they came to play a major shaping role in American classical archaeological scholarship. Short biographical sketches of five of these leading refugee scholars provide insight into the dynamics of this important development in American classical archaeology.

Margarete Bieber (1879–1978) had studied with the most distinguished German classical archaeologists of her generation and by 1932 had gained the exceptional honor of being appointed full professor at the university at Giessen. However, in 1933 she was dismissed by the Nazis because of her Jewish ancestry.[22] She moved to England, but, like Michael Rostovtzeff after the Russian Revolution, found Oxford less hospitable than she had hoped. America proved more generous, and in 1934 she began a new career at Barnard College and Columbia University. As a scholar Bieber brought the best of the German classical archaeology tradition to the United States, as well as the fruits of her research on Hellenistic art and the ancient theater.[23] She provided an excellent role model as a successful academic woman and a humanistic scholar in the best European tradition.

Otto Brendel (1901–1973) was another art historical refugee.[24] Educated in the best German classical humanistic tradition, he loved Goethe, painting and music as much as classical art. He was especially close to Ludwig Curtius (1874–1954), probably the leading German classical archaeologist of the interwar years, with whom he took his doctorate in 1928 and under whom he served as assistant at the German Archaeological Institute from 1932 to 1936.[25] Though not Jewish, Brendel realized by 1936 that the civilized world of Germany, whose traditions he loved and admired, had ceased to exist. He left his native land and after a brief stay in England, entered the United States in 1938.

Brendel's American academic career was spent at Washington University of St. Louis (1938–41), Indiana University (1941–56), and Columbia (1956–73). He brought to the United States among other things an

22. *EHCA* s.v. "Bieber, Margarete (1879–1978)"; Winkes 1974: Bonfante 1981: 250–54.
23. Bieber 1939, 1955.
24. *EHCA* s.v. "Brendel, Otto J. (1901–73)"; Calder 1976, 1988.
25. For Curtius, cf. *EHCA* s.v. "Curtius, Ludwig (1874–1954)."

Figure 16. George Hanfmann, a distinguished example of the German refugee scholars who as a group contributed to American classical archaeology in the years before and after World War II. Courtesy of the Archaeological Exploration of Sardis Archives, Harvard University.

appreciation of the scholarship in the great German-Austrian Roman art historical tradition represented by art historians like Franz Wickhoff (1853–1909) and Alois Riegl (1858–1905).[26] Brendel's approach to this aspect of archaeological scholarship was best captured in the historical introduction to a never completed history of Roman art that appeared in the 1953 *Memoirs of the American Academy in Rome* and was subsequently republished as *Prolegomena to the Study of Roman Art.*[27]

George Hanfmann (1911–1986) was twice a refugee (Figure 16).[28] He was born in St. Petersburg, but his family, like that of Michael Rostovtzeff, fled west from the new Communist government. He spent his youth in

26. *EHCA* s.v. "Riegl, Alois (1858–1905)," "Wickhoff, Franz (1853–1909)."

27. Brendel 1979.

28. *EHCA* s.v. "Hanfmann, George Maxim Anossov (1911–86)"; Mitten 1986; Borbein 1988.

Lithuania but pursued his university education in Germany, mainly in Berlin. His mentor was Gerhart Rodenwaldt (1886–1945), under whom he did his dissertation on Etruscan sculpture.[29] Fearing the consequences of his Jewish ancestry, Hanfmann emigrated to the United States in 1935 and earned a second doctorate at Johns Hopkins. His range of scholarly interests was enormous, with his most influential work focused on Etruscan and Roman art historical scholarship. Hanfmann's textbook *Roman Art,* first published in 1964, was the first general work on the subject published in America.[30] That was an expression of the historical domination of Greek studies in American classical archaeology, but also of the growing interest in things Roman, which was in part due to the arrival of the German refugees. Hanfmann spent his American career at Harvard, where he brought new life to the classical archaeology program.

Richard Krautheimer (1897–1994) had already become a distinguished scholar in early Christian architecture when the Nazi anti-Jewish laws forced him into exile.[31] As a student at Munich, his interests had been turned from law to art history by the lectures of the great German art historian Heinrich Wölfflin. Krautheimer continued his studies at Berlin and at Halle, where he received his doctorate in medieval architectural history in 1923. His interests turned more to early Christian architecture and in 1933 he started what was going to be one of the central projects of his life: directing the Corpus of Early Christian Basilicas in Rome publication project under the sponsorship of the Pontifical Institute for Christian Archaeology.[32]

Expelled from his academic position in Germany, Krautheimer came to the United States in 1935, where he taught at the University of Louisville in Kentucky for two years and then at Vassar College for fifteen. In 1952 he moved to the New York University Institute of Fine Arts, an institution that especially benefited from the refugee phenomenon. It was a relatively new graduate program particularly devoted to art history as *Kunstgeschichte* so that Germans fitted in very well there. In the words of its chairman, Walter Cook, "Hitler is my best friend; he shakes the tree and I collect the apples."[33] Krautheimer's publications ranged from antiquity to the baroque age. However, his special interest was focused on the early Christian period, and he was one of the relatively few scholars in America who appreciated the contribution archaeology could make to

29. *EHCA* s.v. "Rodenwaldt, Gerhart (1886–1945)."

30. One had to wait until 1991 for the publication of the second general textbook, *Roman Art* by Nancy and Andrew Ramage.

31. Eisler 1969: 567, 584–85.

32. Eisler 1969: 584–85.

33. Weitzmann 1955: 332; Eisler 1969: 569–75.

that era of antiquity. When Krautheimer was in his nineties, he participated in excavations in the Cancelleria courtyard in Rome.[34] In his retirement he returned to Rome, where, ironically, he found honored residence in the Herziana, the reopened German art historical research
center.

Another German academic who found a scholarly home at the NYU
Institute of Fine Arts was Karl Lehmann (1894–1960).[35] Lehmann had
enjoyed a golden career in Germany between the wars. He did his doctorate under Wilamowitz-Moellendorff, was assistant director at the German
Archaeological Institute, and then became professor at Munster. He was
dismissed by Hitler in 1933 and in 1935 was appointed to NYU's Institute
of Fine Arts, where he taught until his death. In 1938 he began the
excavations of the Sanctuary of the Great Gods at Samothrace as part of
the institute's graduate teaching and research mission.[36] His publications
ranged widely over the fields of Greek and Roman architecture, Roman
art, and Greek religion. Like those of other archaeologists at the institute,
Lehmann's articles appeared in such diverse classical and art journals as
The Art Bulletin, Hesperia, and *American Journal of Archaeology.*[37] His identification with the values of his new land were expressed in his 1947 book
Thomas Jefferson: American Humanist, in which Lehmann explored the role
classics had played in shaping the thought and work of America's third
president.[38]

The cadre of refugee scholars at the institute received reinforcement
in the immediate postwar years with the arrival of Peter Von Blanckenhagen (1909–1990), who came to the University of Chicago in 1947 and
the NYU Institute in 1949. Von Blanckenhagen was born in Riga, Latvia.
When he was a young boy his family fled the Russian Revolution and
settled in Germany. Although Von Blanckenhagen's lack of German cit-
izenship hindered the early development of his academic career, he
spent most of the war years in relative normalcy as an assistant to Friedrich Matz at Marburg. His appointment in the United States strengthened a developing school of Roman art historians. Von Blanckenhagen's
scholarship was specially focused on Roman architectural decoration and
Roman painting.[39]

The German refugee scholars brought with them an admirable level of

34. Krautheimer 1969: v–xv.
35. *EHCA* s.v. "Lehmann (-Hartleben), Karl (1894–1960); Eisler 1969: 580–81; Fuchs
and Burck 1988.
36. *EHCA* s.v. "Samothrace"; Von Blanckenhagen 1961.
37. Raffett 1983.
38. Lehmann 1947.
39. Harrison 1991.

general culture and a tradition of humanistic art historical scholarship that went back to Winckelmann.[40] Roman art and archaeology were given a significant place in the American academy for the first time. The German scholars also reinforced the complex traditions of *Altertumswissenschaft*, including the painstaking mustering of fact that could both reinforce and stifle creative scholarship. Often the Americans found it easier to adopt the latter German qualities of plodding research and the accumulation of great stacks of index cards than benefit from the rich intellectual humanity of the most creative German scholarship. The general impact of these foreign-born scholars on classical archaeology was limited by the fact that most found positions in art history programs, while the most powerful classical archaeologists were still generally in philology-dominated classics departments. Many were specialists in the art and archaeology of the Hellenistic, Roman, and late antique periods, whereas the focus of American classical archaeology was still overwhelmingly Greek. Although their students contributed to a partial altering of that balance, they did not succeed in overturning the Hellenic hegemony.

The influx of Europeans, which continues today, has also helped foster a sense of inferiority among American classical archaeologists, who came to feel that their native intellectual culture and scholarly attainments were second rate. This self-perception was the opposite of what Emerson and Charles Eliot Norton wanted to cultivate. The Emersonian idea of fostering the distinctive, creative American scholar has too often given place to notions that Europeans are better by virtue of their European education. The problem has been compounded as the generation of European imports has shifted from refugees to deliberate imports. The refugees escaped from a Europe where they faced academic disaster and even physical destruction. Most were extremely grateful to their adopted land. The new imports are drawn here for reasons of professional and economic advancement and often put down much more shallow roots in their new academic communities. Moreover, the Germans came out of an intellectual culture that had become more timid and conventional as a result of the war experience.[41] This attitude has had some unfortunate consequences for American classical archaeological scholarship.

Government Funding and the National Endowment for the Humanities

The postwar era also saw a changed relationship between the federal government and higher education. Increasingly prevalent was an activ-

40. Weitzmann 1955; Marchand 1996: 330–38.
41. Marchand 1996: 354–75.

ist philosophy of government in which Washington was encouraged to create programs that would respond to perceived national needs. America's greater political involvement in world affairs stimulated more international education, and Russian technological challenges produced calls for better graduate preparation in science. This process of federal funding of advanced education began with the GI Bill and continued with the Fulbright program and the National Defense Act fellowships. Science research received increased support from the National Science Foundation, founded in 1950, which had a budget of $360 million by 1961.[42] Key members of the ruling elite in the humanities were clearly concerned that their interests would be neglected in this quest for new government funding. By 1962 there were calls in Congress for a federal role in promoting the humanities.[43]

Such interest in a government role for humanities, especially for archaeology, was not totally new. As early as the late nineteenth century, scholars had commented ruefully on the lack of government support for archaeology, an English and American situation that contrasted sharply with traditions on the Continent. In 1882 one AIA member observed ironically that "it might be a desirable course for the Institute to apply to the U.S. government for assistance, the government being the only Society which had more money than it knew what to do with."[44] Now a changing political climate seemed to make such support possible.

The humanists first had to identify the most important programs that would benefit from such support. To prepare for this new reality, the American Council of Learned Societies (ACLS) appointed a commission in 1963 to look at the state of the humanities in the United States. The interests of classics and classical archaeology were well represented. The report issued in 1964 included general recommendations such as the establishment of a National Humanities Institute and specific reports from constituent institutions including the Archaeological Institute of America.[45]

Several sections of the report relating to the present state and future development of American classical archaeology was prepared by the AIA committee headed by Cedric Boulter of Cincinnati. The committee's outlook was clearly elitist. Its members understood clearly that the "archaeology of the more primitive peoples, in America and elsewhere, will be covered primarily by the report of our colleagues in the American Anthropological Association." They appreciated that the National Sci-

---

42. Arlt 1962: 12–13.
43. Arlt 1962.
44. AIA Archives: Fourth Annual Meeting 20 May, 1882.
45. *Report of the Commission on the Humanities* 1964.

ence Foundation put significant amounts of money into archaeology. But they complained that the NSF's funding priorities put the "archaeologist of advanced civilizations . . . at a disadvantage in comparison with his colleagues in paleolithic and neolithic archaeology." Humanistic (i.e., mainly classical) archaeology needed alternative government support. The classical archaeology this group wished to see funded was very traditional, with disciplinary priorities very much shaped by philological values. The committee members stated emphatically that the most important agenda for mid-twentieth-century classical archaeology was not the forging of improved links with other branches of archaeology, but the promotion of the study of Greek and Latin. The report certainly gave no sense of classical archaeology as a discipline about to rethink itself or learn anything from the debates beginning to rage in other areas of archaeology.[46]

This ACLS report became an important weapon for background lobbying that led to the passage of legislation founding the National Endowment for the Humanities in 1965.[47] The NEH was created as a complement to the NSF. The funding of classical archaeology was, from the beginning, a major area of research activity; this reflected the interests and concerns of the eastern cultural and social elite that played an important role in founding and shaping the early NEH. The first director was Barnaby Keeney (1914–1980), medieval historian and former president of Brown University.[48] The review panels that approved funding were dominated by private, establishment institutions and the grants tended to favor such universities. By 1977 the American Association of State Colleges and Universities complained that only 11 percent of the NEH panelists came from their institutions. In 1975 a congressman noted that Yale had received $3.3 million from the NEH, whereas Ohio State, a much larger and very distinguished public university, had gotten only $134,000.[49]

Although the NEH provided substantial funding for archaeological research from the beginning, it was skewed in other ways toward the establishment world of classical archaeology. For many years all archaeology research funds received from the NEH for projects outside the United States had to be matched by money raised from sources outside regular university budgets. This naturally favored established field programs attached to institutions with major private funding contacts. It

46. This was the period when younger archaeologists like Lewis Binford were laying the foundations of the New Archaeology (Binford 1962; 1972: 1–14; Dyson 1993: 196–98).

47. Berman 1984; S. Miller 1984: 7–29.

48. *WWW America* 7:313 s.v. "Keeney, Barnaby Conrad." Keeney headed the NEH from 1966 to 1970.

49. S. Miller 1984: 66–70.

discouraged small-scale projects and experimentation and helped reinforce the big-dig approach. The situation was compounded by the fact that the NEH and the NSF divided the archaeological domain on a geographical, chronological, and to a certain degree ideological bases. A few Aegean prehistorians got funding from the NSF, but generally it was impossible for classical projects, no matter how anthropological their research orientation might be, to crack the NSF. This rigid funding division served to separate classical archaeology from the dynamic world of anthropological archaeology even further.

The list of NEH interpretive grants (i.e., research projects) in archaeology for 1966–86 provides interesting insight into the structure of American Old World archaeology during this very dynamic period. Geographically, the NEH funded 12 projects for the Near East, 21 for the Levant (Israel and Jordan), 15 for Turkey, 19 for Egypt and North Africa, 14 for Cyprus, 39 for Greece, and 23 for Italy, with some sixty-five institutions receiving money for archaeological field projects. However, thirty-four of these received only one grant. Since a single application was often supported for several years, the grant-to-years-funding ratio is important. The University of Pennsylvania led this category with 8 projects funded for 31 years. Harvard had 6 for 28, Indiana 4 for 25, Bryn Mawr 5 for 17, and Brown 5 for 11.[50]

The balance in favor of digging as opposed to field survey is reflected in the fact that there were 168 funded seasons for excavation as opposed to 34 for survey. Yet this was a period when archaeologists working in anthropological archaeology in the United States and both prehistoric and classical archaeologists in Britain and Italy were demonstrating the importance of survey and settlement archaeology.[51] The lure of established ongoing projects with good connections can be seen in the fact that Aphrodisias of New York University got 18 seasons of funding, Sardis of Harvard 18, and projects related to Corinth 28. NEH programs did much to advance classical field research in the Mediterranean but little to change the directions of the discipline.

Graduate Programs and Field Projects

The late 1940s, 1950s, and 1960s represented a golden age for graduate education and research in classical archaeology. Private funds for excavation were abundant. The GI Bill and later programs like the National Defense Act fellowships increased study opportunities for students without substantial personal means. Colleges and universities were expand-

50. This material compiled from annual and periodic reports of the NEH.
51. Potter 1979: 1–18; Dyson 1982.

ing in response to population growth and increased demands for access to college and university study, making new academy positions available. It was an era when classics and classical archaeology still held central places in the humanities curriculum.

One result of this positive climate for classical archaeology was the growth in the number and size of graduate programs and an accelerated competition for the best faculty and students. Although Princeton remained the dominant program, it faced major challenges from institutions like Harvard, Pennsylvania, Cincinnati, New York University, and Bryn Mawr as well as smaller programs at places like Chicago, Indiana, and Berkeley. Moreover, successful graduate programs required not only distinguished scholars and top-rate library resources but also major field projects. The type of field project undertaken closely expressed both the philosophy of the graduate program and the values and personalities of its leading scholars. In the period from 1945 to 1970 university graduate research and Mediterranean field programs became intertwined in a way that never happened before or since. Even the excavations carried by the American overseas schools generally reflected the values of certain graduate programs historically associated with those institutions. Cosa was the excavation of the American Academy, but it was closely identified with Yale. The Agora remained very much in the sphere of Princeton's influence.

Princeton remained the most important American classical archaeology graduate program during the twenty-five years following World War II. This was not so much owing to the brilliance or the research productivity of its graduate faculty as to its traditional role as a power center. Princeton still had the ability to attract and place the best graduate students and muster impressive financial resources. The university had superb libraries and the program maintained close connections with the foreign schools and the most important Mediterranean excavations. The Agora was de facto if not de jure a Princeton excavation, and Morgantina in Sicily was, for much of its history, a totally Princeton operation. The classical archaeology program stood well balanced between art history and classics, making its graduates very attractive to teaching institutions. The classics section of the Institute for Advanced Study was flourishing and for much of this period (1954–73) the *American Journal of Archaeology,* edited by Richard Stillwell, came out of the Princeton department.

The excavations at Morgantina were central to Princeton's program. After the Athenian Agora, Morgantina was probably the most important American classical excavation in the postwar period. The list of trench supervisors reads like a Who's Who of leading American classical archaeologists of the 1970s and 1980s including Kenan Erim, Ross Holloway, and Kyle Phillips. The excavations were made possible by the Italian government's change in archaeological policy after World War II. For the first time, independent foreign excavations were allowed on Italian soil. In 1955 Princeton followed the lead of the American Academy excavations at Cosa and began digging at a nameless Hellenistic urban site at Serra Orlano in central Sicily later identified as the Greek city of Morgantina.[52]

The selection of Morgantina reflected the interests of the two senior Princeton archaeologists. Richard Stillwell (1899–1982) specialized in Greek architecture. He had an M.F.A. in architecture from Princeton and had been an architectural fellow at the American School. He had undertaken important architectural archaeological work at Corinth.[53] Morgantina provided him with the opportunity to study late classical and Hellenistic urban development at a Greek colonial site with few traces of later occupation. The Swedish archaeologist Eric Sjoqvist (1903–1974), who had extensive archaeological experience in Cyprus and Italy, came to Princeton after the war.[54] Morgantina offered him the possibility of studying the interconnections between Greek and native cultures in the island's interior. His approach to Morgantina as a site that reflected the complex cultural interactions in classical Sicily is clearly articulated in his Jerome lectures, published in 1973 as *Sicily and the Greeks*.[55]

The archaeological methods and mentalities of Corinth and the Agora were imported into Sicily by the Princetonians. During the most active excavation, from 1955 to 1963, emphasis was on clearing major public buildings and dating occupation phases. The archaeologists discovered considerable prehistoric and archaic Greek remains, but excavations focused on the classical and Hellenistic periods. Stillwell and Sjoqvist were already senior scholars when the excavations started, and they did not live to see the excavation publications carried to successful conclusion. After them, Princeton archaeologists lost interest in the excavations. Hubert Allen, a Princeton alumnus at the University of Illinois, directed excavations there from 1968 to 1972. Then it fell to Malcolm Bell, a Princeton-trained archaeologist at the University of Virginia, and a generation of younger archaeologists to advance the final analysis and publication.[56]

Harvard University and the Sardis Excavation

Despite its prestige in American graduate education and the enormous resources at its command, Harvard University had not played a major

---

52. *EHCA* s.v. "Morgantina (Serra Orlando)."
53. *EHCA* s.v. "Stillwell, Richard (1899–1982)"; Shear, Jr. 1983.
54. *WWW* 6: 378 s.v. "Sjoqvist, Erik"; Ostenberg 1976–77.
55. Sjoqvist 1973.
56. Bell 1981 xiii–xv; Cuomo di Caprio 1992; R. Leighton 1993.

role in the development of classical archaeology in the United States since the days of Charles Eliot Norton. The classical archaeologist when George Hanfmann arrived was still George Chase, an amiable Bostonian who had studied with Adolf Furtwängler in Munich and divided his time between Harvard (where he was John E. Hudson Professor of Archaeology from 1916 to 1945) and the MFA, where he engaged in relatively minor projects related to collecting and cataloging.[57]

George Hanfmann changed Harvard's image and reality. In Hanfmann the university had for the first time a classical archaeological scholar of international reputation with degrees from two of the best classical archaeology programs in the world as well as a humanist of wide-ranging interests. He was that rare scholar who felt comfortable working with Greek, Etruscan, and Roman archaeological materials. Hanfmann was also an appealing, interesting person with whom students enjoyed working. These qualities come through best in his book *Letters from Sardis*.[58] During Hanfmann's years at Harvard, the department rivaled Princeton in attracting the brightest, most ambitious American graduate students. The many tributes that appeared before and after his death testify to the affection and respect with which he was held.[59]

Hanfmann was trained as an archaeological art historian and had only limited experience in field archaeology, mainly as a ceramic specialist with Hetty Goldman's excavations at Tarsus. However, as the field archaeological bandwagon developed in the 1950s, an institution as prestigious and self-consciously important as Harvard could not remain aloof toward Mediterranean classical excavation, especially since it already had active archaeological projects in other ares like Mesoamerica.[60] Therefore, in 1958 Harvard, in cooperation with Cornell University and the American Schools of Oriental Research, started digging at Sardis in Turkey.

The American association with Sardis was an old one. Charles Eliot Norton had dreamed of working there. The American excavations of 1910–1922, in spite of the difficulties caused by World War I and the subsequent Greek-Turkish war, had succeeded in clearing and studying the remains of the great temple. George Chase was among those involved in this early project. It was he who suggested publishing the Lydian pottery from the Butler excavations at Sardis to Hanfmann, and this turned Hanfmann to thinking about new excavations at Sardis.[61]

The site attracted Hanfmann for several reasons. Not only did the city

57. Chase 1916, 1924, 1950.
58. Hanfmann 1972.
59. Mitten, Pedley, and Scott 1971; Mitten 1987.
60. Vost and Leventhal 1983.
61. Mitten, Pedley, and Scott 1971: x.

have a long and complex history, but its very position at the crossroads between the Near Eastern and Greek worlds guaranteed its importance as a multicultural center. Sardis had first been a Lydian city. The Lydians were a poorly understood people who had served as a connecting link between the Near East and Greek cultures, and were thought to have had some connections with the Etruscans.[62]

The Sardis excavations that stared in 1958 were an interesting example of how a respected archaeological scholar with limited field experience, sponsored by a power institution without a major classical field tradition, could launch and sustain a massive undertaking. An obituary observation captured Hanfmann's approach to fieldwork: "Care and vigilance in research, thoroughness in recording, flexibility in interpretation, receptivity to new approaches . . . were second nature to him, and he had a great gift for organization" (Greenewalt 1986:124).

The field research was highly respectable, but on the whole not very innovative. This comes through in both of Hanfmann's works on the excavations, *Letters from Sardis* (1972) and *Sardis from Prehistoric to Roman Times* (1983). Despite the initial plan to use Sardis as a site for detailed study of the Lydians, much of the archaeological effort focused on the large Roman and Byzantine structures, such as the bath gymnasium complex, that dominated the site's last urban phase. This suited Hanfmann's talents and interests, for he felt more comfortable with Roman things than most American archaeologists. In fact, the young Sardis excavators helped pioneer an increased interest in Roman art and archaeology in an American classical and art historical community traditionally dominated by Hellenists.

The Sardis excavations absorbed tremendous public and private archaeological resources. Budgets rose from $53,000 in 1958 to $127,000 in 1966. The project's support reflected the archaeological research funding patterns of the postwar period and the way faculty from an institution like Harvard could easily tap into the world of elite foundations, private philanthropy, and even government funding. The initial work was assisted by a grant from the Bollingen Foundation. Other major foundations that supported the research included the Old Dominion Foundation, the Wenner Gren Foundation, the Ford Foundation and the Kress Foundation. The Corning Museum of Glass joined the project in 1961. NEH support was strong and sustained;[63] the 1983 general results report lists twelve separate NEH grants.[64] Turkish archaeology students were

62. Hanfmann 1962.
63. Hanfmann 1967; J. Scott 1990.
64. Hanfmann 1983b: xi.

trained under special grants from the Department of State (1962–65) and other parts of the Sardis budget were sustained by various State Department programs.[65]

The Sardis excavation project, like that of the Athenian Agora, undertook to leave behind a major reconstructed monument as its legacy. Such restorations have become more and more expected in a country like Turkey, where archaeological sites are a major focus for tourism. Harvard invested large sums in the careful physical restoration of the marble court and the synagogue associated with the imperial bath complex.[66] Such reconstruction projects, although justified in terms of international archaeological diplomacy and local economic and cultural needs, raise the cost of modern Mediterranean archaeology enormously. The result is that fewer American institutions can afford fieldwork of any type.

What is Sardis's place in the history of American classical archaeology after World War II? Certainly the excavations produced much important information on the long historical development of a major Asia Minor city. It trained another generation of archaeologists to do megaexcavations well, but pretty much as they have been done in the past. Given Harvard's ability to place graduate students, major graduate programs at institutions like Berkeley and Cornell have been peopled by Sardis alumni. The traditions of big-site archaeology were substantially reinforced at a time when the prospects of other large, Sardis-style projects being launched in the future were declining dramatically.

The University of Pennsylvania

One of the most important graduate programs in classical archaeology in the postwar period was at the University of Pennsylvania. Penn had a solid tradition in classics, had produced some classical archaeologists and, of course, had the impressive and extensive resources of the University Museum. Still, as at most of the Ivy League schools, Penn classical archaeologists did not make a major contribution until after World War II. Their fieldwork in classical archaeology had been previously limited to the short-lived excavations at Minturnae and a longer term but rather isolated excavation at Kourion in Cyprus.[67]

Kourion represented the first significant American venture into Cypriote archaeology since the flamboyant days of Cesnola. The major site selected was called Bamboula: excavations there started in 1934 and soon yielded an important Mycenaean settlement. They were extended into

65. Hanfmann 1967.
66. Yegul 1986.
67. *EHCA* s.v. "Kourion."

the classical city and the sanctuary of Apollo Hylates.[68] The excavators formed an interesting, intergenerational mixture. The aged veteran B. H. Hill was brought in from Athens to provide overall supervision. Both archaeological and financial support came from George McFadden (1911–1953), a Princeton graduate described in his obituary as a "reticent Classical and Christian gentleman whose very profile, recalling the Emperor Augustus, was a gauge of the beauty hidden within," a figure who looked back in interest and attitude to the world of Charles Eliot Norton. Even McFadden's death had a nineteenth century, Romantic quality, for he drowned like Shelley, while sailing in the Mediterranean. As his obituary writer noted, "It is fitting that he should find his end in the Greek and briny sea whence came the goddess of beauty herself to his beloved island — Cyprus."[69] Last but not least, John Franklin Daniel, the young rising star of the immediate postwar years, got his start at Kourion.

A new postwar dynamism came to archaeology at the University of Pennsylvania. Many of the changes were due to increased activity at the University Museum, which entered a golden age. The man largely responsible for the museum's success was Froehlich Rainey (1907–1992) who assumed the directorship in 1947 and held it for some thirty years (Figure 17).[70] The handsome and dynamic Rainey was a *Time* magazine vision of an archaeological chief executive for Henry Luce's American century. He constantly circled the globe, bringing the fruits of American science and especially American technology to the often rather old-fashioned world of archaeology. Rainey was trained in Alaskan archaeology but sponsored and encouraged a bewildering range of Penn projects that were dispatched to all continents.

Rainey was excellent at fund raising and was a master of communications and public relations. Seeing the potential of the new medium of television, he created the archaeological quiz show *What in the World* in the early 1950s. The program was first beamed to the Philadelphia area and then to the nation through the CBS network. Each Sunday afternoon a panel of expert archaeologists and anthropologists struggled to identify archaeological and anthropological objects drawn from the University Museum's vast storerooms. At its height the program was carried by eighty-nine CBS stations, and in 1952 it won a Peabody award. Many young scholars had their interest in archaeology stimulated by *What in the World*.[71]

The Mediterranean section of the University Museum also moved to develop an active, innovative fieldwork program. The new curator was John Franklin Daniel III (1901–1948), a man well suited for the exciting

68. Daniel 1948; Benson 1972; Davis 1989: 164–65.
69. Friend 1954; Flint 1996.
70. Goodenough 1992; Rainey 1992.
71. Dessart 1961; Rainey 1992: 273–78.

Figure 17. Froelich Rainey, director of the University of Pennsylvania Museum from 1947 to 1976, using an underground periscope at the excavations at Sybaris in South Italy. Courtesy of the University of Pennsylvania Museum, Philadelphia.

world of postwar archaeology.[72] Educated at California, in Germany, and at the University of Pennsylvania, where he obtained his Ph.D. in 1941, Daniel had excavated at Kourion from 1934 to 1939 and at Tarsus with Hetty Goldman. As a result of his work in Turkey and Cyprus he had a broader vision of eastern Mediterranean classical archaeology than most American School, Greek-oriented archaeologists. He had the additional macho cachet of having served in the OSS during World War II. Appointed Mediterranean curator at the University Museum in 1946, editor of the *American Journal of Archaeology* in 1947, and professor in 1948, he clearly was a rising star of the profession. Sadly, he died suddenly in Turkey while investigating potential excavation sites.

The chair and field director chosen to replace Daniel was Rodney Young (Figure 18) (1907–1974). Young was a product of Princeton (B.A. 1929, Ph.D. 1940), Columbia (M.A. in classical archaeology), and the pre- and immediate postwar Athenian Agora excavations.[73] His early research interests focused on the Greek geometric period of the ninth and eighth centuries B.C. Young's approach to archaeology was positivistic and pragmatic. As one of his students noted with approval "nothing was as sure to earn his scorn as the excessively theoretical or the dogmatic."[74] Although Rainey's University Museum, with a staff of archaeologists involved in research all over the world, provided the ideal environment for integrating classical archaeology with the rapidly changing field of anthropological archaeology, Young chose to keep his classical archaeology program largely aloof toward such contacts. Representative of this was the fact that he refused to allow his department to move into the new University Museum building with other departments.[75]

Young had one of the strongest personalities of any archaeologist of the period, a complex blend of Greek and Turkish macho, honed by service as an ambulance driver on the Greek-Albanian front at the outbreak of World War II and in the OSS. Given that he presided with an iron hand over one of the most ambitious archaeology programs of the era, Young became a major shaping force in postwar classical archaeology. In the period after 1950, his program turned out some thirty Ph.D.s, many of whom came to play important roles in American classical archaeology.[76]

In 1950 Young started excavations at Gordion in central Turkey. Gordion, located seventy miles southwest of Ankara, was a Phrygian center

72. Swindler 1948.
73. *EHCA* s.v. "Young, Rodney Stuart (1907–74)"; Muscarella 1974; Pritchard 1975; DeVries 1980.
74. DeVries 1980: xvii.
75. Pritchard 1975: 188.
76. Pritchard 1975: 188.

Figure 18. Rodney Young, head of the program in classical archaeology at the University of Pennsylvania in its dynamic post-World War II phase, at the excavation of Gordion, a site in Turkey. Courtesy of the University of Pennsylvania Museum, Philadelphia.

historically associated with the legendary King Midas and with Alexander the Great's cutting of the Gordian knot. The Phrygians had played an important role as intermediaries between the Near Eastern civilizations and the emerging Greek classical world. The great burial mounds of the Phrygian royal family on the site held the promise of hidden treasure.[77]

Gordion was the first of a series of major American excavations started

77. *EHCA* s.v. "Gordion"; Mellink 1959.

in Turkey in the postwar period. Americans had a long tradition of archaeological research in Turkey that went back to Assos and had continued through excavations like Hetty Goldman's at Tarsus. As the number of American field projects in the Mediterranean increased following the war, and the competition for the limited number of Greek permits intensified, the great sites of Turkey looked more and more attractive to American classical archaeologists. Turkish authorities were on the whole open to American projects, and the cost of excavation was even lower than in Greece. Requests for permits did not have to be funneled through one institution.

The Penn excavations at Gordion continued through the 1950s and the 1960s. They represented a complex blend of the conservative, Agora-style archaeology favored by Young and Rainey's more high-tech approach.[78] The use of sophisticated drilling equipment contributed to the most spectacular Gordion find: the 1957 discovery in 1957 of the intact, late eighth-century burial chamber inside the so-called Midas mound.[79] Young's sudden death in 1974 left a major leadership gap in the project, which seriously delayed final publication.

Froehlich Rainey wanted the University Museum to be involved in other expeditions in the classical Mediterranean. He felt that a very important area of archaeology was underrepresented in the museum's field program. He was especially interested in projects that would test the new technology that had become such an important part of the Penn research mission. Rainey also favored missions that would appeal to special donors and patrons. A major excavation at Sybaris in south Italy appeared to meet all these criteria.

No major Greek remains can be seen today at what is the presumed site of ancient Sybaris. Yet the Sybaris of late sixth-century B.C. was one of the richest, even decadent, cities in the archaic Greek world. The English adjective *sybaritic* still evokes a sense of decadence and self-indulgence. Sybaris was destroyed in 510 B.C. by jealous neighboring city-states and was never rebuilt. Buried deep below the silt of the Crati river valley was one of the richest and presumably best preserved cities of sixth-century Greece.[80]

A Penn Museum associated archaeologist, Donald Brown, had already developed an interest in Sybaris and had recovered Greek pottery from geological cores that had been drilled into the deep river silt.[81] A cooper-

78. Rainey 1992: 144–52.
79. Young 1981.
80. *EHCA* s.v. "Sybaris"; Bullitt 1969: 1–68.
81. Brown 1963; Rainey and Lerici 1967: 34–44.

ative project was developed between the University Museum and the scientific-oriented Italian Lerici Foundation.[82] Rainey had confidence that new archaeological remote sensing and drilling machines developed by Penn and Lerici scientists could meet the challenge of the silt beds and find the remains of Sybaris. He interested a wealthy banker, Orville Bullitt, in bankrolling the expedition.[83] In the end, nature proved too overwhelming for the still nascent archaeological technology. Although the sixth-century B.C. levels were reached in a few areas, the combination of magnetometers, borers, and pumps were not able to conquer the deep fill and high ground water level. One of the most expensive projects of the era launched with immense publicity yielded only mediocre results.[84]

George Bass and Underwater Archaeology

If Sybaris demonstrated the limits of high-tech investigations, underwater archaeology revealed its dramatic, if expensive potential. The new era of underwater research was made possible by Jacques Yves Cousteau and Emile Gagnan's introduction of the light, flexible Aqua Lung system in 1942. In 1952 Cousteau excavated the first classical wreck off the Grand Congloue island near Marseilles.[85] However, it was a young University of Pennsylvania graduate student in archaeology named George Bass who demonstrated the full potential of scientific underwater excavation for the first time. The story of Bass's being sent off by Rodney Young to the YMCA pool to learn the fundamentals of scuba diving so that he could do underwater archaeology has become part of modern archaeological lore.[86]

Bass wanted to do more than find ancient wrecks and sunken treasure. He sought to apply the same archaeological questions and modern archaeological methods that were employed with land excavations to the archaeological sites.[87] The pioneering Cape Gelidonya wreck excavation demonstrated that this could be done. The site was a vessel sunk off the coast of Turkey that dated to the thirteenth century B.C. It was by far the oldest shipwreck then known. Bass's innovative and careful excavation provided much important new information on shipping and trade in the Bronze Age Mediterranean.[88] Bass's research and that of his colleagues

82. For the work of the Lerici foundation, cf. *EHCA* s.v. "Lerici, Carlo Maurillo (1890–1981)."

83. Bullitt 1969.

84. Rainey and Lerici 1967.

85. *EHCA* s.v. "Underwater Archaeology"; Munson 1989.

86. Rainey 1992: 267–68.

87. Bass 1966.

88. Bass 1967.

quickly proved the potential of underwater archaeology for illuminating such topics as sea trade and ship construction.

Underwater archaeology was well suited to this go-go era, when the potential for resource growth seemed unlimited. The costs of crew and equipment rise massively when archaeology shifts from land to water. Yet organizations like the National Geographic seemed more than willing to finance the Bass projects. The high point in this support for underwater archaeology came with the construction of a small exploratory submarine, which extended the range and flexibility of underwater exploration, for the University of Pennsylvania.[89] In the end, the submarine proved expensive to maintain, even for the well financed archaeology of the era. However, Bass first at Penn and then at the Institute of Nautical Archaeology at Texas A & M University completed an impressive series of underwater excavations that have rewritten the textbooks on ancient trade and shipping.[90]

New York University and Samothrace

If Penn's programs represented a complex blend of old and new, the excavations of the New York University Institute of Fine Arts at Samothrace and the NYU classics department at Aphrodisias represented the continuation of traditional art and architecture-oriented archaeology. Samothrace is most famous for the statue of Winged Victory now in the Louvre. Although the island had a long history of occupation and religious activity, it achieved special prominence from the fourth century onward when its cults received special patronage from the royal house of Macedon and then from other Hellenistic rulers.[91] Samothrace's Sanctuary of the Great Gods was graced with a number of important monuments that illuminated a key transitional period in Greek architectural history. Karl Lehmann had been drawn to the site before World War II and started excavation in 1938. NYU resumed work there in 1948. Lehmann continued as director until his death in 1960. Excavation has continued under his widow, Phyllis Lehmann, and under James McCredie, a professor at the Institute of Fine Arts and director of the American School of Classical Studies in Athens from 1969 to 1977.[92]

The Samothrace excavation stood squarely in the mainstream of American architectural archaeology. Sanctuary archaeology has long been favored by American field projects. Waldstein's excavations at the temple of Hera at Argos started the tradition. Starting in 1952, Oscar Broneer

89. Rainey 1992: 268–69.
90. Bass 1975, 1982.
91. *EHCA* s.v. "Samothrace"; K. Lehmann 1955: 10–16.
92. *EHCA* s.v. "Samothrace"; for McCredie, *WW America* 1997: 2821.

(1894–1992) of the University of Chicago and then Paul Clement of UCLA worked at the Isthmian sanctuary near Corinth, concentrating especially on the temple of Poseidon, the theater, and the stadium.[93] At various times since the 1920s, American groups have dug at the sanctuary of Nemea.[94] Such excavations have provided useful information on the development of Greek religious architecture.[95] However, with their emphasis on structures, as opposed to more humble evidence for Greek religious practice such as terra-cottas, they have contributed less than they might have to our understanding of Greek popular cult and religious ritual until recently.

Aphrodisias

No recent American excavation in the Mediterranean has produced more in the way of spectacular finds than that at the ancient Turkish center of Aphrodisias. This rich sanctuary and urban center, which developed around a cult center of Aphrodite, flourished in the Roman period. Wealthy patrons provided the city with opulent public buildings such as its stadium and its baths.[96] It was home to a school of sculptors of the Roman imperial period who shipped their products throughout the Mediterranean. The American excavations at Aphrodisias, which started in 1961, were very much the creation of the Turkish-born, Princeton-educated archaeologist Kenan Erim (1929–1990).[97] While important prehistoric research was done at the site by Martha Joukowsky of Brown University,[98] Erim's interests were focused on the remains of the classical, and especially the Roman period.[99] His quest for objects of high art was richly rewarded, particularly with the discovery of the Caesarion, a shrine of the Roman emperors, decorated with a complex program of sculpture glorifying the imperial house of the first century A.D. Such spectacular finds served to stimulate interest in the project by the great foundations such as National Geographic and among the private patrons who supported archaeology during those years.[100] Aphrodisias was very well funded during the years of major excavation. Erim's sudden death reduced activity at the site for many years.

93. *EHCA* s.v. "Broneer, Oscar Theodore (1894–1992)," "Isthmia"; Broneer 1971; Gebhard 1973, 1992.
94. *EHCA* s.v. "Nemea."
95. S. Miller 1995; Birge, Kraynak, and Miller 1992.
96. *EHCA* s.v. "Aphrodisias"; Erim 1986.
97. *EHCA* s.v. "Aphrodisias," "Erim, Kenan Tevfik (1929–90)"; Bowersock, 1991.
98. Joukowsky 1986.
99. Erim 1986.
100. Erim 1986: 12–13.

Bryn Mawr

In the midst of these large university graduate programs with often ample funding sources, it is both surprising and striking to find Bryn Mawr College among the leaders in classical archaeology during the postwar era. Bryn Mawr's long tradition of archaeological teaching and research has already been discussed. However, compared to Princeton, Harvard, Penn, and New York University, Bryn Mawr remained small and poor. It did possess a tradition of archaeological excellence, outstanding library resources, and an impressive network of professional connections. It also enjoyed the services of a small, dedicated, and highly energetic archaeology faculty. That during this era Bryn Mawr produced a president of the AIA and an *AJA* editor is indicative of the group's prestige.

Four names are especially identified with Bryn Mawr archaeology during this period: Macheldt Mellink, Kyle Phillips, Mabel Lang, and Brunhilde Sismondo Ridgway. Macheldt Mellink (1917–   ) received her university education in Holland. However, she excavated at Tarsus with Goldman and in 1949 was invited to join the Bryn Mawr faculty. Her area of expertise is the archaeology of Turkey with special interest in the cultural interactions in the prehistoric and later periods. Mellink was the first woman after Hetty Goldman to direct a major American excavation in the Mediterranean. The site was Karatas-Semayuk in Lycia, which yielded a settlement and burials contemporary with the earliest levels at Troy. Mellink was also deeply involved in professional activities, serving as president of the Archaeological Institute of America.[101]

Kyle Phillips (1934–1988) was educated at Bowdoin College and Princeton, where his mentors were the Swedish archaeologist Eric Sjoqvist and the famed student of late antique art Kurt Weitzman.[102] Phillips excavated at Morgantina and became interested in Italian archaeology. He and R. Ross Holloway of Brown University were the two principal young American archaeologists to use the Morgantina experience as a springboard for distinguished careers in the newly expanding world of Italian archaeology. In 1962 Phillips joined the faculty of Bryn Mawr. His combination of art historical and archaeological interests drew him to Ranuccio Bianchi Bandinelli (1900–1975), one of the most important Italian classical archaeologists of that period.[103] Bianchi Bandinelli interested Phillips in the archaeological possibilities in Tuscany, and especially at Poggio Civitate in the village of Murlo near Siena.[104] Until the postwar period Americans had shown relatively little interest in Etruscan art and

101. *WW America* 1997: 2896 s.v. "Mellink, Machteld."
102. DePuma, Edlund-Berry and Meritt 1989.
103. DePuma and Small 1994: xxvi–xxviii.
104. K. M. Phillips 1993.

archaeology. The Etruscans were located far from the Hellenic epicenter of American classical archaeology and in antiquity had been regarded with suspicion by both the Greeks and the Romans. Prohibitions on excavations in Italy made them even less appealing to American archaeologists. American museums had purchased a certain amount of Etruscan art, unfortunately some of it fraudulent. In other instances, such as when the Met was offered rich objects from the Barberini tombs of Praeneste, museums rejected the opportunity to buy.[105] Much of the rest of the material consisted of ceramics, bronzes, and other small objects from tomb groups, excavated at sites like Narce and Vulci. Arthur Frothingham Jr. had been active in acquiring objects for museums in Chicago, Philadelphia, and Berkeley.[106] Edith Hall Dohan had published collections of Etruscan material that had made their way to the University Museum.[107] George Hanfmann of Harvard had done important research in Etruscan art and archaeology, but he did not become involved in Tuscan fieldwork. One of the first American scholars interested in Etruscan culture was Emeline Hill Richardson (1910–   ). Her interest was stimulated by the small Etruscan bronzes common in private collections. She was educated at Radcliffe and from 1941 to 1949 taught at Wheaton College. Soon after the war Richardson became involved in the American Academy fieldwork at Cosa. Her book *The Etruscans: Their Art and Civilization*, published in 1964, was the first American text on the subject.[108] Deeply involved in research and excavation, Emeline Richardson did not teach regularly again until relatively late in her career.

Murlo was the first Etruscan site excavated by Americans. It was significant as being a settlement or sanctuary site, for up to that time most Etruscan archaeology had been mortuary archaeology, focused on the recovery of art objects from the rich necropolises that surrounded Etruscan cities. The most important discovery at Murlo was of a sixth-century-b.c. courtyard complex variously identified as a shrine or palace complex.[109] This structure yielded an impressive collection of terra-cotta sculpture and terra-cotta plaques depicting scenes from upper-class Etruscan life. Phillips attracted to Bryn Mawr, to Murlo, and to Etruscan archaeology a bright, active group of graduate students, who have since found positions in American colleges and universities. They have helped turn Etruscan studies in the United States from a relative backwater to one of the most dynamic areas within American classical archaeology.

105. DePuma 1986: 1.
106. DePuma 1986: 1–2.
107. *EHCA* s.v. "Dohan, Edith Haywood Hall (1877–1943)"; Dohan 1942.
108. Richardson 1964.
109. K. M. Phillips 1993: 5–49.

Sadly, Phillips died relatively young, leaving much of his research program unfinished.

Mabel Lang (1917–) was most famous during her years at Bryn Mawr for her rigorous teaching of Greek. She was also active in the Athenian Agora excavations and in Mycenaean archaeology. For many years she was a major associate of Carl Blegen's excavations at the palace of Pylos, publishing the late Bronze Age wall paintings discovered there.[110] Ridgway (1929–) represented the continuation of the Rhys Carpenter art-historical tradition at Bryn Mawr. She was of Italian origins and received her early archaeological education at the University of Messina. Ridgway completed her Ph.D. at Bryn Mawr, where she spent her teaching career. She was an enormously productive scholar in the field of Greek art and was a strong mentor and role model for a generation of Bryn Mawr graduate students.[111] Professionally active, she served as editor of the *American Journal of Archaeology* for eight years.

Noble Dreams

Institutions such as Chicago, North Carolina, and Cornell played a secondary, but significant, role in maintaining mainstream American classical archaeology after the war. Almost all these programs operated their field research on the assumption that the larger the excavations and the bigger and more specialized the staff, the more promising the results. Emphasis was on empirical research. Classical archaeology was closely linked to philology and traditional art history. Founding fathers were worshiped as sacred ancestors whose methodologies became rituals to practice and imitate. Mastering Greek and Latin mattered much more than understanding contemporary developments in other branches of archaeology.

An intellectual historian who focused only on the subdiscipline of American classical archaeology during this era would never realize that these decades were among the most tumultuous in the field's history.[112] By the late 1950s a group of archaeological "young Turks" generally located in anthropology departments were demanding that archaeologists reexamine their methodological and theoretical premises and create a real science of archaeology. The movement known as New Archaeology had been launched.[113] Although it would be middle-aged before

110. Lang 1969.
111. Cf. Ridgway 1970, 1976.
112. Willey and Sabloff 1980: 28–266; Dyson 1981, 1993; Trigger 1989: 244–411.
113. Binford 1972.

most classical archaeologists even noticed it,[114] William McDonald of the University of Minnesota and Thomas Jacobsen of Indiana University realized what was happening and tried to move classical archaeology in new directions. Their efforts, successes, and failures say much about the forces and powers shaping classical archaeology in the postwar world.

McDonald and Messenia

During the 1950s and early 1960s William McDonald undertook one of the first field programs that used systematic survey archaeology to reconstruct the settlement history of a region of Greece based on surface survey. American archaeologists in Greece had long conducted topographical research, and their vigorous exploration of the countryside had become the stuff of legend. However, most of this research was directed at identifying sites associated with literary texts and famous historical events. Little attempt had been made to weave the information recovered into broader patterns of settlement history. In general, systematic survey was a little-used method in field archaeology. The English archaeologist O. G. S. Crawford had made an eloquent plea for this approach in 1951:

Excavation is, of course, of fundamental importance, but there is so much else besides to be done, so much that needs doing most urgently, and that is so much easier to do. Field archaeology without digging constitutes the time-exploration of a region, whose space-exploration may (or may not) have been already completed. There are castles, churches, monasteries, forts and even towns to be discovered, photographed and (if possible) planned. There are sites of early occupation to be discovered by mounds and debris of sherds and flints. (2–3)

However, Crawford's appeal fell on deaf ears in the flush, excavation-oriented world of American classical archaeology during the 1950s.

McDonald came to fieldwork with a conventional classical archaeology education including a B.A. in classics and an M.A. in history from Toronto and a Ph.D. from Johns Hopkins (Figure 19). His first excavation experience was with D. M. Robinson at Olynthos. But his work with Carl Blegen at Pylos just before World War II shifted his interests toward Greek prehistory and topographical research. The time was ripe for new investigations in the Pylos countryside. The gradual decipherment of the Linear B tablets was providing important new information on the structure of the rural hinterland around the late Bronze Age palace. The combination of archaeological and literary evidence that had proved so

114. Dyson 1981.

Figure 19. William A. McDonald, one of the first American classical archaeologist to use systematic field survey as a method of reconstructing the settlement history of a particular landscape.

useful for topographical research in the classical period could now be applied to the Bronze Age.[115]

Beginning in 1953, McDonald and and his Canadian colleague Richard Hope Simpson carried out systematic surveys in the Messenia coun-

115. McDonald and Thomas 1990: 355–62.

tryside around Pylos.[116] McDonald described the first stages of this project and the reactions it provoked somewhat ironically:

So MME's [Minnesota Messenia Expedition] initial "strategy" was extremely modest — a search party of one, an undefined area, concentration on population distribution in a specific period (LH IIIB), practically no assured funding, and collegial attitudes ranging from cooperation to apathy to obstructionism. There were then no models for large-scale systematic surface surveys in Greece or (so far as I know) in closely comparable physical environments. (1984: 186)

The point about the lack of previous models needs emphasis, for the methods of the Messenia survey have received a certain amount ex post facto criticism. Little of this type of settlement reconstruction through archaeological survey had been done in Greece at the time. The very influential South Etruria survey, organized by John Ward Perkins of the British School at Rome, was getting underway while McDonald was working in Messenia, and the first significant synthetic publication of that research appeared only in 1968.[117] Even most of the very important Mesoamerican and Peruvian surveys were contemporary or later.[118]

McDonald and his coworkers located sites, collected surface material, mainly ceramics, and used this to reconstruct the ebb and flow of settlement in the area from the early prehistoric to the early modern period. This diachronic approach, which moved from the early prehistoric to the Turkish periods, was a striking innovation for an era when most American archaeology in Greece focused on the Bronze Age to the high Roman era.[119] The final publication of the survey was an impressive interdisciplinary effort involving experts ranging from geologists to ethnoarchaeologists interested in the social and economic structure of the contemporary Messenia countryside.[120]

McDonald used the survey results to select a site he planned to make the object of a modern, scientific excavation. The excavation-oriented research he conducted at Nichoria in Messenia from 1969 to 1975 placed great emphasis on the relatively new discipline of environmental archaeology with its studies of geology, environmental history, and floral and faunal reconstruction.[121] All periods of occupation were considered in

116. McDonald and Hope Simpson 1961, 1964, 1969; McDonald 1984.

117. Ward Perkins et al. 1968; Potter 1979.

118. The first important survey was that undertaken by Gordon Willey in the Viru Valley of Peru (Ford and Willey 1949). For others, cf. Sanders 1965; Parsons 1971; Byers and MacNeish 1967–76; Blanton 1978.

119. *EHCA* s.v. "Minnesota Messenia Expedition"; McDonald and Hope Simpson 1961, 1964, 1969.

120. McDonald and Rapp 1972.

121. *EHCA* s.v. "Nichoria (Rizomylo)": Rapp and Aschenbrenner 1978; Jacobsen 1985: 95.

the research design. The final publications begin with the Neolithic and continue into the Byzantine period.[122]

McDonald's hope of making survey a central part of classical archaeology in Greece was not realized until decades later.[123] Part of this was owing to the Greek government's restrictive archaeological research policies, which hindered systematic surface collections. However, far more was owing to the conservative intellectual and social structure of American classical archaeologists working in Greece. The excavation of public and religious monuments at major sites was still central to the classical archaeological mission. Students were expected to work in the comfortable, ordered world of the big dig and not to go into the field on their own to collect bits of pottery. Contemporary American archaeological field projects in Mesoamerica combined monument excavation with regional settlement reconstruction, while American classical archaeologists excavated their porticoes and temples with little concern for the archaeology of the countryside that supported those centers.

Only in the 1970s did survey become a major part of classical archaeology. In 1972 Michael Jameson, then of the University of Pennsylvania, began a program of survey in the southern Argolid connected with the discovery and excavation of the prehistoric site at Franchthi cave.[124] The result of this research was a sophisticated, diachronic reconstruction of landscape use and settlement change in the region of Greece.[125] Other survey projects were started in Greece, Italy, Cyprus, and Turkey during the 1970s. By 1981 the field had expanded to such an extent that a survey archaeology conference was held in Athens and received sixty-three reports on projects in the Mediterranean. Although still perceived as a stepchild in certain circles of the profession, American Mediterranean survey archaeology had clearly arrived.[126]

McDonald felt that many of the limitations in American classical field archaeology derived from the education American students received in classical archaeology graduate programs. He attempted to apply his ideas on new approaches to graduate education by creating the Graduate Center for Ancient Studies at the University of Minnesota.[127] The center's aim was to break down the barriers that had developed between classics, ancient history, archaeology, and anthropology and produce the truly interdisciplinary scholar needed for the research programs of the late twentieth century. Not only were classical and anthropological archae-

122. McDonald, Coulson, and Rosser 1983; McDonald and Wilkie 1992.
123. Jacobsen 1985.
124. Jameson, Runnels, and Van Andel 1994.
125. Van Andel and Runnels 1987.
126. Keller and Rupp 1983.
127. McDonald 1973.

ologists brought together, but the program included academics from several of the natural sciences. The program received strong initial support and proved very successful for a while. In the end, it fell victim to budget cuts, the lack of strong faculty continuity in key positions, and a general return to academy conservatism.

Franchthi and Indiana Archaeology

Like William MacDonald, Thomas Jacobsen came out of a traditional classical archaeological background. A midwesterner, he took his B.A. at St. Olaf's and an M.A. at Minnesota before going on to a Ph.D. at the University of Pennsylvania and starting what looked like a standard career in classical archaeology. It was his and Michael Jameson's chance discovery in 1967 of a deeply stratified coastal cave at Franchthi near Corinth in Greece that turned Jacobsen's research in new directions. Franchthi proved to be one of the longest occupied sites in Mediterranean archaeology with artifacts going back to 25,000 B.P. Jacobsen recognized the site's potential of the site for multidisciplinary archaeology and created a team that did "total archaeology" with a strong environmental emphasis.[128] He pioneered in many areas of environmental archaeology.[129] The excavations attracted considerable publicity, and during the late 1960s and early 1970s they received a good deal of public and private foundation support. They appealed to both the humanist and the scientist and drew financing from both the National Endowment for the Humanities and the National Science Foundation, a very rare combination in archaeology's history of government funding.

Jacobsen, like McDonald, wanted to carry the lessons of his innovative field back into the graduate school classroom. Indiana University had a well-developed field tradition in mainstream classical archaeology, and had cooperated with the University of Chicago in the excavation of the Corinthian port city of Kenchreai from 1963 to 1968.[130] Jacobsen attempted to combine aspects of these two traditions in a newly created program in classical archaeology in 1971. The mission statement for the new program stated its goal succinctly:

A primary objective, then, in establishing CLAR [program in classical archaeology] at Indiana was to fill this gap by creating a flexible graduate program which, while maintaining traditional academic ties, would encourage and enable students to work in a more broadly interdisciplinary context than had been possible before. It was hoped that the interdisciplinary approach of the field projects in

128. Jacobsen 1976.
129. Hansen 1991.
130. *EHCA* s.v. "Kenchreai"; Scranton, Shaw, and Ibrahim 1978.

Greece could be carried over to the training of graduate students in the classroom. (Indiana University Program in Classical Archaeology, Self-Study Report: 2)

The program's aim was to produce archaeologists who would have a solid background in classical studies but also be comfortable in related disciplines like anthropological archaeology and art history. Those involved in the program were made aware of the theoretical debates surrounding such developments as New Archaeology and were very sympathic to the role that the natural sciences could play in archaeology. For a number of years, the graduate program at Indiana was one of the most active and interesting in the country. Excavations continued at Franchthi, as well as at the Greek urban site of Halieis.[131]

The decline and fall of the Indiana program, which culminated in its formal abolition in 1995, was the result of a variety of factors related to the specifics of the Indiana scene and the general structure of classical archaeology in America. In a classical profession, where philologists dominated most classics departments, the Indiana archaeology graduates with their limited classical language training were placed at a disadvantage in the search for positions. It was only a graduate program, which meant that it lacked the curricular flexibility and enrollment numbers that come with connections to an undergraduate major. Excavations as complicated as Halieis and Franchthi required long postexcavation study and slow publication. That meant the program lacked both the visibility and the new graduate research opportunities provided by ongoing excavations for many years. Although the program no longer exists, its impact continues to be felt through the graduates that it has sent out into the profession.

The Boston University Program in Archaeology

The Boston University Program in Archaeology has proved to be the most successful of the interdisciplinary Old World-oriented archaeology programs, even though although it is in many ways the most radical. The driving force behind its creation has been James Wiseman. Wiseman is a classically trained American School archaeologist from the University of Chicago who became increasingly dissatisfied with the limits imposed on Mediterranean archaeologists by a philologically shaped discipline.[132] He set out to create a department that would reflect his vision of where he thought the discipline should go.

Wiseman's aim was to create a true, interfield program of the type found at British universities. Classical archaeologists, historical archae-

131. Boyd and Rudolph 1976.
132. Wiseman 1980a, b.

ologists, Mayanists, and others would be housed in the same department, and emphasis would be on learning and doing archaeology as a discipline as opposed to archaeology as a branch of classics. The Boston University Program in Archaeology, founded in 1979, included a strong science component with special emphasis on such developing fields as archaeological remote sensing.[133] This Boston philosophy of archaeology also received concrete expression in the *Journal of Field Archaeology*, founded in 1973 by Wiseman and still published by the Boston University archaeology program. Unlike *AJA*, most of whose articles focus on the classical world, *JFA* ranges worldwide, juxtaposing field reports from different areas. One of its most important special features has focused on the antiquities market, raising the consciousness of archaeologists about site looting and destruction, reporting on thefts from sites and museums, and keeping readers current on legal issues related to archaeology and the trade in antiquities.[134]

Although the Boston University program is too young to permit definitive statements on its long-term success, it is flourishing. The program has enjoyed exceptional support from the Boston University administration. James Wiseman, as a highly respected scholar, editor, archaeological administrater, and past president of the Archaeological Institute of America, enjoys high national and international prestige and visibility. Although graduates of the program are making their way into the field, it remains to be seen how they will be received in more conservative disciplines like classical archaeology.

The American School of Classical Studies

As has been made clear from the previous descriptions of the various major graduate schools and their field programs, Greece maintained its position as the center of American classical archaeological activity during the postwar years. The strong American prewar presence in Greece had been enhanced by the contributions the United States had made in defeating the Axis during the war and in supporting the royalist government against the Greek communists afterward. Various initiatives by President Truman had played a major role in stabilizing and reconstructing Greece. This meant that the United States replaced Britain as the hegemonic foreign power in the region.[135]

The Greeks greatly appreciated the ways American archaeologists had supported the Hellenic cause during the war. This was best expressed in the actions of Eugene Vanderpool, Gorham Stevens, and B. H. Hill. Van-

133. Gabel and Petruso 1979.
134. Wiseman 1973.
135. Tsoucalas 1969: 70–113; Iatrides and Wrigley 1995.

derpool decided to stay in Greece when hostilities broke out. He carried on some of his regular Agora activities until he was interned by the Germans in November 1942 and repatriated to the United States in March 1944. However, by January 1945 he was back in Athens, part of an already revived American School. Stevens and Hill also stayed through the war, watching over the Athens and the Corinth facilities and sharing many of the privations of the Greeks.[136]

As the American archaeologists prepared to resume full activities in Athens, they also planned for the future. The 1946–47 annual report of the American School set forth the institution's postwar goals. The most important of these was that "the excavation of the Ancient Agora of Athens must be finished in a scholarly manner, the site itself changed into an attractive archaeological park, and a proper museum built to house the many valuable finds."[137] However, it was argued that the Agora excavations should not hamper the school's other activities. The school's general programs had to serve more students and fellows. The publication program would need more support. The physical plant required attention after the neglect of the war years. The author of the report, old Beaux Arts architect and retired director G. P. Stevens, even urged developing a series of architectural models of the Acropolis and the Agora. Stevens closed his report with a ringing expression of postwar American optimism: "We can, we believe, look forward toward the future with hope and confidence in our hearts. May God bless the School in its work of elevating the Classics in America."[138]

Despite political instability and civil war in Greece, classicists and archaeologists of the American School went back to work quickly. The 1946–47 academic year was spent largely on plant renovation and library updating. By the next year full-blown research was underway, even in the midst of the banditry and political violence associated with the civil war. The 1947–48 annual report noted that "Professor and Mrs. Richard Stillwell arrived in Corinth on March 13, 1948, after a brief delay caused by "andartes [partisan] activities along the Athens-Corinth road." By 1949–50, "termination of revolutionary activity which had plagued Greece ever since the end of the World War made possible travel throughout the country."[139] The American School also benefited greatly from the various U.S. foreign aid and education programs established in Greece after the war. The amount of $20 million was made available for twenty years for pre- and postdoctoral Fulbright fellows. The American School, with its

136. Meritt 1984: 15–24, 30.
137. *Annual Report ASCS* 1946–47: 20.
138. *Annual Report ASCS* 1946–47: 24.
139. Meritt 1984: 46.

important Greek and American connections, became a key player in that selection process. The program peaked with six senior school fellowships in 1951–52 and nine juniors in 1950–51.[140]

Even with increased goodwill toward the Americans by the Greek government, the system of limited permits persisted. Normally the American School received all three of those allocated to the United States, which meant that it continued to control all U.S. excavations in Greek territory.[141] One of these permits was generally used for Corinth. The other two were granted for one long-term and one short-term project (two to five years). Some flexibility was obtained by attaching other field projects to the Corinth permit and through special permits for publication-related research at the sites of former American School excavations. By the 1950s more American universities wanted to excavate in Greece, and competition for permits became fierce.

This golden age was not destined to last forever. By the mid-1960s Greece was changing socially and economically, and the American School could no longer enjoy all aspects of its former comfortable neocolonial existence. The director's annual reports complain increasingly about economic instability and the political chaos caused by the rise of the Greek political left. Greek employees' working hours at the American School had to be reduced, and certain tax and import exemptions long enjoyed by the Americans were reduced or removed.

The American government had long maintained a cozy alliance with conservative political forces in Greece, which in the immediate postwar period centered around the country's royal court. In April 1967 a group of Greek army colonels overthrew the elected government, which they considered too leftist. The United States quickly made its peace with the colonels, regarded as a suitably stable bulwark against the advance of communism.[142] The school proclaimed its political neutrality, although some Greek and American scholars felt that it maintained too close connections with the coup government and some of the conservative, rich Greek-Americans who supported the colonels.

Certainly the school's programs did not suffer under the new military order. The Agora director's report noted that the negotiations for expanded excavations had been interrupted by the coup (euphemistically described as "the change in the Greek government in April of 1967"), but that the new general director of antiquities Spyridon Marinatos (1901–1974) had shown a lively interest in the project. By November 1967 the Greek government had authorized substantial credits for the

140. Meritt 1984: 43–45, 55.
141. Meritt 1984: 89–90.
142. Tsoucalas 1969: 192–208.

acquisition of property in the Agora area.[143] The irony of digging the roots of Greek democracy with the blessing of a group of military dictators who promised to yield power only when the Greek people were "ready for democracy" was apparently lost on some people at the American School.

In 1975 parliamentary government was restored to Athens. The director's annual report of the director noted that the Greeks resented U.S. foreign policy toward the colonels, but held no personal animus against the school.[144] However, tensions increased with the installation of Andreas Papandreou's socialist government and the naming of Melina Mercouri as minister of culture. Mercouri was extremely vocal on such issues as Greece's desire to recover the Elgin marbles and was very concerned about any evidence of archaeological neocolonialism.[145]

The Athenian Agora

The postwar planners at the school had given top priority to completing the Agora excavations. The founding director, T. L. Shear of Princeton, had died in 1945. He was replaced by his prewar assistant, Homer Thompson. Thompson was Canadian, with a B.A. and an M.A. from the University of British Columbia and a Ph.D. from the University of Michigan. He had been an Agora fellow in Athens from 1931 to 1939. After war service in the Canadian navy, he taught at the University of Toronto and in 1947 became professor at the Institute for Advanced Study in Princeton, where he spent the rest of his career. Excavations in the Agora resumed in 1946. This rapid start was in part made necessary by the need to provide immediate employment for long-term employees of the school impoverished by the war and its aftermath.[146] Key Agora staff members were reassembled, and the stage was set for the Agora's postwar dominance American classical archaeology.

The Agora excavations rapidly achieved a pace and scale much larger than those before World War II. New dig concessions were granted in the center of Athens. The permanent staff was expanded each summer by a large body of experts, who arrived from colleges and universities throughout the United States, performed their specialized tasks, and then returned to spread the word about the Agora, its traditions, and its accomplishments to undergraduates and graduate students. Most bright classical archaeology (as opposed to art history) graduate students in America during these years did Greek archaeology, and most spent some

143. *Annual Report ASCS* 1967–68; *EHCA* s.v. "Marinatos, Spyridon N. (1901–74)."
144. *Annual Report ASCS* 1976.
145. Hitchens 1987: 83–105.
146. Thompson 1947.

time at the American School. Many received their initial field training at the renewed excavations at Corinth, but the Agora excavation, visible every time they visited the classical monuments of central Athens, was most influential in shaping their view of what archaeology should be. The Agora's enhanced influence was aided by new programs such as the Fulbright, whose predoctoral and research grants were strongly focused on Agora research.[147]

The school's trustees had given priority to the Agora excavations, but their early statements show that this was initially considered to be a finite commitment, with the anticipation that it would be terminated and that the school would move on to other activities. A 1953 statement by Agora director Homer Thompson seemed to follow that policy:

By the end of the current season it is confidently expected that the excavation of the Agora proper, except that part which lies north of the Athens-Piraeus Railway, will have been completed. By this is meant that all the major monuments will have been exposed and all the accumulation which gathered subsequent to the Herulian sack of A.D. 267 will have been removed. (*Annual Report ASCS* 1952–53: 47)

The statement also makes clear the continuing underlying archaeological philosophy of the excavators. The chronological concerns of the project were clearly defined. The long period of occupation in the Agora area between A.D. 267 and the start of excavation in the 1930s remained of relatively little interest. Artifacts from the period after A.D. 267 were considered mere accumulation rather than material that could provide insight into two thousand years of further human urban activity at the site. The excavation's central aim remained the exposure of public monuments. This view of archaeology in the historical core of a Mediterranean city was not unexpected. In 1953 European urban archaeology was in its infancy, and few excavators studied the full complexity of a city's archaeological.[148] Medieval archaeology had just begun to emerge as a discipline in a country like Britain. The real development of urban and medieval archaeology in the Mediterranean was still a long way off.[149]

Despite these early statements about the finite aims and time span of the Agora project, the excavations had an ongoing momentum that was not to be stopped. The school's project continued to engulf more of the Plaka and dispossess more of its inhabitants. The American archaeologists still operated with an approach that combined aspects of archaeological colonialism with the destructive urban renewal mentality that was just then gutting the historical core of so many American cities. A

147. Meritt 1984: 41.
148. Carver 1993.
149. Carver 1993.

quote from the 1958–59 American School annual report on the confiscation of additional property brings that out very clearly:

None of the occupants were happy about being dispossessed. Some accepted the necessity philosophically and with good grace, and these the School has tried to help in every way possible. We have sought by all means to avoid imposing any severe personal hardships. On the other hand, there is a real urgency about the completion of the whole program. A few of the people owning and occupying the houses have employed every trick and coercion, legal and private, to obstruct or delay the execution of orders, and we must admit that they have shown quite extraordinary ingenuity in devising obstacles. (28)

The Agora excavation was a too well oiled machine to be easily stopped, and its supporters showed tremendous ingenuity in tapping new sources of establishment wealth. By the early 1960s the project did appear to be running out of steam and money. However, the classical archaeological establishment was not going to let it end. The central position of the Agora excavation in the American classical archaeological consciousness of that era can be seen in the 1964 report of the ACLS Commission on the Humanities, the document that helped lay the groundwork for the establishment of the National Endowment for the Humanities. Four of the six classics committee members had close associations with the American School; and it hardly came as a surprise that the report stressed the centrality of the Agora excavations for American classical archaeology. It was described as the "exemplary dig of all time," and a call was made for raising the $4 million needed to complete the project.[150]

The philanthropic establishment, which was interested in the humanities, responded appropriately. On 17 Februrary, 1966 the Ford Foundation announced a grant of $1 million to allow the Agora excavations to resume. It was probably the largest single grant in American archaeological history. The Ford money was to be used only for excavation, with other costs, such as land acquisition, borne by other sources including the Greek government. The focus was to be the north part of the Agora, the area of the Stoa Poikile. This was the Ford Foundation's first contribution of archaeology and again showed the Agora's power to attract establishment funding.

In 1968 it was announced that Homer Thompson was stepping down as director of the Agora and that he was being succeeded by T. L. Shear Jr., assistant professor at Princeton and son of the original director. The appointment of such a young director signaled that the postwar aim of bringing the Agora to a speedy conclusion was not to be realized. The project was destined to continue down to the present day.

150. *Report of the Commission on the Humanities* 1964: 71–76.

The Stoa of Attalus

When excavations resumed in the Agora after the war, the area still had the appearance of a World War II bombed site with great expanses of barren land, blowing dust, and crumbling foundations. Something that would convey the architectural beauty of the area in its glory days was needed. At the same time, the excavation staff required museum space and work and storage areas. The decision was made by the American School to restore one of the ancient Agora's public buildings to be used as a museum, storage, and work area. The structure selected was a stoa erected in the Agora by the Hellenistic king of Pergamon Attalus II, who ruled 159–138 B.C. There was a certain historical irony in Americans choosing to rebuild a structure associated with an ancient despot who wanted to play on the glories of ancient Athens to advance his political causes.[151]

Plans for reconstructing an Agora structure as a museum had been included in the Marshall program of general support for rehabilitating Greek sites and museums. By 1949–50, clearing and excavation of the stoa site were underway. The idea of rebuilding the Stoa of Attalus owed much to the enthusiasm of Gorham P. Stevens. It was to be a project in the manner of the restored structures of colonial Williamsburg. In both instances archaeological and historical evidence were combined to produce accurate, full-scale reconstructions of important public buildings. John D. Rockefeller and the Rockefeller Foundation were instrumental in funding both.

In autumn 1951 two hundred blocks of Piraeus limestone were delivered for the Stoa. They were paid for from the last allotment of Marshall Plan funds devoted to archaeological purposes.[152] In 1953 Ward M. Canady, president of the board of trustees, authorized the start of full-scale construction work. The New York architectural firm W. Stuart Thompson and Phelps Barnum was responsible for the actual building. They worked closely with John Travlos, the architect of the school's excavations. The project benefited from the supply of inexpensive, skilled labor available in postwar Athens: the marble workers and carpenters at the Stoa received $3–4 per day.[153] By 1956 the building had been largely completed, and in September of that year, the gleaming white structure with its museum was dedicated. Prayers were offered by the Greek Orthodox patriarch of Athens in the presence of the Greek king and queen. Speeches were given by leading Greek and American scholars and officials, and Euripides' *Medea* was performed in the odeon of Herodes Atticus for the

151. *EHCA* s.v. "Stoa of Attalos, Athens"; Camp 1986: 172–75.
152. *Annual Report ASCS* 1952: 44.
153. *Annual Report ASCS* 1953–54: 44.

foreign visitors.[154] This was in many ways the high point of postwar American archaeological involvement in Greece. Yet even in the midst of celebrations there were subtle tensions. On 17 September 1956, *Time* magazine reported that

Greek Professor Anastasios Orlandos, the nation's highest authority on ancient monuments, was unable to attend, but he sent a message of dissent. The new Stoa is not a restoration at all, but just a reconstruction, he gruffed, and the gleaming white of its new columns marks an ugly contrast with the weathered beauty of the marbles on the ancient buildings. . . . Many of the Greeks gathered at the old birthplace of free speech shuddered at the professor's breach of form, but American professor John L. Caskey, head of the American School, took it in his stride. "Everyone," he said stoically "is entitled to his opinion."

American Archaeology in Italy

In the years after World War II, Italy was a place of complex and contradictory currents. The country had entered the war on Hitler's side, but a timely switch of sides and the heroic actions of the resistance salvaged much of the situation. Italy was treated very differently from Germany and Japan. Politically the Fascists were discredited, but the position Italy soon assumed as a bulwark against Communism in the Mediterranean meant that conservative forces were soon being reinforced by the U.S. government.[155]

Continuity was also seen in many areas of administration, including the archaeological service. Many of the rising stars of the Fascist antiquities service remained in positions of power and influence after the war. Appreciating a new power reality, they proved very hospitable to outsiders. For the first time since 1870, major foreign archaeological excavations could be started in Italy. At the same time, it was leftist intellectuals like the archaeologist Ranuccio Bianchi Bandinelli who had the greatest appeal to the new emerging generation of university students.[156]

American archaeologists were ill prepared to take advantage of the new opportunities in Italy. The United States had neither a well-developed tradition of Roman field archaeology nor academic support structures in the major graduate institutions. In comparison with its Greek counterpart, Roman archaeology was considered second-class, and opportunities to study either Etruscan archaeology or Italian prehistory were even more limited. Although the German emigres were creating some interest in Roman art history, none was a real field archaeologist. The logical focus for any new interest in Italian field archaeology would

154. *Program* 1956; MacKendrick 1962: 356–61.
155. Clark 1995.
156. Carandini 1979: 121–62.

have to be the American Academy in Rome. However, Albert Van Buren's limited ambitions had meant that the American Academy had not pursued even the limited opportunities available within the parameters of Italian archaeological policy in the 1930s. There was no tradition like Thomas Ashby's topographical research at the British School on which the academy could build.

The academy itself reopened for business in 1947. The director from 1946 to 1960 was Laurence Roberts, expert in Far Eastern art and former director of the Brooklyn Museum. Under Roberts, the academy became one of the most dynamic foreign cultural and social centers in postwar Rome.[157] Classics remained strong at the academy during this period. There was an active fellowship program and good research opportunities for senior scholars. However, the power elite at the academy soon realized that a major excavation was needed if the academy was going to fulfill its role as one of America's major overseas cultural institutions. The scholar best suited to move the Academy into this new world of field archaeology was Frank E. Brown (1908–1988) (Figure 20). Brown had been an undergraduate at Carleton College in Minnesota and had received his Ph.D. under Michael Rostovtzeff at Yale. He had held a fellowship at the American Academy from 1931 to 1933. At the academy G. P. Stevens stimulated his interest in ancient architecture.[158] Rostovtzeff also appreciated Brown's archaeological brilliance and flair and appointed him as a very young field director at Dura Europos for the last phase of excavations just before World War II. After war service in the Near East and a short stint in antiquities administration in Syria, Brown was appointed professor in charge and director of excavations at the American Academy in 1947. As his full title demonstrated, a significant part of his mandate was to explore possible sites for a major academy excavation.[159]

Brown selected the abandoned city center of Cosa, located near the modern city of Orbetello, some one hundred miles north of Rome, as the site for the new academy excavations.[160] On a promontory overlooking the Tyrrhenian Sea, Cosa was a Latin colony founded in 273 B.C. on what was thought to be a preexisting Etruscan settlement. Preliminary survey of the site suggested that the city had been abandoned by the early empire. Hopes that the site would yield significant Etruscan remains were frustrated, since Etruscan Cosa appears to have been located elsewhere. Roman Cosa was a Republican colonial foundation of the third century B.C. with little trace of imperial occupation. Hence it was felt that

157. Valentine and Valentine 1973: 109–18.
158. *EHCA* s.v. "Brown, Frank Edward (1908–88)"; R. T. Scott 1988.
159. *Annual Report AAR* 1943–51: 11; Valentine and Valentine 1973: 132–41.
160. *EHCA* s.v. "Cosa (Ansedonia)"; Brown 1949; Valentine and Valentine 1973: 132–41.

Figure 20. Frank Brown, the most important American archaeologist working in Italy in the post-World War II generation, conducting one of his famous archaeological tours of Cosa, a Roman colonial site on the Tyrrhenian Sea in southern Tuscany.

the site would yield important information on Roman colonial history and the development of Roman architecture during the formative phase of the middle Republic.[161]

The American Academy started excavation at Cosa in May 1948. A special arrangement with a local contractor who was beginning to develop the area as a tourist zone provided academy archaeologists with living quarters and access to skilled workmen. As was customary for the archaeology of that period, the excavations focused on the public buildings. In 1948 Brown was already digging the temples located on the Capitolium.[162] The three field seasons on the Capitolium provided important information on the development of Roman religious architecture in the second century B.C.[163] In 1951 excavations shifted to the forum and its complex of local civic structures.[164] The results there were

161. F. E. Brown 1980.
162. *Annual Report AAR* 1943–51: 24–26.
163. Brown, Richardson, and Richardson 1960.
164. F. E. Brown 1980: 1–46.

equally impressive, for Cosa did indeed provide much new information on the development of Roman public architecture during the late third to early first centuries B.C.[165]

Frank Brown directed the first phase of excavations from 1948 to 1951. In 1952 he was appointed to a professorship at Yale. The position of field archaeologist was given to Lawrence Richardson Jr. (1920–   ), one of Michael Rostovtzeff's last students and a former fellow of the American Academy. He and his wife, Emeline Hill Richardson, were already veterans of the Cosa exacavations. Richardson directed the excavations in the forum in 1953 and 1955. In addition, he undertook excavations in 1955 in the forum at Paestum to explore parallels between the public building of that Roman colony and that of Cosa.[166]

Frank Brown returned as professor at the American Academy in 1963 and digging at Cosa resumed in 1965. Much of the new excavation focused on houses located at the part of the site where the academy wished to build a museum and laboratory. The excavations uncovered several contiguous housing units and produced evidence of a violent destruction of the dwellings around 70 B.C.[167] Much of the reconstruction of Cosa's later urban history has been based on this small residential sample.[168] Only recently has a program of systematic surface survey and test soundings placed it in a wider context of city development.[169] Brown also returned to excavation in the forum, recovering especially useful information on its later history including the remains of a fourth-century sanctuary of the god Liber Pater.[170]

During this final phase, the excavations on the city site were complemented by ambitious research in the harbor area[171] and by settlement survey in the countryside.[172] The harbor studies produced information not only on the port structures and structural development of the republican harbor but also on the economy of the port itself and the related fisheries. The survey in the Cosa hinterland produced evidence of a large number of farmsteads and of a complex settlement history that challenged preconceptions about the history of the Roman countryside.

With both the American Academy research and the ongoing excavations and surveys by other American and Italian teams, Cosa and its

165. Brown, Richardson, and Richardson 1993.
166. *Annual Report AAR* 1951–5: 16–17, 31–36.
167. Bruno and Scott 1993: 146–48.
168. F. E. Brown 1980.
169. Fentress 1994.
170. Collins-Clinton 1977.
171. McCann et al. 1987.
172. Dyson 1978.

territory have become one of the best-known Roman sites in Italy. The final publication history has been uneven. The first two final excavation reports dealing with the general history and topography of the site and the temples of the Arx appeared relatively quickly.[173] Those on the houses and the forum were delayed thirty years.[174] The American Academy sponsored the construction of an excavation laboratory and museum complex, which could have provided a base for ongoing American research in the area. However, declining interest and financial concerns led to a hasty yielding of the facility to the Italian government.

The Cosa excavations impact on the development of American archaeology has been more limited than one might have expected. Part of this was owing to the American Academy's structure and goals. The American Academy of the 1950s, 1960s, and 1970s remained a very diverse, even unfocused institution that tried to encompass all the arts and humanities. Archaeology could never dominate there the way it did at the American School. Moreover, the academy had no special power over other American archaeologists working in Italy the way the American School in Athens did through its control of the Greek permit system. The Academy did not see fostering American archaeology in Italy as part of its role, and generally took relatively little interest in other U.S. projects operating in the peninsula. Compared to their counterparts at the American School in Athens or the British School in Rome, archaeologists operating out of the American Academy tended to have a rather narrow vision of what archaeology should or could be. They knew little of what was going on in the wider universe of archaeology, be it the innovative survey operations at the British School in Rome, the rise of a generation of Bianchi Bandinelli, Marxist-Italian archaeologists, or the convulsed realms of American anthropological archaeology.

In spite of the American Academy's limited direct involvement, Americans have made significant contributions in several areas of postwar Italian archaeology. Kyle Phillips's research has already been considered. The fieldwork of two other archaeologists, R. Ross Holloway of Brown University and Joseph Carter of the University of Texas, represents different but equally important field activity, much of it very innovative technically and some of it done with very limited resources.

Ross Holloway was a graduate of Amherst and Princeton and a veteran of the Morgantina excavations. Appointed professor of archaeology at Brown with a mandate to develop a field program, he first tried to attach Brown to the Agora excavations. When that proved too restrictive, he

173. F. E. Brown 1951; Brown, Richardson, and Richardson 1960.
174. Bruno and Scott 1993; Brown, Richardson, and Richardson 1993.

moved to southern Italy and Sicily, where he has conducted a series of important excavations with a both a prehistoric and a classical focus.[175] He generally worked with relatively small budgets, yet conducted excavations distinguished in their precise field methodology, employment of a variety of scientific analyses, and pioneering application of computer technology. Holloway learned to extend his resources by developing innovative cooperative arrangements with the Italians and other American institutions. He has always published his results with impressive speed and completeness.

Joseph Carter is another Princeton Ph.D. and Morgantina excavation veteran. His research interests cover both classical art history and innovative field archaeology. Operating from his base at the University of Texas at Austin, he has concentrated on reconstructing the history and structure of the countryside around the Greek colonial site of Metapontum in Italy. Working in close collaboration with Professor Dinu Adamesteanu, a pioneer in Italian landscape archaeology and the application of aerial photography to the archaeology of the Italian countryside, Carter has explored many aspects of the Metapontine countryside, from field systems to rural cemeteries.[176]

Special attention should also be paid to the pioneering paleobotanical research in the gardens of Pompeii conducted by Wilhemina Jashemski (1910–   ) of the University of Maryland. American scholars had long been interested in Pompeii and other sites in the Bay of Naples area but had conducted only limited archaeological research there. Albert Van Buren published a few important articles on Pompeii before the war.[177] John D'Arms used archaeological remains extensively in his studies of Roman society around the Bay of Naples.[178] In recent years, Lawrence Richardson of Duke has established a small but significant school of American Pompeian archaeology with a strong art historical and historical focus.[179]

Wilhemena Jashemski's roots and early education were in Nebraska. She completed a Ph.D. at Chicago and did early research in Roman political history. Married to a scientist, she learned to combine standard classical literary and archaeological sources with the information provided by scientific analysis.[180] By the 1960s her interests had focused on gardens and the evidence for agricultural activities within the walls of Pompeii itself. She determined that it was possible to make casts of the

175. Holloway 1970, 1973; Holloway, Joukowsky, and Lukesh 1990.
176. Carter 1981, 1985, 1990, 1992, 1994.
177. Van Buren 1920, 1938.
178. D'Arms 1970.
179. Richardson 1955, 1988; Franklin 1980.
180. R. Curtis 1988: ix–xi.

roots of plants growing in the gardens of Pompeii at the time of the destruction of A.D. 79, to match these root casts with known plant species, and to use that information to reconstruct the gardens associated with certain Pompeii houses.[181] Jashemski has determined that much more lucrative gardening, such as viticulture, went on within the walls of Pompeii than was previously suspected.[182]

Counterpart Fund Archaeology

In 1965 the *American Journal of Archaeology* published a small notice on "The Smithsonian Institution Foreign Currency Program in Archaeology and Related Disciplines." The opening paragraph read:

> The Smithsonian Institution has recently inaugurated a program of foreign currency support for American institutions of higher learning interested in archeological excavation or research in the so-called Public Law 480 excess countries. These are nations in which the United States Government holds amounts of foreign currencies, derived from the sale of surplus agricultural commodities, which the Treasury Department has determined to be excess to the normal requirements of the United States. (365)

The notice identified the relevant countries as Egypt, Israel, Poland, Yugoslavia, Tunisia, India, Ceylon, Pakistan, Burma, and Guinea. The 1966 budget for this program was $1.3 million. This foreign currency program represented a very important development in American classical archaeology during the 1960s. Since foreign aid was paid back by the host country in funds that had to be spent in that country, local archaeology was a good way to use the money. These often quite substantial amounts of research dollars were administered by the Smithsonian Institution in Washington. For a while this program created a miniboom of American field research in countries with rich classical archaeological potential like Yugoslavia and Tunisia.

The history of counterpart fund archaeology also reveals some serious limitations in American classical archaeology. Most American classical archaeologists traditionally focused on Greece, Italy, and Turkey. They were unwilling and unable to respond to the possibilities of this new funding source in unfamiliar areas. Since this counterpart fund money became available at a time when private and even public funding for traditional excavations was still abundant, few in the centers of American archaeological power responded positively to this new challenge. In a few instances, projects came into the hands of archaeologists with somewhat marginal backgrounds and they had an unhappy fate.

181. Jashemski 1979: vii–x.
182. Jashemski 1979.

Other projects were highly successful, helping produce American classical archaeologists with a broader vision of what the discipline could be. An American-based Roman provincial and urban archaeology began to develop. New academic institutions became involved in significant classical fieldwork. Several of these new counterpart fund archaeology projects were headed by women, a situation very different from the male-dominated core world of classical archaeology. Sadly, the program was not destined to last. Shifts in government policy regarding the use of this foreign aid funding and the political upheavals in such key areas as Yugoslavia slowed or stopped much archaeological research just as it was producing significant results. The successes and failures of the counterpart phenomenon can best be appreciated by concentrating on Yugoslavia and Tunisia.

Yugoslavia

Marshal Tito's decision to defy Stalin and look to the West for political support brought large amounts of nonconvertible foreign aid to Yugoslavia. Support of American archaeological research was one of the few ways it could be repaid. Yugoslavia had a rich archaeological heritage that ranged from early prehistoric sites, through Greek and Roman centers, to the important cities of the Middle Ages. Unfortunately, few American classical archaeologists knew anything about Yugoslavia or had much desire to work there.

Most of the archaeological opportunities available in Yugoslavia were at prehistoric, Roman provincial, and medieval sites. The latter two archaeological specialities were not well developed in the United States, although some Americans did move to take advantage of the opportunity. The result was a period of initial confusion and uncertainty, with some rather marginal research. Nevertheless, much important archaeology was done by Americans in Yugoslavia before politics and war terminated most of the field projects. Worthy of special consideration are the prehistoric-Roman provincial investigations undertaken along the Roman Danube frontier, the urban excavations at Split, and Boston University's research at Stobi.

America had no well-developed tradition of Roman frontier or even Roman provincial archaeology before the counterpart fund experience. American classical archaeologists had shown relatively little interest in the core Roman monuments, let alone those of the empire's outlying areas, where classicism could quickly degenerate into barbarism and bad taste. Unlike Britain, Spain, France, and Germany the United States had no monuments of the Roman frontier within its national territory. This began to change with the opportunities provided by counterpart funding. American archaeologists like Edward Ochsenschlager, Fred Winter, and Al Bancroft of Brooklyn College, Michael Werner of SUNY-Albany, John Eadie of Michigan, and Brad Bartel of San Diego became actively involved in the investigation of the Roman frontier and the development of Roman provincial society.[183] Some of these projects combined the approaches of classical and anthropological archaeology in a manner very rare for the period. They also involved a new group of institutions in archaeological field research. Finally, these undertakings required close cooperation with local archaeologists when research goals were often set by the national and local authorities. The Americans had to learn to adjust to new power relationships and, in the case of the Marxist countries, a very different way of looking at archaeology and material culture. The publications were generally financed by the counterpart money and done in the host country. Their quality could not match the American presses' slick productions that were the standard publication mode for the traditional American excavations of the period, and distribution outside the host country was often spotty.

Split

One of the most interesting examples of counterpart fund research was the University of Minnesota project at the harbor city of Split on the Dalmatian coast in what was then Yugoslavia and is today Croatia.[184] Here the Roman emperor Diocletian (ruled A.D. 285–305) built a fortified palace that became his retirement residence. During the Middle Ages, a thriving city developed in and around the ruins of the palace. This strikingly beautiful palace-city site received its first serious architectural study from the eighteenth-century British architect Robert Adam and has become a textbook example of the formal architecture of the late empire.[185] In spite of the confident plans and reconstructions that appear in general books on Roman architecture, most parts of the palace were still relatively poorly known when the Minnesota work began.

The American-Croatian archaeological project directed by Professor Sheila McNally of the University of Minnesota and Dr. Jerko Marasović of the Town Planning Institute of Dalmatia started work in 1968.[186] Their field research focused on the early fourth-century palace.[187] However, since the medieval town of Split had developed within the walls of the

183. Bartel, Kondie, and Werner 1979; Bankoff and Winter 1982.

184. McNally 1994.

185. *EHCA* s.v. "Split (Spalato; Aspalathos)"; L'Orange 1965: 70–71; Marasovic 1982: 33–47; Wilkes 1986.

186. McNally 1975; Marasovic, Marasovic, McNally, and Wilkes 1972: 3–9.

187. McNally 1975; McNally, Marasovic and Marasovic 1976.

palace, any investigation had to be an exercise in sensitive, limited urban archaeology. This could not be an archaeological urban renewal excavation in the destroy-and-clear mode, but a limited excavation working in small, scattered sectors of the city.[188] This limitation on excavation was especially relevant for Split, since the Yugoslavian town planners were very much interested in preserving and enhancing the core historic districts of the town for the purpose of tourist development.[189] American archaeologists at Split had to do the type of work that was part of the developing urban archaeology ethos in countries like Holland, Denmark, and England, with sensitivity to the preservation of the urban fabric.

Despite limitations imposed by the site and the turbulent politics of the region, Split has proven to be one of the most productive of the counterpart fund projects. Important information on the history of the palace has been recovered and the development of the city. An urban revitalization program has been assisted in important ways. The publications have appeared with impressive regularity, and American students have been exposed to a different type of archaeology.

Stobi

Stobi was in some ways the most traditional of the major Yugoslavian projects, for it was a classic excavation of an ancient abandoned urban center. However, by their association with one of the most innovative graduate programs in archaeology, the Stobi excavations have become an excellent example of the blending of old and new in American classical archaeology. The excavations were started in 1970 by Professor James Wiseman, then of the University of Texas. The sponsorship moved to Boston University with Wiseman in 1973–74, where they became an important part of that emerging archaeology program. Much of the excavation has been oriented toward public architecture and the reconstruction of urban development.[190] Important research has been carried on at the theater,[191] the episcopal complex,[192] and a newly discovered synagogue.[193] The site has become a laboratory for the employment of a variety of scientific techniques and approaches that have become a central part of the research initiatives of the Boston Univerity archaeology program.[194]

188. McNally 1975; 1994 fig. 1.
189. Marasovic 1982.
190. *EHCA* s.v. "Stobi"; Wiseman 1986.
191. Gebhard 1981.
192. Aleksova 1981.
193. Wiseman 1986.
194. Folk 1973; Wesolowsky 1975; Wiseman 1978; Wiseman in Anderson-Stojanovic 1992: xxi–xxvi.

These Yugoslavian projects should be remembered in any history of American classical archaeology, not only because of their actual successes and failures but also because they anticipated what will probably be important future developments in American classical archaeology. There will likely be more focus on survey and regional analysis. Research in living cities will become more of a concern for all archaeologists. Close cooperation with local archaeologists and administrators will become increasingly necessary. The violent political events in Yugoslavia are an extreme example of what American archaeologists face in many parts of the world. These international complexities mean that archaeologists will no longer be able to think in the comfortable long-term manner that has become the norm for research in Greece and Italy.

North Africa and Carthage

American archaeologists had early shown an interest in the rich archaeological sites of North Africa, but their efforts there produced limited results. There had been the tragic 1911 expedition to Cyrene, which ended with the death of Fletcher DeCou and the Italian invasion of North Africa. In 1925 Francis Kelsey of the University of Michigan, supported by the Washington society of the AIA, had started excavations in the precinct of Tanit at Carthage. Although launched with great hopes and some impressive initial finds, this project ended with Kelsey's death in 1927.[195]

American interest in the area revived with the availability of foreign aid funding. The first long-term research project to take advantage of the new funding opportunities was the North Africa mosaic survey undertaken by Margaret Alexander of the University of Iowa. The Roman sites of Tunisia are extremely rich in mosaic pavements, some of which have been moved into museums like the Bardo in Tunis. Many others remain in situ in the countryside, often threatened with destruction by man and nature. The Tunisian authorities already had plans under way to start an inventory of these mosaics, when in 1967 Smithsonian funding made possible a joint Tunisian-American project. Alexander and her Tunisian and American colleagues began systematically recording these mosaics and publishing fascicles of the *Corpus des mosaïques de Tunisie*.[196]

Much more ambitious were the two American projects at Carthage itself. As early as 1926, Francis Kelsey had expressed concern about the threat posed to the site of ancient Carthage by the expansion of the modern city of Tunis.[197] By the early 1970s this threat had reached the

195. Kelsey 1926a, b.
196. Alexander and Ennaifer 1973.
197. Kelsey 1926: 22–26.

point where major archaeological intervention was necessary. In 1972 UNESCO and the Tunisian government launched a major operation in salvage archaeology called the International Campaign to Save Carthage. Teams were brought in from various countries to excavate specific sectors within ancient Carthage. The presence of dig personnel from Britain, Bulgaria, Canada, Denmark, France, Germany, Italy, Poland, and the United States, working in close proximity and using their own varied approaches to excavation, provided an ideal international learning environment, which helped reshape the practice in archaeology in several countries.[198]

Two American expeditions participated in this international enterprise. The University of Michigan team under John Humphrey concentrated on a late Roman house and an ecclesiastical complex in the ancient urban area.[199] Lawrence Stager of Chicago and Harvard from 1975 to 1979 focused on the remains of the Punic period with excavations at the tophet and the rectangular harbor area.[200] The American excavations at Carthage, especially those of the University of Michigan, have been impressive in the quality of field techniques, the richness of the finds, and the rapidity and detail of publication. The Carthage projects' immediate influence has been somewhat limited because the type of archaeology that was practiced there did not fit easily into any well-established tradition in American classical archaeology.

However, Carthage did increase U.S. interest in the archaeology of Roman North Africa, and trained a younger generation in new approaches to archaeology. This impact was enhanced by the fact that the Carthage excavations took place at a time when Michigan was rising to the top rank in graduate programs in classical archaeology. American involvement at Carthage has continued with the excavations in the Circus area starting in 1982, carried out by Michigan, the University of Colorado, and the University of Georgia under the codirection of Naomi Norman, Anne Haeckl, and John Humphrey.[201] It has also led to important archaeological survey and settlement history reconstruction in the Tunisian hinterland.[202]

The period from the mid-1940s to the mid-1980s saw more American classical field archaeology than all the previous seven decades combined. The results were often impressive, but generally the projects were limited in innovative imagination. The question of whether this experience positioned American classical archaeologists to deal with the very different situation at the end of the century is considered in the final part of this

198. Ennabli 1978; Pedley 1980.
199. Humphrey 1976, 1988: v.
200. Pedley 1980; Stager 1978, 1980.
201. Humphrey ed. 1988: 1–6.
202. Hitchner 1990.

book. To end this chapter, I want to return to the museum world, its continuities, and its changes.

Museums and Private Collecting

The same economic prosperity that aided field archaeology from the 1950s through the 1970s increased the acquisition budgets of museums and stimulated the growth of private collections on a scale previously unknown. With the increased competition for fine objects, prices for antiquities rose to astounding new heights. This in turn produced an increase in both clandestine excavation and outright theft. By the 1970s concern about the rapid destruction of archaeological resources prompted calls for international action to stem this illicit trade. Thus a major conflict broke out between museums and field archaeologists.

By the end of World War II, the legal export of antiquities from almost all areas in the Mediterranean and the Near East ended, as official colonialism retreated. Countries like Syria and Egypt, whose colonial governments had allowed some export of archaeological material, achieved their independence and stopped such practices. Some antiquities arrived on the market from the recycling of objects in European collections dismantled in the wake of World War II and the economic privations that followed. However, most objects on the market came from clandestine excavations and had to be exported illegally from those countries of origin.

As we have seen, the values shaping the museum world changed dramatically during the early years of this century. Gone was a vision of the museum as an institution that pursued the mandates of Ruskin, Morris, and Norton to improve public taste. The rhetorical stance of promoting idealized Greek beauty was often used to veil the more naked pursuit of the most expensive and most impressive objects to enhance museums' collections. An object's original archaeological context was of little importance. The museum displays of classical art collections were aimed at a cultural and social elite. Museum curators tended to be better educated in the technical aspects of object identification, classification, and dating than in cultural history, art theory, or aesthetics. They gave relatively little thought to innovative ways of presenting Greek and Roman art to a changing American society; that was considered the role of the education department.

The aloof elitism of these curators reflected the philosophy of administrators in most art museums.[203] An expression of this was their reaction to calls for more detailed and educational museum labeling. One mu-

203. Eisler 1969: 590.

seum official commented with disdain that illustrative material "dangerously shifts the attention of the museum visitor away from the art work and on to the information about it." Sherman Lee of the Cleveland Museum, one of the leading figures in museum administration during that period, stated that "Humanists don't understand that a work of art doesn't need words to accompany it. They tend to think that if you understand something through what you see rather than what you read, that it is witchcraft."[204] The implication was that if one had not studied classical art at college, one should probably not be wasting time in a museum.

Museum curators' success in building collections came to depend more and more on their cultivation of private dealers, collectors, and donors. This became truer as prices rose in the antiquities market, and even the wealthiest museums could not always compete with private collectors. Considerable amounts of new postwar money went into ancient art collecting, and for the first time a substantial number of private classical art collections developed. Before World War II, wealthy Americans like James Loeb who were interested in classical art were relatively rare, but now fashionable money sought out Greek and Roman art.

The changing collecting scene can be seen in an exhibition of ancient art from private collections that was staged in three cities in Texas in 1970 and 1971.[205] The pieces ranged from major works of sculpture to large and small bronzes and painted vases down to glass and terra-cottas. Two hundred and thirty pieces were exhibited. Of these, only six were listed as having come from older collections. Most of the rest were presumably products of clandestine excavations and the antiquities market. Indeed, "said to be from" was one of the more commonly used expressions in the catalog.

An article in the Antiques column of the *New York Times* for 23 September 1990 profiled one collecting couple, Leon Levy and Shelby White, and their private classical collection. The occasion for the piece was an exhibition of their collection at the Metropolitan Museum and the publication of a catalog written by Met curators. The Levy-White collection had started with an auction purchase in 1975, when, in Levy's words, "Realizing it was possible to own an ancient bust came as a shock. I could raise my hand and in minutes own something that was 2,000 years old." The $1,300 Levy paid for the Roman bust paled in comparison with the $1.32 million he spent for a neolithic figure in 1986 or the $1.76 million for a Euphronios vase purchase in 1990. Levy saw collecting as a form of trust. As he put it in the *Times* article:

204. S. Miller 1984: 143.
205. H. Hoffman 1971.

We believe very strongly that all of this is borrowed. You borrow it for life and in return for having the pleasure of looking at it, you have the responsibility of taking care of it and finding out as much as you can about it. And then it goes on to somebody else. (Levy 1975)

This was an expression of what was by now a venerable tradition of art historical philanthropy, which had created North America's great museums.

The continued expression of such sentiments was bound to bring joy to a curator's heart. Field archaeologists also appreciated such interests. Cultivated and wealthy individuals helped finance excavations and served on the boards of archaeological societies. Only with the emergence of a greater consciousness about the way the antiquities market contributed to the destruction of archaeological resources did relations between the digger and the collector begin to change. The fact that, of two hundred and thirty objects from the Levy-White collection exhibited in 1990, only two had a specific known origin was bound to raise concern in the archaeological community about the relationship between collecting and site looting and destruction.[206]

The Getty Collection

In the exclusive club of very wealthy Americans Jean Paul Getty stood near the top.[207] Oil had made his fortune, and it was a very large fortune indeed. Getty (1892–1976) had long been interested in ancient art, and in the late 1930s was already acquiring classical pieces.[208] By the 1950s he was greatly interested in ancient art. He purchased extensively, using such distinguished scholars as Professor Bernard Ashmole of Oxford as advisers.[209] Getty's collection of Greek and Roman art became increasingly well known in art history circles for its size and quality.

In his old age Getty decided to achieve cultural immortality by creating an impressive museum structure to house his collection and providing that new museum with a substantial endowment to purchase more art. Getty further impressed the art historical world by creating an extremely wealthy foundation to promote scholarly research, art historical education and conservation. The museum, erected in Malibu, California, was designed as a replica of the Roman Villa of the Papyri excavated at Herculaneum in the eighteenth century.[210] The Getty holdings formed the

206. Gill and Chippindale 1993: 608, 632, 636; Elia 1997: 93.
207. *J. Paul Getty Museum* 1991.
208. *J. Paul Getty Museum* 1991: 5.
209. *J. Paul Getty Museum* 1991: 5–8; Ashmole 1994: 155–61.
210. *J. Paul Getty Museum* 1991: 12–15; Duncan 1995: 79–82.

core of the collection of ancient art, but the enormous acquisitions budget at its disposal allowed its curators to purchase extensively on the international market.[211]

The Getty hired a Czech art historian, Jiri Frel, to mastermind its acquisition program. Frel, who had started his American career at the Metropolitan Museum of Art, was a worthy spiritual descendant of E. P. Warren and John Marshall. He was one of the last curatorial entrepreneurs, who moved rapidly and ruthlessly in the international antiquities market. With Getty money in his pocket, he found that great works of classical art readily appeared for his consideration. The price was usually not of great importance, and the Getty Museum cared relatively little about the original provenance of objects.[212] In a 1973 catalog of the Getty collection of ancient art, eighty-eight of one hundred and eighteen pieces have no listed provenance.[213] This free-wheeling acquisition policy increasingly exposed the Getty to field archaeologists' hostility. Almost immediately, it laid them open to the deceptions of forgers. The Dossenas, the Italians who had placed many fakes with American museums during the interwar period, were dead, but their traditions of skillful forgery lived on.

As one would expect from a new and culturally rather insecure institution, the Getty placed great emphasis on acquiring high-priced works of art produced by famous artists. In the world of ancient art, where secure attributions are rare, this led to three troublesome purchases. One of the Getty's early major acquisitions was a life-size bronze statue they pushed hard to associate with Lysippos, the fourth-century B.C. Greek sculptor who worked for Alexander the Great. This claimed attribution was regarded as wishful thinking by most art historians. The statue caused further trouble when the Italian government claimed that it had been found off the Italian coast.[214]

Even more embarrassing was the acquisition of a marble head of Achilles that was attributed to the fourth-century B.C. Greek sculptor Skopas. Jiri Frel announced its acquisition in florid terms:

Like an apparition from the heavens, a hitherto unknown masterpiece of Greek classic sculpture lights enthusiasm in the heart of everyone who admires it. The name of one of the greatest artists of fourth century B.C. Greece is attached to this marvel. Who would expect to find in a remote French provincial house the over life size marble head of Achilles, the central figure of the west pediment of the temple of Athena Alea in Peloponnesian Tegea, carved in all probability by Skopas himself. (Frel in Stewart 1982)

211. *J. Paul Getty Museum* 1991: 17–63.
212. Hoving 1997: 281–318.
213. Vermeule and Neuerburg 1973.
214. *JFA* 1978: 5; Hoving 1993: 362–68.

Andrew Stewart of the University of California at Berkeley, a leading expert on Skopas, quickly affirmed that it was indeed an authentic piece and probably came from the temple at Tegea. Supposedly it had been carried from Greece to France before 1850.[215] This alleged masterpiece was soon dismissed as an early twentieth-century forgery.[216]

The third and most controversial piece was the so-called Getty kouros. This wonderfully preserved, life-sized, nude male statue supposedly dated to the late sixth century B.C. The purchase price was in the multimillions and the find spot either unknown or concealed.[217] The museum evoked the ever useful "old European collection" explanation, although it was hard to believe something that large and beautiful could have been unknown for so long. Several highly respected experts in Greek sculpture asserted that the kouros was a fake. Other equally respected scholars defended the statue's authenticity. Since it is almost impossible to date marble sculptures by physical-chemical means, the claims of authenticity have to be based on style, and on that question the experts have come to opposite conclusions.[218]

The histories of these three dubious pieces could be duplicated by other examples from the Getty and other American museums. Frel acknowledged as much in an article titled with delicious ambivalence, "Imitations of Ancient Sculpture in Malibu."[219] The ethical issues associated with this trade are discussed below. Less often considered are the intellectual and scholarly consequences of such secretive acquisition policies.[220] For archaic and early classical Greek sculpture, the corpus of accepted originals is very small. With such a small sample, any major new find can significantly alter our intepretation of that key period in the history of Western art. The introduction of numbers of fakes into the corpus undermines the intellectual foundations of the whole enterprise. In their hungry pursuit of decontextualized objects, the museums have ignored these implications, and increasingly have helped to build a reconstruction of the artistic past whose scholarly foundations may be laid in quicksand.

The Met Hot Pot and the Antiquities Trade

Although the Getty drew extensive criticism and censure from the field archaeology community for its actions, the Metropolitan Museum of Art

---

215. Stewart 1982: viii–ix.
216. Hafner 1984, Hoving 1997: 313–18.
217. True 1992.
218. *Getty Kouros Controversy* 1992; Hoving 1997: 279–310.
219. Frel 1981.
220. Gill and Chippindale 1993: 615–36.

really brought the deep conflicts about the high-priced antiquities trade to the public's attention. In November 1972, Thomas Hoving, the museum's director, announced the acquisition of a splendid early red-figured Greek vase attributed to the Athenian pot-painter Euphronios. The price was $1 million, much more than had ever been paid for a Greek vase. The vase had been acquired at the recommendation of Dietrich von Bothmer, the Metropolitan's curator of Greek and Roman art. This purchase was to be the culmination of a career spent enhancing the Met's Greek vase collection.[221]

Problems arose when Hoving and von Bothmer began describing how the Met acquired the Euphronios vase. Hoving's own description combined pride in the predatory zeal of a modern American museum director with the rather uncritical idealization of Greek art, especially Greek figured vases. The Met claimed that the fragmentary vase had long been in the family collection of a Lebanese antiquities dealer from whence it made its way to Switzerland, where the Met acquired it.[222] The Lebanese connections meant that there would be no problems about clandestine excavation or illegal export, an interesting and amusing variation on the "old European collection" ploy used so often by museums to provide a pedigree for objects purchased under dubious circumstances.[223]

The Metropolitan Museum's official explanation was not accepted by many archaeologists nor by the Italian authorities. Most Greek vases in European and American collections have actually been found in Etruscan tombs, the products of a very active international trade in quality ceramics during the sixth and fifth centuries B.C. The looting of Tuscan tombs for these artifacts started in the eighteenth century and continues today. A. L. Frothingham was buying objects directly from Etruscan tombs for American museums at the end of the nineteenth century.

The Italians claimed that the Met vase had been excavated illegally from a tomb near Cerveteri, an Etruscan site north of Rome. Central to the drama was an American antiquities dealer named Robert Hecht, who had studied at the American Academy in Rome and had excavated at Cosa. Basing himself in Europe, and in Italy itself when it was not too "hot," Hecht had made himself well known as one of the most successful operatives in the shadow trade in ancient art.[224]

A few years earlier none of this controversy about a piece's origins would have aroused great consternation. This was the way the interna-

221. Meyer 1973: 86–100; Hess 1974: 141–71; Hoving 1993: 307–40.
222. Dillon and Hoving 1974.
223. Gill and Chippindale 1993: 622–23.
224. Hess 1974: 141–71; Hoving 1993: 308–69.

tional art market operated, and this was how major American museums acquired great works of Greek and Roman art. But the Met purchase came at a time when concern about the looting of archaeological sites throughout the world was becoming especially acute.[225] International pressure had led to the 1970 drafting of a UNESCO convention that would try to stem the illegal traffic in antiquities. As the Met was quick to point out, the United States had not signed onto this treaty. This was partially the result of the efforts of the powerful lobby of antiquities dealers, certain museums, and their wealthy patrons.[226]

The American archaeological community outside the museum world was strongly behind the UNESCO convention. In 1983 the U.S. government finally passed legislation that gave the UNESCO convention force within the United States. The United States was the fifty-first country to ratify the convention and the only major art-importing country to do so.[227] During the debate on ratification the point was made repeatedly that archaeological sites, whether Etruscan tombs, Roman villas, or Mississippian mounds, are a finite resource. The cultures that created them have died. Once the last site of any particular culture is looted and destroyed, that will be the end of our hopes of acquiring new information from undisturbed archaeological contexts. Moreover, while museum curators had learned to treasure the pure beauty of decontextualized objects, for the field archaeologist, the circumstances in which an object was deposited and found were extremely important. Not only does the excavation find spot allow archaeologists to date and authenticate an artifact, but it also makes it possible to relate the artifact to other objects found at a particular archaeological site and thus reconstruct a wide cultural environment. In any Etruscan tomb was not just a Greek pot, but a collection of native and imported pots, wall paintings, grave furniture, and other objects. Studied together these allow the archaeologist to reconstruct the social and economic circumstances, the funerary rituals, and the view of the afterlife of the person buried there.

The differences in the classical archaeological community about the museum-based trade in antiquities produced another crisis when Dr. von Bothmer tried to report on his new find at the annual professional meeting of the Archaeological Institute of America. Instead of receiving the expected praise for a great discovery, the Met curator found himself the object of fierce criticism. This helped catalyze opposition to the antiquities trade. As a result, the AIA passed rules that prohibited either the

225. Winter 1991.
226. Elia 1991: 98.
227. Herscher 1983; Elia 1991: 98.

first presentation of illegally exported material at their annual meeting or its initial publication in the *American Journal of Archaeology*.[228] Individuals who purchased antiquities of dubious origins found themselves closed off from the two most important venues of scholarly presentation in the United States.

Field archaeologists had several reasons for going on record as opposing the antiquities trade. Not only were they more acutely aware of the impact of site looting, but they were also the first to feel the rage of foreign governments, whose cultural resources are being decimated. The American excavators at Morgantina found themselves in a very defensive position when claims were made that a statue of Aphrodite purchased by the Getty had been secretly excavated near that site.[229] Turkish authorities became very specific about their intention to target American field projects when disputes arose over American museums purchasing antiquities illegally exported from Turkey. Not surprisingly, the field-oriented University of Pennsylvania Museum was the first to pledge not to buy objects of unknown or illegal provenance. It was joined by other university-affiliated musems such as those at Harvard.[230]

It took considerable courage for AIA archaeologists to challenge the antiquities establishment, for it led to the alienation of a number of wealthy supporters who were also collectors. This came at a time when research funding was beginning to decline. Yet the controversy did not estrange responsible collectors from the world of field archaeology. A good example was Leon Pomerance of New York.[231] Pomerance was a highly successful businessman who combined collecting and the sponsorship of field archaeology during the 1960s. Although he financed the Greek-American excavations at the Minoan palace site of Kato Zakro, Pomerance was more than just an archaeological patron. He became a recognized expert in the field of Minoan archaeology. Moreover, as concern about the consequences of collecting grew, he distanced himself from that world and focused on field research. The respect with which he was held by the archaeological community is shown by the fact that he held several high offices in the Archaeological Institute of America at a time when the collecting controversy was at its height.

This debate about the antiquities market produced major tensions for classical curators in American museums. They had just been doing business the way it had been done at American museums since the days of Warren and Marshall. Now they found themselves estranged from many

228. Kleiner 1990.
229. Magrini 1988; Elia 1991: 99.
230. Meyer 1973: 73–76.
231. Meyer 1973: 130–32; J. Shaw 1989.

of their professional colleagues, under increased public scrutiny and criticism in the United States and legal and diplomatic pressure from foreign governments. This led to international legal action. In one instance, the Turkish government, which has been especially vigorous in prosecuting illegal archaeological activities, forced the Boston Museum of Fine Arts to return a large hoard of ancient jewelry, illegally excavated and exported from that country.[232] The efforts of important segments of the American archaeological community to combat the antiquities trade have had notable successes and major failures. Organizations like the Archaeological Institute of America and publications like the *Journal of Field Archaeology* have done much to raise public and professional consciousness about the destruction of archaeological resources. An increasing number of major museums, including most recently the Getty itself, have tightened their policies about acquiring antiquities.[233] U.S. government agencies such as the customs service and the courts are increasingly proactive in confiscating and returning illegal antiquities.[234]

Other important museums are blatant in their display of ancient art objects whose origins are dubious at best and in some cases can be traced to known sites in the Mediterranean. Private collecting of archaeological objects has continued unabated, and dealers flourish, justifying their actions and attacking the archaeological community for attempting to stop their lucrative activities.[235] The collectors and dealers have been active in opposing legislation like the UNESCO convention that would tighten the restrictions on that trade.[236] The *Journal of Field Archaeology* and other concerned publications continue their sad chronicle of sites wrecked and museums looted.

232. Rose and Acar 1995.
233. Shestack 1989.
234. Slayman 1998.
235. Brandt 1990.
236. Elia 1991.

Afterword: Archaeology in the 1990s and Beyond

The fall 1988 newsletter of the American School of Classical Studies in Athens opened with the following account:

The Athenian Agora echoed with the rattle of jack hammers and the growl of earth-moving machinery as preparations began in the summer of 1988 for the resumption of excavations. For the first time in a decade, the walls of modern buildings came tumbling down to make way for the excavation of newly acquired properties along the north side of modern Hadrian Street. The demolition of one building was complete by the end of August, and a second structure will be torn down during the winter months.

In actions reminiscent of the 1930s, more of the historic Plaka was destroyed for American topographical investigations. Moreover, the Agora excavations continued to demonstrate their abilities to dominate access to funding sources, even when archaeological research money was diminishing. In 1979 a new program of Agora excavation was able to raise $300,000 from the Packard Foundation, $296,000 from the Mellon Foundation, and $230,000 from the National Endowment for the Humanities. Between 1983 and 1986 the Packard Foundation poured over $350,000 into the Agora.[1] From the perspective of the Agora, American Mediterranean power archaeology in the 1980s had changed little from that of the 1950s or even the 1930s.

However, in the wider world of the Mediterranean, economic, social, and intellectual changes that threatened many aspects of the culture of American classical archaeology were taking place. Development in much of Europe and the Mediterranean meant that economic neocolonialism was dead, and countries like the United States could no longer do archaeology cheaply. The cost of everything related to archaeology, from labor to gasoline has risen to equal or surpass prices in the United States.

The quality difference between American classical archaeologists and the local archaeologists in countries like Italy, Greece, Spain, and Turkey was also disappearing. Improvements in archaeological education and

1. This information is taken from the American School's annual reports.

field training in Europe and the Mediterranean, and changes in the social structure and political ideology of those doing archaeology led to the emergence of a dynamic younger generation of bright and active scholars. Involved in hands-on excavation from the early years of their university careers, these students now generally have considerably more field experience than their American counterparts. Even more embarrassing is the fact that they often know the most recent theoretical literature, including that coming out of the United States, better than their counterparts in American classical archaeology. Probably for the first time in history, American classical archaeologists have little to teach these locals.

The problems for American classical archaeology are compounded by the fact that financial resources are contracting and conservative forces are advancing at a time when change and rethinking are desperately needed. Competitive public funding for classical archaeological funding has almost completely disappeared. The most severe blow came in 1995–96, when the National Endowment for the Humanities, faced with severe budget cuts, eliminated its special archaeology research program.[2] Support of archaeology had been one of the NEH's original goals, and its archaeology program, despite its limitations, had done much to promote an open, democratic spirit in American archaeology. Since internal policy decisions largely exclude classical archaeology from access to National Science Foundation archaeology funding, this branch of archaeology currently has access to only small amounts of governmental research support.

The result of this is a return to the world of the early century when the ability to do archaeological research depended on access to private funding. The classical archaeologists in some university departments have access to considerable sums of institutional money that can be used to develop major programs of field research. In other instances they have access to private sources of wealth. The American economic elite continues to be impressively generous toward archaeology. Some donations are very open; many reflect special interests and special connections.

This growing dependence on private and semiprivate (i.e., special foundation) resources often reinforces but does not create the strong conservative forces that still dominate American classical archaeology. General economic developments explain some of this. Public universities are increasingly hard pressed, and important innovative programs like those at Indiana and Minnesota have disappeared. Elite private education continues to benefit from private philanthropy and alumni generosity. Classical archaeology at Princeton has received impressive new resources.

2. As this is written, the long-term fate of the NEH remains in doubt.

Not everything can be blamed on economic forces. American classical archaeologists have failed to ask hard questions or pursue new directions in most areas of the discipline. Graduate students are trained much the same way they were fifty or even one hundred years ago, without much thought as to changes in either the teaching market or research possibilities. Mastering Greek and Latin remains at the center of much classical archaeology graduate education. However, enrollments in those languages is declining steadily, and classics departments will increasingly survive on their ability to teach classical civilization and harness the great public interest in areas like archaeology. Classics students still generally work in contexts that isolate them from other archaeologists and with methods and problems that in many cases differ little from those learned from the Germans by the founding fathers one hundred years ago. Their field training often comes limited and late, and in a controlled context that inhibits innovation. The important and influential field schools and training programs still tend to focus on major sites, where the student excavator is very much a cog in the greater machine.

American classical archaeology has continued to work largely within the big-dig philosophy, which involves long-term investment in a site, the gathering of a large cadre of experts, and a commitment to long series of study seasons and expensive publication series. Nostalgia continues for the great projects of the past, and American classical archaeologists continue to return to such enterprises as Sardis, Troy, Aphrodisias, and Gordion.[3] Such projects consume a high percentage of diminishing archaeological resources, and it is not clear how long even those will be able to continue.

American classical archaeology can move in two directions. In one scenario, those few who have personal resources or access to private money will control the elite graduate programs and carry on fieldwork in the grand manner. This will represent a return to the world of archaeologists as gentlemen and to Allison Armour and his yacht. Those most likely to benefit will be products of the rich universities and the traditional centers of archaeological power. Those who are less privileged will, if fortunate, receive minor positions in this elite power structure, look on enviously while a privileged few get to do real archaeology, or can content themselves with cataloging and publishing the archaeological leftovers from past generations. Classical archaeology will come to reflect the increasing social and economic stratification evident in so many other areas of American society.

In the other scenario, American classical archaeologists can learn from other former colonial powers such as the British and modify their educa-

3. Gates 1997: 272–74 (Gordion); 288–90 (Sardis), 292–93 (Troy).

tional approach to field research. There is still more archaeology to do than any country has the resources to undertake, and only the most xenophobic national archaeological administrations do not welcome truly cooperative projects. Recent political changes in areas like Eastern Europe and the former Soviet Union have created great opportunities for classical archaeological research, and some Americans have moved to take advantage of these.

Adopting this second scenario will require a major rethinking of the education and field training of the next generation of American classical archaeologists. Like British, Dutch and Scandinavian archaeologists, the Americans may have to develop specialized research niches in fields like environmental analysis or computer data processing. They will need flexible field training that will allow them to see potential in more than one type of archaeological situation and to move out on their own. Although few countries will allow outsiders to excavate sites of great national importance, they will welcome assistance in salvage, survey, and conservation projects, and in the development of archaeological sites as tourist resources. This new universe will demand archaeologists who can range widely and think about how their discipline relates to a wide academic and nonacademic public.

Bibliography

Abrams, A. (1985) *The Valiant Hero*. Washington, D.C.

Abse, J. (1981) *John Ruskin: The Passionate Moralist*. London.

Adams, H. (1961) *The Education of Henry Adams*. Boston.

Adams, L. (1925) *The Faliscans in Prehistoric Times*. Proceedings and Memoirs of the AAR 5.

Adams, W. H. (1976) *The Eye of Thomas Jefferson*. Washington, D.C.

Adelson, H. (1958) *The American Numismatic Society, 1858–1958*. New York.

Agard, W. (1953) "Classical Scholarship." In M. Curti, ed., *American Scholarship in the Twentieth Century*, 146–67. New York.

Aleksova, B. (1981) "The Presbyterium of the Episcopal Basilica at Stobi and Episcopal Basilica at Bargala." In B. Aleksova and J. Wiseman, eds., *Studies in the Antiquities of Stobi III*, 29–46. Skopje.

Alexander, M., and M. Ennaifer. (1973) *Corpus des mosaïques de Tunisie*. Vol. 1. Tunis.

Allen, C. E., A. Beatty, S. Goodnight, and A. Laird. (1935) "Professor Grant Showerman." *Annual Bulletin AIA*: 22–23.

Allen, S. H. (1995) "'Finding the Walls of Troy': Frank Calvert, Excavator." *AJA* 99: 379–407.

Allesbrook, M. (1992) *Born to Rebel: The Life of Harriet Boyd Hawes*. Oxford.

Alsop, J. (1964) *From the Silent Earth*. New York.

Amandry, P. (1992) *La Redécouverte de Delphi*. Paris.

American Academy in Rome, Report, 1943–1951. (1951). New York.

American Academy in Rome, Report, 1951–1955. (1955). New York.

Anderson, M. (1987) *Pompeian Frescoes in the Metropolitan Museum of Art*. New York.

Anderson, P. (1980) *Promoted to Glory: The Apotheosis of George Washington*. Northampton, Mass.

Anderson-Stojanovic, V. (1992) *Stobi: The Hellenistic and Roman Pottery*. Princeton, N.J.

Andrews, W. (1964) *Architecture, Ambition, and Americans*. New York.

Arlt, G. O. (1962) "A National Humanities Foundation." *ACLS Newsletter* 13.7: 11–18.

Arnold, D., ed. (1994) *Belov'd by Ev'ry Muse*. London.

Arrias, P. E. (1995) "Il mito dell'archeologia italiana: Due 'patres conscripti' all'inizio delle leggi sulle antichita dopo il 1870." *Rendiconti della Classe di Scienze morali, storiche e filologiche dell'Accademia dei Lincei* 9.6: 137–45.

Ascherson, N. (1996) *Black Sea*. London.

Ashmole, B. (1970) "Sir John Beazley." *Proceedings of the British Academy* 56: 443–61.

———. (1985) "Sir John Beazley (1885–1970)." In Kurtz (1985a), 57–71.

———. (1994) *An Autobiography*, ed. D. Kurtz. Malibu, Calif.

Bacon, F. H., ed. (1902–21) *Investigations at Assos*. Boston.

Bagnani, G. (1955) "Winckelmann and the Second Renaissance, 1755–1955." *AJA* 59: 107–18.

Baker, P. (1964) *The Fortunate Pilgrims: Americans in Italy, 1800–1860*. Cambridge, Mass.

———. (1992) "Stanford White and Italy." In *The Italian Presence in American Art, 1860–1920*, 158–72. New York.

Baldwin, M., and M. Torelli. (1979) *Latin Inscriptions in the Kelsey Museum: The Dennison Collection*. Ann Arbor, Mich.

Bandelier, A. (1884) *Report of an Archaeological Tour in Mexico in 1881*. Papers of the Archaeological Institute of America. American Series, vol. 2. Boston.

Bankoff, A., and F. Winter. (1982) "The Morava Valley Project in Yugoslavia: Preliminary Report, 1970–1980." *JFA* 9: 149–64.

Barber, R. (1990) "Classical Art: Discovery, Research and Presentation, 1890–1930." In Cowling and Mundy, 391–411.

Barker, G., ed. (1986) *Thomas Ashby: Un archeologo fotografa la Campagna Romana tra '800 e '900*. Rome.

Barker, G., R. Hodges, and O. Ferrari. (1989) *Archeologia a Roma nelle fotografie di Thomas Ashby, 1891–1930*. Naples.

Bartel, B., V. Kondie, and M. Werner. (1979) "Excavation at Kraku'lu Yordan, NE Serbia, Preliminary Report 1973–6." *JFA* 6: 127–50.

Bartlett, I. H. (1996) "Edward Everett Reconsidered." *New England Quarterly* 69: 416–60.

Bass, G. (1961) "A Bronze Age Shipwreck." *Expedition* 3.2: 2–11.

———. (1966) *Archaeology Under Water*. London.

———. (1967) *Cape Gelidonya: A Bronze Age Shipwreck*. Transactions of the American Philological Society n.s. 57, pt. 8. Philadelphia.

———. (1975) *Archaeology Beneath the Sea*. New York.

———. (1982) *Yassa Ada*. College Station, Tex.

Baur, P. V. C. (1912) *Centaurs in Ancient Art: The Archaic Period*. Berlin.

———. (1922) *Catalogue of the Rebecca Darlington Stoddard Collection of Greek and Italian Vases in Yale University*. New Haven, Conn.

———. (1947) *The Excavations at Dura-Europos Final Reports*, ed. M. I. Rostovtzeff et al., Part 4.3: *The Lamps*. New Haven, Conn.

Beazley, J. D. (1918) *Attic Red-Figured Vases in American Museums*. Cambridge, Mass.

———. (1920) *The Lewes House Collection of Ancient Gems*. Oxford.

———. (1941) "Warren as Collector." In Burdett and Goddard (1941), 331–56.

Becker, M., and P. Betancourt. (1997) *Richard Berry Seager*. Philadelphia.

Bell, M. (1981) *Morgantina Studies I: The Terracottas*. Princeton, N.J.

Bell, W. J. (1967) "The Cabinet of the American Philosophical Society." In W. M. Whitehill, ed., *A Cabinet of Curiosities*, 1–34. Charlottesville, Va.

Bender, T. (1987) *New York Intellect*. Baltimore.

Bennett, C. E. (1890) "The Work and Aims of the Archaeological Institute of America." *Report of the First Annual Meeting of the Wisconsin Society–Archaeological Institute of America*, 15–24.

Bennett, T. (1995) *The Birth of the Museum*. London.

Benson, J. (1972) *Bamboula at Kourion: The Necropolis and the Finds*. Philadelphia.
Berman, R. (1984) *Culture and Politics*. New York.
Biddle, N. (1993) *Nicholas Biddle in Greece*, ed. R. A. McNeal. University Park, Pa.
Bieber, M. (1939) *The History of the Greek and Roman Theater*. Princeton, N.J.
——. (1955) *The Sculptures of the Hellenistic Age*. New York.
Binford, L. (1962) "Archaeology as Anthropology." *American Antiquity* 28: 217–25.
——. (1972) *An Archaeological Perspective*. New York.
Binni, L., and G. Pinna. (1989) *Museo*. Milan.
Birge, D., L. Kraynak, and S. Miller. (1992) *Nemea I: Topographical and Architectural Studies: The Sacred Square, the Xenon, and the Bath*. Berkeley, Calif.
Bishop, M. (1962) *Early Cornell, 1865–1900*. Ithaca, N.Y.
Blake, M. E. (1947) *Ancient Roman Construction in Italy from the Prehistoric Period to Augustus: A Chronological Study Based in Part upon the Material Accumulated by the Late Dr. Esther Boise Van Deman*. Washington, D.C.
——. (1958). "Esther Van Deman." *DAB* 11, 2 (supp. 2).
——. (1973) *Roman Construction in Italy from Nerva Through the Antonines*, ed. D. T. Bishop. Philadelphia.
Blanton, R. (1978) *Monte Alban*. New York.
Bledstein, B. (1976) *The Culture of Professionalism*. New York.
Blegen, C. W. (1921) *Korakou: A Prehistoric Settlement near Corinth*. New York.
——. (1922) "Excavations in Greece in 1921." *Art and Archaeology* 13: 209–16.
——. (1923) "Excavations at Zygouries, Greece, 1921." *Art and Archaeology* 15: 85–89.
——. (1925) "The American Excavation at Nemea, Season of 1924." *Art and Archaeology* 17: 175–84.
——. (1925a) "Excavations at the Argive Heraeum." *AJA* 29: 413–18.
——. (1926) "The December Excavations at Nemea." *Art and Archaeology* 22: 127–37.
——. (1928) *Zygouries: A Prehistoric Settlement in the Valley of Cleonae*. Cambridge, Mass.
——. (1952) "Leicester Bodine Holland (1882–1952)." *Yearbook of the American Philosophical Society*: 316–19.
——. (1958) "In Memoriam: Bert Hodge Hill, 1874–1958." *Yearbook of the American Philosophical Society*: 15–16.
——. (1963) *Troy and the Trojans*. London.
Blegen, C. W., J. L. Caskey, M. Rawson, and J. Sperling. (1950–58) *Troy I–IV*. Princeton, N.J.
Blegen, C. W., and M. Rawson. (1966–73) *The Palace of Nestor at Pylos in Western Messenia*. Princeton, N.J.
Bloom, H., ed. (1986) *John Ruskin*. New Haven, Conn.
Boak, A., ed. (1933) *Karanis, The Temples, Coin-Hoard, Botanical and Zoological Reports, Seasons 1924–31*. Ann Arbor, Mich.
Boak, A., and Peterson. (1931) *Karanis*. Ann Arbor, Mich.
Boardman, J. (1988) "Classical Archaeology: Whence and Whither." *Antiquity* 62: 795–97.
Bober, P. P., and R. O. Rubinstein. (1986) *Renaissance Artists and Antique Sculpture*. Oxford.
Bodel, J. (1983) *Roman Brick Stamps in the Kelsey Museum*. Ann Arbor, Mich.
Bolger, D. (1994) "Ladies of the Expedition: Harriet Boyd Hawes and Edith Hall in Mediterranean Archaeology." In C. Claassen, ed., *Women in Archaeology*, 41–50. Philadelphia.

Bonfante, L. (1981) "Margarete Bieber (1879–1978): An Archaeologist in Two Worlds." In Sherman, 239–74.

———. (1988) "Margarete Bieber, 1879–1978." In Lullies and Schiering, 196–97.

Borbein, A. (1988) "George M. A. Hanfmann." In Lullies and Schiering, 313–14.

Boston Museum of the Fine Arts: A Companion to the Collection (1887). Boston.

Bosworth, R. J. B. (1979) *Italy, the Least of the Great Powers: Italian Foreign Policy Before the First World War.* Cambridge.

Bowersock, G. (1991) "Kenan Tevfik Erim, 1929–1990." *AJA* 95: 281–83.

Boyd, T., and W. Rudolph. (1976) "Excavataions at Porto Cheli and Vicinity, Preliminary Report IV: The Lower Town of Halieis." *Hesperia* 47: 333–35.

Bradeen, D. W. (1967) *Lectures in Memory of Louise Taft Sample.* Princeton, N.J.

Bradley, I. (1978) *William Morris and His World.* London.

Bradley, J. and I. Ousby (1987) *The Correspondence of John Ruskin and Charles Eliot Norton.* Cambridge.

Brandt, A. (1990) "Room for Cynicism." *Connoisseur* (January): 92–117.

Braun, E. (1990) "Political Rhetoric and Poetic Irony: The Uses of Classicism in the Art of Fascist Italy." In Cowling and Mundy, 345–58.

Breasted, C. (1943) *Pioneer to the Past.* New York.

Breasted, J. (1924) *The Oriental Forerunners of Byzantine Art.* Chicago.

Brendel, O. (1953) "Prolegomena to a Book on Roman Art." *Memoirs of the American Academy in Rome:* 9–73.

———. (1979) *Prolegomena to the Study of Roman Art.* New Haven, Conn.

Briggs, W. W. (1987) *The Letters of Basil Lanneau Gildersleeve.* Baltimore.

———. (1990) "Basil L. Gildersleeve (1831–1924)." In W. Calder and W. Briggs, eds., *Classical Scholarship: A Biographical Encyclopedia,* 93–119. New York.

———. (1995) "Basil L. Gildersleeve: The Formative Influence." In H. Geitz, J. Heideking, and J. Herbst, eds., *German Influences on Education in the United States to 1917,* 245–56. Cambridge.

Briggs, W. W., and H. Benario. (1986) *Basil Lanneau Gildersleeve.* Baltimore.

Brinkerhoff, D. (1958) "Greek and Etruscan Art in the Museum of the Rhode Island School of Design." *Archaeology* 11.3: 150–52.

Broneer, O. (1971) *Isthmia: The Temple of Poseidon.* Princeton, N.J.

Brooks, V. W. (1940) *New England Indian Summer.* Boston.

———. (1958) *The Dream of Arcadia.* New York.

Broughton, T. R. S. (1983) "Inez Scott Ryberg (1901–1980)." *Yearbook of the American Philosophical Society:* 426–29.

———. (1988) "Valentin Müller." In Lullies and Schiering, 244–45.

———. (1990a) "Louise Adams Holland *In Memoriam.*" *APA Newsletter* (December): 13–14.

———. (1990b) "Tenney Frank." In W. Calder and W. Briggs, eds., *Classical Scholarship: A Biographical Encyclopedia,* 68–76. New York.

Brown, A. (1983) *Arthur Evans and the Palace of Minos.* Oxford.

Brown, D. (1963) "In Search of Sybaris: 1962." *Expedition* 5.2: 40.

Brown, F. E. (1949) "Cosa: Exploration in Etruria." *Archaeology* 2: 2–10.

———. (1969–70) "Albert William Van Buren." *Rend. Pont. Accad. d'Arch.* 42: 31–36.

———. (1980) *Cosa: The Making of a Roman Town.* Ann Arbor, Mich.

Brown, F. E., E. H. Richardson, and L. Richardson, Jr. (1960) *Cosa II: The Temples of the Arx.* Memoirs of the American Academy in Rome 26.

———. (1993) *Cosa III: The Buildings of the Forum.* Memoirs of the American Academy in Rome 37.

Browne, H. (1917) *Essays on the Reform and Revival of Classical Studies.* London.
Bruno, V., and R. T. Scott. (1993) *Cosa IV: The Houses.* Memoirs of the American Academy in Rome 38.
Bryan, W. R. (1925) *Italic Hut Urns and Hut Urn Cemeteries.* Rome.
Bullitt, O. (1969) *Search for Sybaris.* New York.
Burdett, O., and E. H. Goddard. (1941) *Edward Perry Warren: The Biography of a Connoisseur.* London.
Burt, N. (1977) *Palaces for the People.* Boston.
Bury, M. (1991) "Introduction to *Plaster and Marble.*" *Journal of the History of Collections* 3: 121–24.
Bushman, R. (1993) In Cooper, *Classical Taste in America, 1800–1840.* Baltimore.
Butler, E. M. (1958) *The Tyranny of Greece over Germany.* Boston.
Butler, H. C. (1903) *Publication of an American Archaeological Expedition to Syria in 1899–1900.* New York.
———. (1921) "The Investigations at Assos." *Art and Archaeology* 12: 17–26.
———. (1922) *Sardis, v. 1, The Excavation 1910–1914.* Leiden.
———. (1925) *Sardis v. 2, The Architecture, Pt. 1, The Temple of Artemis.* Leiden.
Byers, D., and R. S. MacNeish. (1967–76) *The Prehistory of the Tehuacan Valley.* Austin, Tex.
Cahill, N. (1991) *Olynthus: Social and Spacial Planning in a Greek City.* Ann Arbor, Mich.
Calder, W. E., III. (1976) "Biographical Note." *In Memoriam Otto Brendel,* x–xi. Mainz.
———. (1984) *Studies in the Modern History of Classical Scholarship.* Naples.
———. (1988) "Otto Brendel 1901–1973." In Lullies and Schiering, 283–84.
Camp, J. (1986) *The Athenian Agora.* London.
———. (1989) "William Bell Dinsmoor, 1923–1988." *AJA* 93: 233–34.
———. (1990a) *The Athenian Agora: A Guide to the Excavation and Museum.* Athens.
———. (1990b) "Eugene Vanderpool 1906–1989." *AJA* 94: 291–92.
Campbell, S. (1988) *The Mosaics of Antioch.* Toronto.
Capps, E. (1933) "Foreword." *Hesperia* 2: 89–95.
Carandini, A. (1979) *Archeologia e cultura materiale.* Bari.
Carpenter, R. (1921) *The Aesthetic Basis of Greek Art of the Fifth and Fourth Centuries B.C.* New York.
———. (1925) *The Greeks in Spain.* New York.
———. (1933) *The Humanistic Value of Archaeology.* Cambridge, Mass.
———. (1966) *Discontinuity in Greek Civilization.* Cambridge.
———. (1967) "Mary Hamilton Swindler." *Yearbook of the American Philosophical Society:* 148–50.
Carter, J. (1906) *The Religion of Numa.* London.
Carter, J. (1981) "Rural Settlement at Metaponto." In G. W. Barker and R. Hodges, eds., *Archaeology and Italian Society,* 167–78. Oxford.
———. (1990) "Metapontum — Land, Wealth, Population." *Essays in Honour of A. D. Trendall,* 405–41. Canberra.
Carver, M. O. H. (1993) *Arguments in Stone: Archaeological Research and the European Town in the First Millennium.* Oxford.
Cashman, S. D. (1984) *America in the Gilded Age.* New York.
Caskey, J. L. (1972) "William Taft Semple." *AJA* 76: 81–82.
———. (1972) "Carl William Blegen (1887–1971)." *Yearbook of the American Philosophical Society:* 121–25.
Caskey, L. (1922) *Geometry of Greek Vases.* Boston.

————. (1925) *Catalogue of Greek and Roman Sculpture in the Museum of Fine Arts, Boston.* Cambridge, Mass.

Cesnola, L. P. di (1878, 1991) *Cyprus: Its Ancient Cities, Tombs, and Temples.* New York.

Chadwick, J. (1958) *The Decipherment of Linear B.* New York.

Chase, G. H. (1908) *The Loeb Collection of Arretine Pottery.* Cambridge, Mass.

————. (1912) "The New Criticism of Roman Art." In H. W. Smyth, ed., *Harvard Essays on Classical Subjects,* 1–32. Cambridge, Mass.

————. (1916) *A Catalogue of Arretine Pottery in the Museum of Fine Arts.* Boston.

————. (1919) "Archaeology in 1918." *Classical Journal* 15: 294–99.

————. (1924) *Greek and Roman Sculpture in American Collections.* Cambridge, Mass.

————. (1944) "Arthur Fairbanks." *Annual Bulletin AIA*: 33.

————. (1950) *MFA Department of Classical Art, Greek and Roman Antiquities: A Guide to the Classical Collections.* Boston.

Cherry, J. (1992) "Beazley in the Bronze Age: Reflections on Attributions in Aegean Prehistory." *Aegaeum* 8: 123–41.

Christ, K. (1972) *Von Gibbon zu Rostovtzeff.* Darmstadt.

Clark, G. (1989) *Prehistory at Cambridge and Beyond.* Cambridge.

Clark, J. H. (1974) *The Autobiography of an Architect.* Portale Valley, Calif.

Clark, K. (1974) *The Gothic Clark.* New York.

Clark, M. (1995) *Modern Italy, 1871–1982.* London.

Clarke, G. W. (1989) *Rediscovering Hellenism.* Cambridge.

Clarke, J. T. (1879) "The Hypaethral Question: An Attempt to Determine the Mode in Which the Interior of a Greek temple Was Lighted." *Papers of the Harvard Club* 1. Cambridge, Mass.

————. (1882) *Report on the Investigations at Assos, 1881.* Boston.

————. (1885) "Trojan and Assian Cranology." *AJA* 1:195–202.

————. (1898) *Report on the Investigations at Assos: 1882, 1883.* New York.

————. (1902) "A Plea for Archaeological Instruction." In G. S. Hall, ed., *Methods of Teaching History,* 90–103. Boston.

Cohon, R. (1996) *Discovery and Deceit: Archaeology and the Forger's Craft.* Kansas City, Mo.

Colburn, G. B. (1914) "Civita Lavinia, Site of Ancient Lavinium" *AJA* 18: 18–31, 185–98, 363–80.

Cole, M. (1997) "Exhibits with a Pulse." *Perspectives* (February): 31–34.

Coleman, L. V. (1939) *The Museum in America.* Washington, D.C.

Colini, A. M. (1938) "Esther Boise Van Deman." *Bullettino della Commissione archeologica communale di Roma* 66: 323–24.

Collins-Clinton, J. (1977) *A Late Antique Shrine of Liber Pater at Cosa.* Leiden.

Congdon, L. K. (1974) "The Assos Journals of Francis H. Bacon." *Archaeology* 27.2: 83–95.

Connor, P. (1989) "Cast-Collecting in the Nineteenth Century: Scholarship, Aesthetics, Connoisseurship." In G. W. Clarke, 187–235.

Cook, A. B. (1931) *The Rise and Progress of Classical Archaeology.* Cambridge.

Cook, B. (1964) "The Boscoreale Cubiculum." *Bulletin of the Metropolitan Museum of Art* 22: 166.

————. (1985) *The Townley Marbles.* London.

————. (1991) "The Archaeologist and the Art Market." *Antiquity* 65: 533–37.

Coolidge, J. (1989) *Patrons and Architects.* Fort Worth, Tex.

Cooper, W. (1993) *Classical Taste in America, 1800–1840.* Baltimore.

Cordasco, F. (1960) *Daniel Coit Gilman and the Protean Ph.D.* Leiden.

Cowling, E., and J. Mundy, eds. (1990) *On Classic Ground*. London.

Crane, S. (1972) *White Silence*. Coral Gables, Fla.

Craven, W. (1968) *Sculpture in America*. New York.

———. (1979) "The Grand Manner in Early Nineteenth Century American Painting." *American Art Journal* 11: 5–43.

Crawford, J. S. (1974) "The Classical Orator in Nineteenth Century American Sculpture." *American Art Journal* 6.2: 56–72.

———. (1979) "The Classical Tradition in American Sculpture — Structure and Surface." *American Art Journal* 11.3: 38–52.

Crawford, O. G. S. (1951) *Antiquity* (Spring 1981): 2–3.

Cuomo di Caprio, N. (1992) *Morgantina Studies III: Fornaci e officine da vasaio tardo-ellenistiche*. Princeton, N.J.

Curti, M., J. Greev, and R. Nash. (1963) "Anatomy of Giving: Millionaires in the Late 19th Century." *American Quarterly* 15: 416–35.

Curtis, C. D. (1919) "The Bernardini Tomb." *MAAR* 3: 9–90.

———. (1925) "The Barberini Tomb." *MAAR* 5: 9–52.

Curtis, R. (1988) *Studia Pompeiana and Classica in Honor of Wilhelmina F. Jashemski*. New Rochelle, N.Y.

Curtius, L. (1941) "In Memoriam: Edward Perry Warren and John Marshall." In Burdett and Goddard, 412–13.

Damrosch, D. (1995) "The Scholar as Exile." *Lingua Franca* 5: 56–60.

Daniel, G. (1962) *The Idea of Prehistory*. Harmondsworth.

———. (1976) *A Hundred and Fifty Years of Archaeology*. Cambridge, Mass.

Daniel, J. (1948) "Kourion, Past Achievements and Future Plans." *Bulletin of the University Museum* 13.3: 7–15.

D'Arms, J. (1970) *The Romans on the Bay of Naples*. Cambridge, Mass.

Davis, T. W. (1989) "A History of American Archaeology on Cyprus." *Biblical Archaeologist* (December): 163–69.

DeCou, H. F. (1912) *Antiquities from Boscoreale in Field Museum of Natural History*. Publications of the Field Museum of Natural History 152. Anthropological Series 7, no. 4. Chicago.

Deetz, J. (1977) *In Small Things Forgotten*. New York.

DePuma, R. (1986) *Etruscan Tomb Groups*. Mainz.

DePuma, R., I. E. M. Edlund-Berry, and L.S. Meritt. (1989) "Kyle Meredith Phillips, Jr., 1934–1988." *AJA* 93: 239–40.

DePuma, R., and P. Small. (1994) *Murlo and the Etruscans*. Madison, Wis.

Dessart, G. (1961) "What in the World." *Expedition* 4.1: 37–39.

DeVisscher, C. (1949) *International Protection of Works of Art and Monuments*. Washington, D.C.

DeVries, K., ed. (1980) *From Athens to Gordion: The Papers of a Memorial Symposium for Rodney S. Young*. Philadelphia.

Diehl, C. (1978) *Americans and German Scholarship*. New Haven, Conn.

Diggins, J. P. (1972) *Mussolini and Fascism: The View from America*. Princeton, N.J.

Dillon, D., and T. Hoving. (1974) *The Metropolitan Museum of Art, The Euphronius Krater: A Report to the Members of the Corporation*. New York.

Dimaggio, P. (1982a) "Cultural Entrepreneurship in Nineteenth-Century Boston: The Creation of an Organizational Base for High Culture in America." *Media, Culture, and Society* 4: 33–50.

———. (1982b) "Cultural Entrepreneurship in Nineteenth-Century Boston, Part II: The Classification and Framing of American Art." *Media, Culture, and Society* 4: 303–22.

Dimmick, L. (1991) "An Altar Erected to Heroic Virtue Itself: Thomas Craw-
ford and His Virginia Washington Monument." *American Art Journal* 23: 4–
73.
Dinsmoor, W. (1943) "Early American Studies of Mediterranean Archaeology."
Proceedings of the American Philosophical Society 78.1: 70–104.
———. (1950) *The Architecture of Ancient Greece.* New York.
DiVita, A. (1986) "Tripolitania e Cirenaica nel carteggio Halbherr: fra politica e
archeologia." In V. La Rosa, ed., *L'Archeologia italiana nel Mediterraneo*, 73–92.
Catania.
Dohan, E. H. (1942) *Italic Tomb Groups in the University Museum.* Philadelphia.
Döhl, H. (1981) *Heinrich Schliemann.* Munich.
Dolmetsch, J. (1970) "Prints in Colonial America, Supply and Demand in the
Mid-Eighteenth Century." In J. D. Morse, ed., *Prints in and of America to 1850*,
53–74. Charlottesville, Va.
Donahue, A. (1985) "One Hundred Years of the *American Journal of Archaeology.*"
AJA 89: 3–30.
D'Ooge, M. L. (1906) *Catalogue of the Gallery of Art and Archaeology in the Univesity of
Michigan.* Ann Arbor, Mich.
———. (1908) *The Acropolis of Athens.* New York.
Dörpfeld, W. (1904) *Troja und Ilium.* Athens.
Dort, A. V. (1954) "The Archaeological Institute of America-Early Days." *Archaeol-
ogy* 7.4: 195–201.
Dow, S. (1980) "A Century of Humane Archaeology." *Archaeology* (May–June):
42–51.
Dowling, L. (1994) *Hellenism and Homosexuality in Victorian Oxford.* Ithaca, N.Y.
Downey, G. (1961) *A History of Antioch in Syria.* Princeton, N.J.
Duffy, T. (1996) "The Gender of Letters: Charles Eliot Norton and the Decline of
the Amateur Intellectual Tradition." *New England Quarterly* 69: 91–109.
Duncan, C. (1995) *Civilizing Rituals.* London.
Dunham, D. (1950) "The Status of Excavating in Egypt and the Sudan." *Archaeol-
ogy* 3: 2–3.
Dyson, S. L. (1978) "Settlement Pattern in the Ager Cosanus: The Wesleyan
University Survey." *JFA* 5: 251–68.
———. (1981) "A Classical Archaeologist's Response to the New Archaeology."
BASOR 242: 7–13.
———. (1982) "Archaeological Survey in the Mediterranean: A Survey of Recent
Research." *American Antiquity* 47: 87–96.
———. (1985) "Two Paths to the Past: A Comparative Study of the Last Fifty Years
of *American Antiquity* and the *American Journal of Archaeology.*" *American Antiquity*
50: 452–63.
———. (1989) "The Role of Ideology and Institutions in Shaping Classical Archaeology in the Nineteenth and Twentieth Centuries." In A. L. Christenson, ed.,
Tracing Archaeology's Past, 127–35. Carbondale, Ill.
———. (1993) "From New to New Age Archaeology: Archaeological Theory and
Classical Archaeology—A 1990s Perspective." *AJA* 97: 195–206.
———. (1994) "Archaeological Lives." *AJA* 98: 159–62.
Edlund, I., A. M. McCann, and C. R. Sherman. (1981) "Gisela Marie Augusta
Richter (1882–1972): Scholar of Classical Art and Museum Archaeologist." In
Sherman, 275–300.
Egbert, D. D. (1980) *The Beaux Arts Tradition in French Architecture.* Princeton, N.J.
Egbert, J. (1919) "Presidential Address." *Annual Bulletin AIA* 3: 4.

Ehrich, R. (1974) "The Yugoslavian Interlude." In *A Symposium in Memory of Hetty Goldman, 1881–1972,* 38–42. Princeton, N.J.

Einaudi, K. (1979) *Fotografia archeologica, 1865–1914.* Rome.

Einaudi, K., ed. (1991) *Esther B. Van Deman.* Rome.

Eisler, C. (1969) "*Kunstgeschichte* American Style: A Study in Migration." In D. Fleming and B. Bailyn, eds., *The Intellectual Migration,* 544–629. Cambridge, Mass.

Elderkin, G. (1934) *Antioch on the Orontes.* Princeton, N.J.

Elia, R. (1991) "Popular Archaeology and the Antiquities Market: A Review Essay." *JFA* 18: 95–103.

———. (1997) "Looting, Collecting, and the Destruction of Archaeological Resources." *Nonrenewable Resources* 6: 85–98.

Emerson, A. (1889) "Recent Progress in Classical Archaeology." *Tenth Report of the Archaeological Institute of America:* 47–94.

Emerson, E. W. (1912) "Charles Eliot Norton: The Man and the Scholar." *Annual Bulletin AIA* 3: 83–128.

Engels, D. (1990) *Roman Corinth.* Chicago.

Ennabli, A. (1978) "La Campagne internationale de fouille et de mise en valeur de Carthage (Tunisie), 1973–78." *Acta of the XI International Congress of Classical Archaeology,* London: 165–69.

Erim, K. (1986) *Aphrodisias.* London.

Evans, E. (1939) *The Cults of the Sabine Territory.* New York.

Evans, J. (1954) *John Ruskin.* New York.

Fairbanks, A. (1907) *Athenian Lekythoi.* New York.

———. (1910) *A Handbook of Greek Religion.* New York.

———. (1914) *Athenian Lekythoi with Outline Drawing in Matt Color on a White Ground.* New York.

———. (1933) *Greek Art: The Basis of Later European Art.* New York.

Fawcett, T. (1986) "Graphic Versus Photographic in the Nineteenth Century Reproduction." *Art History* 9: 185–212.

Fentress, L. (1994) "Cosa in the Empire: The Unmaking of a Roman Town." *JRA* 7: 208–22.

Feyler, G. (1987) "Contribution à l'histoire des origines de la photographie archéologique: 1839–1880." *MEFR* 99: 1019–47.

Finch, E. (1947) *Carey Thomas of Bryn Mawr.* New York.

Fiske, T. L., and K. Lummis. (1975) *Charles F. Lummis: The Man and His West.* Norman, Okla.

Fitton, J. L. (1996) *The Discovery of the Greek Bronze Age.* Cambridge, Mass.

Flexner, A. (1940) *I Remember.* New York.

———. (1960) *An Autobiography.* New York.

Flexner, J. T. (1952) "Benjamin West's American Neo-Classicism." *New York Historical Quarterly* 36: 5–51.

———. (1969) *The Light of Distant Skies: American Painting, 1760–1835.* New York.

Flint, N. (1996) "An American in Cyprus: George McFadden in Episkopi Village." *CAARI News* (November): 1–3.

Folk, R. (1973) "The Geologic Framework of Stobi." In J. Wiseman, ed., *Studies in the Antiquities of Stobi I,* 37–57. Belgrade.

Ford, B. (1985) "The Englishman in Italy." In G. Jackson-Stops, ed., *The Treasure Houses of Britain,* 40–49. New Haven, Conn.

Ford, J., and G. Willey. (1949). *Surface Survey of the Viru Valley, Peru.* New York.

Fotou, V. (1993) *New Light on Gournia.* Liege.

Fowler, H. N. (1908a) "Charles Eliot Norton." *AJA* NS 12: 395–97.

———. (1908b) "Thomas Day Seymour." *AJA* NS 12: 1–2.

———. (1909) "John Henry Wright." *AJA* NS 13: 1–2.

———. (1918) "In Memoriam James Rignall Wheeler." *AJA* 22: 71–72.

———. (1921) "Samuel Ball Platner." *Annual Bulletin AIA*, 151–53.

———. (1922) "The American School of Classical Studies at Athens." *Art and Archaeology* 14: 171–91.

———. (1923) "Arthur Lincoln Frothingham." *AJA* 17: 381–82.

———. (1924) "American Work on the Erechtheum." *Art and Archaeology* 17: 153–59.

———. (1944) "Alfred Emerson." *AJA* 48: 76–77.

Fowler, H. N., and R. Stillwell. (1932) *Corinth*. Vol. 1, pt. 2, *Introduction. Topography. Architecture*. Cambridge, Mass.

Fowler, H. N., and J. R. Wheeler. (1909) *A Handbook of Greek Archaeology*. New York.

Frank, T. (1924) *Roman Buildings of the Republic*. Rome.

Franklin, F. (1910) *The Life of Daniel Coit Gilman*. New York.

Franklin, J. (1980) *Pompeii: The Electoral Programmata, Campaigns and Politics A.D. 71–79*. PMAAR 28. Rome.

Fraschetti, A. (1982) "Per Bartolomeo Borghesi: Antiquari e 'tecnici' nella cultura italiana dell'ottocento." In A. Calbi, ed., *Bartolomeo Borghesi, Scienza e Liberta*, 135–57. Bologna.

Frazer, G. (1932) "Roman Baths at Leptis Magna, Architectural Reconstruction." *MAAR* 10: 129–34.

Freely, J. (1990) *Classical Turkey*. San Francisco.

Frel, J. (1981) "Imitations of Ancient Sculpture in Malibu."

———. (1983) "Observations on Classical Bronzes." *Getty Museum Journal*: 117–22.

French, J. (1946) *A History of the University Founded by Johns Hopkins*. Baltimore.

Frend, W. H. C. (1996) *The Archaeology of Early Christianity*. London.

Freund, T. (1987) "Art and Money." *New England Monthly* (October): 49–57, 103–5.

Friend, A. M. (1954) "George H. McFadden." *AJA* 58: 154.

Frothingham, A. L., Sr. (1894) "The Philosophy of Art." *AJA* 9: 165–201.

Frothingham, A. L., Jr. (1904) "A Revised List of Roman Memorials and Triumphal Arches." *AJA* 8: 1–34.

———. (1905) *The Monuments of Christian Rome from Constantine to the Renaissance*. New York.

———. (1910) *Roman Cities in Italy and Dalmatia*. London.

———. (1914) "Discovery of the Capitolium and Forum of Verona." *AJA* 18: 129–45.

———. (1915) "The Roman Territorial Arches." *AJA* 19: 155–74.

Fuchs, W., and E. Burck. (1988) "Karl Lehmann 1894–1960." In Lullies and Schiäering, 262–63.

Furtwängler, A. E. (1990) "Adolf Furtwangler." In W. Calder and W. Briggs, eds., *Classical Scholarship: A Biographical Encyclopedia*, 84–92. New York.

Gabel, C., and K. Petruso. (1979) "Interdisciplinary Archaeology at Boston University." *JFA* 6: 124.

Gardiner, E. (1909) "A Series of Sculptures from Corinth." *AJA* 13: 158–69, 304–27.

Gaslund, B. (1987) *The Birth of Prehistoric Chronology*. Cambridge.

Gates, C. (1996) "American Archaeologists in Turkey: Intellectual and Social Dimensions." *Journal of American Studies of Turkey* 4: 47–68.

Gates, M.-H. (1997) "Archaeology in Turkey." *AJA* 101: 241–306.

Gazda, E., ed. (1978) *Guardians of the Nile.* Ann Arbor, Mich.

———. (1983) *In Pursuit of Antiquity: Thomas Spencer Jerome and the Bay of Naples (1899–1944).* Ann Arbor, Mich.

Gebhard, E. (1973) *The Theatre at Isthmia.* Chicago.

———. (1981) "The Theater at Stobi: A Summary." In B. Eleksova and J. Wiseman, eds., *Studies in the Antiquities of Stobi III*,13–28. Skopje.

———. (1992) "Oscar Theodore Broneer, 1894–1992." *AJA* 96: 543.

Geffcken, K. (1991) "Ester Van Deman: A Profile." In Einaudi, 7–13.

J. Paul Getty Museum Handbook of the Collections. (1991) Malibu, Calif.

Getty, J. P. (1976) *As I See It.* London.

The Getty Kouros Colloquium. (1992). Athens.

Getz-Preziosi, P. (1987) *Sculptors of the Cyclades.* Ann Arbor, Mich.

Gill, D. W., and C. Chippindale. (1993) "Material and Intellectual Consequences of Esteem for Cycladic Figures." *AJA* 97: 601–60.

Gilman, D. C. (1906) *The Launching of a University.* New York.

Goessler, P. (1951) *Wilhelm Dörpfeld.* Stuttgart.

Goldman, H. (1931) *Eutresis.*

———. (1950–63) *Excavations at Gozu Tarsus.* Princeton, N.J.

———. (1955). Speech at Bryn Mawr College.

Goodchild, R. G. (1976) *Libyan Studies.* London.

Goodchild, R. G., J. Pedley, and D. White. (1976) *Apollonia, the Port of Cyrene, Excavations by the University of Michigan 1965–1967.* Tripoli.

Goodenough, W. (1993) Froehlich Gladstone Rainey, 1907–1992." *AJA* 97: 355–66.

Goodwin, M. (1990) "Objects, Belief and Power in Mid-Victorian England: The Origins of the Victoria and Albert Museum." In S. Pearce, ed., *Objects of Knowledge*, 9–49. London.

Goring, E. (1988) *A Mischievous Pastime.* Edinburgh.

Govan, T. P. (1959) *Nicholas Biddle, Naturalist and Public Banker.* Chicago.

Grafton, A. (1983) "Polyhistor into *Philolog*: Notes on the Transformation of German Classical Scholarship, 1780–1850." *History of Universities* 3: 159–92.

Granger, A. H. (1972) *Charles Follen McKim.* New York.

Graslund, B. (1987) *The Birth of Prehistoric Chronology* Cambridge.

Grayson, D. (1983) *The Establishment of Human Antiquity.* New York.

Greco, E. (1981) *Magna Grecia.* Rome.

Green, M. (1989) *The Mount Vernon Street Warrens.* New York.

Greenewalt, C. (1986) "George Maxim Anossov Hanfmann." *Yearbook of the American Philosophical Society*: 120–26.

Griffin, J. (1985) "The Formation of the Society for American Archaeology." *American Antiquity* 50: 261–71.

Guarducci, M. (1980) *La Cosidetta fibula prenestina: Memorie della Accademia Nazionale dei Lincei* 24, fasc. 4.

———. (1992) "Per la storia dell'instituto archeologico germanico." *Romische Mitteilungen*: 307–27.

Gulick, C. B. (1956) "Harold North Fowler, 1859–1955." *Annual Report of the ASCS*: 16–17.

Gummere, R. (1963) *The American Colonial Mind and the Classical Tradition.* Cambridge, Mass.

Guralnick, E., ed. (1990) *The Ancient Eastern Mediterranean.* Chicago.

Gutman, J. (1973) *The Dura Europos Synagogue.* Missoula, Mont.

Hadley, R. (1987) *The Letters of Bernard Berenson and Isabella Stewart Gardner.* Boston.
Hafner, G. (1984) " 'Ungemein schön und seelenwoll'-zum 'Kopf de Bry' in Malibu." *Antike Welt* 15.2: 27–32.
Halbherr, F. (1896) "Report on the Expedition of the Institute to Crete." *AJA*: 525–611.
Halbherr, F., P. Orsi, L. Mariani, and A. Taramelli. (1897) "The Cretan Expedition of the Institute III." *AJA* 1: 159–311.
Hall, E. (1914–15) "Excavations at Vrokastro, Crete, in 1912." *Art and Archaeology* 1: 33–36.
Hamlin, T. (1944) *Greek Revival Architecture in America.* London.
———. (1955) *Benjamin Henry Latrobe.* New York.
Handbook of the Collection in the William Rockhill Nelson Gallery of Art and Mary Atkins Museum of Fine Arts. (1959) Kansas City, Mo.
Hanfmann, G. (1944) "Review of *Italic Tomb Groups in the University Museum* by Edith Hall Dohan." *AJA* 48: 114–16.
———. (1961) "Excavations at Sardis." *Scientific American* (June): 124–35.
———. (1962) "Sardis-Lydian, Hellenistic and Byzantine: Excavations into 2000 Years of the City's History." *ILN* (April 7): 542–44.
———. (1967) "Sardis." *Newsletter of the Harvard Graduate Society for Advanced Study and Research* (March 31).
———. (1972) *Letters from Sardis.* Cambridge, Mass.
———. (1974) "Hetty Goldman and the Iron Age." In *A Symposium in Memory of Hetty Goldman, 1881–1972,* 12–22. Princeton, N.J.
———. (1983a) *Ehrenpromotion Georg M.A. Hanfmann am Fachbereich Altertumswissenschaften der Freien Universitate Berlin am 21 Mai 1982.* Berlin.
———. (1983b) *Sardis from Prehistoric to Roman Times.* Cambridge, Mass.
Hansen, J. (1991) *The Palaeoethnobotany of Franchthi Cave.* Bloomington, Ind.
Harden, D. B. (1927) "Punic Urns from the Precinct of Tanit at Carthage." *AJA* 31: 197–310.
Harland, J. P. (1963) "Stephen Bleecker Luce, 1887–1962." *Annual Report ASCS.*
Harris, N. (1962) "The Gilded Age Revisited: Boston and the Museum Movement." *American Quarterly* 14: 545–66.
———. (1982) *The Artist in American Society.* Chicago.
———. (1990) *Cultural Excursions.* Chicago.
Harris, W. F. (1908) "Charles Eliot Norton, Address Delivered Before a General Meeting of the Archaeological Institute of America," 43–59.
Harrison, E. (1991) "Peter Heinrich von Blanckenagen, 1909–1990." *AJA* 95: 155–56.
Haskell, F., and N. Penny. (1981) *Taste and the Antique.* New Haven, Conn.
Haspels, C. H. E. (1971) *The Highlands of Phrygia.* Princeton, N.J.
Hawes, C. H., and H. Boyd Hawes. (1909) *Crete: The Forerunner of Greece.* London.
Hawes, H. B., et al. [1908] *Gournia, Vasiliki, and Other Prehistoric Sites on the Isthmus of Hierapetra.* Philadelphia.
Hawkins, H. (1960) *Pioneer: A History of the Johns Hopkins University, 1874–1889.* Cambridge, Mass.
Herbert, K. (1964) *Ancient Art in Bowdoin College.* Cambridge, Mass.
Herscher, E. (1983) "The United States Implements the UNESCO Convention." *JFA* 10: 350–62.
Hess, J. (1974) *The Grand Acquisitors.* Boston.
Hibbert, C. (1987) *The Grand Tour.* London.
Higham, J. (1979) "The Matrix of Specialization." In Oleson and Voss, 3–18.

Hill, D. K. (1949) *Catalogue of the Classical Bronze Sculpture in the Walters Art Gallery*. Baltimore.

——. (1974) "The Classical Collection and Its Growth." *Apollo* 100: 352–59.

Hines, T. (1974) *Burnham of Chicago*. New York

Hinsley, C. (1985) "From Shell-Heaps to Stelae: Early Anthropology at the Peabody Museum." In G. Stocking, ed., *Objects and Others*, 49–74. Madison, Wis.

——. (1986) "Edgar Lee Hewett and the School of American Research in Santa Fe, 1906–1912." In Meltzer, Fowler, and Sabloff, 217–33.

Hiss, P., and R. Fansler. (1934) *Research in Fine Arts in the Colleges and Universities of the United States*. New York.

Hitchens, C. (1987) *The Elgin Marbles: Should They Be Returned?* London.

Hitchner, B. (1990) "The Kasserine Archaeological Survey — 1987." *Antiquités Africaines* 26: 231–59.

Hoffmann, D. (1994) "The German Art Museum and the History of the Nation." In D. Sherman and I. Rogoff, eds., *Museum Culture*. London.

Hoffmann, H. (1971) *Collecting Greek Antiquities*. New York.

——. (1981) *Ten Centuries That Shaped the West: Greek and Roman Art in Texas Collections*. Mainz.

Hogarth, D. (1910) *Accidents of an Antiquarian Life*. London.

Holland, L. A. (1961) *Janus and the Bridge*. Rome.

Holland, L. A., and L. B. Holland. (1950) "Down the Tiber on a Raft." *Archaeology* 3: 87–94.

Holland, L. B. (1944) "Lacey Davis Caskey." *Annual Bulletin AIA*: 32.

Holloway, R. R. (1970) *Satrianum*. Providence, R.I.

——. (1973) *Buccino: The Eneolithic Necropolis of S. Antonio*. Rome.

Holloway, R. R., M. Joukowsky, and S. Lukesh. (1990) *La Muculifa: The Early Bronze Age Sanctuary*. Providence, R.I.

Hope Simpson, R. (1985) "William A. McDonald and the Minnesota Messenia Expedition." In Wilkie and Coulson, xviii–xxi.

Hopkins, C. (1972) *Topography and Architecture of Seleucia on the Tigris*. Ann Arbor, Mich.

——. (1979) *The Discovery of Dura Europos*. New Haven, Conn.

Hoppin, J. H. J. (1897) *Greek Art on Greek Soil*. Boston.

——. (1917) *Euthymides and His Fellows*. Cambridge.

——. (1919) *A Handbook of Attic Red-Figured Vases*. Cambridge, Mass.

——. (1924) *A Handbook of Greek Black-Figured Vases*. Paris.

Hoppin, J., and A. Gallatin. (1926) *Hoppin and Gallatin Collections*. Paris.

Horowitz, H. L. (1994) *The Power and Passion of M. Carey Thomas*. New York.

Hoving, T. (1993) *Making the Mummies Dance*. New York.

——. (1997) *False Impressions*. New York.

Howe, W. E. (1946) *A History of the Metropolitan Museum of Art. Vol. 2, 1905–1941*. New York.

Hudson, K. (1987) *Museums of Influence*. Cambridge.

Humphrey, J. (1976) *Excavations at Carthage, 1975, Conducted by the University of Michigan*. Tunis.

——. (1988) *The Circus and a Byzantine Cemetery at Carthage*. Vol.1. Ann Arbor, Mich.

Hurlbut, J. L. (1921) *The Story of Chautauqua*. New York.

Hussey, M. (1934) "The Pompeii of Palestine." *Art and Archaeology* 35.1: 3–17.

Hyman, L. (1976) "The *Greek Slave* by Hiram Powers, High Art as Popular Culture." *Art Journal* 35: 216–23.

Iakovidis, S. (1989) "George Emmanuel Mylonas, 1898–1988." *AJA* 93: 235–37.
Iatrides, I. and L. Wrigley. (1995) *Greece at the Crossroads*. University Park, Pa.
Irwin-Williams, C. (1990) "Women in the Field: The Role of Women in Archaeology Before 1960." In G. Kass-Simon and P. Farnes, eds., *Women of Science: Righting the Record*, 1–41. Bloomington, Ind.
Jacobsen, T.W. (1976) "17,000 Years of Greek Prehistory." *Scientific American* 234 (June): 76–87.
———. (1985) "Another Modest Proposal: Ethnoarchaeology in Greece." In Wilkie and Coulson, 91–108.
James, H. (1903) *W. W. Story and His Friends*. Boston.
———. (1914) *Novelists with Some Other Notes*. New York.
———. (1995) *Italian Hours*. Harmondsworth.
Jameson, M., C. Runnels, and T. van Andel. (1994) *A Greek Countryside: The Southern Argolid from Prehistory to the Present Day.*. Stanford, Calif.
Jarausch, K. H. (1995) "American Students in Germany, 1815–1914: The Structure of German and U.S. Matriculants at Göttingen University." In H. Geitz, J. Heideking, and J. Herbst, eds., *German Influences on Education in the United States to 1917*, 195–211. Cambridge.
Jashemski, W. (1979) *The Gardens of Pompeii, Herculaneum, and the Villas Destroyed by Vesuvius*. New Rochelle, N.Y.
Jenkins, I. (1992) *Archaeologists and Aesthetes*. London.
Jenkyns, R. (1991) *Dignity and Decadence*. Cambridge, Mass.
Jerome, T. S. (1923) *Aspects of the Study of Roman History*. Ann Arbor, Mich.
Jessen, H. (1988) "Eduard Gerhard, 1795–1867." In Lullies and Schiering, 20–21.
Johnson, B. K. (1932) "The 'Terme Nuove' at Ostia." *MAAR* 10: 143–44.
Johnson, J. (1932) "The Excavation of Minturnae." *Art and Archaeology* 32: 283–93.
———. (1933) *Excavations at Minturnae II*. Rome.
———. (1935) *Excavations at Minturnae I*. Philadelphia.
———. (1957) "Anniversary." *Archaeology* 10: 30–31.
Jones, A. H. M. (1952) "Michael Ivanovitch Rostovtzeff." *Proceedings of the British Academy*: 347–61.
Jones, F. F. (1974) "A Quartette of Excavations." In *A Symposium in Memory of Hetty Goldman, 1881–1972*, 1–11. Princeton, N.J.
Joukowsky, M. S. (1986) *Prehistoric Aphrodisias*. Providence, R.I.
Kahane, A., L. Murray-Threipland, and J. B. Ward-Perkins. (1968) "The Ager Veientanus North and East of Rome." *PBSR* 36: 1–218.
Keller, D. R., and D. W. Rupp. (1983) *Archaeological Survey in the Mediterranean*. Oxford.
Keller, J. D., and K. A. Breisch. (1980) *A Victorian View of Ancient Rome*. Ann Arbor, Mich.
Kelsey, F. W. (1910–11) "The Tragedy at Cyrene." *Bulletin of the AIA* 2: 111–14.
———. (1919) "Richard Norton." *Art and Archaeology* 8: 329–35.
———. (1920) "The Burnt Areas of Constantinople and Proposal for a City Plan." *Art and Archaeology* 10: 163–70.
———. (1926a) "Carthage, Ancient and Modern." *Art and Archaeology* 21: 55–67.
———. (1926b) *Excavations at Carthage*. New York.
———. (1926c) "Mitchell Carroll." *Art and Archaeology* 21: 103–12.
Kenna, V. (1970) "Richard Berry Seager: An American Archaeologist in Crete, 1882–1925." *Archaeology* 23: 322–32.
Kennedy, R. (1990) *Orders from France*. Philadelphia.
Kirker, H. (1969) *The Architecture of Charles Bulfinch*. Cambridge, Mass.

Kirker, H., and J. Kirker. (1964) *Bulfinch's Boston, 1787–1817*. New York.
Kleiner, F. (1990) "On the Publication of Recent Acquisitions of Antiquities." *AJA* 94: 525–27.
——. (1996) "The *American Journal of Archaeology* and the Archaeological Institute of America." *AJA* 100: 1–4.
Klindt-Jensen, O. (1975) *A History of Scandinavian Archaeology*. London.
Koehler, C. G. (1996) "Virginia Randolph Grace, 1901–1994." *AJA* 100: 153–56.
Kohl, B., W. Linker, and B. Kavelman. (1995) *The Centennial Directory of the American Academy in Rome*. New York.
Kopff, E. C. (1986) "Gildersleeve in American Literature: The 'Kaleidoscope Style.'" In Briggs and Benario, 56–81.
Kostoff, S. (1973) *The Third Rome, 1870–1950: Traffic and Glory*. Berkeley, Calif.
Kraeling, C. H. (1956) *The Excavations at Dura-Europos Final Reports*, ed. M. I. Rostovtzeff et al. Part 8.1, *The Synagogue*. New Haven, Conn.
——. (1967) *The Excavations at Dura-Europos Final Reports*, ed. M. I. Rostovtzeff et al. Part 8.2: *The Christian Building*. New Haven, Conn.
Krautheimer, R. (1969) *Studies in Early Christian, Medieval, and Renaissance Art*. New York.
Krohn, C. D. (1993) *Intellectuals in Exile*. Amherst, Mass.
Kuklick, B. (1996) *Puritans in Babylon*. Princeton, N.J.
Kurtz, D., ed. (1985a) *Beazley and Oxford*. Oxford.
——. (1985b) *Occasional Papers on Antiquities*. Getty Museum 3.
LaFarge, C. G. (1925) "The American Academy in Rome." *Art and Archaeology* 19.2: 60–62.
Laing, J. O. (1912) "An Ancient Roman Villa in the Maltese Islands." *Annual Bulletin AIA* 3.3: 178–80.
Lamont, T. (1941–42) "Address of Thomas W. Lamont at a Dinner Given to George II, King of the Hellenes, by the American Educational Institutions of the Near East." *Annual Report ASCS*: 10–14.
Lanciani, R. (1897; 1967) *The Ruins and Excavations of Ancient Rome*. New York.
——. (1901) *New Tales of Old Rome*. Boston.
——. (1894) *Ancient Rome in the Light of Recent Discoveries*. Boston.
——. (1988) *Notes from Rome*. Rome.
Lang, M. (1969) *The Palace of Nestor at Pylos in Western Messenia*. Vol. 2, *The Frescoes*. Princeton, N.J.
——. (1980) "Rhys Carpenter, 1889–1980." *American Philosophical Society Yearbook*: 555–60.
Lange, C., and C. Riley. (1996) *Bandelier*. Salt Lake City, Utah.
La Rosa, V. (1986) "Federico Halbherr e Creta." In V. La Rosa, ed., *L'Archeologia italiana nel Mediterraneo*, 53–72. Catania.
Larrabee, S. (1957) *Hellas Observed*. New York.
Larson, M. (1977) *The Rise of Professionalism*. Berkeley, Calif.
Lattimore, R. (1980) "Elegy for Rhys Carpenter." Bryn Mawr, Pa.
Laurence, R. (1993) "Architects, Planners and the Classical City." *History Today* (November): 7–10.
Lavin, A. M. (1983) *The Eye of the Tiger*. Princeton, N.J.
Lees-Milne, J. (1947) *The Age of Adam*. London.
Lehmann, K. (1955) *Samothrace*. New York.
——. (1985) *Thomas Jefferson, American Humanist*. Charlottesville, Va.
Lehmann, P. W. (1953) *Roman Wall Paintings from Boscoreale in the Metropolitan Museum of Art*. Cambridge, Mass.

———. (1968) "Harriet Boyd Hawes: Introductory Remarks." In *A Land Called Crete*. Northampton, Mass.

Leighton, H. (1984) "The Lantern Slide and Art History." *History of Photography* 8: 107–18.

Leighton, R. (1993) *Morgantina Studies IV: The Protohistoric Settlement on the Cittadella*. Princeton, N.J.

Lerman, L. (1969) *The Museum*. New York.

Levi, D. (1947) *Antioch Mosaic Pavements*. Princeton, N.J.

Levine, L. (1988) *Highbrow/Lowbrow*. Cambridge, Mass.

Levine, P. (1986) *The Amateur and the Professional*. Cambridge, Mass.

Lindquist-Cook, E. (1979) "Stillman, Ruskin and Rossetti: The Struggle Between Nature and Art." *History of Photography* 3: 1–14.

Lloyd, S. (1980) *Foundations in the Dust*. New York.

Lock, P. (1990) "D. G. Hogarth (1862–1927): A Specialist in the Science of Archaeology." *PBSA* 85: 175–200.

Lord, L. (1947) *A History of the American School of Classical Studies at Athens, 1882–1942*. Cambridge, Mass.

———. (1949–50) "Walter Miller." *Annual Report ASCS*: 18–19.

Low, T. L. (1948) "Who Uses the Archaeological Material in American Museums." *Archaeology* 1.1: 52–54.

Lowenthal, D. (1988) "Classical Antiques as National and Global Heritage." *Antiquity* 62: 726–35.

Luce, S. (1933) CVA RISD.

———. (1942) "Ralph Van Deman Magoffin." *AJA* 46: 412.

———. (1949) "William Nickerson Bates." *AJA* 53: 388.

———. (1950a) "James Egbert." *AJA* 54.

———. (1950b) "Walter Miller." *AJA* 54: 73.

———. (1952a) "George Henry Chase." *AJA* 56: 180–81.

———. (1952b) "Victor Christopher Baur." *AJA* 56: 67.

Lullies, R. (1988) "Wolfgang Helbig, 1839–1915." In Lullies and Schiering, 71–72.

Lullies, R., and W. Schiering, eds. (1988) *Archaeologenbildnisse*. Mainz.

MacKendrick, P. (1962) *The Greek Stones Speak*. New York.

Magoffin, R., and E. C. Davis. (1930) *The Romance of Archaeology*. Baltimore.

Magrini, L. (1988) "La Venere di Morgantina." *Archeologia* 27.6–7: 1.

Manacorda, D., and R. Tamassia. (1985) *Il piccone del regime*. Rome.

Manners, V., and G. C. Williamson. (1976) *Angelica Kauffmann, R.A., Her Life and Her Works*. New York.

Marabini Moevs, M. T. (1971) *Fra marmo pario e archeologia*. Bologna.

Marasovic, J., T. Marasovic, S. McNally, and J. Wilkes. (1972) *Diocletian's Palace: Report on the Joint Excavation in the Southeast Quarter, Pt. I*. Split.

Marasovic, T. (1982) *Diocletian's Palace*. Belgrade.

Marchand, S. (1996) *Down from Olympus*. Princeton, N.J.

Marks, A. S. (1981) "The Statue of George III in New York and the Iconology of Regicide." *American Art Journal* 13.3: 61–82.

Marquand, A. (1909) *Handbook of Greek Architecture*. New York.

Marsh, A. R. (1886) "Review of C. Waldstein, *Essays on the Art of Pheidias*." *AJA*: 182–87.

Mau, A. (1902) *Pompeii: Its Life and Art*. New York.

Mazower, M. (1993) *Inside Hitler's Greece*. New Haven, Conn.

McAdams, R., and C. Schelling. (1976) *Corners of a Foreign Field Working Papers: The Rockefeller Foundation.* New York.

McCann, A. M., et al. (1987) *The Roman Port and Fishery of Cosa.* Princeton, N.J.

McCaughey, R. (1974) "The Transformation of American Academic Life: Harvard University, 1821–1892." *Perspectives in American History* 8: 239–335.

McClees, H. (1924a) *The Metropolitan Museum of Art: The Daily Life of the Greeks and Romans.* New York.

———. (1924b) "The Daily Life of the Greeks and Romans." *Bulletin of the Metropolitan Museum of Art* 19: 18–19.

McCredie, J., et al. (1990) *Eugene Vanderpool, August 3, 1906–August 1, 1989.* Princeton, N.J.

McDonald, W. A. (1973) "Archaeology in the Graduate School." *JFA* 1: 371–73.

———. (1984) "The Minnesota Messenia Survey: A Look Back." In *Studies Presented to Sterling Dow on His Eightieth Birthday*, 185–92. Durham, N.C.

McDonald, W. A., W. D. E. Coulson, and J. Rosser. (1983) *Excavations at Nicoria in Southwest Greece.* Vol. 3, *Dark Age and Byzantine Occupation.* Minneapolis.

McDonald, W. A., and R. Hope-Simpson. (1961) "Prehistoric Habitation in Southwestern Peloponnese." *AJA* 65: 221–60.

———. (1964) "Further Exploration in Southwestern Peloponnese, 1962–1963." *AJA* 68: 229–46.

———. (1969) "Further Exploration in the Southwestern Peloponnese." *AJA* 73: 123–77.

McDonald, W. A., and G. R. Rapp, Jr. (1972) *The Minnesota Messenia Expedition.* Minneapolis.

McDonald, W. A., and C. Thomas. (1990) *Progress into the Past.* Bloomington, Ind.

McDonald, W. A., and N. C. Wilkie. (1992) *Excavations at Nicoria in Southwestern Greece.* Vol. 2, *The Bronze Age Occupation.* Minneapolis.

McFadden, E. (1971) *The Glitter and the Gold.* New York.

McFadden, G. (1950) "Kourion: The Apollo Baths." *Bulletin of the University Museum* 14.4: 14–26.

McGuire, W. (1982) *Bollingen: An Adventure in Collecting the Past.* Princeton, N.J.

McNally, S. (1975) "Diocletian's Palace, Split in the Middle Ages." *Archaeology* 28: 248–59.

———. (1994) "The Joint American-Croatian Excavations in Split (1965–1974)." *AnTard* 2: 107–21.

McNally, S., J. Marasovic, and T. Marasovic. (1976) *Diocletian's Palace, Report on Joint Excavations, Pt. 2.* Split.

McNeal, R. A. (1995) "Athens and Nineteenth Century Panoramic Art." *International Journal of the Classical Tradition* 1: 81–97.

Mellink, M. (1959) "The City of Midas." *Scientific American* (July): 100–109.

———. (1974) "Contribution to the Study of the Orient." In *A Symposium in Memory of Hetty Goldman, 1881–1972*, 30–37. Princeton, N.J.

Meltzer, D., D. Fowler, and J. Sabloff, eds. (1986) *American Archaeology Past and Future.* Washington, D.C.

Meritt, L.S. (1984) *History of the American School of Classical Studies at Athens, 1939–1980.* Princeton, N.J.

Metropolitian Museum of Art. (1949–50) "The Collections: Strengths and Weaknesses." *Bulletin of the Metropolitan Museum of Art* 8: 290–94.

Metropolitan Museum of Art: Tentative List of Objects Desireable for a Collection of Casts of Sculpture and Architecture Intended to Illustrate the History of Plastic Art. (1891). New York.

Meyer, K. (1973) *The Plundered Past.* New York.

Miller, L. B. (1966) *Patrons and Patriotism: The Encouragement of the Fine Arts in the United States, 1790–1860.* Chicago.

Miller, S. (1984) *Excellence and Equity:The National Endowment for the Humanities.* Lexington, Ky.

Miller, S. G., ed. (1995) *Nemea: A Guide to the Site and Museum.* Berkeley, Calif.

Miller, W. (1931) "The Athenian Agora." *Art and Archaeology*: 99–108, 175–85.

Miraglia, M. (1996) "Giorgio Sommer's Italian Journey: Between Tradition and Popular Image." *History of Photography* 20: 41–48.

Mirick, H. D. (1933) "The Large Baths at Hadrian's Villa." *MAAR* 11: 119–26.

Mitchell, L. M. (1883, 1894) *A History of Ancient Sculpture.* New York.

Mitten, D. (1987) "George Maxim Anossov Hanfmann, 1911–1986." *AJA* 91: 259–66.

Mitten, D., J. Pedley, and J. Scott. (1971) *Studies Presented to George M. A. Hanfman.* Mainz.

Moltesen, M. (1987) *Wolfgang Helbig.* Copenhagen.

Momigiliano, A. D. (1966) *Studies in Historiography.* New York.

Monga, L., ed. (1987) "Americans in Italy." *Bollettino del C.I. R.* 1.

Montgomery, C., and P. Kane. (1997) *American Art, 1750–1800: Toward Independence.* New Haven, Conn.

Moore, C. (1929) *The Life and Times of Charles Follen McKim.* Boston.

Morey, C. R. (1925) "Allan Marquand, Founder of the Department of Art and Archaeology." *Art and Archaeology* 20: 105–8, 136.

———. (1934) *Antioch on the Orontes.* Vol 1. Princeton, N.J.

———. (1938) *The Mosaics of Antioch.* New York.

Morgan, C. H. (1942) *Corinth 11, Byzantine Pottery.* Cambridge, Mass.

———. (1972) *The Art Collection of Amherst College.* Amherst, Mass.

Morison, S. E. (1930) *The Development of Harvard College.* Cambridge, Mass.

Morris, I. (1994) "Archaeologies of Greece." In I. Morris, ed., *Classical Greece: Ancient Histories and Modern Archaeologies.* Cambridge: 8–47.

Morrison, T. (1974) *Chautauqua: A Center for Education, Religion, and the Arts in America.* Chicago.

Mumford, L. (1931) *The Brown Decades.* New York.

Mumford Jones, H. (1964) *O Strange New World.* New York.

Munson, R. (1989) *Cousteau: The Captain and His World.* New York.

Muscarella, O. (1974) "Rodney Stuart Young 1907–1974." *JFA* 1: 406–8.

———, ed. *Ancient Art: The Norbert Schimmel Collection.* Mainz.

Mylonas, G. (1940) "Greek Vases in the Collection at Washington University in St Louis." *AJA* 44: 187–211.

———. (1951) *Studies Presented to David Moore Robinson.* St. Louis, Mo.

———. (1957–58) "In Memoriam David Moore Robinson, 1880–1958." 15–16.

———. (1963) "Hazel Dorothy Hansen, 1899–1962." *ASCS Newsletter*, 17.

Myres, J. L. (1914) *Handbook of the Cesnola Collection of Antiquities from Cyprus.* New York.

Neils, J. (1996) "The Cleveland Painter." *Cleveland Studies in the History of Art* 1: 12–29.

Noble, J. V. (1959–60) "A New Gallery of Models and Casts." *Bulletin of the Metropolitan Museum of Art* 18: 138–44.

Norton, C. E. (1859) *Notes of Travel and Study in Italy.* Boston.

———. (1885) "The First American Classical Archaeologist." *AJA* 1: 3–9.

———. (1904) *The Letters of John Ruskin to Charles Eliot Norton.* Boston.

———. (1909–10) "The Work of the Archaeological Institute of America." *Bulletin of the AIA* 1: 251–66.

———. (1913) *The Letters of Charles Eliot Norton.* Cambridge, Mass.

Norton, R. (1910–11a) "The Excavations at Cyrene: First Campaign, 1910–1911." *Bulletin of the AIA* 2: 141–63.

———. (1910–11b) "From Bengazi to Cyrene." *Bulletin of the AIA* 2: 57–67.

Norton, R., J. Hoppin, C. D. Curtis, and A. F. S. Sladden. (1910–11) *The Excavations at Cyrene: First Campaign.* New York.

Novick, P. (1988) *That Noble Dream: The Objectivity Question and the American Historical Profession.* Cambridge, Mass.

Nye, R. B. (1960) *The Cultural Life of the New Nation, 1776–1830.* New York.

Oldfather, W. A. (1936) "In Memoriam Grant Showerman of Wisconsin and Rome." *American Scholar* 5: 367–72.

Oleson, A., and J. Voss. (1979) *The Organization of Knowledge in Modern American, 1860–1920.* Baltimore.

Ostenberg, C. E. (1976–77) "Erik Sjoqvist." *Rend. Pont. Accad. Rom. Arch.* 49: 11–16.

Packer, J. (1989) "Politics, Urbanism, and Archaeology in 'Roma capitale': A Troubled Past and a Controversial Future." *AJA* 93: 137–41.

Panofsky, E. (1955) "Three Decades of Art History in the United States." In I. Lavin, ed., *Meaning in the Visual Arts,* 321–46. Garden City, N.Y.

———. (1956) "Charles Rufus Morey (1877–1955)." *Yearbook of the American Philosophical Society*: 482–91.

Pappas, P. (1985) *The United States and the Greek War for Independence.* New York.

Parsons, J. R. (1971) *Prehistoric Settlement Patterns in the Texcoco Region of Mexico.* Ann Arbor, Mich.

Patterson, T. (1986) "The Last Sixty Years: Toward a Social History of Americanist Archaeology." *American Anthropologist* 88: 7–26.

———. (1995) *Toward a Social History of Archaeology in the United States.* New York.

Pedley, J. (1980) *New Light on Ancient Carthage.* Ann Arbor, Mich.

Perkins, A. (1973) *The Art of Dura Europos.* Oxford.

Perkins, C. (1864) *Tuscan Sculptors.* London.

———. (1870) "American Art Museums" *North American Review* 228 (July): 1–29.

———. (1883) *Historical Handbook of Italian Sculpture.* New York.

Petricioli, M. (1990) *Archeologia e Mare Nostrum.* Rome.

Pevesner, N. (1975) *Pioneers of Modern Design.* Harmondsworth.

Pfister, R., and L. Bellinger. (1945) *The Excavations at Dura-Europos Final Reports,* ed. M. I. Rostovtzeff et al. Part 4.2, *The Textiles.* New Haven, Conn.

Phillips, C. R. (1989) "Classical Scholarship Against Its History." *AJP* 110: 636–57.

Phillips, K. M. Jr. (1993) *In the Hills of Tuscany.* Philadelphia.

Pickard, J. (1919) "The Future of the College Art Association." *Art Bulletin* 2: 5–9.

Pickman, D. (1970) "Museum of Fine Arts Boston: the First One Hundred Years." *Archaeology*: 114–19.

Pierson, W. (1970) *American Buildings and Their Architects: The Colonial and Neocolonial Styles.* Garden City, N.Y.

Place, C. A. (1968) *Charles Bulfinch: Architect and Citizen.* New York.

Platner, S. N. (1904, 1911) *Topography and Monuments of Ancient Rome.* Boston.

Pollak, L. (1994) *Römische Memoiren.* Rome.

Pompeii as Source and Inspiration (1977) An Exhibition Organized by the 1976–1977 Graduate Students in the Museum Practice Program. Ann Arbor, Mich.

Popovic, V., and E. Ochsenschlager, eds. (1971) *Sirmium II.* Belgrade.

——. (1973) *Sirmium III.* Belgrade.

Potter, T. (1979) *The Changing Landscape of South Etruria.* New York.

Potts, A. (1994) *Flesh and the Ideal.* New Haven, Conn.

Powers, H. H. (1928) *The Message of Greek Art.* New York.

Prezzolini, G. (1933) *Come gli Americani scoprirono l'Italia.* Milan.

Price, T. D. (1932) "A Reconstruction of Horace's Sabine Villa." *MAAR* 10: 135–42.

Pritchard, J. (1975) "Rodney Stuart Young (1907–1974)." *Yearbook of the American Philosophical Society:* 186–90.

Program: The Celebration of the Seventy-Fifth Anniversary and the Dedication of the Stoa of Attalus as the Museum of the Athenian Agora. (1956). Athens.

Raffett (1983)

Rainey, F. (1992) *Reflections of a Digger.* Philadelphia.

Rainey, F., and C. Lerici. (1967) *The Search for Sybaris, 1960–1965.* Rome.

Ramage, A. (1987) "Lydian Sardis." In E. Guralnick, ed., *Sardis: Twenty Years of Discovery,* 6–16. Chicago.

Rand, E. K. (1914–15) "The School of Classical Studies of the American Academy in Rome." *Art and Archaeology* 1: 13–20.

Rapp, G., Jr., and S. E. Aschenbrenner. (1978) *Excavations at Nicoria in Southwest Greece.* Vol. 1, *Site, Environs, and Techniques.* Minneapolis.

Rather, S. (1992) "Rome. and the American Academy: Art Mecca or Artistic Backwater." In Joffe, ed., *The Italian Presence in American Art, 1860–1920,* 214–28. New York.

Reichardt, W. L. (1933) "The Vestibule Group at Hadrian's Villa." *MAAR* 11: 127–32.

Reinhold, M. (1946) "Historian of the Classic World: A Critique of Rostovtzeff." *Science and Society* 10: 361–91.

——. (1984) *Classica Americana.* Detroit.

Renfrew, C. (1980) "The Great Tradition Versus the Great Divide." *AJA* 84: 287–98.

Report of the Commission of the Humanities (1964) New York.

Richard, C. (1994) *The Founders and the Classics.* Cambridge, Mass.

Richardson, E. H. (1964) *The Etruscans: Their Art and Ciivlization.* Chicago

Richardson, L. (1955) *Pompeii: The Casa dei Dioscuri and Its Painters. MAAR* 23 Rome.

——. (1988) *Pompeii: An Architectural History.* Baltimore.

Richardson, R. (1911) *A History of Greek Sculpture.* New York.

Richter, G. M. A. (1915) *Greek, Etruscan, and Roman Bronzes in the Metropolitan Museum of Art.* New York.

——. (1917, 1920) *Handbook of the Classical Collection,* Metropolitan Museum of Art. New York.

——. (1929) "Forgeries of Greek Sculpture." *Bulletin of the Metropolitan Museum of Art* 24: 3–5.

——. (1937) *Etruscan Terracotta Warriors in the Metropolitan Museum of Art.* Metropolitan Museum Papers No. 6. New York.

——. (1938) "The Exhibition of Augustan Art." *Bulletin of the Metropolitan Museum of Art* 33: 272–79.

——. (1940) *Handbook of the Etruscan Collection.* , Metropolitan Museum of Art. New York.

——. (1950) *The Sculpture and Sculptors of the Greeks.* New York.

——. (1942, 1960, 1970) *Kouroi: Archaic Greek Youths.* New York.

———. (1969) *A Handbook of Greek Art.* New York.

———. (1970) "The Department of Greek and Roman Art: Triumphs and Tribulations." *Metropolitan Museum Journal* 3: 73–95.

———. (1972) *My Memoirs.* Rome.

Ridgeway, B. (1970). *The Severe Style in Greek Sculpture.* Princeton, N.J.

———. (1976). *The Archaic Style in Greek Sculpture.* Princeton, N.J.

Ridgway, D. (1981) "The Forgers and the Fibula." *Times Literary Supplement* (June 19): 691.

Ridley, R. T. (1992) *The Eagle and the Spade.* Cambridge.

Rieche, A. (1979) *Die Satzungen des deutschen archaologischen Instituts, 1828–1972.* Mainz.

Riggs, A. S. (1927) "Francis Willey Kelsey." *Art and Archaeology* 23: 272, 284.

———. (1931) "The American Excavations in Athens." *Art and Archaeology* 32: 88–90.

Rippy, J. F. (1935) *Joel R. Poinsett: Versatile American.* Durham, N.C.

Robertshaw, P. (1980) ed., *A History of African Archaeology.* Portsmouth, N.H.

Robertson, M. (1985) "Beazley and Attic Vase Painting." In Kurtz (1985a), 19–30.

Robinson, D. M. (1917) "Reproductions of Classical Art." *Art and Archaeology* 5: 221–34.

———. (1924) "A Preliminary Report on the Excavations at Pisidian Antioch and Sizm." *AJA* 28: 435–44.

———. (1925) "The Archaeological Museum at the Johns Hopkins University." *Art and Archaeology* 19: 265–67.

———. (1934–38) *CVA: The Robinson Collection in Baltimore.* Fasc. 1–3. Cambridge, Mass.

———. (1951–52) "Paul Victor Christopher Baur, 1872–1951." *Annual Report ASCS*: 26–27.

———. (1952) "Olynthus: The Greek Pompeii." *Archaeology* 5.4: 228–35.

Robinson, E., ed. (1908, 1910) *Metropolitan Museum of Art: Catalogue of the Collection of Casts.* New York.

Rodenwalt, G. (1931) "The Archaeological Institute of Germany." *Art and Archaeology*: 25: 67–76, 141.

Rogers, M. F. (1974) "Nydia." *Antiques* 97: 374–78.

Roma Antiqua. (1992) Rome.

Rose, M., and O. Acar. (1995) "Turkey's War on the Illicit Antiquities Trade." *Archaeology* (March–April): 44–56.

Rostovtzeff, M. (1922) *Iranians and Greeks in South Russia.* Oxford.

———. (1927) *Mystic Italy.* New York.

———. (1932) *Out of the Past of Greece and Rome.* New Haven, Conn.

———. (1935) "Dura Europos and the Problem of Parthian Art." *Yale Classical Studies*: 5.

———. (1938) *Dura Europos and Its Art.* Oxford.

———. (1942) "How Archaeology Aids History." *Yale Review*: 713–29.

Roth, L. M. (1983) *McKim, Mead and White Architects.* New York.

Rowell, H. T. (1948) "Ostia on the Tiber" *Archaeology* 1.1: 34–43.

Ryberg, I. S. (1940) *An Archaeological Record of Rome.* Philadelphia.

Saibanti, C. (1990) *Fotografi a Pompei nell' 800 dalle collezioni del Museo Alinari.* Pompeii.

St. Clair, W. (1972) *That Greece Might Still Be Free.* London.

Salmon, J. B. (1984) *Wealthy Corinth: A History of the City to 338 B.C..* Oxford.

Samuels, E. (1979) *Bernard Berenson: The Making of a Connoisseur.* Cambridge, Mass.

Sanborn, A. (1956) "Henry North Fowler." *AJA* 60:285.

Sanders (1927) "Francis Willey Kelsey." *CP* 22: 308–310.

Sanders, W. T. (1965) *The Cultural Ecology of the Teotihuacan Valley*. University Park, Pa.

Sanders, W. T., J. R. Parsons, and R. S. Santley. (1979) *The Basin of Mexico: Ecological Processes in the Cultural Evolution of a Civilization*. New York.

Santayana, G. (1945) *The Middle Span*. New York.

Savage, E. (1977) *Seleucia on the Tigris*. Ann Arbor, Mich.

Sayce, A. H. (1927) "David George Hogarth." *Proceedings of the British Academy*, 379–83.

Schnapp, A. (1982) "Archéologie et tradition académique en Europe aux XVIIIe et XIXe siècles." *Annales*, 760–77.

Schwartz, H. (1956) *Samuel Gridley Howe: Social Reformer*. Cambridge, Mass.

Scott, I. (1929) "Roman Tradition in the Light of Archaeology." *MAAR* 7: 7–118.

Scott, J. (1990) Editor's preface. In J. Crawford, *The Byzantine Shops at Sardis*. Cambridge, Mass.

Scott, R. T. (1988) "Frank Edward Brown, 1908–1988." *AJA* 92: 577–79.

Scranton, R., J. Shaw, and L. Ibrahim. (1978) *Kenchreai: Eastern Port of 'Corinth*. Vol. 1. *Topography and Architecture*. Leiden.

Serra, J., ed. (1986) *Paestum e la memoria moderna del dorico, 1750–1830*. Florence.

Seymour, T. D. (1902) *The First Twenty-Five Years of the American School of Classical Studies at Athens. Bulletin of the School of Classical Studies at Athens* 5. Norwood, Mass.

———. (1903) "Archaeological Investigations in Greece and Asia Minor." *Carnegie Yearbook* 2: 213–42.

Shand-Tucci, D. (1995) *Boston Bohemian*. Amherst, Mass.

Shaw, B. (1992) "Under Russian Eyes." *JRS* 82: 216–28.

Shaw, J. (1989) "Leon Pomerance, 1907–1988." *AJA* 93: 459–60.

———. (1990) "North American Archaeological Work in Crete." *Expedition* 32.3: 6–14.

———. (1992) "James Walter Graham, 1906–1991." *AJA* 96: 325–26.

Shear, T. L. (1927) "Recent Excavations at Corinth." *Art and Archaeology* 23: 109–15.

———. (1932) "Excavations in the Athenian Agora: The Program of the First Campaign in 1931." *Hesperia* 1: 97–109.

Shear, T. L., Jr. (1983) "Richard Stillwell, 1899–1982." *AJA* 87: 423–25.

Sheftel, P. (1979) "The Archaeological Institute of America 1879–1979: A Centennial Review." *AJA* 83: 3–17.

Sherman, C. R., ed. (1981) *Women as Interpreters of the Visual Arts, 1829–1979*. Westport, Conn.

Shestack, A. (1989) "The Museum and Cultural Property: The Transformation of Institutional Ethics." In P. Messenger, ed., *The Ethics of Collecting Cultural Property*. Albuquerque, N.M.

Showerman, G. (1924) "Darkness and Light in the Old World." *University of California Chronicle* (July): 238–52.

Silk, G. (1982). *Museums Discovered: The Wadsworth Athenaeum*. Fort Lauderdale, Fla.

Sjoqvist, E. (n.d.) *The Life and Death of a Sicilian City*. New York.

———. (1956) "Charles Rufus Morey (1877–1955)." *Colloqui del Sodalizio*: 3–10.

———. (1973) *Sicily and the Greeks*. Ann Arbor, Mich.

Slayman, A. (1998) "Case of the Golden Phiale." *Archaeology* 51.3: 36–41.

Sloan, B., and B. Swinburne. (1981) *College Art Museums and Galleries*. Carbondale, Ill.

Smith, C. S. (1989) "Museums, Artifacts, and Meanings." In P. Vergo, ed., *The New Museology*, 6–21. London.

Smith, E. B. (1912) *The Study of the History of Art in the Colleges and Universities of the United States*. Princeton, N.J.

——. (1925) "Howard Crosby Butler." *Art and Archaeology* 19: 3–17.

Smith, H. (1913) "Problems of the College Art Association." *Bulletin of the College Art Association* 1: 1–5.

Smith, R. R. R., and C. Ratte. (1996) "Archaeological Research at Aphrodisias in Caria." *AJA* 100: 5–33.

Smyth, C., and P. Lukehart. (1993) *The Early History of Art History in the United States*. Princeton, N.J.

Snodgrass, A. M. (1985) "The New Archaeologist and the Classical Archaeologist." *AJA* 89: 31–37.

——. (1987) *An Archaeology of Greece*. San Francisco.

Solberg, W. (1968) *The University of Ilinois, 1867–1894: An Intellectual and Cultural History*. Urbana.

Soles, J. (1979) "The Early Gournia Town." *AJA* 83: 149–67.

——. (1991) "The Gournia Palace." *AJA* 95: 17–78.

——. (1992) *The Prepalatial Cemeteries at Mochlos and Gournia and the House Tombs of Bronze Age Crete*. Princeton, N.J.

Sox, D. (1987) *Unmasking the Forger*. New York.

——. (1991) *Bachelors of Art*. London.

Springer, C. (1987) *The Marble Wilderness*. Cambridge.

Stager, L. (1978) "A Metropolitan Landscape: The Late Punic Port of Carthage." *World Archaeology* 9: 334–46.

——. (1980) "The Rite of Child Sacrifice at Carthage." In J. Pedley, ed., *New Light on Ancient Carthage*. Ann Arbor, Mich.

Starr, C. G. (1991) "Ancient History in the Twentieth Century." *Classical World* 84: 177–88.

Stein, R. (1967) *John Ruskin and Aesthetic Thought in America, 1840–1900*. Cambridge, Mass.

Sterrett, J. (1888a) *Epigraphical Journey to Asia Minor*. Boston.

——. (1888b) *Wolfe Expedition to Asia Minor*. Boston.

——. (1911) *A Plea for Research in Asia Minor and Syria Authorized by Men Whose High Achievements and Representative Character Make the Project a Call for Humanity at Large for Light in Regard to the Life of Man in the Cradle of Western Civilization*. Ithaca, N.Y.

Stevens, G. P. (1925) "The Architect of the American Academy in Rome." *Art and Archaeology* 19: 81–85.

——. (1955) *Restorations of Classical Buildings*. Princeton, N.J.

Stewart, A. (1982) *Skopas in Malibu*. Malibu, Calif.

Stieg, M. F. (1986) *The Origins and Development of Scholarly Historical Perodicals*. University, Ala.

Stillman, W.J. (1888) *On the Track of Ulysses*. Boston.

——. (1897) *The Old Rome and the New*. Boston.

——. (1901) *Autobiography of a Journalist (1828–1901)*. Boston.

——. (1976). *Articles and Despatches from Crete*. Austin, Tex.

Stillwell, R. (1938) *Antioch on the Orontes II, The Excavations, 1933–1936*. Princeton, N.J.

———. (1941) *Antioch on the Orontes III, The Excavations, 1937–1939.* Princeton, N.J.

———. (1945) "Theodore Leslie Shear." *AJA* 49: 582–83.

———. (1952) *The Theatre: Corinth Excavations.* Vol. 2. Princeton, N.J.

Stoneman, R. (1987) *Land of Lost Gods.* Norman, Okla.

Strong, E. (1928) "La formazione delle accademie e scuole straniere di Roma." *Capitolium* 4: 94–111.

Susini, G. (1969–70) "Lilly Ross Taylor, storica di Roma." *Rendiconti Pont. Accad. d'Arch.* 42: 41–45.

———. (1970) "Albert Van Buren." *Rendiconti Pont. Accad. d'Arch.* 42.

Suttenfeld, M., ed. (1993) *One Hundred Years at the Art Institute: A Centennial Celebration.* Chicago.

Swindler, M. H. (1929) *Ancient Painting.* New Haven, Conn.

———. (1948) "John Frankin Daniel III." *AJA* 52: 483–84.

Szegedy-Maszak, A. (1987) "True Illusions: Early Photographs of Athens." *J. Paul Getty Museum Journal* 15: 125–38.

———. (1988) "Sun and Stone: Images of Ancient, Heroic Times." *Archaeology* (July–August): 20–31.

Tarbell, F. (1896, 1927) *A History of Greek Art with an Introductory Chapter on Art in Egypt and Mesopotamia.* New York.

———. (1897) *Illustrated Catalogue of Carbon Prints on the Rise and Progress of Greek and Roman Art.* Boston.

———. (1909) *Catalogue of Bronzes in the Field Museum of Natural History Reproduced from Originals in the National Museum of Naples.* Chicago.

Taylor, F. H. (1936–37) "In Defense of the Classics." *Worcester Art Museum Annual* 1: 1–27.

Taylor, L. R (1912) *The Cults of Roman Ostia.* Bryn Mawr, Pa.

———. (1920) "The Worship of Augustus in Italy During His Lifetime." *TAPA* 51: 116–33.

———. (1923) *Local Cults of Etruria.* PMAAR 2. Rome.

Tharp, L. H. (1965) *Mrs. Jack.* Boston.

Thomas, T. (1990) *Dangerous Archaeology: Francis Willey Kelsey and Armenia (1919–1920).* Ann Arbor, Mich.

Thompson, H. A. (1945) "Theodore Leslie Shear." *Annual Bulletin AIA*: 43–45.

———. (1947) "The Excavation of the Athenian Agora." *Hesperia* 16: 193–212.

———. (1949) "Stoa of Attalus." *Archaeology* 2: 124–30.

———. (1954, 1976) *The Athenian Agora: Guide to the Excavations.* Athens.

———. (1973) "Gisella M. A. Richter (1882–1972)." *Yearbook of the American Philosophical Society*: 144–50.

———. (1974a) "Introductory Remarks." In *A Symposium in Memory of Hetty Goldman 1881–1974*, vii–x. Princeton, N.J.

———. (1974b) "William Bell Dinsmoor (1886–1973)." *Yearbook of the American Philosophical Society*: 156–63.

———. (1980) "In Pursuit of the Past: The American Role, 1879–1979." *AJA* 84: 263–70.

———. (1991) "J. Walter Graham 1906–1991." *Newsletter of the American School of Classics Studies at Athens* 28 (Fall): 15.

Thorp, W., M. Myers, and J. S. Finch. (1978) *The Princeton Graduate School: A History.* Princeton, N.J.

Tomkins, C. (1970) *Merchants and Masterpieces.* New York.

Tomlinson, R. (1991) *The Athens of Alma Tadema.* Wolfeboro Falls, N.H.

Tonks, O. (1913) "Museum of Art and Teachers of the Classics." In S. Axon, ed., *Art Museums and the Schools*, 97–144. New York.

Traill, J. S. (1990) "Benjamin Dean Meritt (1899–1989)." *AJA* 94: 483–84.

Travlos, J. (1981) "Athens After Liberation, Planning the New City and Exploring the Old." *Hesperia* 50: 391–407.

Triantaphyllopoulos, (1991) "Doro Levi: Trieste 1898–Roma 1991." *Rivista St. Ant.* 21: 243–46.

Trigger, B. (1985) "Writing the History of Archaeology: A Survey of Trends." In G. Stocking, ed., *History of Anthropology 3*, 218–35. Madison, Wis.

———. (1989) *A History of Archaeological Thought*. Cambridge.

True, M. (1987) "A Kouros at the Getty Museum." *Burlington Magazine* 129: 3–11.

———. (1992) "The Getty Kouros: Background on the Problem." In *The Getty Kouros Colloquium*. Athens.

Truettner, W., and A. Wallach. (1994) *Thomas Cole: Landscape into History*. New Haven, Conn.

Tsigakou, F. M. (1981) *The Rediscovery of Greece*. London.

Tsoucalas, C. (1969) *Greek Tragedy*. Harmondsworth.

Tucker, L. L. (1967) " 'Ohio Show-Shop': The Western Museum of Cincinnati, 1820–1867." In W. M. Whitehill, ed., *A Cabinet of Curiosities*, 73–105. Charlottesville, Va.

Valentine, L., and A. Valentine. (1973) *The American Academy in Rome, 1894–1969*. Charlottesville, Va.

Van Andel, T., and C. Runnels. (1987) *Beyond the Acropolis*. Stanford, Calif.

Van Buren, A. (1919a) "Francis John Haverfield." *Classical Journal* 15: 169–72.

———. (1919b) "The Past Decade of Pompeian Studies." *Classical Journal* 15: 404–16.

———. (1926) "C. Densmore Curtis." *AJA* 30: 99–100.

———. (1938). *A Companion to the Study of Rome and Herculaneum*. Rome.

Vance W. L. (1989) *America's Rome in Classical Rome*. New Haven, Conn.

Van Deman, E. (1909) *The Atrium Vestae*. Washington, D.C.

———. (1912) "Methods of Determining the Date of Roman Concrete Monuments." *AJA* 16: 230–51, 387–432.

Vanderbilt, K. (1959) *Charles Eliot Norton*. Cambridge, Mass.

Vanderpool, E. (1982) *Studies in Attic Epigraphy, History and Topography Presented to Eugene Vanderpool*. Princeton, N.J.

Van Ingen, W. (1939) *Figurines from Seleucia on the Tigris*. Ann Arbor, Mich.

Ventris, M. and J. Chadwick (1956) *Documents in Mycenaean Greek*. Cambridge.

Vergo, Peter, ed. (1989) *The New Museology*. London.

Vermeule, C. (1964) *European Art and the Classical Past*. Cambridge, Mass.

———. (1968) *Roman Imperial Art in Greece and Asia Minor*. Cambridge, Mass.

———. (1981) *Greek and Roman Sculpture in America*. Berkeley, Calif.

———. (1987) *The Cult Images of Imperial Rome*. Rome.

Vermeule, C., and A. Brauer. (1990) *Stone Sculptures: The Greek, Roman, and Etruscan Collections of the Harvard University Art Museums*. Cambridge, Mass.

Vermeule, C., and M. B. Comstock. (1988) *Sculpture in Stone and Bronze*. Boston.

Vermeule, C., and N. Neuerburg. (1973) *Catalogue of the Ancient Art in the J. Paul Getty Museum*. Malibu, Calif.

Vermeule, E. (1987) "The Key to the Fields: The Classics at Bryn Mawr" In P. H. Labalme, ed., *A Century Recalled*, 161–72. Bryn Mawr, Pa.

———. (1995) "Sterling Dow, 1903–1995." *AJA* 99: 729–30.

Veysey, L. (1965) *The Emergence of the American University*. Chicago.

Vickers, M. (1985–86) "Imaginary Etruscans: Changing Perceptions Etruria Since the Fifteenth Century." *Hephaistos* 7–8: 153–68.

———. (1987) "Value and Simplicity, Eighteenth Century Taste and the Study of Greek Vases." *Past and Present* (116: 98–137).

Vogt, E., and R. Leventhal. (1983) *Prehistoric Settlement Patterns: Essays in Honor of Gordon R. Willey.* Cambridge, Mass.

Von Blanckhenhagen, P. (1961) "Karl Lehmann." *AJA* 65: 307–8.

Von Blanckhenhagen, P., and C. Alexander. (1990) *The Augustan Villa at Boscotrecase.* Mainz.

Von Bothmer, D. (1961) *Ancient Art from New York. Private Collections.* New York.

———. (1985) "Beazley the Teacher." In Kurtz (1985a), 5–19.

———, ed. (1990) *Glories of the Past, Ancient Art from the Shelby White and Leon Levy Collection.* New York.

———. (1991) "Etruria and American Collecting: The Early Years." In *Gens antiquissima Italiae*, 47–50. Perugia.

———. (1975) "A Curator's Choice." In T. Hoving, ed., *The Chase, the Capture: Collecting at the Metropolitan*, 111–22. New York.

Von Bothmer, D., and J. V. Noble. (1956–57) "Greek Vases from the Hearst Collection." *Bulletin of the Metropolitan Museum of Art* 15: 165–67.

———. (1961) *An Inquiry into the Forgery of the Etruscan Terracotta Warriors in the Metropolitan Museum of Art.* New York.

Von Mach, E. (1905) *A Handbook of Greek and Roman Sculpture.* Toronto.

Waldstein, C. (1885) *Essays on the Art of Pheidias.* Cambridge.

———. (1893) *The Work of John Ruskin.* New York.

———. (1902, 1905) *The Argive Heraeum.* Boston.

———. (1914) *Greek Sculpture and Modern Art.* Cambridge.

Walker, A., and H. Goldman. (1915) "Report on Excavations at Halae of Locris." *AJA* n.s. 19: 418–37.

Wallach, A. (1994) "Thomas Cole: Landscape and the Course of American Empire." In Truettner and Wallach, 23–112.

Ward, R., and P. Fidler. (1993) *The Nelson-Atkins Museum of Art: A Handbook of the Collection.* New York.

Ward Perkins, J. (1958) "Four Roman Garland Sarcophagi in America." *Archaeology* 11.2: 98–104.

———. (1962) "Etruscan Towns, Roman Roads, and Medieval Villages." *Geographical Journal* 128: 389–405.

Washington, H. S. (1923) "Excavations at Phlius in 1892." *AJA* 27: 428–46.

Waterhouse, H. T. (1988) *The British School at Athens: The First Hundred Years.* London.

Watkin, D. (1980) *The Rise of Architectural History.* London.

———. (1982) *Athenian Stuart.* London.

Watson, W. (1980) *Images of Italy: Photography in the Nineteenth Century.* South Hadley, Mass.

Weber, S., and F. Malandrini. (1996) "Fratelli Alinari of Florence." *History of Photography* 20: 49–56.

Weeks, E. (1966) *The Lowells and Their Institution.* Boston.

Weinberg, S. (1956) *The Aegean and the Near East: Studies Presented to Hetty Goldman on the Occasion of Her Seventy-Fifth Birthday.* New York.

Weitzmann, K., ed. (1955) *Late Classical and Medieval Studies in Honor of Albert Mathier Friend, Jr.* Princeton, N.J.

Weller, A. S. (1992) *100 Years of Teaching Art History and Archaeology, University of Missouri, Columbia.* Columbia, Mo.

Welles, C. B. (1956) "Michael I. Rostovtzeff." *Historia* 5: 351–88.

Welles, C. B., R. O. Fink, and J. Gilliam. (1959) *The Excavations at Dura-Europos Final Reports*, ed. M. I. Rostovtzeff et al. Part 1, *The Parchments and Papyri.* New Haven, Conn.

Wes, M. A. (1990) *Michael Rostovtzeff, Historian in Exile: Russian Roots in an American Context.* Stuttgart.

Wesolowsky, A. B. (1975) "The Pathology of Human Remains at Stobi." *Studies in the Antiquities of Stobi II*, 143–60. Belgrade.

West, A., ed. (1917) *Value of the Classics.* Princeton, N.J.

Wharton E. (1934) *A Backward Glance.* New York.

Whitehead, P. B. (1927a) "The Church of SS Cosma e Damiano in Rome." *AJA* 31: 1–18.

———. (1927b) "The Church of Anastasia at Rome." *AJA* 31: 405–29.

Whitehill, W. M. (1970) *Boston Museum of Fine Arts: A Centennial History.* Cambridge, Mass.

Wiebe, R. (1967) *The Search for Order, 1877–1920.* New York.

Wiebenson, D. (1969) *Sources of Greek Revival Architecture.* London.

Wiesen, D. (1981–82) "Cornelius Felton and the Flowering of Classics in New England." *Classical Outlook* (December–January): 44–48.

Wilkes, J. (1986) *Diocletian's Palace, Split, Residence of a Retired Roman Emperor.* Sheffield.

Wilkie, N., and W. Coulson, eds. (1985) *Contributions to Aegean Archaeology.* Minneapolis.

Willey, G., and J. Sabloff. (1980) *A History of American Archaeology.* San Francisco.

Williams, C., and O. Zervos. (1996) "Franks in Corinth 1995." *Hesperia* 65: 1–55.

Williams, E. R. (1984) *The Archaeological Collection of the Johns Hopkins University.* Baltimore.

Wills, G. (1984) *Cincinnatus.* Garden City, N.Y.

———. (1992) *Lincoln at Gettysburg.* Garden City, N.Y.

Wilmerding, J. (1976) *American Art.* Harmondsworth.

Wilson, J. (1964) *Signs and Wonders upon Pharaoh.* Chicago.

Winkes, R. (1974) "Margarete Bieber zum 95 Gebürtstag." *Giessner Universitatsblatter* 1: 68–75.

———. (1993) "The Influence of Herculeaneum and Pompeii on American Art of the Eighteenth and Nineteenth Centuries." In L. F. dell'Orto, ed., *Ercolano, 1738–1988.* Rome.

Winter, F. (1991) "Who Owns the Past? Ethical Dilemmas in Contemporary Archaeology." *Explorers Journal* 69: 128–33.

Wiseman, J. (1973) "Editorial Comment." *JFA* 1: 2–3.

———. (1978) "Stobi in Yugoslavian Macedonia, Archaeological Excavations and Research, 1977–78." *JFA* 5: 391–429.

———. (1980a) "Archaeology as Archaeology." *JFA* 7: 149–51.

———. (1980b) "Archaeology in the Future: An Evolving Discipline." *AJA* 84: 279–85.

———. (1983) "Conflicts in Archaeology: Education and Practice." *JFA* 10: 1–9.

———. (1986) "Archaeology and History at Stobi, Macedonia." In C. B. McClendon, ed., *Rome and the Provinces: Studies in the Transformation of Art and Archaeology in the Mediterranean World.* New Haven, Conn.

Wiseman, J., and D. Mano-Zissi. (1971) "Excavations at Stobi, 1970." *AJA* 75: 395–411.

———. (1972) "Excavations at Stobi, 1971." *AJA* 76: 407–24.

———. (1981) "Stobi, 1970–1977: A Review." In B. Aleksova and J. Wiseman, eds., *Studies in the Antiquities of Stobi*, 133–46.

Wittlin, A. (1970) *Museums: In Search of a Usable Future.* Cambridge, Mass.

Wittman, O. (n.d.) *Greek Vases in the Toledo Museum of Art.* Toledo, Ohio.

Wren, P. (1995) "Remembering 'Aunt Hetty': Excavations at Halai Now and Then." *AIA Newsletter* 1: 5.

Wright, N. (1963) *Horatio Greenough.* Philadelphia.

Yegul, F. (1986) *The Bath-Gymnasium Complex at Sardis.* Cambridge, Mass.

———. (1991) *Gentlemen of Instinct and Breeding.* Oxford.

Young, C. H. (1895) "Augustus Chapman Merriam." *AJA* 10: 227–29.

Young, R. (1958) "The Gordion Tomb." *Expedition* 1.1: 3–13.

———. (1981) *Three Great Early Tumuli*, Gordion Excavations. Final Reports I, University Museum Monographs, Philadelphia.

Young, W. (1972) "The Fabulous Gold of the Pactolus Valley." *Boston Museum Bulletin* 70: 5–13.

Index

Adam, Robert, 2, 7–8, 269
Adamesteanu, Dinu, 266
Adams, Henry, 35
Aegina, 31, 123
Aeschines, 9
Agnes Hoppin memorial fellowship, 59–60
Albani, Cardinal Alessandro, 3, 123
Alexander, Christine, 153
Alexander, Margaret, 271
Alinari Brothers, 63
Allen, Hubert, 233
Allston, Washington, 11
Altertumswissenschaft, 25, 54, 160, 218, 228
American Academy in Rome, ix, 38, 110,
    114, 159, 167, 170, 172, 189, 208–15, 220,
    232, 262–65, 278; summer school, 162,
    207–9
American Academy of Fine Arts, 11, 22
American Antiquity, 161
American Council of Learned Societies,
    229–30, 259
American Exploration Society, 90
American Journal of Archaeology, x, 46–8, 52,
    62, 91, 97, 104, 160–61, 164, 166–67,
    191, 206, 222–23, 232, 239, 247, 254, 280
American Lyceum Movement, 49
American Numismatic and Archaeology
    Society, 26
American Oriental Society, 26, 40
American Philosophical Society, 40
American School of Architecture, 111
American School of Classical Studies in
    Athens, ix, 33, 38, 53–55, 58–60, 64, 67–
    68, 73, 78, 82–83, 85–88, 92, 94–95, 99,
    102–3, 159, 162, 168–70, 173, 208, 243,

254–57, 282; summer school, 162, 209–
    10
American School of Classical Studies in
    Rome, 38, 76, 78, 109–10, 112, 114–15,
    162, 172–73, 175–77, 185, 200, 208–9,
    220
American Schools of Oriental Research,
    234
Amherst College, 66
amphorae, 184
Andalusia, 10
Antichita di Ercolano, 6
Antioch on the Orontes, 120, 161, 167–68,
    199, 216
Antioch in Pisidia, 194
antiquities trade, 72, 135–39, 152, 156–57,
    273–76, 278–81
Aphrodisias, 231, 244, 284
Apollo Belevedere, 16, 23, 128
Appelby, Thomas, 135
Archaeological Institute of America, viii,
    xiii, 1, 32, 38–39, 42, 65, 68, 71–73, 82–
    83, 85–86, 98, 104, 124, 160–61, 200–
    204, 217, 221–22, 245, 254, 279–81; An-
    nual Meeting, 51–53, 201–2; Baltimore
    Society, 42, 97; Boston Society, 103; Chi-
    cago Society, 43; Detroit Society, 43; Lec-
    ture Program, 49–51, 202–3; New York
    Society, 42; Philadelphia Society, 42;
    Pittsburgh Society, 43; Southwest Society,
    45; St. Louis Society, 201; Washington So-
    ciety, 46, 187, 200–201, 203, 206, 271;
    Wisconsin Society, 43
Archaeology, 205, 211, 217, 221–22
Argive Heraeum, 76, 83–84, 103, 177, 243